CONTENTS

ABOUT THE AUTHORS

Angela Dare and Margaret O'Donovan come from backgrounds of health visiting, midwifery and teaching. They worked together for many years at City and Islington College, London, on nursery nursing and other childcare courses. Margaret O'Donovan also taught for a number of years at The Chiltern College, Caversham. Angela Dare was for several years an External Moderator for CACHE courses.

Miranda Walker has worked with children from birth to 16 years in a range of settings, including her own day nursery and out-of-school clubs. She has inspected nursery provision for Ofsted, and worked at East Devon College as an Early Years and Playwork lecturer and NVQ assessor and internal verifier. She is a regular contributor to industry magazines and an established author.

DEDICATIONS

To Kieran and Kate; and to Leilah and Dominic.

Good Practice in

Caring for Children with Special Needs

3rd Edition

Angela Dare
Margaret O'Donovan

Series Editor: Miranda Walker

Nelson Thornes

First published in 1997 by Stanley Thornes (Publishers) Ltd

Second edition published in 2002 by Nelson Thornes Ltd

This edition published in 2009 by:
Nelson Thornes Ltd
Delta Place
27 Bath Road
CHELTENHAM
GL53 7TH
United Kingdom

09 10 11 12 13 / 10 9 8 7 6 5 4 3 2 1

A catalogue record for this book is available from the British Library

ISBN 978 1 4085 0490 1

Illustrations by Angela Lumley
Page make-up by Northern Phototypesetting Co. Ltd

Printed and bound in Spain by GraphyCems

ACKNOWLEDGEMENTS

The authors would like to thank their colleagues for the ongoing interest and encouragement they have shown, particularly Anna O'Brien and Cynthia Isaac at City and Islington College, also Christine Hobart and Teresa O'Dea.

The authors gratefully acknowledge the help received from Theresa le Bas, Marie Owen, Catherine Thomas, Maureen Cotterell and Francesca, Ben and Beth O'Brien. They are also indebted to Marita Jackson (head teacher) and Cate Westrup (SENCO) from St Joseph's Combined School, Poole, for their support and assistance.

They are most appreciative to staff, parents and children for permission to use photographs taken in Bromley Hall School, Poplar, London E.14; and of the London Borough of Greenwich Portage Scheme.

The Scope bookmark on page 43 is reproduced by kind permission of Scope.

The photograph on page 68 is reproduced by kind permission of WRK Developments.

The photographs on pages 252, 253 and 254 (both right) are reproduced by kind permission of the Cystic Fibrosis Trust and Camilla Jessel.

The photograph on page 66 is reproduced by kind permission of The Soft Brick Company Ltd.

The photograph on page 67 is reproduced by kind permission of Bounce Krazee.

The photograph on page 251 is reproduced by kind permission of Alamy.

Crown copyright © material is reproduced under Class Licence No. CO1 W 0000195 with the permission of the Controller of HMSO and the Queen's Printer for Scotland.

PART 1
Introduction

Early Years workers require particular knowledge to enable children with special needs to take part in play, learning and social activities alongside their peers in a variety of settings. The earlier a child's special need is recognised and assessed, the sooner effective and ongoing help and family-centred support can be provided.

Part One of the book covers a range of issues associated with disability and special needs, such as the medical and social models of disability, disability awareness, discrimination and stereotyping. The subject of access and inclusion is also addressed. Throughout the text there is recognition of the uniqueness and individuality of every child, and the role of the Early Years worker in caring for, and supporting, the different needs of young children and their families. Statutory and voluntary provision for young children with special needs is identified.

Relevant legislation is included. The guidance in the Special Educational Needs Code of Practice 2002 is explained, with particular reference to its implementation in Early Years settings.

Emphasis is placed on the importance of parents and their role as partners within the Early Years team, teachers and specialists in implementing care and education programmes for their child. The right of children with special needs to be listened to, make choices and express an opinion about decisions that affect them is also reflected in the text.

Sections on Early Years Development and Childcare Partnerships, Parent Partnership Service, the Sure Start initiative and the Early Years Foundation Stage are incorporated into Part One of the book.

1 BACKGROUND TO DISABILITY AND SPECIAL NEEDS

This chapter covers:
- Disability
- Special needs
- Definitions of impairment and disability
- Types of special need
- Possible causes of special needs
- Towards prevention and early identification of special needs
- Meeting the needs of parents and family
- Multiprofessional teams

This chapter considers some of the issues surrounding disability. The term 'special needs' is explained and types of special need, with some possible causes, are identified. Families of children with special needs have their own particular concerns and worries, and the chapter looks at ways to help and support parents and siblings.

Professionals from the multidisciplinary team that provides medical, educational and social care for a child with special needs are specified in the text. Early Years workers are always valued members of this team.

Disability

Everyone has their own perception of disability, which varies according to personal knowledge and experience. Perhaps you know a child or adult who is disabled and understand something of his or her needs. Perhaps you are also aware of the different attitudes of society towards people with disabilities and the barriers they frequently encounter in their everyday living – social barriers of **discrimination** (being treated differently and unequally), prejudice and isolation, as well as physical barriers of **access**. Or, perhaps your only understanding of disability is seeing disabled people out and about from time to time, watching an occasional documentary programme about disability or reading fleeting references to disabled people in books or articles. Many disabled people are 'invisible' because they have no easy access to an environment planned and constructed by able-bodied people.

KEY POINT
- Disability extends beyond wheelchair users to include people with sensory impairments, medical conditions and mental health problems.
- Children and adults with disabilities are entitled to the same rights and opportunities as other members of society.

Professionals involved in caring for children with disabilities must listen sensitively to what the children and their parents are saying about their situation.

Activity

Imagine you are a wheelchair user going out and about in your local neighbourhood.

1 How easy or difficult is it for you to get around the streets and shops?
2 Are there any particularly accessible facilities such as public transport, leisure and entertainment services? If so, identify what makes them user-friendly.
3 What specific improvements would be necessary to make your neighbourhood physically accessible to wheelchair users?

The physical environment must be accessible to all children

Throughout the ages disabled people have been pushed to the margins of society and even today there are differing attitudes towards those considered 'abnormal'. A disabled relative, frequently considered a 'shame' on the family, was sometimes cast aside to make do as best they could, while others were left to die or were even killed – especially in societies where everyday life was such a struggle for survival that those who were unable to contribute fully to their society were rejected. Even Aristotle called the deaf 'senseless and incapable of reason'.

The 'insane' were often thought to be possessed by the devil and were put to death. In ancient Rome deformed children were drowned in the Tiber. Women who gave birth to disabled children were often assumed to be witches and both mother and baby would be killed. Disabilities in babies were sometimes deemed to be 'God's punishment' for the sins of the parents, while in other cultures people with disabilities had mystical powers attributed to them.

Most disabled people, though, have been tolerated in varying degrees. In rural societies, as Britain once was, disabled people made a valuable contribution to their family and community by undertaking the less demanding work around the farms and helping in the traditional cottage industries of weaving and basket and chair making. However, in the nineteenth century, when large sections of the population moved to the bigger towns and cities as a consequence of the Industrial Revolution, there was little work for those who were disabled. Many were abandoned by their families. The more liberal members of society and church organisations founded institutions where abandoned disabled people could find shelter and basic care. Gradually, more and more families used these institutions as a way of unburdening themselves either of the financial or 'shameful' burden of disabled relatives.

With the advance in medical treatment doctors sought to 'cure' disabled people and return them to society. Most of those who could not be cured remained in the institutions to live out their lives there, often completely abandoned by their families.

In Britain today, which in world terms is rich, disabled people's expectations are for equality, inclusion and equal opportunity. Large long-stay institutions have disappeared. As far as possible disabled children and adults are supported within their own families or in small community homes. These residential homes are often frowned upon by some members of local communities who would prefer them to be elsewhere. The same people are often outspoken about the cost of medical care, both in hospital and the community and the general financial cost to the tax payer of ongoing support and resources. People may have these reactions because they lack knowledge of disabilities or, perhaps, believe perpetuated myths about disabled people.

KEY POINT

Society frequently sees the birth of a baby with a disability as a tragedy, so subscribing to the medical model of disability (see Chapter 2, pages 32–3). Friends may offer condolences rather than congratulations because they do not know what to say.

PROGRESS CHECK

1 What social and physical barriers do people with disabilities encounter in their everyday lives?
2 Why are disabled people often 'invisible'?
3 Why is it important to understand past attitudes towards disability?

Over the last twenty years attitudes and assumptions have been slowly changing. Through *education* and moves towards *integration* and inclusiveness there is better awareness of the issues surrounding disability.

EDUCATION

- Campaigns by disability organisations have resulted in greater 'disability awareness', equal rights and opportunities for disabled people.
- Disability awareness and equality training helps people to examine their own attitudes towards disabled people, and to implement good practice and courtesy towards them in their workplace and wider environment. Professionals caring for people with disabilities need to learn about disability directly from disabled people. For blind people, for example, the biggest problem is often the lack of skills in sighted people, which are needed when assisting a blind person.
- For details of legislation for equal rights and opportunities, see Chapter 3.
- Attempts are being made by the media to portray people with disabilities positively (although images on the television tend to remain rather negative).
- National and international sporting events for disabled people such as the paralympics and marathon races, although exclusive activities, raise the profile and visibility of disability.

INTEGRATION

- Disabled people now have a higher profile in the community and in all areas of public life.
- Inclusive day care and education settings enable children with special needs to play and learn alongside their peers and neighbourhood friends.
- There is better access to public transport, libraries, social activities, local amenities (such as sports facilities) and holiday venues.

All these changes have led to a more informed society and have benefited children and adults with disabilities by promoting confidence and removing social isolation.

KEY POINT

In spite of legislation and greater efforts to educate people about disability, there is still much to be done towards achieving a fully inclusive society.

PROGRESS CHECK

1 Explain how education and integration have contributed to a greater awareness of disability within society.
2 How does a more informed society benefit disabled people?

Special needs

Whether caring for children in an Early Years, school or home setting you are constantly identifying, responding to and satisfying children's ordinary, everyday needs.

Satisfying children's ordinary, everyday needs

The term 'special needs' is used by childcare and educational professionals in relation to children whose development is atypical, that is, not following the recognised pattern seen in most children. All children are on a continuum of development – they start out at the beginning of the same track and move along in a continuous process of development. However, as you know from observing children in your workplace, not all children of similar ages are at the same stage of development. Children with special needs are simply at different points on the developmental continuum. The term 'special educational needs' (SEN) is used when a child learns differently from most children of the same age and may need extra or different help to learn. Not all disabled children need extra or different help to learn – it depends on their individual needs. The term 'SEN' is used by national and local education departments.

KEY POINTS

- Children with special needs have the same requirements for love, security and protection as the other children you care for. They have individual personalities, likes and dislikes, some will be strong-willed and others easygoing.
- Take time to get to know children with special needs and give them plenty of

attention and encouragement. Ensure you offer them the opportunity to make and maintain friendships and help them to become independent.

> **Activity**
> Carry out a detailed written record observation on each of three children of the same age in your work setting. The aim of your observation must be the same for all three children. Your evaluations should be clear and objective. Compare the developmental stages and abilities of each child. Are all the children at the same stage and level of development or are there obvious differences?

LABELLING CHILDREN

Labels such as 'handicapped' and 'subnormal' (see Chapter 2, page 74) are no longer used; they focus on a particular disability and conceal a child's unique character, personality and determination. 'A child may be unable to walk, yet may be confident and determined, able to use elbow crutches to move around the room. Labelling this child "physically handicapped" focuses on his disability only, and tells nothing of how he is coping with that difficulty' (*Children with Special Needs*, Woolfson, 1991).

KEY POINTS

- There is no group of children called 'the disabled' or 'the handicapped' but there are individual children who happen to have different conditions. Current preferred terms are 'children with learning difficulties', 'disabled children', 'children with special needs' and 'children with special educational needs (SEN)'.
- Using the term 'special needs' recognises the uniqueness of each child and acknowledges each child's particular strengths, abilities and level of development. It focuses positively on the 'need' rather than the disability, enabling appropriate levels of care and resources to be provided to support the child in everyday life. However, the term is seen by some as just another label implying separateness and segregation.

PROGRESS CHECK

1 What do you understand by a 'continuum of development'?
2 What is wrong with using labels such as 'handicapped' and 'subnormal'?

Definitions of impairment and disability

Although definitions may help to identify and explain a degree of need more readily and assist in planning future services, there are no universal, precise definitions. Any definition is subject to the views, attitudes and influences of those formulating it and there is continuing debate about acceptable definitions and terminology. What really matters is the individual child, how the child's needs are met and the attitudes of society towards the child. However, you may find the definitions on page 10 interesting and helpful.

STATISTICS

There are approximately nine to ten million disabled people in Great Britain, many of whom would not consider themselves part of this statistic, particularly older people who have developed conditions or impairments in later life. Within this figure there are 360,000 children with impairments.

Nationally, 20 per cent (one in five) of *all* children may have a particular special educational need at some time during their pre-school or school years and 2 per cent (one in fifty) of *all* children will receive a **statement of special educational needs** (see Chapter 3, pages 89–94). In 2001, an estimated 258,000 children in all schools in England received statements. This is an increase of 13.6 per cent over the five years since 1996. Of the total number of children who received statements in 2001, 61 per cent attend mainstream schools (nursery, primary and secondary). The Special Educational Needs and Disability Act 2001 strengthens the rights of children with special educational needs to be educated in mainstream schools (see Chapter 3, pages 78-9).

Types of special need

There are many types of special need. As Early Years workers you will need to find out about the degree of difficulty a child is experiencing. This requires a good knowledge of child development. The developmental charts on pages 397–401, will help you. In addition, through talking to the child, her parents and the professionals caring for her, you will be able to understand a child's particular needs. Not all children with special needs have a special educational need, but, when necessary, special educational provision is determined through a process of assessment (detailed in Chapter 3).

KEY POINTS

■ Remember, the word 'types' refers to the special need, not to the child.
■ Many children may, at some time, have short-term special needs, for example, following bereavement or other emotional trauma, or a period of illness or hospitalisation. Unless their needs are adequately met at the time they may develop emotional, social or learning difficulties.

You may care for children with any of the special needs identified in the table on page 11. The key points on page 11 are explained in more detail in Part Two.

DEFINITIONS OF IMPAIRMENT AND DISABILITY

1. The **Disability Discrimination Act 1995** describes disability as 'a *physical or mental impairment* which has a *substantial* and *long term* adverse effect on a person's ability to carry out *normal day-to-day activities*'. (Italics added.)

   - *Physical impairment*: refers to conditions that weaken or adversely change part of the body. They may be **congenital** or a result of illness or accident. Examples are poor vision or hearing, blindness, deafness, inability to walk, heart and respiratory diseases.
   - *Mental impairment*: includes recognised mental illness and learning difficulties.
   - *Substantial*: more than minor or trivial, but does not have to be severe.
   - *Long term*: the impairment has lasted or is likely to last more than twelve months.
   - *Normal day-to-day activities*: the impairment affects: mobility; ability to lift and carry; speech, hearing or eyesight; memory or ability to concentrate, learning or understanding.

2. **The Children Act 1989** states that: 'a child is disabled if he is blind, deaf or dumb or suffers from mental disorder of any kind or is substantially and permanently handicapped by illness, injury or congenital deformity or such other disability as may be prescribed.'

3. Based on definitions from the **World Health Organization (WHO)**:
   - *Impairment*: any loss or abnormality of psychological, physiological or anatomical structure or function – a limitation or loss of function of part or parts of the body.
   - *Disability*: any restriction or lack (resulting from impairment) of ability to perform an activity in the manner or within the range considered normal for a human being.

   Examples of difficulties or inabilities due to impairment include: mobility and postural difficulties; poor vision and hearing, blindness and deafness; recognised mental illness; inability to make and maintain effective relationships or to maintain codes of behaviour.

4. Adopted by **'Disabled Peoples International' 1981**: 'Disability is the loss or limitation of the ability to take part in the normal life of the community on an equal level with others due to physical and social barriers.'

5. Based on the **Social Model of Disability** (see page 33):
   - *Impairment*: a limitation of function of the body. Some part of the body is not working properly, due to illness, injury or congenital condition. Examples include loss of whole or part of a limb; vision or hearing loss; learning difficulties.
   - *Disability*: the exclusion of people with impairments from community life and social activities, on an equal level with others, due to the attitudes and situations imposed by society – personal and social disadvantage. For example, (a) a child using a wheelchair is unable to manage steps into a building – society disables the child if no ramp is provided; (b) a person with visual impairment is disadvantaged if information is not readily available in large print or Braille.

Check the table on page 11 for examples of particular types of disability and special needs.

Activity

Look at the definitions of disability above. In what way is the definition of disability in the Social Model different from, or similar to, the other definitions?

TYPES OF SPECIAL NEED

	Physical conditions	Speech, language and sensory impairment	Learning difficulties	Emotional and behavioural difficulties
Cause	Damage to the body and its physical functions, including injuries: ■ to the brain and spinal cord ■ to the body systems ■ affecting the control of movement.	*Speech and language (see also page 296)* ■ hearing, learning and articulation difficulties. *Sensory (see also pages 335–64)* ■ familial tendency ■ maternal rubella in pregnancy ■ prematurity.	Various: a child has a learning difficulty if she has greater difficulty in learning than most children of her age (see also Chapter 3). Learning difficulties can be mild, moderate, severe or profound.	■ emotional events and experiences ■ learning difficulties ■ physical conditions or sensory impairments ■ illness.
Examples	Physical conditions include: ■ cerebral palsy ■ spina bifida ■ cystic fibrosis ■ sickle cell condition ■ arthritis ■ muscular dystrophy ■ epilepsy, asthma, eczema.	Speech and language difficulties include: ■ stammering ■ poor pronunciation ■ difficulty in understanding the meaning or structure of language. Sensory difficulties include: ■ Vision and hearing impairment.	Learning difficulties include: ■ Down syndrome ■ fragile X syndrome ■ autism ■ speech and language impairment ■ sensory impairment.	Children can become: ■ unhappy ■ disruptive ■ angry ■ aggressive ■ withdrawn ■ anti-social ■ uncooperative.
Key points	■ The effects of every condition will vary from child to child. ■ Children with some physical conditions frequently require physiotherapy to help with posture, balance and mobility. Many children will have specialist equipment such as wheelchairs, walking frames, braces, crutches, callipers or artificial limbs to help them to get around. They may use particular feeding aids and require help in feeding, dressing and toileting routines. Lifting, handling and positioning techniques are important to avoid injury to the child or carer. Dietary requirements, medication and hospital care will vary from child to child.	■ The degree of hearing difficulty will vary according to the level of impairment. ■ Early identification of speech and language difficulties is important for a child's emotional and social development and for later school performance. ■ Support for children with sensory impairments includes adapting materials and providing opportunities and stimulation to promote independence and confidence. Children will benefit from special equipment such as spectacles, hearing aids and amplification systems.	■ A specific learning difficulty is a difficulty in a clearly identified area and includes dyslexia and dyspraxia. ■ Careful observation of children with learning difficulties is necessary in assessing needs. Activities and learning programmes must match their actual level, not the level expected for their age.	■ Emotional and behavioural difficulties may also arise from factors within a school environment, e.g. bullying. A high adult-to-child ratio, one-to-one care and small group activities are beneficial for children with emotional and behavioural difficulties. Alternatively, individual education programmes and behaviour management may be appropriate. The education welfare officer or social services department may become involved with the child and family.

Which child has a special need?

Activity

Find out as much as you can about particular equipment and different aids available for children with special needs. The physiotherapy and occupational therapy departments of your local hospital may be able to help and show you how different equipment works. Voluntary organisations, whose addresses can be found throughout Part Two and on pages 408–12, often have leaflets or brochures and manufacturers usually advertise in telephone directories. Parents are always excellent sources of information and most would be willing to help you in your research. Build up your own file of specialist equipment.

PROGRESS CHECK

1 Name the four types of special need.
2 What do you understand by the term 'learning difficulties'?
3 Name two conditions that are classed as 'specific learning difficulties'.
4 Why might a young child have emotional and behavioural difficulties?

Possible causes of special needs

Special needs may be caused by:
- hereditary factors
- prenatal, birth and postnatal developments
- childcare and parenting factors.

Sometimes it is not possible to identify a clear cause.

Recognising special needs

Special needs may be recognised:

- prenatally
- at birth
- through child health promotion and surveillance programmes
- by follow-up to a parent's observation and concern
- by professional observation of children in the home and in care and education settings
- following an accident or serious illness.

The table on page 15 sets out possible causes of special needs.

Towards prevention and early identification of special needs

Preconceptual care reduces many of the risks to the unborn child and helps to make the womb a healthy environment in which the baby can safely grow. Prenatal care aims to prevent, as far as possible, any problems with a pregnancy. Special tests such as amniocentesis, chorionic villus sampling, ultrasound scanning and particular blood tests may identify certain conditions but cannot alter them.

Parents and society naturally expect perfect babies. The emphasis on special tests, with the expectation that a mother will seek a termination if there is something wrong with the baby that cannot be 'cured', puts great pressure on women. Sophisticated testing can cause confusion and ongoing anxiety in parents as questions and queries cannot always be answered. Waiting for the results of invasive tests or deciding whether or not to have a test at all is stressful for them. Mothers especially have to consider the following:

- what they would do if results do not give peace of mind, but point to a high risk of abnormality
- how they would feel if a test diagnosed Down **syndrome** or other **chromosome** disorder
- The possibility (one in one hundred) of a miscarriage following amniocentesis or chorionic villus sampling
- how accurate the tests are and the possibility of terminating a healthy pregnancy or giving birth to a baby with special needs.

KEY POINTS

- Parents have a right to all available information about special needs. While some special needs may be identified before birth, the importance of every child as a unique individual with their own potential must be recognised and valued.
- Parents may need information about an **inherited** condition and the risk of

passing it on to children or grandchildren. **Genetic counselling** can advise a couple on the probability or degree of risk and the choices they need to think about. It is a sensitive area of medicine, and professionals should support a couple in the decision they make.

Activity

Find out about the special tests of pregnancy. At what stage of a pregnancy would these tests be offered? How are the tests carried out? What specific conditions might these tests identify?

GOOD PRACTICE

- Throughout infancy and childhood, child health promotion and surveillance programmes are offered. Observation of children by family doctors, health visitors, Early Years and school staff and parents can identify, at an early age, those who may have special needs. Appropriate help can often limit or reverse the difficulties or delay.
- Immunisation is an effective form of preventive care for infants and young children. It is offered routinely from the age of two months. Occasionally, for specific medical reasons, the doctor will advise against a child receiving immunisation.

The boxed text below, 'Towards prevention and early identification of special needs', sets out measures that may prevent, or identify, special needs at an early stage.

TOWARDS PREVENTION AND EARLY IDENTIFICATION OF SPECIAL NEEDS

- Genetic counselling.
- Preconceptual care: medical care and positive health advice given to a couple before starting a pregnancy. It includes self-care by continuing or changing to a healthy lifestyle.
- High standards of prenatal, perinatal and neonatal care.
- Immunisation programmes.
- Comprehensive child health services for child health promotion, screening and developmental assessment programmes; and efficient referral systems for specialist care and investigations.
- Loving and secure emotional environments in which children can thrive and be happy.
- Healthy and safe environments that lessen the risk of childhood illnesses, infections and accidents.

SOME POSSIBLE CAUSES OF SPECIAL NEEDS

Hereditary factors

Genetic inheritance	Cystic fibrosis, sickle cell and thalassaemia conditions, phenylketonuria, Tay-Sachs disease and others (some of these are discussed in Chapter 7).
Chromosomal inheritance	Down syndrome, fragile X syndrome (see Chapter 9).
Sex-linked inheritance	Haemophilia, Duchenne muscular dystrophy (see Chapter 7).

KEY POINTS

- Inherited disorders are passed on from parents to their children and are *always present at birth* even if not immediately identifiable.
- *One or more* special need may be present but *one* may predominate.

Prenatal factors	Substances: drugs, tobacco, alcohol. Maternal infections, including: rubella, toxoplasmosis, cytomegalovirus, listeriosis, HIV and some sexually transmitted diseases (STDs). Threatened miscarriage.
At birth	Anoxia (lack of oxygen), **prematurity**, postmaturity, low birth weight, difficult delivery.
Postnatal factors	Infections including: bacterial meningitis, measles, mumps, diphtheria, poliomyelitis. Accidents/injuries: particularly those damaging the brain and spinal cord. Childhood cancers: leukaemia, sarcomas, retinoblastoma, Wilm's tumour. Child abuse of any kind. Allergic reactions, including asthma and eczema (see Chapter 6).
Childcare and parenting factors	Frequent changes in prime carers during early years. Emotional deprivation. Family stress. Difficulties with parenting.
Unknown factors	Sometimes it is not possible to identify a clear cause for a special need.

KEY POINTS

- Conditions present at birth are said to be congenital.
- Congenital conditions are not necessarily hereditary, for example congenital heart disease, congenital dislocation of the hip.
- Special needs may not become obvious until a baby grows and develops, hence the importance of health promotion and developmental assessment programmes.

PROGRESS CHECK

1 What do you understand by (a) hereditary, (b) congenital?
2 Name three prenatal factors that may have adverse effects on the unborn baby.
3 What particular infections in infancy or childhood may result in a baby or young child having special needs?
4 What is preconceptual care?
5 Other than through preconceptual care, how else might special needs be prevented or identified at an early stage?

Meeting the needs of parents and family

PARENTS

Parents do not expect their child to have developmental delay, require additional help, perhaps undergo intrusive medical procedures or even to die in early life. The whole sudden experience of having a baby with special needs can be deeply upsetting and isolating.

Recognising a special need

Sometimes the diagnosis is very obvious and clear at, or just after, birth. For some children and their families it may be many months or even years before a diagnosis can be made. When a special need is recognised in a child the parents inevitably need time to understand, adapt and accept. They need time to adjust and learn about their child as an individual with her own personality and potential. Often, the only information parents have about certain conditions is affected by the prejudice of society. Their own experience may be very limited.

KEY POINT

A child's special need may affect only a minor part of the child's life, or it may be a major and challenging factor.

Parents' reactions

Many parents will go through the different emotional stages associated with bereavement – grieving for their apparently 'lost' child – before they are able to accept, adjust and take pleasure in her. Such reactions are seen across all cultures and social classes. Typically parents experience:

- shock, grief, numbness and confusion, inability to come to terms or fully comprehend and take in what has happened
- denial of any long-term disabling condition, feeling their child 'will grow out of it' or 'catch up later'; of an older child they may say she's 'just lazy' or 'shy'
- feelings of guilt and apportioning blame, particularly if the child has an inherited condition or the mother smoked or drank heavily during pregnancy. Anger and blame may be directed at the doctor for not recognising or preventing the special need prenatally or at birth. Parents may blame

themselves or each other if their child is disabled following an accident or serious illness.

■ gradual orientation, acceptance and adjustment – they are able to relate to their child as an individual with her own personality and potential.

KEY POINT

There is no time limit to this process of acceptance and adjustment; it may take up to several years. Parents work through the stages in their own time.

Adjustment

In spite of the sadness and stress they feel, most parents learn to love their child and are aware of the greater degree of dependency and responsibility there is always going to be. Their protective instincts are usually heightened, sometimes to the point of overprotection. Adjusting to the implication that their child will not get better and striving to provide the care, opportunity and stimulation required by the child (often despite the attitudes of society) can be a challenging process.

KEY POINT

Some parents find it difficult to cope and may never reach this stage of adjustment. They may be reluctant to share their anxieties either with family or a professional carer. Some children with special needs are fostered or adopted.

Questions parents ask

Initially, many questions are asked – 'Why did it happen?', 'What is it?', 'Why us?' Parents want quick answers to questions such as 'Will she die?', 'Will she learn to walk and talk?', 'Will she be able to go to ordinary school?' or 'What quality of life will she have?' There may be no ready answers. Sometimes, the cause is never determined, possibly making the situation harder for the parents to accept, although knowing the cause does not automatically make it easier.

PROGRESS CHECK

1 Describe the typical emotional stages parents go through when their baby is born with a special need.
2 Why might parents feel guilty or seek to blame themselves?
3 How long might it take parents to reach the stage of acceptance and adjustment?

Areas of difficulty

Mother–baby bonding

For medical reasons mother and baby may be separated from each other, or a mother may be reluctant to hold, cuddle and feed her baby, fearful of yet more powerful emotions should her baby die. Parents may find their baby's physical appearance upsetting. The baby may be rejected.

KEY POINT

A mother may have mixed feelings of love and dislike, particularly if there are feeding difficulties or she receives no response from her child to caring overtures.

GOOD PRACTICE

While family and friends may be attentive and caring it is important that sensitive professional counselling and support is available. Parents need to be listened to and helped to recognise and express their feelings.

Relationships

Family routines tend to revolve around a child with special needs. Twenty-four-hour care is often necessary, with parents taking 'turns'. As their child gets bigger and heavier, routines of carrying, lifting and bathing may become more difficult and parents feel exhausted. The child may be sleeping in the parents' room or a parent may sleep with the child in her room.

Financial pressures can occur from loss of earnings due to caring responsibilities, extra laundry, heating and lighting costs. Transport costs to and from appointments and assessments plus possible adaptations to the home (there may be grants towards these) all quickly add up. Stress and anxiety can lead to irritability and arguments. Strained relationships, separation and divorce are not uncommon. For many families, though, relationships grow stronger as they find the determination and energy to face the difficulties and strive to find the support and provision they know is best for their child.

Isolation

Parents may feel isolated from family, friends and their local community because their child is 'different' and does not fit into the normal pattern. They may feel they are the only people to have a child with a special need. Their isolation can be partly self-enforced as a way of coping or to avoid the hurt and embarrassment of unsocial behaviour, for example whispering or turning away – many people today still have little awareness of special needs. Equally, there is less time for socialising. Day-to-day activities, which most mothers and young children do together, are limited, especially while the child is not walking.

Supporting the parents' needs

When the needs of parents are recognised and supported there is less stress and anxiety within the family, often reducing the length of time towards acceptance and adjustment.

KEY POINT

Support and advice from the different agencies (statutory and voluntary) must be offered sensitively, and with understanding and direction.

In particular, parents need:

- information about their child's condition and the help available. They have a right to know about their child's difficulties and where to go for help – not knowing is confusing and stressful.
- support for their own emotional needs. As a child reaches the age at which she would have achieved particular milestones such as sitting up, walking and talking, the sense of loss and sadness frequently re-emerges. Unsupported needs have damaging and destructive effects on the whole family.
- practical help in the home. This may be offered by relatives, friends or the social services department.
- contact and friendship with other parents whose own experiences provide valuable insights into many aspects of special needs. Special needs support groups or self-help groups provide the opportunity to share feelings and concerns, perhaps saying things that could not be comfortably shared with the professionals. Information about play and school facilities, financial benefits, babysitting and childminding and so on are available within these groups. Parents whose children are older can say what did and did not help them. (More details of befriending schemes are included on pages 182–3.)
- time to be with other members of their family and meet their needs.

KEY POINTS

- Parents need assurance that their emotions are normal reactions. Pretending they do not exist does not make them go away.
- Help and counselling are available. A 'special needs' health visitor can be a vital point of professional contact. A health visitor is outside the family circle, someone in whom parents may find it easier to trust and confide.

GOOD PRACTICE

Link workers from ethnic minorities should be available from both statutory and voluntary agencies to enable families to obtain the support, information and resources they need. Similarly, parents for whom English is not their home or community language or who have communication difficulties, need interpreters and translators who are skilled in special needs issues, as well as information presented on tapes, in large print and in Braille.

KEY POINTS

- Over-saturation with information and conflicting advice is a common experience. Parents need to pull back from time to time and listen to their own feelings and instincts.
- Parents from ethnic minorities may experience lack of effective communication from the professionals. They may be unclear about the specific roles of the professionals and the terminology they use.

PROGRESS CHECK

1 Why is it important to support parents' emotional needs? How can this be done?
2 How can the needs of parents from ethnic minorities be identified and supported?

Activity

You are employed as a nanny caring for a baby, now ten days old, with special needs. The baby's mother is distressed and reluctant to hold, cuddle and care for her baby although she will offer her the bottle.

Think of ways in which you could help and support the mother to get close to and relate to her baby.

THE CHILD

Most children with special needs are loved and accepted within their families but some experience loss of love and approval from the important people in their lives. The negative attitudes of many in society lead to discrimination and isolation. For a child with restricted mobility there is greater dependence on parents, perhaps resulting in over-protection and greater control in the child's life.

Supporting the child's needs

All children with special needs have a right to be part of a family, a community and society. They also have a right to:
- love, security, respect and stability of care
- be valued for who they are
- appropriate specialist care and therapy
- play opportunities, stimulation and social interaction
- inclusive daycare and education with key worker support and flexible provision.

GOOD PRACTICE

Professional carers must help parents to find a healthy balance between caring and protecting and allowing their child to develop the confidence necessary for independence and quality of life.

KEY POINT

Too great a preoccupation with her special need or using it to gain attention is damaging to a child's social and emotional development.

Further references
Throughout this book there is emphasis on the uniqueness and value of every child. Chapter 2 details ways in which you can help a child develop self-esteem and confidence. Most chapters identify specific support and provision such as health care, play and education opportunities. Chapters 4 and 5 describe the role of a key worker in caring for children with special needs.

THE SIBLINGS

The effects on brothers and sisters vary according to their ages, birth order and the number of children in the family.

Siblings may experience:

■ over-protection or, possibly, neglect
■ resentment at the amount of attention given to their brother or sister, including continual discussion about the child between parents and other adults
■ jealousy
■ a shift in the family balance, which means they may have to take on a domestic role
■ worry and anxiety that they will 'catch' their brother or sister's condition
■ fear and concern at witnessing their parents' distress or rejection of the child
■ teasing and social isolation
■ emotional swings, from being loving and protective to disturbed behaviour such as regression, attention-seeking, moodiness, anxiety, low self-esteem, embarrassment or guilt.

Siblings may feel anxious and concerned

KEY POINTS

- Not all siblings will experience such emotional or social disadvantage. Much depends on individual personality and the bond between them and their brother or sister with special needs. Many remain happy and well adjusted.
- You may care for siblings in an Early Years, school or home setting. Observation of their play and behaviour (perhaps in the home corner), or of their drawings, painting and general demeanour, may indicate they are experiencing difficulties. They may exhibit regressive behaviour, resort to temper tantrums or become withdrawn and clinging.

Supporting the siblings' needs

Siblings may be supported by:

- individual attention and reassurance that they are loved and valued
- one-to-one key worker provision for a child in a daycare or education setting
- opportunity for older children to express their feelings and be listened to uncritically by parents, carers or professionals such as the family doctor, health visitor, Early Years worker or child psychiatrist
- time on their own with parents
- correct information appropriate to their level of understanding – there may be a misunderstanding or lack of knowledge about the special need that is causing unnecessary worry
- encouragement to care for their brother and sister in small everyday ways just as an older child normally would for a younger member of the family. This includes cuddling, talking and playing with her and fetching nappies and clothes during bathing and changing routines.

Siblings need individual quality time with parents

GRANDPARENTS AND OTHER CLOSE FAMILY MEMBERS

Grandparents, other close family members and involved adults may initially feel confused and lacking in confidence. They can be encouraged to treat the child just as they would any other child in the family. They will quickly learn the care and management routines, often becoming great sources of strength and support, both practically and emotionally.

CASE STUDY

Sammy was three-and-a-half years old and had attended a day care setting since he was eighteen months old. He had always been a happy, sociable and helpful little boy. An only child, he was particularly looking forward to the birth of his baby brother or sister and kept telling the day care staff how he was going to bring 'his' baby to the nursery every day so that he could look after 'it'.

Sibling participation in a caring routine

Susan was born six months later with cerebral palsy and a visual impairment. She was cared for in the special baby unit for two months before coming home.

Her parents cared for her with love and commitment but were, naturally, very worried, especially as she had marked developmental delay. They were also very tired. Inevitably, they had less time for Sammy, who still wanted to take Susan to the nursery and could not understand why she was not smiling and chuckling when he talked to her or gave her a tickle.

At the nursery the staff noticed Sammy had started to suck his thumb again (he had given that up a long time ago) and had become rather clingy. He also had had several 'accidents', although he had been clean and dry since he was two-and-a-half.

Several times Sammy threw the bricks he was playing with across the floor and spoilt a friend's painting.

1   Would you have been concerned about Sammy? Give reasons for your answer.
2   In what ways could the Early Years staff have supported Sammy and his family?

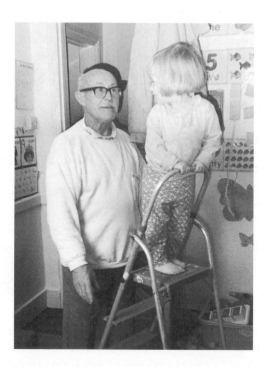

'Hello Grandad.' Grandparent support for a sibling

Multiprofessional teams

All children have a range of needs, including needs for health, education and care. Traditionally, services for young children have been organised separately to meet these needs through:

■ health services
■ education services
■ social care services.

Workers from health, education and social care services will liaise and work together with children and families when necessary. This enables them to meet families' needs in a co-ordinated way. Childcarers will liaise with workers from each of these services when appropriate. Health service workers include:

■ health visitors
■ doctors
■ nurses
■ physiotherapists
■ speech therapists.

Education workers include:

■ teachers
■ specialist teachers
■ classroom assistants
■ learning support workers
■ psychologists
■ educational welfare officers.

Social care workers include:

■ social workers
■ residential care workers
■ outreach workers
■ youth workers
■ probation officers.

It is becoming more common for professionals from these separate services to work to together on a day-to-day basis, perhaps alongside professionals from the voluntary and private sectors. We call this a multi-agency, multidisciplinary or multiprofessional team.

The purpose of the team is to work closely together for the benefit of children and families. Team members will share their knowledge, skills, understanding and perceptions (opinions). This is good for families because it means professionals can provide them with a fully co-ordinated service that meets their needs holistically (meaning wholly, or altogether). The professionals within the team will be aware of each other's work with the family at every stage.

When professionals work together from the same premises, it is much more convenient for families to access services on a practical level. For example, multiprofessional teams can be based within:

■ Sure Starts, where workers organising projects for families and young children might include Early Years workers, social workers, health visitors and outreach workers

- Children's trusts, which are new organisations for families, children and young people. Trusts bring together health, education and social care services locally. Some trusts have responsibility for all children's services, where others do not at present. Workers might include Early Years workers, social workers with different specialities, health visitors, speech therapists, educational psychologists, youth workers, playworkers and teachers.

Parents are always considered valuable members of the team and should be invited to participate in meetings concerning their child.

KEY POINTS

Early Years workers are members of the multidisciplinary team. They have a unique child health, education and social care training, enabling them to recognise early signs of difficulty in children. Opportunities exist for them to work in a variety of settings such as daycare, education, the home and hospital. In some areas Early Years workers assist health visitors in caring for families with young children in the community.

PROFESSIONALS AND THEIR SPECIALIST SKILLS

Health service professionals

Paediatrician (hospital or community based)
Paediatricians are doctors specialising in the diagnosis of illness, disorders and special needs in children and the provision of medical care. They work in hospitals or as members of the community child health service and may become involved with children with disabilities or special needs in the maternity unit, paediatric ward, out-patient department or a child development centre.

Consultant/specialist
Consultants/specialists care for children in hospital who have short-term or long-term serious medical or surgical needs. They have in-depth expertise and skill in specific conditions. An important aspect of their work is liaising with the family doctor and the school medical officer. They also contribute to assessments or reassessments of any child for whom they are caring.

Child psychiatrist
Child psychiatrists have a medical degree and specialise in child mental illness. They work in hospital child psychiatry units and community child and family guidance centres providing individual, family or group therapy for children with emotional or behavioural difficulties. In particular, child psychiatrists work as consultants giving insight and understanding to the origin of a child's problems, so enabling members of the team working directly with the child to offer effective help.

Child psychologist

Child psychologists are non-medical professionals working in child development centres and child and family guidance centres. They observe and assess children's social, emotional and behavioural development and needs. Understanding the dynamics, relationships and circumstances of the family is an important part of their work. Particularly, they offer advice on how to manage difficult or unusual behaviour.

Child psychotherapist

Child psychotherapists work in child and family guidance centres and are concerned with child development and the way relationships develop within the family. They help children and families to work through their problems.

Family doctor

The family doctor (or general practitioner) is the key professional in the primary health care team and an important person in the lives of all families, especially those with young children. She is often the first point of call for worried parents. A family doctor may work from a health centre or surgery and will care for the general health needs of a child with special needs, including attending to everyday ailments and carrying out child health surveillance and immunisation programmes. Children are referred by their doctor for specialist care and therapy. Access to accurate and updated information about service provision enables the family doctor to discuss options of care and management for the child and support for the family – for example, Portage (see pages 176–9) and **respite care**.

Health visitor

Health visitors have a background in nursing, obstetric training and the health and development of infants and young children. They are members of the primary health care team working in the community with people of all ages. They have particular responsibilities towards all children under five years, visiting them and their families at home. A health visitor may be the first person to identify a possible special need in a child and is frequently the Named Person (see Chapter 3, page 75) for a child under five years with a special need.

Many health authorities employ specialist health visitors to work with families who have a child with a special need. They offer help, counselling, support and advice, and provide a link between the hospital and community services. They know how to access the right statutory and voluntary services and provide information about local support groups, playgroups and toy libraries. At all times they work and liaise with a family's regular health visitor.

A regular or specialist health visitor will visit the family as often as necessary to offer early support and build up an in-depth relationship with the child and the family.

Community paediatric nurse

Community paediatric nurses are specialist children's nurses working in the community from a hospital or health centre base. They help and support children in their own homes who require nursing care and who, without this service, would need to remain in hospital. Through an assessment process they are able to identify the nursing and equipment needs of babies and children with profound and complex special needs. They liaise and co-ordinate care with the hospital and primary health care team.

School medical officer and school nurse
School medical officers are concerned with the health needs of school children and advise the local education authority on the medical aspect of children's development. They provide medical supervision for children with special needs in the school and may be part of a multidisciplinary team assessing pre-school children with special needs. They do not directly treat any medical condition but refer a child to the family doctor or appropriate specialist.

School nurses discuss health issues with children and their parents offering health-promotion advice and referring children when necessary to the school medical officer. They may carry out selective vision and hearing screening tests. Many work in special schools where they supervise the routine medical care of children with special needs.

Speech and language therapist
Speech and language therapists are concerned with all aspects of communication. They assess children's hearing, speech and language, and check mouth and tongue movements. They prepare individual programmes of activities and exercises for children to help them acquire language and use speech. Children with a cleft lip and/or palate, cerebral palsy, a hearing impairment or a stammer are particularly helped by speech therapy. Children with speech and communication difficulties often have secondary behavioural and social problems. Speech and language therapists work either in the community, hospital clinics or schools.

Paediatric physiotherapist
Physiotherapists assess children's motor skills and help those with movement, positioning or balancing difficulties. Their aim is to provide exercises and activities to improve these skills. They demonstrate exercises to help breathing and coughing in children with cystic fibrosis, which parents or carers can carry out at home or in school. Physiotherapists work in hospitals, health centres and schools.

Occupational therapist
Occupational therapists are concerned with the practical and functional skills needed for everyday living. They particularly assess children's fine and gross motor skills in relation to their ability to feed, wash and dress themselves appropriate to their age. They give advice regarding toys and suitable home equipment, which will help a child to play constructively, move around, sit and position themselves independently. Occupational therapists work either in hospitals or in the community.

Dietician/nutritionist

Dieticians or nutritionists give advice on a range of special diets. Children with diabetes, cystic fibrosis and coeliac condition have dietary requirements, which enable them to remain healthy. The dietician or nutritionist will support the child and family in managing the special diet and offer ongoing advice as the child grows or a dietary need alters. They may work in hospitals and in the community.

Play therapist

Play therapists work with individual children or groups of children in paediatric wards, or sometimes in day nurseries, to alleviate stress and anxiety through play. They provide a range of play experiences for children to help them 'play out' emotions such as fear, discrimination or aggression. Play therapists may hold an Early Years childcare and education award and may also have the Hospital Play Specialist Board Certificate.

PROGRESS CHECK

1 Which health professionals work in a child and family guidance centre?
2 Describe how the family doctor might be involved in caring for children with special needs.
3 How can specialist health visitors help children with special needs and their families?
4 Which health service professional would assess the nursing needs of a child with special needs being cared for at home?
5 How does a paediatric physiotherapist help a child with cystic fibrosis?

Education service professionals

Educational psychologist

Educational psychologists are trained and experienced teachers with additional qualifications in education psychology. They advise teachers and parents about children who may be experiencing learning or behavioural difficulties and prepare educational assessments for children requiring a statement of special educational needs (see Chapter 3, pages 90–4).

Education welfare officer/education social worker

Education welfare officers provide a link between children and their families, the school and the local education authority. In particular, they are concerned with the welfare of children whose school attendance is irregular. They may negotiate alternative education provision for excluded pupils and can be a main contributor of social information in any assessment procedure.

Special needs support teacher

Special needs support teachers, sometimes called learning support teachers, are teachers with additional training and experience. They may be appointed to work in a particular school teaching individual children or they may be **peripatetic** – moving from place to place – teaching children in different education settings and visiting pre-school children with special needs in their own homes. In particular, they work with children with vision, hearing, speech and language impairments.

Special needs adviser

Special needs advisers are peripatetic teachers with specific expertise, who visit the schools of a particular local education authority giving specialist advice and support both to children with special educational needs and to the teaching staff.

Special needs assistant

Special needs assistants (also known as learning support assistants or special schools assistants) are non-teaching members of staff who provide extra help and support for children with special needs and are seen as members of the school team. They may be qualified Early Years workers or may hold the Certificate in Learning Support. Some may be trained teachers who do not want the responsibility of a full teaching role, while others may have no formal qualifications but have worked with children in a variety of ways. They provide learning support for individual children or groups of children, some of whom may have received a statement of special educational needs (see Chapter 3, pages 90–4). Specific training will be needed when working with children who require medical routines such as physiotherapy.

PROGRESS CHECK

1 Describe the work of an educational psychologist.
2 A special needs support teacher may be 'peripatetic'? What do you understand by the word peripatetic?

Social service professionals

Social worker

Social workers are employed mainly by local authorities but may also work for voluntary organisations. They are based in hospitals or a local area office. They hold a social work qualification and undertake different kinds of social welfare responsibilities for children with special needs and their families, including advising on accessing resources, benefits and services to which children and parents are entitled and acting as an **advocate** to enable them to obtain these services. They offer counselling and support to parents or carers and help them to understand the special needs of their child. Social workers are involved in assessment for daycare, respite care and family aide provision. They have statutory child protection duties towards children with special needs and are responsible for the quality of care for those looked after in residential care homes.

A psychiatric social worker has special expertise in working with school children with emotional, behavioural and learning difficulties and is often a member of the child and family guidance centre team.

Residential social worker/childcare officer

Residential social workers or childcare officers provide day-to-day care and support for children, including those with special needs, living in long-term or short-term residential care homes. They may also be key workers for individual children in these homes maintaining an overall interest in their welfare.

PROGRESS CHECK

How might social workers be involved in supporting children with special needs and their families?

Activity

1   Find out further information about any three of the professionals listed above. Write down your findings.
2   In what circumstances might an Early Years worker caring for children with special needs liaise with (a) a health visitor; (b) a paediatric physiotherapist; (c) a speech and language therapist; (d) a social worker?

KEY TERMS

You need to know what these words and phrases mean. Go back through the chapter and make sure that you understand:

disability	multiprofessional team
disability awareness and equality	social service professionals
education service professionals	stages of bereavement
health service professionals	types of special need
impairment	

2 PERCEPTIONS OF DISABILITY: ACCESS AND INCLUSION

> **This chapter covers:**
> - **The medical and social models of disability**
> - **Disability awareness**
> - **Positive images of disability and special needs**
> - **Language used, attitudes and behaviour**
> - **Discrimination and stereotyping**
> - **The child's self-image**
> - **Access and inclusion**
> - **The Early Years Foundation Stage**
> - **Play materials and toys**

The medical and social models of disability, describing two different approaches to disability, are explained in this chapter. The text also focuses on discrimination, **stereotyping** and the use of inappropriate language in relation to children with special needs and stresses the importance of challenging these behaviours. Strategies for helping children with special needs to develop a positive self-image are identified and the prominent issues of access and inclusion are addressed. The principles of inclusive day care are also set out in the chapter.

The medical and social models of disability

The medical and social models of disability provide a framework to explain, in simple terms, two differing perceptions of disability.

THE MEDICAL MODEL

The medical model of disability, also called the 'individual' or 'personal tragedy' model, sees a child or adult as a problem because of their disability or special need. It focuses on what a disabled person cannot do. It labels disabled people as 'ill' and in need of treatment, and may fail to take into account a disabled person's own views and feelings, leaving them powerless, without choice and dependent on others. The medical model contributes to disabled people being thought of as patients, reluctant to give up the 'sick role'. The phrase 'suffering from' Down syndrome and so on) is commonly heard. This encourages dependence on professionals, family and friends, and leads to over-protection and social isolation, often with the result that disabled people are less likely to challenge exclusion from mainstream society. Parents may feel guilty and at fault for their child's impairment and perhaps try to compensate by seeking different medical opinions, cures and alternative therapies, and take on the role of 'nurse' to their child.

Within the medical model society responds to disability by determining where disabled children should be cared for, go to school and, later, where they should live and what type of work would be suitable for them. This attitude reinforces reliance on others, giving disabled children no control over their lives and denying them opportunities for choice.

The Disability Movement (a growing group of disabled people and supporters) rejects the medical model of disability because it discriminates, patronises and fails to accord disabled people the opportunities and rights available to others.

However, inherent in the medical model are the positive values of pain relief, medication and provision of specialist resources such as surgery and a range of therapies. Without medical treatments and therapies many children with disabilities would die. For example, regular physiotherapy, medication and dietary management are essential if children with cystic fibrosis are to remain well. Babies born with spina bifida may require life-saving surgery with ongoing nursing care and physiotherapy.

THE SOCIAL MODEL

The social model of disability came about through the Disability Movement, and other organisations, campaigning for equal rights, opportunities and choices for disabled people. It rejects the medical model of disability but does not deny the need for medical care. Within the social model it is society that is the problem, not the disabled child or adult. It is society that disables and excludes children and adults from mainstream life by creating barriers of rejection, discrimination, negative attitudes and poor social organisation. The social model acknowledges those with disabilities as people first and foremost. It emphasises the need for structural and social change to enable disabled people to take charge of their own lives in a society that is inclusive, accessible and supportive of personal rights, choice and freedom.

Changes and reorganisation (some of which are now enshrined in law) should include: creating physical access to buildings, transport and housing; providing access to information (large print, Braille, signing, tapes, different languages); establishing equal opportunities and inclusion in education, employment, play and recreation; challenging discrimination, stereotyping and inappropriate language from whatever source; and adapting management practices in the workplace.

We (disabled people) reject the inhumanity of the 'medical model' of thinking, involved in labelling and identifying people by their impairing conditions. Calling someone a 'Down's child' or a 'spina bif' makes the child no more than their condition . . . the social model of disability identifies prejudice and discrimination in institutions, policies, structures and the whole environment of our society as the principle for our exclusion . . . we must reject the legacy of the past that has excluded us and see children as they really are – not 'categories' but as citizens and with contributions to make, if we let them (Micheline Mason, 1994).

Internationally, disabled people are now united to stand up to oppression and discrimination, to challenge society and confront all those in authority, including professionals, in the fields of health and social care.

How would you describe and present to your peer group the perceptions of disability as described in the medical and social models?

Disability awareness

Disability awareness means understanding, valuing and embracing difference and diversity, responding positively to what disabled children and adults consider important in their lives and respecting the human and civil rights of all disabled people. Particular principles include:

- understanding and positively responding to the social model of disability
- professionals, parents, carers and all members of society listening and talking to disabled children and adults, so learning directly from them
- breaking down barriers facing people with disabilities; recognising and challenging all forms of discrimination, bias, stereotyping, inappropriate language and behaviour; being firm and confident in response to such behaviours so that the person concerned understands that their approach was wrong and insensitive
- displaying and using positive images of children and adults with disabilities in books, playthings and in the media
- understanding the need for social change and an accessible, **inclusive environment**.

Social interaction and inclusion

DISABILITY AWARENESS AND EQUALITY TRAINING

Disability awareness and equality training, available through courses and learning packs, is prepared and given by disabled people themselves. The resources can be adapted to meet the needs of particular groups. Training seeks to raise people's awareness of the issues surrounding disability, equal opportunities and the disabling nature of society. It promotes the social model of disability and inclusive practice and examines the preoccupation of society with 'perfect babies' and intolerance to difference. Training also explores discrimination, negative perceptions of disability and the language used to describe disability. The impact these attitudes have on the lives of disabled people, and strategies for challenging them, is examined. Role play and case studies are usually included in the training. Those working with disabled young children in inclusive care and education settings may wish to consider using this facility both for the staff and parents. Providers of training include the Disability Resource Team and Disability Equality Training Network. Addresses and websites can be found on pages 408–12.

'Please will someone come and play with me?'

GOOD PRACTICE

Equal opportunities policies in Early Years settings, schools and childminding facilities must make reference to children with disabilities and special needs, indicating how their needs will be met and setting out agreed procedures for dealing with incidents of disability discrimination or harassment.

FEAR AND EMBARRASSMENT

Many people have deep-seated fears about disability or are embarrassed by it, particularly if they have no experience or understanding of it. They may be unsure how to approach or speak to someone who is disabled, often assuming a child or adult with a physical condition is also deaf (especially if they use a wheel-chair). They may be disturbed by the physical appearance of people with Down syndrome and feel threatened by people with mental disabilities. To overcome fear and embarrassment they may stare at, ignore, ridicule or speak disparagingly of disabled people, possibly not fully realising how offensive and hurtful their behaviour and remarks are.

As an Early Years worker you may have similar concerns and worries and may be alarmed at the strength of your feelings. Always discuss any anxieties you have with your supervisor or a senior member of staff. Becoming familiar with special needs issues and caring for children with special needs reduces anxieties and fears and leads to an understanding and appreciation of different abilities.

PROGRESS CHECK

1   What do you understand by the phrase 'disability awareness'?
2   What facility could you use to learn more about disability awareness and equality?

EQUAL OPPORTUNITIES

All children are equal and must be loved, accepted, valued and respected for who they are. For some children sign language will be their first language, for others mobility will be by wheelchair. Being unable to walk or communicate verbally are differences, not failures. Children with disabilities and special needs are children first and foremost and, while they may require special learning programmes or different forms of therapy, they also need plenty of opportunities to play, make choices and interact with their carers, friends and peers. Like all children they will have particular interests and talents, for example in music, reading and drawing, which must be encouraged and supported.

Further references to equal opportunities are threaded through the text of this book.

Some children will have a particular interest and talent

- Always look beyond the disability and make sure children's 'special needs' do not overshadow their 'ordinary needs'. Be positive and think about what each child can do, not what the child cannot do.
- No child should be left out of any activity because of his disability or special need. Make sure you help non-disabled children to understand that all children have a right to be included in the activities of the setting at their individual levels.
- Non-disabled and disabled children (including those who use wheelchairs) can learn about each other through 'pairing' in activities such as music and dance, ball games and so on. After a while the children will initiate pairing themselves.

KEY POINT

Children with disabilities and special needs also have 'ordinary' needs, which must not be overlooked.

DEVELOPING CARE SKILLS

As an Early Years worker, perhaps a key worker, you may initially feel uncomfortable and unsure about caring for children with disabilities and special needs, and feel you lack the necessary skills and knowledge to be an effective care-giver.

You may be cautious when lifting and handling children with physical disabilities in case you hurt them or you may be worried about helping a child at meal and snack times who has difficulty in chewing and swallowing.

Communicate and talk directly with the children and ask them how they like to be moved, positioned and helped with eating and drinking. Members of staff with expertise and specialist carers, such as a physiotherapist, occupational therapist or member of a particular voluntary organisation, can offer practical advice about moving, lifting and positioning children so that they are supported and comfortable at all times. They will also suggest ways to help children at mealtimes. A good relationship with parents is essential as they are the real experts in caring for their child. They will tell you what the child can and cannot manage in mobility and independence skills and help you to communicate directly with him. As you get to know individual children's likes and dislikes, how to make them comfortable and the level of physical contact they prefer, you will gain in confidence. (See also Chapter 5, pages 163–70.)

Some children with special needs require considerable help when eating

GOOD PRACTICE

When caring for children who do not find verbal communication and self-expression easy, be patient and wait until the child indicates by a sound, eye movement, nod or other small gesture that a need has been expressed or a choice made. It may take time and many guesses before you get it right.

PARENT WORKSHOPS

Workshops, organised by an Early Years setting or school, can offer guidance, support and encouragement to parents. The sessions need careful planning. Specialist speakers, or parents with a particular expertise in the area of special needs, can be invited to give talks and lead discussions on topics chosen by those attending the workshops. Examples might be:

- adapting play materials and activities
- accessing support services
- the process of **statementing**
- how to prepare for a special educational needs Appeal Tribunal.
- **advocacy** training (Chapter 3, pages 114–5).

These workshops enable parents to support each other, become more confident in their ability to help their child and find their way through what, at times, may seem a mass of red tape.

GOOD PRACTICE

Establishing a relationship of respect and trust with parents is essential for the well-being of children with disabilities and special needs.

KEY POINT

Setting up workshops for parents enables them to become informed, develop confidence and gain new skills to help their children.

Positive images of disability and special needs

Positive images of children and adults with disabilities and special needs from different cultures should be represented in care and education settings through books, pictures, posters, displays and puzzles, and in the home corner.

Persona dolls are valuable in helping children to gain positive, accurate and visible information about differences and disability. The dolls (toddler sized, with different skin tones and special needs) have their own individual personalities and life histories. They can represent both boys and girls in wheelchairs, wearing glasses, or using hearing aids, crutches and splints. The children can be shown how particular aids are used and their importance in helping children and adults to see, hear and walk. The dolls do not stay in the home corner but are introduced to the children at story or circle times, or in one-to-one or small group situations. Early Years workers can then encourage the children to ask questions, explore their feelings and engage in discussion about special needs. Dolls, in particular, help children to understand how someone can be different in one respect but similar in other ways, for example, a doll with a disability still needs to be bathed, fed and cuddled. Training on the use of persona dolls is available – see address on page 411.

Books that include a child or adult with special needs (not with an exaggerated profile or simply as a token gesture, but as an integral part of the story) help children to develop sensitive understanding of disability. Read and talk about the stories with the children before they look at the book for themselves.

KEY POINTS

■ Active, adult interaction with the children in exploring 'special needs' dolls and stories helps them to understand concepts of special needs and how particular aids are used. Children can learn more about disability by playing with the dolls in the home corner and looking again at the stories in the book corner.
■ Always check the safety of any special needs aids for the home corner before offering them to children.

Activity
Check the contents of the home corner in your setting; also look at the books, pictures and posters you provide. Do they encourage the children to gain an awareness of physical differences and special needs? Are there any other resources you could offer the children to help them to learn about children and adults with special needs?

SPECIAL EQUIPMENT

Modern, computerised technology is increasingly used to help children with special needs. Some pieces of medical and educational equipment, for example, computer systems, complex nutritional equipment, voice synthesisers and electronically controlled wheelchairs, are fairly technical and parents, carers, teachers and the children themselves need help to understand how they work. One-to-one demonstrations and advice, information booklets and programmes, plus training videos, may be necessary for some of the more sophisticated items. In addition, for every piece of such equipment a child in your care uses, ask yourself:
■ How dependent is the child on it?
■ What could go wrong with it and how would the child be affected if it failed in some way?

- How accessible is twenty-four-hour emergency back-up support and advice if there is a problem with it?
- How must it be stored?
- What essential aspects of maintenance such as cleaning and daily safety checks must be carried out? (Check manufacturer's instructions.)

KEY POINT

By helping children to understand the specific technology on which they depend, you are encouraging them to be independent and take control of a part of their life.

Less complicated aids include walking frames, standing frames, artificial limbs, glasses and different hearing aids. Some children may be curious about these items. Talk to them about the different aids, how they are used and cared for. They may ask if they can try out an item used by their friend. Always ask permission from the child or his parents to do this, make sure the equipment is not damaged and that it is returned to the owner after use.

Language used, attitudes and behaviour

Language carries many powerful messages It *reflects* and *shapes* attitudes. The use of inappropriate words and terms when talking about disability is insulting and not only devalues disabled children but also labels and categorises them, so reinforcing negative attitudes and influencing the way society perceives disability.

Incorrect and offensive terminology oppresses, offends and patronises. It contributes to poor self-image and lack of self-esteem among children with disabilities.

Choose your words and terminology carefully. Children will copy the language used by their adult carers and older children. It is easy to be negative or cause offence without realising it. Talk about an individual child and his personality, not his special need. Say what you mean but be careful to say it positively. Check with the Scope bookmark 'Think About The Words You Use', on page 43, for appropriate words and phrases to use.

INAPPROPRIATE LANGUAGE

Examples of inappropriate language include:
- abnormal, deaf and dumb, dummy
- daft, lunatic, mental, mongol
- spastic, cripple, hop-a-long
- the disabled, the handicapped
- the Down boy in reception class, the deaf baby in the nursery, the cerebral palsied child.

Such language is hurtful to a child's dignity. It also focuses primarily on the disability rather than the child.

'It hurts when I'm called names. I just go away and cry.'

Through education and the work of disability organisations, society is now much more aware of what is acceptable and preferred language. Non-disabled people should always be guided by disabled people in the language they use.

CHILDREN'S AWARENESS OF DISABILITY AND SPECIAL NEEDS

Children are naturally curious. They usually become aware of disability some time around three years of age and will ask many questions about a child they perceive as being different. Children need accurate and developmentally appropriate information about their own and others' disabilities. They may wonder if a condition is catching or if it hurts. Ignoring their questions or failure to resolve any fears and anxieties they may have can reinforce myths and lead to later bias and discrimination.

GOOD PRACTICE

- Always use appropriate language yourself and teach children correct words and terms if they are known.
- Do not criticise children for being curious and asking questions. Answer them as honestly as you can.

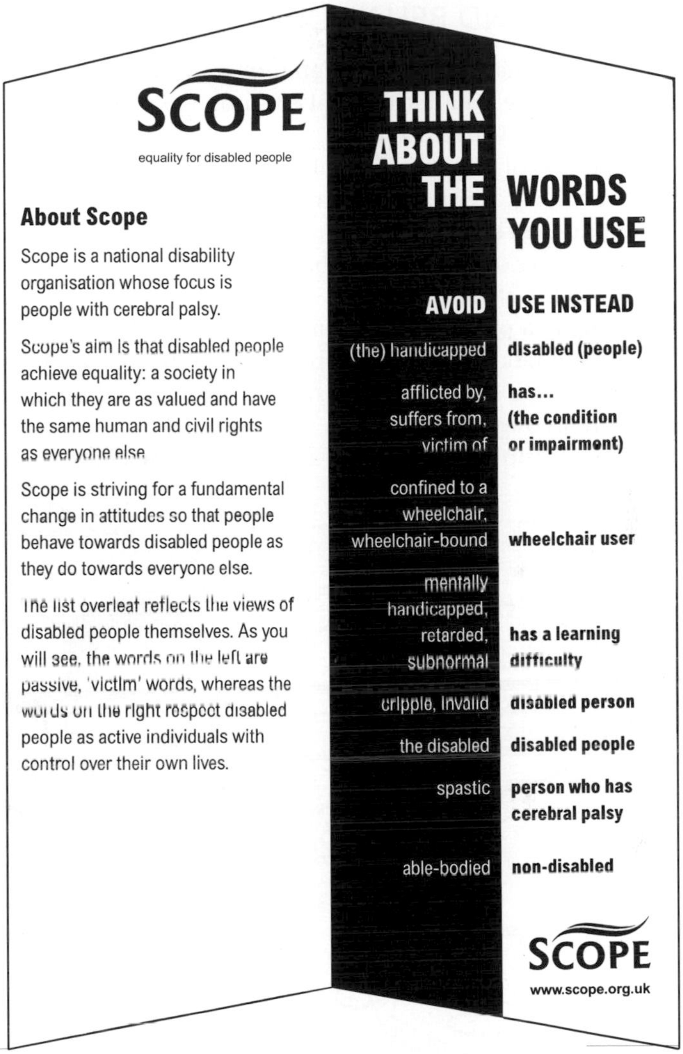
SCOPE
equality for disabled people
About Scope
Scope is a national disability organisation whose focus is people with cerebral palsy.
Scope's aim is that disabled people achieve equality: a society in which they are as valued and have the same human and civil rights as everyone else.
Scope is striving for a fundamental change in attitudes so that people behave towards disabled people as they do towards everyone else.
The list overleaf reflects the views of disabled people themselves. As you will see, the words on the left are passive, 'victim' words, whereas the words on the right respect disabled people as active individuals with control over their own lives.
THINK ABOUT THE WORDS YOU USE
AVOID
USE INSTEAD
(the) handicapped
disabled (people)
afflicted by, suffers from, victim of
has... (the condition or impairment)
confined to a wheelchair, wheelchair-bound
wheelchair user
mentally handicapped, retarded, subnormal
has a learning difficulty
cripple, invalid
disabled person
the disabled
disabled people
spastic
person who has cerebral palsy
able-bodied
non-disabled
SCOPE
www.scope.org.uk

The Scope bookmark sets out appropriate words and terms

Activity

Create a notice or a poster for the nursery or school indicating 'Words We Use'.

PROGRESS CHECK

1 How does inappropriate use of words and terms affect children with disabilities?
2 Why must you be careful about the language you use?
3 Why is it important not to ignore children's questions about disability?

ATTITUDES AND BEHAVIOUR

The following unacceptable and offensive attitudes and behaviour can have a negative influence and detrimental effect on the way children and their families react to and cope with disability:

- brusqueness of professionals during conversations or assessments
- talking to the carer instead of to the child
- assuming the child is deaf or unable to understand and communicate
- concentrating on a child's disability rather than his ability
- staring at the child
- behaving in a patronising way towards the child
- seeing and talking about children with disabilities as objects of curiosity and pity, deserving sympathy, for example 'Poor little thing', 'What a pity he can't walk on his own'
- pushing, teasing, name calling and bullying the child.

'I'm happy when you talk to ME.'

KEY POINT

Children's perceptions of special needs are greatly influenced by the attitude of their adult carers towards disability.

Discrimination and stereotyping

DISCRIMINATION

Instances of discrimination or prejudice on the grounds of disability or special needs must be challenged in the same way as any racial, religious or gender discrimination. Children can be upset or frightened by disability and may reject a disabled child. Give them the opportunity to talk about how they feel in an open and honest way. A child who has been discriminated against, perhaps by being teased or bullied or excluded from an activity or game, needs comfort, support and help to talk about how he is feeling. The other children will need reminding of the rules of the setting and through stories, role play and small-group work you can emphasise and reinforce what is hurtful and what is acceptable behaviour.

STEREOTYPING

Stereotyping, in the context of this book, means making assumptions, categorising or having pre-conceived fixed ideas or images about children with disabilities and special needs. This behaviour, which emphasises the differences between 'them' and 'us', usually occurs because of ignorance about disability and disabled children. Children with disabilities may be seen as:

■ tragic victims to be pitied
■ weak, oversensitive and a burden
■ helpless, unable to make decisions or to take responsibility for themselves
■ in need of care by 'normal' people
■ less intelligent than their non-disabled peers
■ deaf
■ infectious.

Physical appearance is important in our society. Books, theatrical productions and films often portray their characters as disabled to provide greater atmosphere and dramatic effect or to emphasise wickedness (Long John Silver in *Treasure Island* – blind in one eye and with a wooden leg; and Captain Hook in *Peter Pan* – only one hand).

Instances of discrimination against a child with special needs must always be challenged

In some countries children are deliberately maimed and disfigured before being put out to beg in the hope of evoking pity, guilt and a greater financial contribution from passers-by.

GOOD PRACTICE

Support and care for all children's needs without bias or discrimination and challenge any attitude or behaviour, from wherever it comes, that stereotypes, hurts or unfairly treats children with disabilities.

Activity
Write a story suitable for children aged three to five years. Without making any assumptions or being in any way patronising include a child or children with special needs in the story.

PROGRESS CHECK

1 In what ways might children with disabilities be discriminated against?
2 What do you understand by the word 'stereotyping'?

The child's self-image

All children need to feel good about themselves with a clear sense of who they are in order to develop into well-adjusted and independent members of society. Terms such as 'self-image', 'self-esteem' and 'positive identity' are all used in referring to how a child perceives himself.

KEY POINT

Children develop their self-image and identity from the attitudes of others towards them and the way their family, friends and carers interact with them.

A POOR SELF-IMAGE

Children compare themselves with others. A disabled child may have a poor self-image and lack confidence because of the differences (especially physical differences) he sees between himself and his friends or because of inappropriate comments made about his lack of progress in a particular developmental area. He may also hear adults make comments such as 'I don't know how you manage to look after him'. Over-enthusiastic attempts to make a child walk or talk at all costs and too much emphasis on treatment and cure will have a negative effect on a child's attitude towards himself.

PROMOTING A CHILD'S SELF-IMAGE

There are many ways in which you can help a child with a disability or special need to develop a positive self-image:

- See the child before the disability or special need; value the child for himself.
- Always use the child's name.
- Encourage the child himself, and others, to use positive language. Challenge any inappropriate language or behaviour from other children or adults.
- Help the child to be aware of the needs of others, to develop social behaviour skills and operate within the rules of his peer group.
- Develop good listening skills and be sensitive to non-verbal communications, for example, body language.
- Be positive; do not underestimate ability.
- Offer choices and allow him to make decisions, e.g. 'Which jumper would you like to wear?', 'Would you like jam or honey in your sandwich?', 'You choose the colours you would like to use for your painting'.
- Avoid rigid expectations and set realistic goals and targets that he is likely to attain. Frustration and boredom lower self-esteem.
- Encourage success and independence by breaking down activities and skills into slow, small steps in correct sequence.
- Always praise effort and achievement, however small.
- Make sure the child plays with other children, is included in team games and is never isolated. This helps him to develop social skills and make friends.

- Care for the child's intimate personal needs with sensitivity.
- Value and support parents and listen to any concerns they may have. Take into account their ideas and wishes in any care or learning programme.

Offer activities that are pleasurable as well as stimulating

Storytime at playgroup – adult role model

KEY POINT

Disabled children need disabled adult role models who feel good about themselves if they, too, are to grow up with a positive self-image.

PROGRESS CHECK

1 Why might a child with special needs have a poor self-image?
2 How can you prevent a child with special needs from becoming frustrated and bored?
3 How can you help a child with special needs to take part in activities?

Access and inclusion

Access and inclusion are words frequently used in relation to disability. *Access* means a way into, or freedom to obtain or use something. Planners, architects and policy makers have a responsibility to design environments and create opportunities that are open and accessible to everyone. *Inclusion* means sharing equally; removing barriers to participation in society; making sure everyone has the same chance to be part of society and contribute to it at their own particular level of ability. For the environment and society to be inclusive, children with special needs must have equal access to:

- the physical (built) environment – indoors and outdoors
- the learning environment – all levels of education and activity according to their needs and abilities
- appropriate health and social care provision
- training and employment opportunities when they are older
- information about services available to them, including financial benefits, as and when they can understand them
- sports, leisure and holiday facilities.

INCLUSIVE EARLY YEARS SETTINGS

Inclusive Early Years settings provide opportunities for children with and without special needs to learn, play and socialise together. The environment, curriculum, and resources should reflect the ethos (belief, principle) that children with special needs are welcomed, cared for, respected and valued *equally* with other children.

KEY POINT

Appropriate networks of support must be available to enable children with special needs to participate in all activities of the setting. The chart on page 50 offers suggestions for Early Years workers to consider.

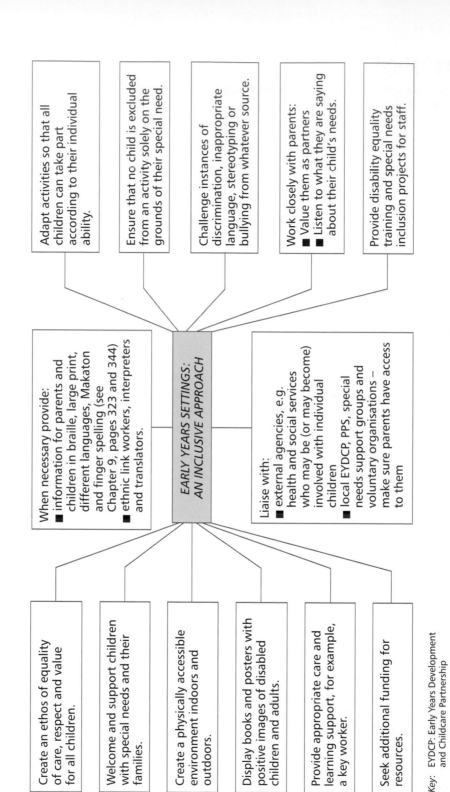

Adapt activities so that all children can take part according to their individual ability.

Ensure that no child is excluded from an activity solely on the grounds of their special need.

Challenge instances of discrimination, inappropriate language, stereotyping or bullying from whatever source.

Work closely with parents:
■ Value them as partners
■ Listen to what they are saying about their child's needs.

Provide disability equality training and special needs inclusion projects for staff.

EARLY YEARS SETTINGS: AN INCLUSIVE APPROACH

When necessary provide:
■ information for parents and children in braille, large print, different languages, Makaton and finger spelling (see Chapter 9, pages 323 and 344)
■ ethnic link workers, interpreters and translators.

Liaise with:
■ external agencies, e.g. health and social services who may be (or may become) involved with individual children
■ local EYDCP, PPS, special needs support groups and voluntary organisations – make sure parents have access to them

Create an ethos of equality of care, respect and value for all children.

Welcome and support children with special needs and their families.

Create a physically accessible environment indoors and outdoors.

Display books and posters with positive images of disabled children and adults.

Provide appropriate care and learning support, for example, a key worker.

Seek additional funding for resources.

Key: EYDCP: Early Years Development and Childcare Partnership
PPS: Parent Partnership Service

Early Years settings: an inclusive approach

KEY POINT

The local authority, disability organisations and disabled people themselves advise on access design.

GOOD PRACTICE

The Health and Safety Policy of an Early Years setting must make reference to (a) particular safe practices and procedures for caring for children and adults with special needs in emergency situations and (b) their safety during the day-to-day routine of the setting, for example, children with different needs moving from one location to another (see also Critical incidents and emergency procedures, Chapter 2, page 62). To maintain a safe environment always follow these safety principles:

- Familiarise yourself with the Health and Safety policy of your workplace. In particular, know the procedures for fire practice, dealing with accidents, prevention of infection and handing children over at 'home time'.
- Make sure the adult:child ratio meets local authority requirements.
- Maintain appropriate supervision of children both indoors and outdoors.
- Be a role model for safe practice – the children will copy you.
- Check equipment, furniture and toys regularly. Make sure gates and fences are secure and in good repair.
- Avoid clutter in playrooms and corridors – this is especially important for children with visual impairment or mobility difficulties.

Children with special needs must have equal access to inclusive sports and recreational facilities

A higher staffing level will be needed in an inclusive setting to care for children requiring a great deal of help with mobility, eating, drinking and toileting routines.

PROGRESS CHECK

1   What do you understand by the words *access* and *inclusion*?
2   Explain how the environment and society can be made accessible and inclusive for children with special needs.
3   What do you understand by the phrase 'an inclusive Early Years setting'?
4   Which particular practices and procedures must be included in the Health and Safety Policy of Early Years settings?

The Early Years Foundation Stage

Since September 2008 the Early Years Foundation Stage (EYFS) has been mandatory for:
■ all schools
■ all Early Years providers in Ofsted-registered settings (including nurseries, pre-schools and childminders).
It applies to children from birth to the end of the academic year in which the child has their fifth birthday.

In the Statutory Framework for the Early Years Foundation Stage the Department for Education and Skills tells us that:

> *Every child deserves the best possible start in life and support to fulfil their potential. A child's experience in the early years has a major impact on their future life chances. A secure, safe and happy childhood is important in its own right, and it provides the foundation for children to make the most of their abilities and talents as they grow up. When parents choose to use early years services they want to know that provision will keep their children safe and help them to thrive. The Early Years Foundation Stage (EYFS) is the framework that provides that assurance. The over-arching aim of the EYFS is to help young children achieve the five* Every Child Matters *outcomes.*

EVERY CHILD MATTERS

Every Child Matters is the government agenda that focuses on bringing together services to support children and families. It sets out five major outcomes for children:
1   being healthy
2   staying safe
3   enjoying and achieving

4 making a positive contribution
5 economic well-being.

The EYFS aims to meet the Every Child Matters outcomes by:

- **Setting standards** for the learning, development and care young children should experience when they attend a setting outside their family home. Every child should make progress, with no children left behind.
- **Providing equality of opportunity and anti-discriminatory practice.** Ensuring that every child is included and not disadvantaged because of ethnicity, culture, religion, home language, family background, learning difficulties or disabilities, gender or ability.
- **Creating a framework for partnership working between parents and professionals**, and between all the settings that the child attends.
- **Improving quality and consistency in the early years** through standards that apply to all settings. This provides the basis for the inspection and regulation regime carried out by Ofsted.
- **Laying a secure foundation for future learning** through learning and development that is planned around the individual needs and interests of the child. This is informed by the use of ongoing observational assessment.

Note: The EYFS replaces the Curriculum Guidance for the Foundation Stage, the Birth to Three Matters Framework and The National Standards for Under 8s Daycare and Childminding, which are now all defunct. Settings following the EYFS must have regard to the Special Educational Needs Code of Practice 2002.

EVERY DISABLED CHILD MATTERS

Every Disabled Child Matters is a campaign to get rights and justice for every disabled child. It is jointly led by four organisation that work with disabled children and their families: Contact a Family, Council for Disabled Children, Mencap and the Special Educational Consortium. The organisation 'will challenge politicians and policy-makers to make good on the government's commitment that every child matters.' Visit www.edcm.org.uk for further details.

THEMES, PRINCIPLES AND COMMITMENTS OF THE EYFS

The EYFS is based around four **Themes**. Each theme is linked to a **Principle**. Each Principle is supported by four **Commitments**. The Commitments describe how their Principle can be put into action. The Themes, Principles and Commitments are shown in the table on page 54.

Theme	Principle	Commitments
1. A Unique Child	Every child is a competent learner from birth who can be resilient, capable, confident and self-assured	1.1 Child development 1.2 Inclusive practice 1.3 Keeping safe 1.4 Health and well-being
2. Positive Relationships	Children learn to be strong and independent from a base of loving and secure relationships with parents and/or a key person	2.1 Respecting each other 2.2 Parents as partners 2.3 Supporting learning 2.4 Key person
3. Enabling Environment	The environment plays a key role in supporting and extending children's development and learning	3.1 Observation, assessment and planning 3.2 Supporting every child 3.3 The learning environment 3.4 The wider context
4. Learning and Development	Children develop and learn in different ways and at different rates. All areas of learning and development are equally important and interconnected	4.1 Play and exploration 4.2 Active learning 4.3 Creativity and critical thinking 4.4 Areas of learning and development

Additional statements are provided within the EYFS to explain each Commitment in more detail. You can see these on the Department for Education and Skills' 'Principles into Practice' poster, an extract of which is reproduced on page 55.

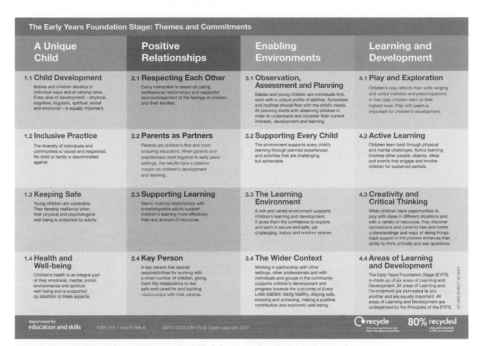

Department for Education and Skills' 'Principles into Practice' poster

AREAS OF LEARNING AND DEVELOPMENT

Theme 4, Learning and Development, also contains six Areas of Learning and Development. These are shown on the diagram below.

Areas of Learning and Development

Each Area of Learning and Development is divided up into Aspects. You can see these on the Department for Education and Skills' Learning and Development card, reproduced below. Together, the six areas of Learning and Development make up the skills, knowledge and experiences appropriate for babies and children as they grow, learn and develop. Although these are presented as separate areas, it is important to remember that for children everything links and nothing is compartmentalised. All areas of Learning and Development are connected to one another and are equally important. They are underpinned by the principles of the EYFS. Each Area of Learning also has a list of ELGs. The aim is for children to reach the goals by the end of their Reception year.

Department for Education and Skills' Learning and Development card

As you will read below, there are a set of EYFS Resource Cards for practitioners. This includes a card for each Area of Learning that provides guidance on what practitioners must do to promote children's development, and outlines what this means to children.

WELFARE REQUIREMENTS

Settings to which the Early Years Foundation Stage applies must meet the EYFS welfare requirements. These fall into the following five categories:

Safeguarding and promoting children's welfare
- The provider must take necessary steps to safeguard and promote the welfare of children.
- The provider must promote the good health of the children, take necessary steps to prevent the spread of infection, and take appropriate action when they are ill.
- Children's behaviour must be managed effectively and in a manner appropriate for their stage of development and particular individual needs.

Suitable people
- Providers must ensure that adults looking after children, or having unsupervised access to them, are suitable to do so.
- Adults looking after children must have appropriate qualifications, training, skills and knowledge.
- Staffing arrangements must be organised to ensure safety and to meet the needs of the children.

Suitable premises, environment and equipment
- Outdoor and indoor spaces, furniture, equipment and toys must be safe and suitable for their purpose.

Organisation
- Providers must plan and organise their systems to ensure that every child receives an enjoyable and challenging learning and development experience that is tailored to meet their individual needs.

Documentation
- Providers must maintain records, policies and procedures required for the safe and efficient management of the settings and to meet the needs of the children.

So what does all this mean?
Childcarers working in settings following the EYFS need to meet the standards for learning, development and care. Their responsibilities include:
- planning a range of play and learning experiences that promote all of the Aspects within all of the Areas of Learning
- assessing and monitoring individual children's progress through observational assessments
- using the findings of observational assessments to inform the planning of play and learning experiences
- ensuring that children's individual interests and abilities are promoted within the play and learning experiences.

In their 'Key Elements of Effective Practice' (KEEP) the Department for Education and Skills tells us that:

Effective practice in the early years requires committed, enthusiastic and reflective practitioners with a breadth and depth of knowledge, skills and understanding. Effective practitioners use their own learning to improve their work with young children and their families in ways which are sensitive, positive and non-judgemental.

*Therefore through initial and ongoing training and development
practitioners need to develop, demonstrate and continuously improve their:*

- *relationships with both children and adults*
- *understanding of the individual and diverse ways that children learn and develop*
- *knowledge and understanding in order to actively support and extend children's
  learning in and across all areas and aspects of Learning and Development*
- *practice in meeting all children's needs, learning styles and interests*
- *work with parents, carers and the wider community*
- *work with other professionals within and beyond the setting.*

EYFS RESOURCES FOR CHILDCARERS

The EYFS pack of resources for providers includes the following:

The Statutory Framework for the Early Years Foundation Stage
This booklet sets out:

- The welfare requirements, which set out providers' duties to ensure children's
  welfare and well-being within the setting
- The learning and development requirements, which set out providers' duties
  under each of the six areas of Learning and Development.

Practice Guidance for the Early Years Foundation Stage
This booklet provides further guidance on:

- legal requirements
- the areas of Learning and Development
- the EYFS principles
- assessment.

24 cards
These give the Principles and Commitments at a glance, with guidance on putting the principles into practice. They include an overview of child development.

CD-ROM
This contains all the information from the booklets and cards. It includes information on effective practice, research and resources. This can also be accessed via the EYFS website (www.standards.dcsf.gov.uk/eyfs/). It is a good idea to take the overview tour to familiarise yourself with the site on your first visit. You can then follow the links to the Areas of Learning and read more about the Aspects, then follow the links to the 'Principles in practice' for examples of how practitioners following the EYFS work with children within their settings.

NURSERY EDUCATION GRANT FUNDING

All three and four year olds are entitled to free nursery education in regis-tered early years settings. The offer (currently 12.5 hours per week) will be increased to 15 hours per week in all local authorities in 2010. Fifteen per cent of the most disadvantaged families in each local authority area will also receive the offer of free nursery education for two year olds. Children with special needs benefit from the bustle and atmosphere of a mixed ability group. Many may have remained sheltered and isolated within the home, perhaps with lit-tle awareness of other children and adults in the wider community. With inclusive day care provision all the children come to understand, accept and value differences and diversity, developing greater self-esteem as they play and learn together. Children with special needs have opportunities to play and acquire language and social skills within their peer group from the local community. Non-disabled children learn about, respect and accept different abilities, at the same time developing a range of caring skills. Additionally, a local Early Years setting provides social contact and support for both the child and family.

GOOD PRACTICE

In an inclusive day care setting:
- all children are valued equally
- the environment, equipment and curriculum are accessible to *all* the children, enabling them to participate, interact and socialise at their individual levels
- participation and choice in play and learning is encouraged – consistent with the stage of development and the overall ability of each child
- children are listened to and carers learn the necessary skills to interact with a child using his particular method of communication
- key worker support and care is provided for all children
- a one-to-one keyworker or personal assistant (PA) may work with children with severe or complex disabilities
- trusting and supportive partnerships with parents are created
- children's 'ordinary needs' are cared for as well as their special needs.

KEY POINTS

- A stimulating day care environment, with a wide variety of experiences, will extend all-round physical development and enable children to progress in learning, social and independence skills.
- Day care provision can be offered to siblings if parents of a child with complex special needs may otherwise find attendance at hospital or clinic impossible.

PARTNERSHIPS AND PARENTS

Co-operation and partnership with parents is an essential part of good practice and helps effective communication and sharing of information. A daily or weekly record or diary, filled in by both parents and staff, can provide details of a child's progress or any area of concern and offer helpful suggestions for activities at home. Most day care settings are happy for parents to enquire about their child at any time and flexible visiting times can be arranged.

Activity
What particular information about their child might parents wish to share with the day care staff on a daily basis?

EARLY YEARS DEVELOPMENT AND CHILDCARE PARTNERSHIPS (EYDCPS)

Early Years Development and Childcare Partnerships are a government initiative resulting from the National Childcare Strategy 1998. The nationwide partnerships, convened by local education authorities (LEAs), bring together representatives from local statutory bodies and private and voluntary organisations (including representatives from Primary Care Trusts and social services). EYDCPs meet regularly to discuss and advise on the work of Early Childhood Services in response to the National Sure Start Guidance. (See pages 160–1 for information about Sure Start.)

KEY POINT
Early Years workers should make sure parents receive information about their local EYDCP group.

Activity
1 Find out about the Early Years Development and Childcare Partnership in your own local area.
2 Which services and organisations are represented in the partnership? In particular, how does the partnership help children with special needs and their families?
3 How often does the partnership hold meetings? If possible, attend an EYDCP meeting – perhaps your tutor will help you to arrange this – and then discuss with your colleagues the issues debated and the decisions made.

PROGRESS CHECK

1 Explain the advantages of inclusive day care for children with and without special needs.
2 What is the Nursery Education Funding entitlement for three and four year olds?
3 What are the EYFS welfare requirements?
4 Who inspects early years settings?
5 Name three functions of an Early Years Development and Childcare Partnership.

STAFF DEVELOPMENT INITIATIVES

All adults working with disabled children and children with special needs may benefit from a range of initiatives such as:
- disability equality training
- the principles of inclusive practice
- attending seminars and workshops run by voluntary organisations – they offer specialist help and advice for parents and professionals caring for children with special needs, such as lifting and positioning techniques, helping children with their food and drink and use of specialist cutlery, bowls and plates, administering medication and use of appropriate and specialist equipment
- a current first aid training and qualification
- liaising with local support groups and disability agencies in the local community for up-to-date information on disability issues
- inviting specialist speakers, such as a Portage home visitor, a speech and language therapist or an occupational therapist, to talk to staff about their work with children with special needs.

PARENTAL CONCERNS

If there are no children with special educational needs currently in attendance at a setting, parents of children already attending the setting may be concerned their children will not receive adequate care and attention if a child with special needs begins to attend. Offer them the opportunity to discuss their anxieties with you. Reassure them about the value for all children of an inclusive policy and the opportunities for non-disabled children to learn about children with different abilities who require particular help. By developing a caring ethos that embraces all children equally and promotes awareness of disability, staff can allay any fears and misgivings that parents may have. Some parents may prefer a specialist rather than an inclusive setting for their young children. Their choice must be respected.

An inclusive day care setting welcomes children with and without special needs

CRITICAL INCIDENTS AND EMERGENCY PROCEDURES

All members of staff in Early Years care and education settings must be familiar with the systems for managing a critical incident and implementing emergency procedures identified in their Health and Safety Policy.

Evacuation of children and staff from the setting may be necessary because of a fire, bomb or gas alert or other serious incident. The local Fire Prevention Officer, and some voluntary organisations, offer advice about necessary adaptations to the environment and alarm systems for children with special needs. They also provide guidance in best practice for evacuating children with vision and/or hearing impairment or with mobility difficulties.

Once the alarm sounds the priority is to evacuate all the children and staff quickly and safely and call the emergency services. These two activities should be carried out simultaneously. Early Years staff must know:

■ how to raise the alarm
■ who is responsible for contacting the emergency services
■ their own role in the evacuation procedures
■ how the children are to be evacuated and which evacuation route is to be used by each room or department
■ where the children will be cared for if they are evacuated to 'off site' premises for any length of time.

They also need to know who is responsible for:

■ helping children with special needs
■ checking specific areas (such as the lavatories) for remaining children

- reassuring and taking care of shy and 'settling-in' children and those for whom English is not their first language
- checking the registers at the assembly point
- declaring the building(s) empty.

KEY POINT

Always await clearance from the emergency services or a senior member of staff before re-entering the building.

Play materials and toys

Young children are naturally curious, eager to explore and investigate their environment and discover how things work. They do this through play. Children with special needs may not always show this natural curiosity. This does *not* mean they are uninterested in playing or cannot play, but it *does* mean they need more encouragement and help to become involved, so developing interest and skills in play activities.

KEY POINT

Avoid the temptation to overprotect children with special needs. They need opportunities and freedom to test their limits in a safe and supervised environment.

Play materials and toys must be:
- safe and well made
- attractive, colourful and enjoyable
- stimulating and versatile
- appealing to the children.

Special books and catalogues are useful sources of help in choosing suitable items. The health visitor, occupational therapist and child development centre will be able to offer advice about special toys. Parents, too, may know of particularly appropriate toys and activities.

Equipment should be a mixture of standard and specialist. Safe, sturdy versions of standard equipment and playthings, together with existing facilities and resources, can often be imaginatively adapted for children with special needs. The local authority and voluntary organisations may provide help and parents with creative DIY skills can often make particular pieces of equipment. Discuss children's specific needs with their parents.

KEY POINT

Some children require special equipment to enable them to take part safely in everyday play activities. Planning advice and suggestions about equipment and furniture can be provided by specialist teachers, educational psychologists, physiotherapists and occupational therapists, as well as voluntary organisations.

PLAY OPPORTUNITIES

You may find the following suggestions helpful in stimulating children's play and learning:

- Match activities and toys to the actual level of development not the level you would expect for age.
- Prompt a child to pick up a toy and encourage him to actively explore it.
- Offer toys that guarantee 'success' when played with. For example, there is no right or wrong way to play with a ball or a pile of bricks, whereas posting shapes into a box is dependent on getting the correct shape into the correct hole. Children become frustrated and lose interest when they cannot succeed.
- Place a toy in the hands of babies and children with visual impairment and cerebral palsy. Move their fingers over it so that they can understand its shape, texture and what it does.
- Provide activities that are graded in sequence of difficulty. This promotes confidence and a sense of achievement as each small step is mastered.
- Creative play materials and jigsaws made of light but strong foam plastic benefit children with poor hand control.
- Push-and-pull toys, tricycles, climbing frames, rope ladders and swings promote muscle tone, co-ordination and balance.
- Allow children to progress at their own pace and consolidate achievement at one level before suggesting something more difficult.
- Always be positive in outlook, encourage and praise. Never show disappointment or anxiety at any perceived lack of progress.
- Encourage signs of independence and avoid over-protection.

GOOD PRACTICE

- Make sure *all* children take part in the activities of the setting. Do not exclude any child.
- Remember to offer toys, games and activities that promote all-round developmental skills – physical, sensory, cognitive, social and emotional. Change the activity if it becomes too difficult or boring.

KEY POINT

Certain adaptations to the environment and equipment will be dictated by individual special needs.

For children with mobility difficulties
- Ramps, lifts in multi-storey settings, grab-rails, wide entrances and automatic doors provide easy access.
- Plenty of empty, uncluttered and well-planned space allows wheelchairs to wheel around and children to crawl, ride and slide around in safety. Make sure there are clearly defined spacious routes from one activity to another.

- Large toilet, washing and changing facilities are essential. A separate toilet for disabled children is unnecessary as large toilets can accommodate wheelchairs and walking frames.
- Long-handled taps are easier to manage than the rotating type.
- Suitable seating is needed: adjustable chairs with attachable trays for eating, drawing and playing; specially designed tables with space cut out for a child in a wheelchair enable him to engage with his peers in group play or at mealtimes; corner seats for sitting at floor level.

A special table and seat

- Soft play areas, beanbags or soft mattresses facilitate crawling, rolling and jumping. Ball pools stimulate the whole body and help muscle tone and posture.
- Sloping foam or canvas wedges support a child lying prone, enabling floor play with free arms.
- Sand and water trays with detachable legs allow children to lie on sloped wedges round the trays and enjoy the tactile stimulation of the sand and water.
- Prams and other pushing toys weighted with sandbags assist balance and walking.

Going ... ... *going ...* ... *gone!*

A soft play area

Soft play equipment

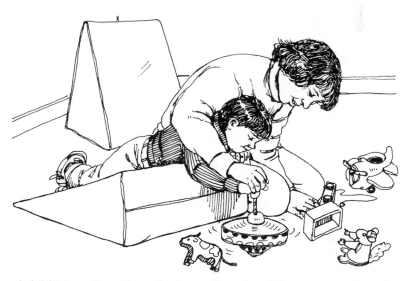

Carer and child interaction. Floor play is possible when lying prone on a wedge

- Children may have their own particular equipment:
  - a prone board that gives the sensation of standing and enables play at a table
  - a mobile standing frame (for a child who cannot stand unaided) or a wheelchair
  - a tricycle with pedal straps to support the feet and a seat belt
  - head sticks for painting and drawing – easels must be secure and stable.

Adjustable bikes for children with special needs

For children with visual impairment
- Lay out equipment and activities in a familiar pattern each day.
- Provide plenty of light.
- Ensure there is no clutter.
- Brightly coloured arrows should lead to areas such as the toilet and outdoors with bright day-glo strips on the edges of steps, including steps to the climbing frame.
- Use different textured surfaces to indicate specific outdoor areas such as the climbing frame area and the sand pit area.
- Raised or beaded edges to activity tables prevent objects falling off.
- 'Feelie' bags and boards help to develop muscle tone and flexible hands – necessary when using Braille facilities.
- Provide large print names, signs and symbols, magnifiers, and signs in Braille.
- Provide large print books, talking books, tactile books and tapes.
- Clear Vision (print and Braille) books can be read by a sighted or visually impaired person to children to begin to familiarise them with Braille in the same way that sighted children become familiar with print.

For children with hearing impairment
- A system for recognising the fire alarm is necessary.
- Provide access to language and communication through a signing system and speech therapy programmes.
- Ensure there are lots of signs, pictures and symbols.

KEY POINTS

- Children with learning difficulties and emotional/behavioural difficulties will also benefit from many of the facilities set out above. In addition, they may follow structured activity and learning programmes and take part in small group activities with the help of a key worker.
- A sensory area providing a range of visual, auditory and tactile experiences provides pleasure and learning opportunities for all the children in the setting.
- An enlarged home corner enables children with mobility, vision and hearing difficulties to engage in imaginative play.

You will find further provision for children with mobility difficulties in Chapters 5 and 7, vision and hearing impairment in Chapters 8 and 9, and learning difficulties and emotional and behavioural difficulties in Chapters 8 and 9.

Activity
Plan a sensory area for the benefit of all the children in a day care setting.

MUSIC ACTIVITIES

Making music is an activity that can be enjoyed by all children. It is an especially beneficial therapy for children with severe learning and communication difficulties. They are often isolated with little control over their lives. Choosing and taking turns with different instruments and being offered the opportunity to 'lead' the group enables them to take the initiative, so building confidence. Through music children can express emotions such as pleasure, anger or frustration in a safe, accepting environment. They also interact with each other and the carer or therapist, at the same time learning about sharing and taking turns.

Ben has always enjoyed making music. For a time he attended a music therapy project where this photograph was taken

KEY POINT

In addition to the usual musical instruments (bells, drum, tambourine, triangle), offer shakers and different safe containers filled with items such as small pebbles, corks, fir cones or chestnuts, which make a variety of sounds.

Activity

Think about the care setting where you work. What specialist equipment or adaptations exist? Do these effectively meet the needs of the children they are intended for? If not, what alternatives could be provided?

CASE STUDY

Adam was seven years old and had just started a new school. He had visual impairment and wore glasses with thick lenses. Through PTA fund raising the school provided an outdoor grassed area where the children could enjoy ball games, group activities and races. Adam loved being outside playing with his classmates. However, several children in Adam's class had recently ganged up on him, excluding him from joining in their games. They called him 'four eyes' and laughed at him when he missed catching or kicking a ball. On one occasion they broke his glasses.

1 How would you have cared for and supported Adam's needs?
2 Give possible reasons for the children's behaviour.
3 How might you have challenged the other children's inappropriate language and behaviour? How could you have helped them to understand the rules of the setting?

KEY TERMS

You need to know what these words and phrases mean. Go back through the chapter and make sure that you understand:

access and inclusion
Clear Vision books
critical incidents
disability awareness
disability equality training
models of disability

Early Years Foundation Stage welfare
   requirements
inappropriate language
inclusive day care provision
preferred language

3 LEGAL FRAMEWORK; CODE OF PRACTICE; CHILDREN'S RIGHTS

This chapter covers:

- The Warnock Report 1978
- The Education Act 1981 and the Education Act 1996
- The Education Reform Act 1988
- The Special Educational Needs and Disability Act 2001 and revised regulations
- The Special Educational Needs Code of Practice 2002
- The Disability Discrimination Act (DDA) 1995
- The Disability Rights Commission (DRC) and the Equality and Human Rights Commission
- The National Health Service (NHS) and Community Care Act 1990
- The Health Act 1999
- The NHS Act 2006
- The Children Act 1989
- Every Child Matters
- The Children and Young People's Plan
- Children's rights, empowerment and advocacy

This chapter identifies current legislation relevant to children with special needs and special educational needs. Anyone providing services for children with special needs – health, education or social service departments, as well as voluntary organisations – must act within the legal framework. Legislation can change at any time and all health, education and social care practitioners, also Early Years workers, should be alert to new Acts and Regulations.

Acts of Parliament and Regulations are the law. Reports may make recommendations but are not legal documents. However, their recommendations may be accepted by the government and enshrined in Acts or Regulations, so becoming legislation. Codes of Practice are the official guidelines on how an Act or Regulation(s) should be interpreted and put into practice. While not the law, they must be implemented to demonstrate compliance with the law.

Empowerment and advocacy, important aspects of caring for children with special needs, are discussed at the end of the chapter.

KEY POINTS

- There are no 'Good practice' headings in the legislation text. Complying with the law is, in itself, good practice.
- Reports are not legally binding. Legislation is the law of the land.

- The words 'handicap' and 'handicapped' were used at the time of the Warnock Report 1978 and thus feature in the text below.

The Warnock Report 1978 – 'Special educational needs – the education of handicapped children and young people'

BACKGROUND TO THE REPORT

Mary Warnock chaired a committee of inquiry into 'the education of handicapped children and young people'. It was the first inquiry to review educational provision for all handicapped children in the UK since 1889. The considerations were based on the philosophy that all children are entitled to an education whatever their disabilities and stressed the importance of focusing on a child's educational need rather than on his or her disability.

SUMMARY OF THE REPORT

- The report recognised the 'special responsibility' of health visitors for children under five and their families, and their important role in detecting disabilities.
- Of professionals other than those in the health service the report says:

> *they may be instrumental in the discovery of handicapping conditions in children attending nurseries, nursery schools, nursery classes and those playgroups with which they have effective contact. The staff of day nurseries and playgroups have excellent opportunities to discover such conditions among children in their care.*

- While concluding that up to one child in five (20 per cent) is likely to require special educational provision at some time in their school career, the committee believed that 'no child should be sent to a special school who can satisfactorily be educated in an ordinary one'.
- A child's educational needs and special provision should be identified through a process of assessment.
- The practice of categorising and labelling children according to their handicap should be abolished. It creates a distinction between the handicapped and the non-handicapped.
- The report recognised the important role of early education for handicapped children under five years.
- At all times there should be a partnership of trust and understanding between the parents and those offering a professional service to the family.
- Parent workshops could be a valuable form of support, provided they met the specific needs of parents of different backgrounds.

Early Years workers in a day care setting observing and interacting with children. Opportunities exist to identify children who require extra help

RECOMMENDATIONS OF THE REPORT

KEY POINTS

■ While continuing to use the terms 'sensory disabilities' and 'physical disabilities', labels such as 'remedial', 'maladjusted', 'educationally sub-normal' or 'mentally handicapped' would be replaced by 'children with learning difficulties'.

■ Learning difficulties could be described as 'mild', 'moderate' or 'severe'. Children with particular difficulties, such as specific reading or writing difficulties, might be described as having 'specific learning difficulties'.

The following further recommendations were made in the report:

■ the adoption of the term 'special educational need' – this would take into account a child's abilities as well as disabilities

■ a five-stage assessment process, with an annual review of progress, to identify a child's specific educational needs – at all stages parents would be fully involved and informed

■ access to the school curriculum through (a) specialist help adapted to the particular needs of each child; (b) provision of ramps or handrails to the classroom; and (c) equipment such as hearing aids or techniques for teaching through Braille. A special curriculum would be provided for children with severe learning difficulties. Some children would benefit from being taught in small groups or a special class.

- the integration of children with special educational needs into mainstream schools whenever possible. Three forms of integration were envisaged:
  locational – special classes in an ordinary school but with little opportunity for contact with other pupils
  social – children from a special class would mix with other pupils at assemblies, playtimes and mealtimes
  full – pupils with special educational needs would be taught in the same classes as the other pupils and mix freely with them at all times.

RECOMMENDATIONS FOR THE UNDER FIVES

- A Named Person would provide the family with a point of contact for advice and support. An obvious choice for a very young child would be the family health visitor. For an older child it might be a social worker or a teacher. This person would be someone who understood the family's cultural and ethnic background, making sure their special needs and anxieties were followed up and supported. The Named Person would provide a link between the parents, the family doctor and specialist health services, teachers (including home visiting teachers), social services, support groups and voluntary organisations.
- There should be provision of nursery education in nursery schools/classes for children with special needs.
- There should be a range of provision, such as day nurseries, playgroups and opportunity groups to provide crucial early learning opportunities for young children with special needs.
- A peripatetic teaching service should be provided for children with hearing and visual impairment, physical disabilities and learning difficulties of any kind. Teachers would visit children either at home or in a day nursery setting.

More than two hundred recommendations were made in the Warnock Report, many of which were included in the Education Act 1981.

KEY POINT

Terms such as 'special educational needs', 'children with learning difficulties' and 'specific learning difficulties' were promoted in the Warnock Report.

PROGRESS CHECK

1 In what ways did the Warnock Report envisage children with special educational needs gaining access to the school curriculum?
2 Briefly describe the three levels of integration suggested in the Warnock Report.
3 What specific provision did Warnock recommend for children under five with special needs?
4 What do you understand by a peripatetic teaching service?

The Education Act 1981 and the Education Act 1996

THE EDUCATION ACT 1981

The Education Act 1981 plus the Education (Special Educational Needs) Regulations 1983 were a direct result of the Warnock Report. The Act was concerned only with children with special educational needs and brought about major changes for their education.

KEY POINT

In particular the Act recognised the essential role of parents as partners with the school in the education of their children.

Principles of the Education Act 1981

- Labelling a child according to handicap was abolished and the concept of special educational needs, focusing on a child's learning needs, was introduced.
- Statutory duties were placed on local education authorities (LEAs) and school governors to meet learning needs through special educational provision.
- Procedures were introduced for continuous classroom assessment, statutory assessment and preparation of a statement of special educational needs.
- Where possible, children with special educational needs would be educated in mainstream schools, provided that this was compatible with the provision of well-organised education for the other children being educated and the efficient use of resources.
- The role of parents in education was seen as crucial to children's progress. Parental wishes on integration into mainstream school had to be taken into account.
- Parents were given a right of appeal against local education authority decisions about their child.

Activity
1 Find out who your local councillor is and discuss with him or her your local authority's policy on inclusive education. Prepare your questions beforehand.
2 If possible, observe a council session on relevant education matters.

THE EDUCATION ACT 1996

The Education Act 1996 (Part IV) 1996, plus the Special Educational Needs and Disability Act 2001 and Revised Regulations legislate for children with special educational needs in England and Wales (see opposite). Comparable legislation for Scotland is the Education (Scotland) Act 1980 and for Northern Ireland the Northern Ireland Education Order 1997, Education (Special Educational Needs) Regulations 1997 and the Special Educational Needs Tribunal Regulations 1997.

Parent and sibling involvement in education

DEFINITION OF SPECIAL EDUCATIONAL NEEDS (SEN)

Children have special educational needs if they have a learning difficulty, which calls for special educational provision to be made for them.

Children have a learning difficulty if they.
(a) have a significantly greater difficulty in learning than the majority of children of the same age
(b) have a disability which prevents or hinders them from making use of the educational facilities of a kind generally provided for children of the same age in schools within the area of the local education authority
(c) are under compulsory school age and fall within the definition at (a) or (b) above or would do so if special educational provision was not made for them.
Children must not be regarded as having a learning difficulty solely because the language, or form of language of their home, is different from the language in which they will be taught.

Special educational provision means:
(a) for children of two or over, educational provision that is additional to, or otherwise different from, the educational provision made generally for children of their age in schools maintained by the LEA, other than special schools, in the area
(b) for a child under two, educational provision of any kind
(Section 312, Education Act 1996).

Special educational needs occur because of physical, learning, sensory, emotional and behavioural difficulties, or difficulties with speech or language or social interaction. Needs may be mild, severe or complex and long term. Sometimes they are only temporary.

KEY POINTS

- Children have special educational needs if they have learning difficulties that make it much harder for them to learn than most children of the same age and they require special educational provision.
- Children do not have learning difficulties just because the language, or form of language, in their home is different from the language in which they will be taught.

Most children with special educational needs are educated in mainstream schools and have their needs met from the resources already available to maintained Early Years education settings and schools.

PROGRESS CHECK

1 Why was the Education Act 1981 so important?
2 What are the main principles of the Act?
3 Which Education Act sets out the current legislation for children with special needs in England and Wales?
4 What do you understand by the term 'special educational need'?

The Education Reform Act 1988

The Education Reform Act 1988 introduced:
- a national curriculum, which all children, including those with special educational needs, are expected and entitled to follow. This inclusive approach has meant a move away from separate special classes for children with special educational needs to a policy of in-class support teaching.
- the rights of all parents to send their children to the school of their choice provided it has room for them
- a school's right to opt out of local education authority control, if a majority of parents voted in its favour, under the new concept of Local Management of Schools (replaced in 1999 in England by the Fair Funding system).

The Special Educational Needs and Disability Act 2001 and revised regulations

The Special Educational Needs and Disability Act (SENDA) 2001 placed new statutory duties on LEAs, schools and Early Years settings with regard to special educational needs, additional to those set out in the Education Act 1996 (Part IV), for example:

- a stronger right for children with SEN to be educated in mainstream school
- reinforcement of the right of children with physical and behavioural difficulties to be taught in mainstream classes
- the requirement for LEAs to provide advice and information services for parents of children with SEN, and offer a means of resolving disputes
- a requirement for schools and relevant nursery education providers to tell parents when they are making special educational provision for their child
- the right of schools and relevant nursery education providers to request a statutory assessment of a child.

Part II of the Special Educational Needs and Disability Act 2001 places additional anti-discrimination duties on LEAs and schools. Schools cannot treat disabled pupils less favourably because of their disability, and must take reasonable steps to ensure that they are not placed at a substantial disadvantage compared to those who are not disabled.

The Special Educational Needs Code of Practice 2002

The Special Educational Needs Code of Practice was updated in 2002. Local education authorities, all Early Years education settings that receive government funding (including private nurseries, pre-schools and accredited childminders working as part of an approved network), and health and social services departments, must 'have regard' to the guidance in the SEN Code of Practice when fulfilling their statutory obligations, under the Education Act 1996 (Part IV), towards children with special educational needs.

The Code itself does not set out statutory duties, nor does it tell settings what they must do, but it does recommend the steps and procedures they must consider to enable children with special educational needs to reach their full potential – for example, implementing a staged approach of action and intervention and developing positive partnerships with parents. The Code of Practice builds on the rights of parents to be involved in all stages of planning and implementing their child's special educational needs programme.

Advice and support in interpreting and implementing the Code is provided by Local Education Authority Development Officers, Early Years Development and Childcare Partnerships, Sure Start and Parent Partnership Services.

The guidance in the Code is informed by the following general principles:

- A child with special educational needs should have their needs met.
- The special educational needs of children will normally be met in mainstream schools or settings.
- The views of the child should be sought and taken into account.
- Parents (this includes all those with parental responsibility) have a vital role to play in supporting their child's education.
- Children with special educational needs should be offered full access to a broad, balanced and relevant education, including the appropriate curriculum.

KEY POINT

The manager or head teacher of an Early Years setting, working closely with the SENCO (Special Educational Needs Co-ordinator) is responsible for the overall provision for children with special educational needs. The delegation of particular responsibilities is a matter for individual settings.

A summary of the SEN Code of Practice–Guidance for Early Years Settings is shown in the chart on page 81. The chart is complementary to the text below.

IMPLEMENTING THE SEN CODE OF PRACTICE

Special Educational Needs policy

Maintained schools and registered settings are expected to develop and publish a Special Educational Needs policy, whether or not they currently care for a child with SEN. The SEN policy must take account of the SEN Code of Practice.

Accredited childminders who are part of an approved network, may work together to develop an SEN policy. Advice for providers who are writing a policy for the first time may be obtained from LEA Development Officers, Early Years Development and Childcare Partnerships, Sure Starts, Parent Partnership Services and other neighbourhood Early Years settings.

Special Educational Needs policies will be structured to meet the needs of individual settings, but should contain a policy statement (the aims of your setting); organisation (roles and responsibilities of the staff within the setting); and arrangements (how you carry out your aims). The format and wording of the policy must be easy for staff and parents to understand. Where all practitioners in the setting work together to develop an SEN policy, there is a sense of shared ownership and a greater commitment to a successful implementation of the policy. Settings may wish to consider suggestions from parents for inclusion in the policy. When necessary, the policy must be available in different languages, large print, Braille or on tape.

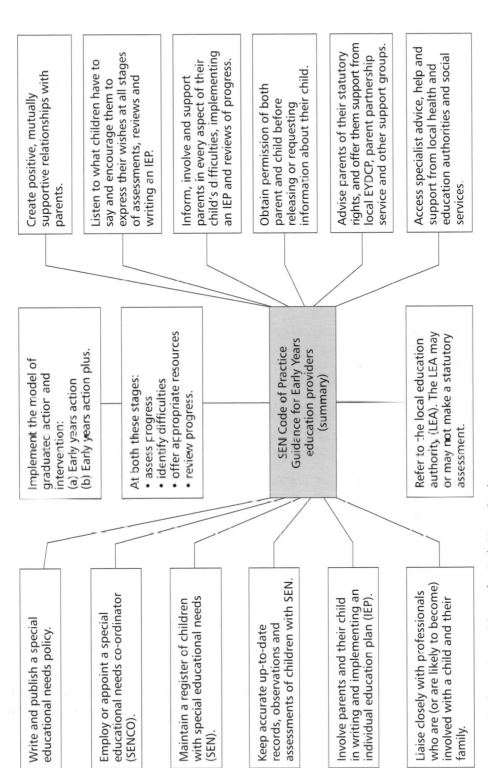

Create positive, mutually supportive relationships with parents.

Listen to what children have to say and encourage them to express their wishes at all stages of assessments, reviews and writing an IEP.

Inform, involve and support parents in every aspect of their child's difficulties, implementing an IEP and reviews of progress.

Obtain permission of both parent and child before releasing or requesting information about their child.

Advise parents of their statutory rights, and offer them support from local EYDCP, parent partnership service and other support groups.

Access specialist advice, help and support from local health and education authorities and social services.

Implement the model of graduated action and intervention:
(a) Early years action
(b) Early years action plus.

At both these stages:
- assess progress
- identify difficulties
- offer appropriate resources
- review progress.

SEN Code of Practice Guidance for Early Years education providers (summary)

Refer to the local education authority (LEA). The LEA may or may not make a statutory assessment.

Write and publish a special educational needs policy.

Employ or appoint a special educational needs co-ordinator (SENCO).

Maintain a register of children with special educational needs (SEN).

Keep accurate up-to-date records, observations and assessments of children with SEN.

Involve parents and their child in writing and implementing an individual education plan (IEP).

Liaise closely with professionals who are (or are likely to become) involved with a child and their family.

SEN Code of practice–guidance for Early Years Settings

KEY POINT

Like all the policies of your setting, a Special Educational Needs policy is not static. It must be monitored, evaluated and reviewed regularly. Minor amendments can be inserted, but when new legislation is introduced or procedures and practices in the setting change, the policy must be rewritten.

On page 83 you will find a framework for a Special Educational Needs policy, which Early Years teams may find helpful.

Special Educational Needs Co-ordinator (SENCO)

All Early Years education providers must employ an SEN Co-ordinator, or designate an existing member of staff to take on the role and responsibilities of SENCO. For accredited childminders the role of SENCO may be shared between the co-ordinator of their network and individual childminders.

The SENCO works closely with the head teacher, or manager, and other colleagues and is responsible for monitoring and co-ordinating the SEN Code of Practice. The SENCO will:

- oversee the day-to-day operation of the SEN policy, maintain the SEN register and accurate, relevant, up-to-date records of individual children
- co-ordinate provision and support for children with SEN at stages Early Years Action and Early Years Action Plus, also at stages School Action and School Action Plus
- make sure appropriate Individual Education Plans (IEPs) are in place and implemented
- collate and present relevant records, assessments, observations and progress reports to the LEA when a child is referred for statutory assessment
- liaise with parents of children with SEN and with specialists from outside agencies who are involved with the child and her family, for example, the LEA psychology service, health and social services and voluntary organisations
- provide parents with information about services offered by their LEA, the local EYDCP and Parent Partnership Service, and other local voluntary and support groups
- support and advise the Early Years team, contribute to in-service training of staff and, with the manager or head teacher, arrange staff training on issues such as the Code of Practice, writing a Special Educational Needs Policy, Disability Equality and other relevant subjects.

KEY POINT

It is important to observe the confidentiality code of the setting. Always obtain parental permission before making an approach to any person or agency, for example, health or social services, to either ask for or release information about their child. If parents do not wish details of their child to be passed on to third parties, their wishes should be respected.

FRAMEWORK FOR A SPECIAL EDUCATIONAL NEEDS POLICY

Policy statement

In the policy statement a setting will include a commitment to:

- the ethos of inclusion, difference and diversity
- writing the aims and objectives of the setting with regard to children with SEN
- early identification of children with SEN
- encouraging and assisting children with SEN to reach their full potential
- establishing positive partnerships with parents
- providing the organisation and arrangements for implementing the SEN policy
- providing resources for SEN support
- providing staff training relating to SEN issues.

Organisation

- An organisational chart naming the members of the Early Years SEN team and stating their titles is helpful for staff, parents and external specialists.
- The responsibilities and duties of each member of the team should be described in detail.

Arrangements

The setting should describe (among other things) the arrangements for:

- developing an inclusive approach within the setting
- welcoming children with SEN and their parents to the setting
- providing interpreters, translators, signers and ethnic link workers when necessary
- physical access – modifications and adaptations
- identifying and assessing children's special educational needs
- delivering the curriculum
- reviewing children's progress
- accessing and allocating resources, and co-ordinating provision
- creating links with external agencies, for example, health and social services, Early Years Development and Childcare Partnerships (EYDCPs), Parent Partnership Services (see pages 96–7), voluntary organisations and other special needs support groups
- creating a partnership with parents and informing them of their rights
- maintaining confidentiality both within the setting and with external specialists and agencies
- staff training
- resolution of disputes.

Partnership with parents

Parents know their child best and have a critical role to play in their education. A positive, trusting and supportive partnership between the setting, the parents and the local education authority is central to a child's education and overall progress. The SEN Code of Practice puts greater emphasis than before on the involvement of parents in all decision-making processes, such as identification of their child's SEN, action and intervention programmes, review processes and assessments. It is important that the Early Years team takes time to listen to parents' views and concerns and welcomes the knowledge and expertise they can offer about their child. All professionals and specialists attending the child in the setting or in the community (physiotherapist, occupational therapist, speech and language therapist, educational psychologist, support teachers), as well as Early Years practitioners, rely on parents to reinforce and consolidate care and learning plans in the home. The processes of statutory assessment and making a statement of special educational needs (see below) can be a stressful time for parents. They need support at all times and to be kept fully informed on the range of available local provision, including schools. At the time of a proposed statement of special educational needs, local education authorities *must* remind parents about the Parent Partnership Service (see Chapter 3, pages 96–7) and the dispute resolution services (see Chapter 3, pages 95–6).

Listening to children

The SEN Code of Practice states that children have important and relevant information to offer about their education. Always encourage children, including very young ones, to express any wish or difficulty and prompt them to make even the smallest choices and decisions. Avoid making assumptions about the level of understanding of any child. Older children may welcome the opportunity to talk privately about their education. Children of any age with learning, communication or sensory difficulties, may need extra help to make their views and wishes known. For children who are unable to express a wish or choice, or have no one to speak on their behalf, the services of an advocate will be beneficial (see advocacy, pages 114–15).

GRADUATED MODELS OF ACTION AND INTERVENTION

Where a child is experiencing particular or general learning difficulties, the Early Years setting or school should offer that child different opportunities or alternative approaches to learning.

Early Years graduated approach

Children's progress is monitored and assessed throughout the Early Years Foundation Stage of education (from the age of three years to the end of the reception year). If a child appears to be experiencing general or particular learning difficulties the Early Years setting will need to consider different approaches and procedures to assist learning and help the child to make progress.

Early Years Action and *Early Years Action Plus* are the two stages of graduated *action* and *intervention* set out in the Code of Practice and recommended for use in Early Years settings.

Early Years Action

Early Years Action is the first stage of intervention aimed at helping a child who is experiencing learning difficulties. When the Early Years team or SENCO identifies a child with special educational needs, they provide interventions that are *additional to* or *different from* those provided in the setting's usual curriculum.

Triggers for Early Years Action

The Early Years team or SENCO might be concerned that a child, despite receiving appropriate early learning experiences:

- makes little or no progress, even when teaching approaches are structured to meet the child's identified needs
- works at levels far below those expected for children of similar age, in certain areas
- exhibits persistent emotional and/or behavioural difficulties, which are not relieved by the behaviour management strategies in place in the setting
- has poor communication and interaction skills, which require specific learning support
- has sensory or physical problems even when provided with personal aids and equipment.

KEY POINT

Early Years Action may also be triggered by the concerns of parents who may instinctively feel that 'there is something wrong' with their child.

Early Years practitioners should sensitively advise parents of their concerns and explain how the SENCO can help. Encourage parents to discuss particular worries (health, behaviour, physical) they have about their child and any difficulties she is experiencing. The SENCO will liaise with external specialists who may already be involved with the child. Accurate records of the child's progress and particular needs will be required, including observations of any behavioural difficulties, noting where, when, why, with whom and how often they occur.

The SENCO and Early Years team, in discussion with the parents and child, devise an Individual Education Plan (IEP) to help the child achieve maximum learning and progress. An IEP sets out only particular teaching strategies that are *additional to* or *different from* the **differentiated** curriculum plan the child already follows. The IEP also identifies particular short-term targets for the child, specifies a review date and records the outcomes when the IEP is reviewed. Arrangements and resources for teaching and learning strategies may include individual, group or out-of-hours support (breakfast or lunch-time clubs); different learning materials or special equipment; LEA support services for advice on strategies or equipment; and LEA staff training to provide effective intervention without the need for regular and ongoing input from external agencies.

- The key to Early Years Action is effective, individualised arrangements for teaching and learning.
- An IEP must be changed and restructured without waiting for the next review date if little or no progress is made. Always discuss with the parents the child's progress and why the IEP is being changed.
- An IEP is reviewed frequently – at least once every term, or more frequently if necessary.

Early Years Action: the period of individual support

Despite extra individual support and an IEP the child may not make adequate progress and you will need to move forward to:

Early Years Action Plus

Early Years Action Plus is the second stage of intervention aimed at helping a child who is experiencing learning difficulties. When the Early Years team or SENCO identifies that the child requires further assistance to make adequate progress they seek help from the external support services so that interventions that are *additional to* or *different from* those provided for the child through Early Years Action can be put in place and a new IEP drawn up.

Triggers for Early Years Action Plus

The SENCO and Early Years team seek help from external support services when, despite following an individualised programme and/or concentrated support, the child:

- continues to make little or no general progress in certain areas over a long time

- follows an Early Years curriculum well below that expected of children of similar age
- displays emotional or behavioural difficulties that substantially and regularly interfere with the child's own learning or that of the group, despite an individualised behaviour management programme
- experiences ongoing communication and interaction difficulties that adversely affect her social relationships and learning
- has sensory or physical needs and requires additional equipment or regular help from an outside specialist.

The SENCO, Early Years team and parents meet to review the child's IEP and discuss ongoing difficulties and needs. A request for help is made to the external support services and all relevant information (observations, assessment or test results, IEP and progress reports) is made available to them. It is likely a specialist will observe the child in the setting and then: offer advice on a new IEP, identify particular targets and teaching strategies; provide more specialist assessments; advise on the use of new or specialist materials; and provide support for particular activities. Parents are consulted and involved in drawing up the IEP.

External support services for Early Years settings in the maintained sector can be accessed through the LEA Special Educational Needs Officer, the local health authority or social services department. Specialists (with access to further advice and resources) include: the paediatrician; the educational psychologist; support teachers for sensory, learning or behavioural difficulties; speech and language therapists; and physiotherapists. Technicians are also available to support children with physical and/or sensory impairment.

KEY POINTS

- The different kinds of advice and support available to Early Years settings may vary according to local policies.
- The two-stage Early Years graduated approach of action and intervention is based within the setting.

PROGRESS CHECK

1 What is the SEN Code of Practice?
2 Identify three principles in the SEN Code of Practice relating specifically to parents of children with special educational needs.
3 For what reasons would Early Years staff implement
   (a) Early Years Action and (b) Early Years Action Plus?
4 What is the *particular* characteristic of Early Years Action Plus that is not also part of Early Years Action?

Infant/primary phase graduated approach

A child's special educational needs may or may not have been identified before compulsory school age and teachers in reception year or year 1 should be alert to the outcome of the baseline assessment that may give an indication of particular difficulties a child may have. A child with identified SEN is unlikely to have received a statement of special educational needs in an Early Years setting, however, the school should have access to earlier records and IEPs, which will have been written in the context of the Foundation Stage curriculum.

A 'pupil record' for a child with SEN in infant school includes information about a child's progress and behaviour from the school, the child's Early Years education setting, parents and health and social services.

The SEN Code of Practice sets out a two-stage model of graduated action and intervention for children in infant school. The stages are *School Action* and *School Action Plus*.

School Action

School Action is the first stage of intervention aimed at helping a child who is experiencing learning difficulties. Interventions that are *additional to* or *different from* the school's usual differentiated curriculum are implemented by the class teacher and the SENCO.

Triggers for School Action

School Action is indicated when the class teacher or SENCO identifies that a child:

- makes little or no progress and experiences difficulty in developing mathematics and literacy skills, even with a specially targeted teaching approach
- displays persistent emotional or behavioural problems, which are not relieved through the behaviour management strategies of the school
- experiences sensory or physical difficulties although specialist equipment is provided; or has communication and/or interaction difficulties even with a differentiated curriculum.

Interventions include writing an IEP that sets out particular teaching strategies and provisions, short-term targets, review date and the outcomes when the IEP is reviewed. To help the child to progress, group or individual support may be offered and different learning materials and equipment provided. The class teacher remains responsible for working with the child on a daily basis and for planning and delivering an individualised programme.

School Action Plus

School Action Plus is the second stage of intervention aimed at helping a child who is experiencing learning difficulties. Following a review of the IEP by the SENCO, teachers and parents, a request for help from the external support services (curriculum, literacy and numeracy co-ordinators and external specialists) is made.

Triggers for School Action Plus

School Action Plus is indicated if a child continues to:

- make little or no progress and works at National Curriculum levels well below that expected of children of similar age
- experience difficulty with literacy and mathematics skills

- display emotional or behavioural problems, which interfere with the child's own learning or that of the class group
- experience communication or interaction difficulties, which impede social relationships and are a barrier to learning
- has sensory or physical problems that require specialist equipment or regular advice or visits from a specialist service.

Support service and external specialists advise on a new IEP, with fresh and appropriate strategies for supporting the child's progress. They make arrangements for specialist assessment, for example, from the educational psychologist, and advise on a range of different teaching approaches and appropriate equipment and teaching materials, including the use of technology.

If the class teacher, SENCO, other colleagues and parents continue to be concerned about a child's progress a request for statutory assessment can be made to the LEA.

KEY POINT

At all times the parents and the child are involved with the class teacher, SENCO and specialist support services in discussions and decisions with regard to the child's special educational needs.

STATUTORY ASSESSMENT AND STATEMENT OF SPECIAL EDUCATIONAL NEEDS

Statutory assessment

A statutory assessment is a detailed multi-agency review and consideration of a child's special needs and necessary educational provision. Early Years settings and schools, in consultation with parents and external specialists, may request the LEA to make a statutory assessment if, despite intervention and help through Early Years Action and Early Years Action Plus or School Action and School Action Plus, a child has not achieved expected progress and there is significant cause for concern.

KEY POINT

Parents are entitled to request an assessment or a child may be referred for assessment by another agency, for example, the health service.

The SENCO and external specialists fully discuss the details of assessment with the parents and child. LEAs make their decision whether or not to make a statutory assessment only when they have: studied reports and assessments and evidence of achievement in the early learning goals; reviewed documentation and IEPs from all those who have been involved with the child; assessed all the identified difficulties the child is experiencing; and examined the intervention strategies implemented by the Early Years or school setting.

KEY POINTS

- An LEA may decide that the intervention and action already taken by the setting is appropriate, or suggest further fine-tuning of strategies and resources to meet the child's needs, and that a statutory assessment is not necessary
- The LEA must notify parents of their decision *not* to make a statutory assessment, give reasons for their decision and set out the provision they feel would best meet their child's needs.

If a decision to make an assessment is made, a named LEA Officer acts as a source of information between the LEA and parents. Parents are also entitled to independent advice and help throughout the process of assessment. A Named Person or Independent Parental Supporter (IPS) (see Parent Partnership Services, pages 96–7) can offer support to parents by attending meetings with them, encouraging them to participate with the professionals in all efforts and discussions on their child's behalf and helping them to understand the SEN framework. The Named Person or IPS may be someone from a voluntary organisation, the local Parent Partnership Service, another parent who perhaps has a child with special needs and understands the system, or a friend.

KEY POINT

At all times the parents and child are fully involved, their views are sought and they are advised of the objectives and method of assessment.

Following statutory assessment, the LEA decides whether:
- the child's needs can be adequately met by the Early Years setting's or the school's resources or
- to make a statement of the child's special educational needs.

If the LEA decides *not* to make a statement, a 'note in lieu' is usually sent to the parents explaining the decision and recommending further appropriate provision for their child.

Statement of Special Educational Needs

A Statement of Special Educational Needs is a legal document detailing a child's special educational needs and setting out the provision the LEA considers necessary for the child. It forms the basis for the child's future education plans. The framework of a statement is included below. Parents are advised that Parts 2, 3 and 4 of a statement are legally binding on the LEA, but Parts 5 and 6 are not. A draft, or proposed, statement is sent to the parents. If they accept it, the contents become final and a copy of the completed statement is given to them. The time taken from the statutory assessment to the final statement must not exceed twenty-six weeks.

As far as possible, arrangements are made for a child's education to continue in a mainstream school of the parents' choice. For some children with multiple and complex SEN, the facilities, specialist teaching, expertise and adapted environment of a special school may be of greater benefit.

A statement is reviewed every year (every six months if the child is under five years). It may last for the whole or part of a child's school career. It ceases at sixteen if the child leaves school at that age. An LEA may maintain the statement if a child remains at school until nineteen years of age.

Provision of resources identified in a statement can be expensive. Budgets are generally over-stretched and tightly controlled. It is often felt that a statement is resource-led rather than needs-led and parents may express concern that their child is not receiving the level of support indicated in the statement.

KEY POINT

It is the duty of LEAs to *decide whether or not* statutory assessments should be made. It is also their duty *to make* both statutory assessments and statements of special educational needs.

Writing the statement
A statement is set out in six parts.
Part 1 *Introduction*: the child's name and address and date of birth. The child's home language and religion. The names and address(es) of the child's parents.

Part 2 *Special Educational Needs* (learning difficulties): clear details of the nature and severity of each and every one of the child's special educational needs, as identified by the LEA during statutory assessment, and of the advice received and attached as appendices to the statement.

Part 3 *Special Educational Provision*: the special educational provision that the LEA considers necessary to meet the child's special educational needs.
(a) the *objectives* that the special educational provision should aim to meet
(b) the *special educational provision*, which the LEA considers appropriate to meet the needs set out in Part 2 and to meet the objectives
(c) the *arrangements* to be made for monitoring progress in meeting those objectives, particularly for setting short-term targets for the child's progress and for reviewing the child's progress on a regular basis.

Part 4 *Placement*: the type and name of school where the special educational provision set out in Part 3 is to be made or the LEA's arrangements for provision to be made otherwise than in school.

Part 5 *Non-educational needs*: all relevant non-educational needs of the child as agreed between the health services, social services or other agencies and the LEA.

Part 6 *Non-educational provision*: details of relevant non-educational provision required to meet the non-educational needs of the child as agreed between the health services and/or social services and the LEA, including the agreed arrangements for its provision.
Signature and date
(From the Special Educational Needs Code of Practice)

Advice attached to the statement *must* include educational, medical, psychological and social services advice, plus advice the LEA has asked for from any other body and considers to be relevant. Parental evidence and any views expressed by the child are also included.

A 'preferred' school

Parents have a right to state a preference for a particular school including the one their child already attends. The local education authority will take into consideration the needs of the other children in the school and available resources before making its decision.

Parents have a right of appeal against Parts 2, 3 and 4 of a statement of special educational needs.

KEY POINTS

- The recommended special educational provision identified in Part 3 of a statement may include speech and language therapy, learning support assistance or specialist equipment.
- Non-educational needs in Part 5 of a statement may include physiotherapy, occupational therapy, help to develop self-care and independence skills, mobility training or respite care.
- The actual provision set out in Part 6 may include arrangements for particular therapies and respite care, and a special needs assistant to help with self-care and independence skills.
- In exceptional cases special travel arrangements may also be provided.

PROGRESS CHECK

1 Who is responsible for (a) making a statutory assessment; and (b) writing a statement of special educational needs?
2 What must the advice attached to a statement include?
3 Against which parts of a statement of special educational needs may parents (a) appeal and (b) not appeal?
4 Why might a special school be more appropriate for some children with special educational needs?
5 Describe the non-educational needs a child might have.

Activity

A parents' evening has been arranged in your setting to discuss the principles of the Early Years graduated approach of Action and Intervention, Statutory Assessment and a Statement of Special Educational Needs. Prepare a leaflet, or construct a flow chart, to present to the parents clearly identifying these procedures.

STATUTORY ASSESSMENT AND STATEMENT FOR YOUNG CHILDREN

Children under compulsory school age and over two years

Health authorities and National Health Service (NHS) Trusts must inform parents and the appropriate LEA if they consider a child under compulsory school age and over two years may have special educational needs (section 332, Education Act 1996). A child development centre may provide a multi-specialist assessment of the child's difficulties. The LEA will want to know about the difficulties identified by the Early Years setting (if the child attends one) and whether or not outside specialist help for the child's physical health and overall development has been requested. If a child's educational needs appear complex and likely to be ongoing, or there is a need for specialist intervention to support the child's difficulties and developmental delays, then it is likely the LEA will make both a statutory assessment and a statement of special educational needs. The statement will follow the same format as for older children (see above).

Children under two years

When a child under two years is referred to the LEA it is likely that a parent or the child health services have first identified a special need. Sure Start (see Chapter 5, pages 160–1) may also identify a child with special needs and co-ordinate access to appropriate services. A statutory assessment for a child under two years can only be made if a *parent gives consent* for it. An LEA *must* make the assessment if a parent requests it. An assessment at this age is generally based on medical and developmental observations made in a child development centre.

A statement for a child under two years is rare. However, it may be appropriate if a child's needs are complex or if it will help her to access a particular service or area of support.

Special educational provision for children under compulsory school age
Parents have a right to be consulted about the type of help and support they would like to receive for their child. Some may prefer to combine home-based care and support with centre-based provision, while others may prefer totally centre-based help and support.

Special educational provision for very young children includes:

- the Portage Home Visiting Programme
- peripatetic teacher support for children with vision or hearing impairment
- advice from a clinical or educational psychologist for a child with behavioural difficulties
- attendance (or continued attendance) in a mainstream Early Years setting
- attendance in a specialist setting.

The LEA and local EYDCP hold information on nursery school/class provision for children with SEN, also the availability of places in a range of Early Years settings such as family centres, day nurseries and playgroups in the area.

For children and families for whom English is not their home language, LEAs should provide information through translators, interpreters and signers, on tapes and in Braille (according to need), at all stages of intervention and action (both in Early Years settings and infant schools), and during the procedures of a statutory assessment and a statement of special educational needs.

Steven, aged twenty months, with a Portage home visitor

KEY POINTS

- Any concerns the staff in an Early Years setting may have about a child's developmental progress should be shared as early as possible with the parents and the local education authority.
- Parents must be kept informed, involved and consulted throughout all the decision-making processes concerning their child.

SPECIAL EDUCATIONAL NEEDS TRIBUNAL

The special educational needs tribunal considers appeals by parents against local authority decisions about their child's SEN. It is an independent tribunal, unconnected to any local education authority. A decision is made after considering all written and verbal evidence, including whether the local education authority has acted within the guidance set out in the Code of Practice. The government cannot influence the tribunal's decisions.

Reasons for appeal

Appeals will be considered if:

- the local education authority decides against making a statutory assessment or does not make a statement of special educational needs after a statutory assessment
- made against the description of a child's special educational needs and/or the special educational provision the local education authority has identified
- made against the school named in the statement or the local education authority refuses to change the school named in the statement
- the local education authority refuses a request for a further assessment or ceases to maintain a statement.

KEY POINT

Appeals *cannot* be made against the way the local education authority carried out the assessment; the length of time the assessment took; Parts 5 and 6 of a statement of special educational needs; or the way the Early Years setting or the school is meeting a child's special educational needs.

Information for parents

Parents must make their appeal within two months of the LEA decision. While they are usually encouraged to attend the appeal hearing they are not obliged to do so. An Independent Parental Supporter (see below) should be available to advise parents about the procedures of a tribunal and to attend the tribunal hearing with them if it is the parents' wish. Children may attend the tribunal or present a written statement if they have a particular view they wish to express about their education. The appeal application can be withdrawn any time before the hearing. The appeals procedure usually takes between four to five months from the time the appeal is received to the tribunal's decision. Parents and the local education authority have to accept the decision of the tribunal.

KEY POINT

Parents can obtain advice about the special educational needs tribunal, and access help in preparation for their appeal from the LEA; the SENCO of their child's Early Years setting or school; their local EYDCP and PPS; an Independent Parental Supporter; or a voluntary society representing their child's particular special need, for example the Down's Syndrome Association or the National Autistic Society.

PROGRESS CHECK

1 What particular rights do parents have regarding statutory assessment if their child is *under* two years of age?
2 For which children under the age of two years might a statement of special educational needs be appropriate?
3 What special educational provision is likely to be offered to a child under compulsory school age?
4 Describe the function of a special educational needs tribunal. Why might parents wish to make an appeal to the tribunal?

Parent Partnership Service (PPS)

The government Green Paper, Excellence for all Children: Meeting Special Educational Needs, stressed the importance of effective partnerships with parents. All local education authorities are required to offer a Parent Partnership Service (whether LEA based or bought in from another provider) to encourage partnership between parents, LEAs, schools and voluntary organisations and to ensure parents receive the necessary information and guidance in relation to the special educational needs of their child. A PPS aims to provide a menu of flexible services for parents whose children have SEN in order to enable them to play an active role in their child's education and make appropriate, informed decisions and choices. Partnerships also make sure parents have access to an Independent Parental Supporter (IPS) (if they would like one) and are referred to other agencies, organisations or parent support groups for further help and advice. Supporters are volunteers, often members of a voluntary organisation or parents who have experience in caring for a child with special needs. They receive specific training to offer independent, accurate and neutral advice to parents about:

- the legal aspects of a Statutory Assessment and Statement of Special Educational Needs, also Special Educational Needs Tribunal procedures
- SEN provision
- their rights when requesting a mainstream school place for their child
- interpreting letters and reports concerning their child's SEN
- agencies such as health and social services that may be caring for their child
- sources of help such as the Children's Information Service, voluntary organisations and other support groups
- state benefits available for children with special needs and their families
- resolution of disputes.

KEY POINT

Parent Partnership Services ensure that information for parents is available through appropriate methods of communication and in appropriate community languages.

Resolution of disputes

Local education authorities must make arrangements for resolution of disputes and appoint independent persons to help in avoiding or resolving them. Good communication and the sharing of information between parents and schools, and between parents and the LEA will, hopefully, prevent any disputes arising. PPSs can help with early, informal resolution by preventing disagreements as soon as difficulties arise, negotiating with or between the parties involved and identifying areas of compromise.

Ben – a true story

Ben is a five-year-old boy with Down syndrome, who lives with his parents and two-year-old sister Beth. Outgoing and sociable, Ben readily makes friends with other children and adults, and with members of his wider family, who are all very important people in his life – loving, caring for and supporting Ben, his parents and his sister. Ben is a treasured son, brother, grandson and nephew.

Ben was a happy baby and toddler and made slow, steady progress. He had repeated upper respiratory tract infections, which lessened over the years, although he still has frequent catarrh. His development was regularly assessed and Ben received all his immunisations.

Between the ages of eight months and two-and-a-half years (when he began to attend day nursery) Ben received weekly help from a Portage home visitor, which proved extremely beneficial for him. He was usually able to perform the weekly set task before the next session. His family were involved and enthusiastic participants in the programme. Physiotherapy, speech and language, and occupational therapy services were all provided. Ben always enjoyed his therapy and exercise sessions although they could be tiring for him.

Ben walked at two years. When he was four years old he attended gym sessions for children with special needs, which increased his physical ability and confidence. He learnt to walk along a form, climb wall ladders, commando-crawl under, over and through hoops and tunnels and, with help, hang by his hands. Now, at five years, he can run around and climb up and down steps and stairs.

'Whoops! Mummy didn't tell me about the landing!'

Although he would rather just play with the water, Ben makes a good effort at washing his hands and face and cleaning his teeth. Dressing and undressing can be tricky. He can take off his shoes, socks, trousers and sometimes a top item, like a tee-shirt, with help. He can put on and pull up his trousers but needs help to get them over his bottom; he also needs help to get his socks over his toes and heels. Undoing a zip poses no problem but he is unable to manage buttons, press studs or buckles.

Ben demonstrates symbolic play and hand–eye co-ordination

Ben is an enthusiastic but slow eater. He is able to use a spoon and fork (and sometimes a knife) independently but there are times when he prefers someone to feed him – particularly when he sees Beth being fed. He eats a range of food and has been able to chew properly since the age of three. Ben has learnt to push his plate away when he has had enough as he is unable to say 'I've had enough' or 'I'm not hungry'. He drinks from a training beaker.

Ben is in control. He signs for others in the setting to be quiet. They can 'wake up' when he signals by loud banging on the tambourine

Ben has a well-developed pincer grasp, although his hands are weaker than those of a child without special needs. He manages simple three-piece jigsaw puzzles, threads beads and can turn large objects such as taps. He plays enthusiastically and is able to engage in simple sequencing activities. His play, at a little over four years, was assessed at the developmental level of two-and-a-half years.

Ben's comprehension is improving. He understands positional language such as in, on, under, up and down, and he readily fetches things and responds to little commands. He has a spoken vocabulary of about twenty words and is beginning to pick up simple phrases he hears Beth using such as 'Go away' and 'Get away!'. Ben uses up to a hundred and fifty Makaton signs. Beth copies her brother's signing – a positive example of sibling interaction.

Because Ben has no way of expressing himself verbally he does become frustrated. He may throw things or refuse to get dressed. When being read a story he may push the book away. At times he will rush around in a state of high spirits.

Ben received a statement of special educational needs when he was four-years-and-four-months old. His parents were unhappy at the recommendation that Ben should attend a special school. They felt strongly it would be more beneficial for Ben's overall development if he attended his ordinary, neighbourhood school.

They appealed to the special educational needs tribunal and their appeal was upheld.

Family interaction – even Beth joins in signing

Ben is now settled and integrated into the school of his parents' choice. Two special needs assistants provide a total of thirty-five hours' help per week. Ben also has one session of speech and language therapy per month. Full-time education is tiring but, apart from a few tears, particularly at the beginning of term, Ben is happy. He is making all-round progress and can now join up the dots of his name. Since attending school he has learnt to sit on and use a child's toilet.

The Disability Discrimination Act (DDA) 1995

The Disability Discrimination Act 1995 aims to end the discrimination faced by many disabled people (both children and adults). Under this Act, it is unlawful to treat disabled people less favourably than other people for reasons related to their disability. It is also unlawful for those who provide goods, facilities and services to discriminate against disabled people. In addition, service providers must make 'reasonable adjustments' to their procedures, policies and practices and offer information on tape, or provide an interpreter or reader, to make it easier for disabled people to use the service. Where there are physical barriers that restrict or prevent access for disabled people, providers must make 'reasonable adjustments' to overcome them. For example, if steps into the building pose a physical barrier, a ramp or alternative entrance may be provided to overcome the barrier. It is good practice for settings to anticipate and overcome common barriers, such as steps, even if a disabled person does not currently use the setting.

However, it would be extremely difficult to anticipate every eventuality, so it is important that providers continue to identify the barriers that may affect their users and respond by making reasonable adjustments as required.

The Disability Discrimination Act supports the policies and requirements of the Education Act 1996 to provide all children with special educational needs with an education and school place appropriate to their requirements.

KEY POINT

Examples of service providers are: businesses and organisations including those that offer childcare and services for families; shops, pubs and restaurants; sports and leisure facilities; libraries, museums, theatres and cinemas; employment agencies; and bus and railway stations.

A disabled person is defined in the DDA 1995 as someone who has a physical or mental impairment that adversely affects their ability to carry out normal day-to-day activities. This will be long term – it will have lasted for 12 months or be likely to last for more than 12 months. This includes some chronic illnesses, such as ME, which affect some people's ability to carry out normal day-to-day activities.
(Definition of SEN)

The Disability Rights Commission (DRC) and the Equality and Human Rights Commission

The Disability Rights Commission was established under the Disability Rights Commission Act 1999. It was an independent body set up by the government to secure and protect the civil rights of disabled people and had powers to:

- work to eliminate discrimination against disabled people
- promote equal opportunities for disabled people
- encourage good practice in the treatment of disabled people
- review the working of the DDA and assist disabled people to secure their rights by offering information, advice and support in taking cases forward
- provide information and advice to employers and service providers about their duties under the DDA
- ensure children with special needs can join in a wide range of play and leisure activities.

The Disability Rights Commission is now closed. Its responsibility for helping secure civil rights for disabled people transferred to the new Equality and Human Rights Commission in 2007, who tell us:

How we live together is one of the big challenges of the twenty-first century: as serious as climate change and more immediate.
A milestone along the road to a fairer, more equal Britain, the new Equality and Human Rights Commission opened on 1 October 2007.

The new commission is working to eliminate discrimination, reduce inequali-ty, protect human rights and to build good relations, ensuring that everyone has a fair chance to participate in society.

The previous commissions – the Equal Opportunities Commission, the Commission for Racial Equality, and the Disability Rights Commission – have made enormous advances, changing Britain into a fairer place. But much remains to be done.

The new commission is building on their legacy to achieve change to benefit some of the most disadvantaged and voiceless people in our society.

The new commission brings together the work of the three previous equality commissions and also takes on responsibility for the other aspects of equality: age, sexual orientation and religion or belief, as well as human rights.The Equality and Human Rights Commission acts not only for the disadvantaged, but for everyone in society, and can use its new enforcement powers where necessary to guarantee people's equality. It also has a mandate to promote understanding of the Human Rights Act.

The Equality and Human Rights Commission is a non-departmental public body (NDPB) established under the Equality Act 2006 – accountable for its pub-lic funds, but independent of government.

The National Health Service (NHS) and Community Care Act 1990

The National Health Service and Community Care Act 1990 made provisions for setting up National Health Service Trusts, which are responsible for the ownership and management of hospitals. All NHS hospitals in the country are now run by NHS Trusts. Under the Act, local authorities have a duty to make assessments of need for community care services (nursing and physical care, help in the home, equipment or adaptations to the home). For children with special needs community care means providing health and social care services, as well as support, to enable them to live as independently as possible in their own family homes or in homely settings. A 'seamless' care plan should demonstrate a holistic approach to assessment and provision.

The Health Act 1999

The Health Act 1999 set out changes to the way the NHS is run in England, Wales and Scotland. The Act abolished general practitioner fund-holding in England, Wales and Scotland and established:
- new arrangements aimed at improving the quality of care within the NHS
- a new statutory body, known as the Commission for Health Improvement, to monitor and improve the quality of health care provided by the NHS
- Primary Care Trusts in England and Wales.

The Health Act also placed a duty of quality of care on health authorities, NHS Trusts and Primary Care Trusts.

The NHS Act 2006

The NHS Act 2006 provided a framework enabling money to be pooled between health bodies and health-related local authority services. It also allowed functions, resources and management structures to be integrated. This facilitated the 'joining-up' of existing and new services.

PRIMARY CARE TRUSTS

Primary Care Trusts (or Groups) are groups of general practitioners, nurses, midwives, health visitors and allied professionals such as social workers, dentists, pharmacists and opticians, who look after health needs in a specific community. They are independent, statutory NHS organisations accountable to their health authority. Their aim is to shape services that will provide better health care, leading to better health, for local communities. Trusts have their own budgets for delivering a range of community health and social care services and running community hospitals. They provide community paediatric services, including multidisciplinary assessment of children with special needs. Primary Care Trusts liaise with LEAs in providing for the health needs of children with SEN.

Designated medical officer

A **designated medical officer for SEN**, appointed by the health authority, is responsible for co-ordinating the health care for children with SEN and will:
- make sure schools know how to obtain medical advice for children with SEN – the usual channel is through the school health service
- co-ordinate health service advice for a statutory assessment and all review meetings. Advice may come from the child's general practitioner and health visitor, the school doctor and school nurse, therapists, child psychiatrist and/or psychologist and hospital specialists such as the paediatrician or heart or orthopaedic consultant
- help general practitioners and therapists to prepare reports for schools and LEAs on the medical history and health needs of children with SEN
- co-ordinate health service provision set out in Part 6 of a statement of SEN
- arrange therapy and nursing services provision with the health authority or Primary Care Trust for a child with SEN.

KEY POINT

The designated medical officer may be a member of the local EYDCP (or will liaise with it), so that information on accessing health advice is consistent across the whole area.

The Children Act 1989

The Children Act 1989 is the legal framework for the *care and protection* of children in England and Wales. It established a new approach in England and Wales to services for children and their families. The Act recognises the importance of families and that, wherever possible, children are brought up within their own families.

Children with disabilities are included in children's legislation as a legal category. Local authority social services departments are required to register children with disabilities and provide care services for them.

The Act encourages better co-ordination of services between local health, education and social services departments.

Families are important

DEFINITIONS FROM THE CHILDREN ACT

The Children Act states that a 'child in need' can be helped most effectively if there is a co-operative and trusting partnership between the parents and the local authority.

The Act (Part III, section 17) defines children as being in need if the following apply:

■ The child is unlikely to achieve or maintain, or to have the opportunity of achieving or maintaining a reasonable standard of health or development without provision for that child of services by a local authority under this Part (of the Act).

- The child's health or development is likely to be significantly impaired, or further impaired without the provision for that child of such services.
- *The child is disabled.*
  The Children Act states that:

  A child is disabled if he is blind, deaf or dumb or suffers from mental disorder of any kind or is substantially and permanently handicapped by illness, injury or congenital deformity or such other disability as may be prescribed.

KEY POINT

Children in need refers to children, including those with disabilities, who require specific help and services to ensure 'a reasonable standard of health and development'.

PRINCIPLES IN THE CHILDREN ACT

The following principles are enshrined in the Children Act:
- The welfare of the child (whether disabled or not) is paramount and should be safeguarded and promoted at all times by those providing services.
- Children with disabilities are children first with the same rights as all children to services.
- Parents and families are important in children's lives. Local authorities should support them in carrying out their responsibilities.
- Parents should be valued as partners with local authorities and other agencies such as health and education services.
- Children have a right to be consulted and listened to when decisions about them are being made. Their views and the views of their parents must always be taken into account.
- Health, education and social services for children with disabilities should be co-ordinated.

REGISTRATION

Local authority social services departments are required to keep a register of children with disabilities – where possible, a joint register between local health, education and social services departments. Such a register makes it easier to plan and co-ordinate services for a child and her family. Inclusion on the register is voluntary and parents have a right to see what is written. Provision of services is not dependent on registration.

KEY POINT

A register of children with disabilities is totally separate from, and has no connection with, a child protection register.

PROGRESS CHECK

1   What is the *main* objective of the Children Act 1989?
2   What do you understand by the phrase 'children in need'?
3   What are the principles of the Children Act?

Every Child Matters

Every Child Matters is the government agenda that focuses on bringing together services to support children and families. It sets out five major outcomes for children:

- being healthy
- staying safe
- enjoying and achieving
- making a positive contribution
- economic well-being.

Further information is provided on pages 52–3.

The Children and Young People's Plan

Building brighter futures sets out a compelling challenge: to make England the best place in the world for children and young people to grow up. The government tells us that:

> This means world-class health outcomes, services of the highest quality, minimising inequalities, and tackling poverty. The Children and Young People's Plan (CYPP) is a powerful force in helping realise these ambitions - it drives better local integration of children's services; helps strengthen local partnership arrangements; and describes what improvements will be achieved in the local area, and when these improvements will be delivered.
>
> Local areas will build on their experience of developing CYPPs and bring a step-change to improving children's outcomes. By 2010 all areas are expected to have consistent and high quality arrangements in place for prevention, early identification and early intervention in order to narrow gaps and improve outcomes for all.
>
> New non-statutory CYPP guidance for local authorities has been published to help achieve these aims. The new guidance replaces previous guidance

on the Children and Young People's Plan issued in 2005 and 2007. It brings together the 2005 and 2007 CYPP regulations in one place, reflects the new performance management arrangements including Local Area Agreements, and sets out the proposed legislative changes for 2011.

For further information, including updates on the progress made towards realising the plan, visit www.dfes.gov.uk/publications/childrensplan.

Children's rights, empowerment and advocacy

CHILDREN'S RIGHTS

Children are dependent on their parents for basic needs such as food, warmth, shelter, clothing, protection and love, but they are also subject to adult preferences, rights and power. Adults may not always understand or meet children's needs.

Children have rights enshrined in laws. Technically, the days when children were 'seen and not heard' are over. Action has been taken to ensure children, and their families, know what their rights are and how to put this entitlement into practice. Children must be empowered to secure their rights and make their voice heard. Young children can be represented by an advocate to speak and interpret on their behalf.

KEY POINT

Remember, the fact that children have been granted legal rights does not automatically mean those rights will be respected.

The Convention on the Rights of the Child

In 1959 the United Nations, formerly the League of Nations, made a Declaration of the Rights of the Child. During the International Year of the Child in 1979, Poland proposed a Convention on the Rights of the Child. It was an important step in recognising the child as a person worthy of respect and with rights. The Convention was completed and adopted by the United Nations General Assembly in 1989 and ratified (formally approved) by the UK government in December 1991. Countries that have ratified the Convention are known as States Parties and are legally bound by its provisions.

Activity

Find out the current number of States Parties to the Convention on the Rights of the Child. Are there any countries that have not ratified the Convention?

The Convention on the Rights of the Child declares that children have the following rights:

- life
- an adequate standard of living – food, shelter, medical care
- education, play, leisure and cultural activities – access to information and freedom of thought
- protection against all forms of abuse, neglect and exploitation, including child labour and sexual exploitation
- a say in matters affecting their lives and opportunities to take part in the activities of their society in preparation for responsible adulthood

Article 23 of the Convention (summarised) states that 'a disabled child has the right to special care, education and training to help him or her enjoy a full and decent life in dignity and achieve the greatest degree of self-reliance and social integration possible'.

KEY POINT

The Convention on the Rights of the Child recognises the rights of parents or carers and in no way promotes conflict between them and their children.

The World Summit for Children in 1990 created a Committee for the Rights of the Child to monitor the way in which States Parties implement the provisions of the Convention.

KEY POINT

In spite of the Convention, many governments are ignoring its principles and children world-wide continue to be exploited, neglected and abused.

Rights of children with special needs

Children with special needs in the UK have, through Acts of Parliament, a right to education, health care and a range of services, which promote and safeguard their welfare. Local education authorities, local health authorities (through their hospital and community health provision) and social services departments have duties to provide appropriate care and support programmes through continuous assessment and review procedures. Multiprofessional teams (see Chapter 1, pages 24–31) work and plan with the parents and child, to provide a 'package of care and support' to meet individual and changing needs.

KEY POINT

Any care and support plan must be flexible. The overall aim is, as far as possible, to maintain and support children with special needs within their own families. Children being looked after by foster carers or living in residential homes have a right to be placed near their family homes – often placements are many miles away making parental visits time consuming and expensive.

Listening to children

The Children Act 1989 and the Special Educational Needs Code of Practice require that children are listened to, consulted and involved in decision making, which will affect their lives. Young children with special needs must be listened to, whatever their age, and their wishes and choices respected and encouraged. It is sometimes hard for people, including professionals, to understand that children have rights independently of the adults around them, especially their parents. Newell (1988), commenting on the Cleveland child abuse crisis in which the professionals were clearly not listening to what the children were saying, but rather they were acting in the children's best interests, wrote 'let no one forget after Cleveland that "best interests" are no substitute for "rights".' Lord Justice Butler-Sloss in her Cleveland Report said 'the child is a person, and not an object of concern'.

'Now, will somebody please listen to me!'

KEY POINT

The family's Named Person is able to act as a co-ordinator in securing the appropriate information, help and support.

PROGRESS CHECK

1   What is the importance of the Convention on the Rights of the Child?
2   What does Article 23 of the Convention say about the rights of disabled children?

3 To which particular services do children with special needs have a right in the UK?
4 What comments were made by Newell and Lord Justice Butler-Sloss with regard to the Cleveland child abuse crisis?

EMPOWERMENT

The word **empower** means to enable, to give power or authority. Young children with special needs must be enabled to make their wishes known to their adult carers and to make choices, however small, in matters affecting their everyday lives. The motto of the National Children's Bureau is 'The powerful voice of the child'. All children, including those with special needs, have the right to be heard and given a sense of control over their lives. Frequently, children 'fall in' with whatever plans their parents and other adults have for them without being asked whether or not they have any choice or preference. Listening to children, taking into account their views, allowing them to exercise choice and involving them in planning and decision-making procedures come within the remit of the Children Act 1989, and the SEN Code of Practice.

Offering choices

How often are non-disabled children given the chance to make a choice or say 'yes' or 'no' during the course of a day? Typically, you ask them 'What would you like for your lunch?', 'Would you like an orange or an apple?', 'Which story would you like?', 'Where shall we go for our walk today?'
    The Children Act 1989 says:

Learning to make well-informed choices and making some mistakes should be part of every child's experience. Children and young people should be given the chance to exercise choice and their views should be taken seriously if they are unhappy about the arrangements made for them.

GOOD PRACTICE

Make sure you offer choices to children with special needs and encourage them to speak for themselves and make decisions in care, education and home settings.

On a small scale you can offer children similar choices to those above, such as which clothes they would like to wear, what activity they would like to do next or whether they would like a rest. Choice of a music tape, appropriate television programmes or a special treat can also be offered. Older children can be actively involved in decisions about education and be given certain responsibility within the school environment. They can be asked their views on management of their health care and medical needs.

KEY POINTS

- A balance must be struck between giving children a voice and offering them choices and decisions about which they cannot make an appropriate judgement on their own.
- Giving children the opportunity to choose and make decisions in small ways increases self-image and promotes the confidence and independence to make later major decisions affecting all areas of their lives.

Scott makes a choice

Activity

If you are caring for children with special needs think how many times you offered them choices today. How were the children with complex special needs able to respond to your offers?

Child protection

Children need protection from all types of child abuse. Children with special needs are particularly vulnerable to the possibility of abuse and must be empowered to recognise appropriate and inappropriate touching, as well as behaviours such as verbal abuse and discrimination. They should be given the words and language to use in any court procedures.

Special attention must be given to children with learning and communication difficulties when they wish to express their feelings or recall events. Careful assessment of demeanour and body language is important and alternative communication systems may be used. Interpreters and facilitators can ensure the child's best interests are served. Early Years workers must always follow the procedures laid down in the Child Protection Policy of their setting.

GOOD PRACTICE

Your role and responsibility as an Early Years worker in protecting children with special needs and identifying possible abuse is the same (if not more so) as protecting other children (see Chapter 9, pages 394–5).

Understanding and interpreting children's needs

Not all children with special needs will be able to make their voices heard through the spoken word. Even so their vocal communications, actions, demeanour and behaviour can reveal their wishes and feelings. You will need to be patient and learn to interpret their clues and gestures, such as nodding or shaking their heads, pointing, facial expressions as well as recognising the messages they give through their play and creative activities. Children with severe learning difficulties or communication skills can be helped to make their needs and preferences known through sign language, large print, Braille and information technology. Interpreters and facilitators are also of great help.

Children communicate in a variety of ways

KEY POINT

Through observing children you can pick up any stress, anxiety, aggression or pleasure, which may indicate a particular need or a wish to express a view.

Empowering parents

The Children Act 1989, the Education Act 1996 and the SEN Code of Practice empower parents of children with special needs to enter into a partnership of support and co-operation with the professionals. This concept recognises that parents know their children best and professional services cannot be wholly effective without their support. However, families cannot be empowered unless they are informed. Professionals should ensure that families receive appropriate information about the range of services available. Information should also be freely accessible through outlets such as public libraries, local child health and development centres, day care and education settings, hospitals and surgeries.

KEY POINT

Information must always reflect the needs of families from a variety of ethnic and cultural groups.

Activity

Check in various outlets, such as those mentioned above, in your own locality for leaflets or information sheets on services available to children with special needs and their families. Do you have information available in your work setting? Is the information available for families of different ethnic groups and those with sensory impairment?

PROGRESS CHECK

1   What do you understand by the word 'empowerment'?
2   Why is it important to offer young children with special needs the opportunity to make choices and decisions?
3   In what non-verbal ways might children with special needs make their wishes and choices known to you?

ADVOCACY

The movement for child advocacy started in America in the 1960s. It is now enshrined in the Children Act 1989. Children with special needs are those least likely to be able to speak up for themselves and their rights. Those who are unable to make themselves heard or who are denied appropriate services and support need an adult to act as advocate, interpreting and articulating for them. An advocate will *listen, interpret, liaise* and *negotiate* to secure children's rights. Parents can be enabled to speak on their child's behalf (or another advocate can speak their words for them). Where a child's needs appear to be overruled or ignored an advocate can help the parents to gain information and support. This may be a professional such as the family health visitor or social worker (perhaps in their capacity as Named Person), an EYDCP representative, an ethnic link worker, or someone from a voluntary organisation. Some local authorities employ children's rights officers as independent advocates for older children with special needs to make sure they are 'heard' when plans for their future are being discussed.

When advocacy is helpful

Advocacy is helpful when:

- parents have insufficient knowledge of English to make themselves understood
- parents lack knowledge about services and resources available to their child and family
- professionals will not listen to the child or the parents.

Advocacy and school children

Children with special needs attending school have a right to be involved in their own school-based and local authority assessments and decision-making processes.
The SEN Code of Practice states:

> *Children with special educational needs … should, where possible, participate in all the decision-making processes that occur in education including the setting of learning targets and contributing to IEPs, discussions about choice of schools and contributing to the assessment of their needs. They should feel confident that they will be listened to and that their views are valued.*

The Code of Practice does, however, stress the balance between giving children a voice and encouraging them to make informed decisions, and expecting them to make decisions when they have insufficient experience, knowledge and support.

KEY POINTS

- Advocacy may be important if parents are unsure about the statutory assessment procedures or how to appeal against a statement of special educational needs.
- Children looked after by the local authority may require access to an independent advocate.
- Where children's rights have been obstructed or violated, the child, or an advocate (parent, carer, social worker, the police, social service department or other person or organisation) can seek help for the child through the courts.

Advocacy and parents

Advocacy training programmes for parents enable them to become confident and assertive advocates for their children. They gain information about the rights of children with special needs and learn how to access the resources available for them.

Self-advocacy is a form of self-help in that it empowers parents to speak out effectively for their own needs.

PROGRESS CHECK

1 What do you understand by the word 'advocacy'?
2 Who might act as an advocate on behalf of a child with special needs?
3 Why might the parents of a child with special needs require an advocate?

CASE STUDY

A family recently moved from abroad to join their extended family in Britain. Both parents had limited English. Their five-year-old child, Leila, was to join her cousins in the local infant school.

On admission to school Leila was found to have marked developmental delay and arrangements were made for her to be formally assessed and receive a statement of special educational needs.

Leila's parents had no knowledge of the education system, the support available or their rights. There was unanimous agreement at a case conference that Leila's needs would be best represented by an advocate and an ethnic link worker. The assessment and statementing procedure was commenced.

1 In what other situations might an advocate be better suited than a parent to represent a child's needs?
2 How could Leila's parents gain access to the information needed to make a suitable choice of school for their daughter?

KEY TERMS

You need to know what these words and phrases mean. Go back through the chapter and make sure that you understand:

advocacy
Children Act 1989
children's rights
Children and Young People's Plan
Disability Discrimination Act 1995
Disability Rights Commission
Early Years Action
Early Years Action Plus
Education Act 1981
Education Act 1996
empowerment
Equality and Human Rights
   Commision
Every Child Matters
Health Act 1999
individual education plan

learning difficulty
NHS Act 2006
NHS and Community Care Act 1990
Parent Partnership Service
reports and legislation
resolution of disputes
School Action
School Action Plus
special educational needs
Special Educational Needs and
   Disability Act 2001
Special Educational Needs Code of
   Practice
special educational provision
Warnock Report 1978

4 STATUTORY SERVICES AND SUPPORT FOR CHILDREN AND THEIR FAMILIES

This chapter covers:
- **Health service systems and support**
- **Social services systems and support**
- **Education authority systems and support**
- **Office for Standards in Education (Ofsted)**
- **Benefits**

This chapter sets out the statutory care and support available for children with special needs and their families. Laws, or statutes, are passed by Parliament and either impose a *duty* (must do) or give a *discretionary power* (may do) to central or local government departments or agencies to provide a service or carry out certain obligations. The three main statutory service providers for children with special needs are:
- the health service
- social services
- education authorities.

Across these three areas of service there is a wide range of support and care for children and their families. Professionals from the different disciplines interlink to offer appropriate provision, for example, a child with cerebral palsy may receive physiotherapy and speech and language therapy from the health service, family support and counselling from social services and, later on, special educational provision from the local education authority. Research shows that families appreciate services being accessible in one integrated centre – accessing help when services are spread over a wide area often causes frustration and delay.

KEY POINTS

- The key to successful assessment, review procedures and provision of services is an effective working partnership between the family and all those providing a service. This is particularly important for children who have wide-ranging and complex needs.
- Sometimes a particular service is offered by one or more providers, for example, health and social services may both provide respite care, or social services and the local education authority may have joint responsibility for combined nursery centres.

Health service systems and support

The National Health Service (NHS) in the UK was introduced in 1948. It is a comprehensive service providing health care, within available resources, for all members of the community.

HEALTH SERVICE PROVISION FOR YOUNG CHILDREN WITH SPECIAL NEEDS

Hospitals
- in-patient care
- out-patient care

Community child health services

Consultant/specialist advice and care
- neonatologists
- paediatricians
- neurologists
- ophthalmologists

- ear, nose and throat specialists,

Primary health care team

Family doctors
- prescriptions
- care of unwell child
- referrals
- child health promotion
- immunisation

Health visitors / special needs health visitors

Community midwives

Community paediatric nurses
- nursing care
- support
- equipment loans

Hospital/hospice respite care

Child psychiatric clinics

Designated medical officer for special educational needs

KEY POINT

The following services may be hospital or community based: speech and language therapy, occupational therapy, paediatric physiotherapy, hearing and eye clinics, and nutrition and dietary advice.

Child health clinics
Child development centres
Child and family guidance services

School health service
Dental services

Toy libraries
(also social services provision)

SOCIAL SERVICES SUPPORT
FOR YOUNG CHILDREN WITH SPECIAL NEEDS AND THEIR FAMILIES

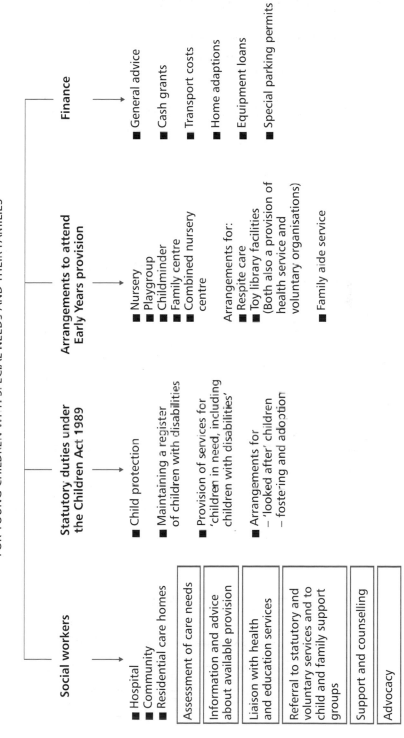

Social workers

■ Hospital
■ Community
■ Residential care homes

Assessment of care needs

Information and advice about available provision

Liaison with health and education services

Referral to statutory and voluntary services and to child and family support groups

Support and counselling

Advocacy

Statutory duties under the Children Act 1989

■ Child protection

■ Maintaining a register of children with disabilities

■ Provision of services for 'children in need, including children with disabilities'

■ Arrangements for
  – 'looked after' children
  – fostering and adoption

Arrangements to attend Early Years provision

■ Nursery
■ Playgroup
■ Childminder
■ Family centre
■ Combined nursery centre

Arrangements for:
■ Respite care
■ Toy library facilities
(Both also a provision of health service and voluntary organisations)

■ Family aide service

Finance

■ General advice
■ Cash grants
■ Transport costs
■ Home adaptions
■ Equipment loans
■ Special parking permits

EDUCATION AUTHORITY PROVISION
FOR YOUNG CHILDREN WITH SPECIAL EDUCATIONAL NEEDS

Mainstream or specialist education settings

- Combined children's centres
- Nursery schools
- Nursery classes
- Infant schools (including reception classes)
- Special schools
- Hospital school service (joint education and health service provision)

Specialists

- Educational psychologist
- Educational welfare officer (also known as Education Social Worker)
- Special Educational Needs Co-ordinator (SENCO)

Teachers

- Head teacher
- Classroom teachers
- Special needs teachers
  - advisory
  - specialist } including peripatetic
  - support
- Special needs assistants

Statutory assessment and writing a statement of special educational needs

- A named LEA officer
- Pre-school portage service

The Department of Health has overall responsibility for the National Health Service.

All children with special needs are entitled to have their needs assessed (the Children Act 1989). Usually, the first professionals a child and his family see are from the medical profession. For many children identified with special needs through the health service the most likely causes will be a physical condition, sensory impairment or developmental delay. Sometimes needs can be assessed in a child health clinic or surgery but usually children are seen in a child development centre that provides multidisciplinary assessment.

KEY POINT

Children with special needs may require hospital care. Some will receive health care at home from the family doctor and community paediatric nursing team. Ongoing physiotherapy, occupational or speech and language therapy can be provided in hospital, the local child health clinic, an Early Years setting, school or at home.

HEALTH SERVICE SUPPORT AND PROVISION

Health service support and provision includes the following.

Health service professionals
See pages 26–30.

Specialist/consultant care
Many children need specialist assessment, treatment and care including surgery, investigations and a range of therapies. Parents are often overawed by a hospital environment and are particularly vulnerable when waiting for new information, such as the results of tests or investigations, or are bringing new concerns to the doctor's attention.

KEY POINT

Any visit to hospital can be a stressful and difficult time. A sensitive approach by the doctors and other staff can allay fears and anxieties.

Primary health care
Routine health care for children with special needs is always available in the community from the primary health care team. The family doctor cares for day-to-day health problems and concerns. Home nursing care and loans of medical equipment, such as suction apparatus, injection pumps, feeding support equipment, oxygen and mobility aids, are provided by the community paediatric nursing service. The health visitor sees the family at home, offering advice, support and information often in the role of Named Person.

A special needs health visitor may also visit the family.

Home nursing care equipment and mobility aids

Assessment of needs

Assessment of a child's needs usually takes place in a child development centre in either a community or hospital setting. The centre provides facilities for health and developmental assessment, ongoing therapy and care for children with special needs. The centre is a 'single door' through which children and their families have access to the necessary services. Referral is usually through the family doctor or, sometimes, through Sure Start (see Chapter 5, pages 160–1).

Typically, the core members of a centre's multidisciplinary team would be: paediatrician, child psychologist, social worker, health visitor, play specialist, teacher, speech and language therapist, physiotherapist and occupational therapist, community paediatric nurse and Early Years workers. The parents are always valued members of the team – they have the day-to-day knowledge of their child's progress and needs. Developmental assessment may take place in a playgroup setting at the centre over a period of a few weeks. For parents, it can either be a time of worry and anxiety or a relief that, at last, something is being done for their child.

Play activities are provided with the Early Years team observing behaviour and play skills. Other professionals assess the child in their own field of expertise. Continuing support and therapy is frequently required with further assessment every six months or so.

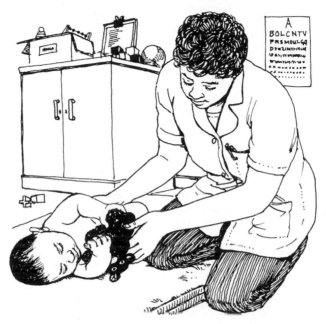

Physiotherapist assessing muscle tone in a child development centre

GOOD PRACTICE

Child development centres serving ethnic communities provide community link workers to interpret and advise as necessary.

A child development centre
A child development centre offers the following benefits:
- an accessible setting for children and their families with familiar layout and staff
- opportunities to meet other families with children with similar special needs. Families can share experiences and knowledge and learn about family support groups and other voluntary organisations
- a link worker to advise, interpret and support families of different cultures
- day care or playgroup facilities
- transport arrangements for children who live far away or who have mobility difficulties.

Child and family guidance service

The child and family guidance service may be based in a child development centre, child health clinic or hospital. The service offers help, guidance and support for children with emotional, behavioural and school difficulties, and their families. Professional staff include a child psychiatrist, psychologist and psychiatric social worker and, usually, a psychotherapist and family therapist. Because of the link between disturbed behaviour and home/social circumstances the service is orientated towards family as well as child therapy. Typically, a child would be referred to the child and family guidance service because of emotional problems such as fear, anxiety, sadness or unhappiness or because of aggressive, anti-social and defiant behaviour. Parents experiencing difficulties in adjusting to a child with special needs can also be helped by the child and family guidance team.

Parent and child attend a therapy session

KEY POINT

The aim of child and family guidance intervention is to help children live a more normal life both individually and within the family so that they can grow up settled and secure.

Activity

Think of reasons why a young child might display (a) anxiety and (b) aggressive behaviour over a short-term or long-term period.

Child health promotion programmes

Child health promotion programmes contribute to good health and the prevention of illness. Programmes aim to: promote optimum child health and development; prevent illness, accidents and child abuse; detect and eliminate, if possible, problems affecting development, learning and behaviour; and detect difficulties at an early stage. Immunisation and child health surveillance (growth and development assessment and screening programmes) are essential provisions of any child health promotion programme. Assessments and screening may take place in a child development centre, child health clinic, hospital or surgery, or in schools (including special schools) as part of the school health service.

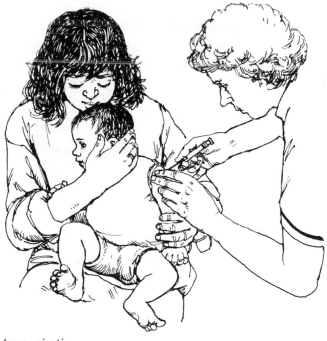

Immunisation

A hearing test: the baby locates the sound stimulus

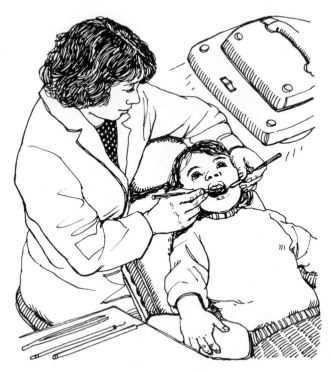

Dental care is important for all children

A speech and language therapy session; communication through signing

Activity

Obtain a current immunisation schedule from your local health centre or surgery. In which circumstances would it be unsafe for immunisation to be carried out?

Dental care

Dental care is offered by the family or community dentist. Specialist dental care is provided in a hospital dental clinic.

Therapy services

Many children with special needs require either physiotherapy, occupational therapy and/or speech and language therapy. Therapists assess and help children at home, and in child development centres, clinics, hospitals or schools.

Aids and equipment

Equipment such as wheelchairs, special seating, standing frames and hearing aids are available either on loan or free of charge. Radio hearing aids are not necessarily free. In some areas health and social services have joint equipment stores.

Prescriptions and medication

Children with special needs may require long-term or short-term medication. Drugs and medicines are free of charge. They can be in liquid or tablet form, injections, inhalers or suppositories. Certain special dietary foods are also free on prescription.

Never give a child an injection or a suppository without prior training and parental permission.

Respite care

The health service provides respite care for families caring for children with serious health problems and substantial medical and nursing needs. Children should be cared for in small, home-like, locally based settings – such as Honeylands (see Chapter 5, pages 158–9). Children's hospices and paediatric wards may offer respite care for children with complex disabilities or terminal illness.

School health service

The school health service offers health advice and support to children with SEN in education settings through health professionals such as doctors, school nurses, speech and language therapists, physiotherapists and occupational therapists. Provision, which may vary nationwide, can also include selective screening and dental care.

PROGRESS CHECK

1   What special equipment might children with special needs require in their own homes?
2   What is the function of a child development centre?
3   What benefits does a child development centre offer to a child and his family?
4   Why might a child be referred to the child and family guidance service? What is the aim of this service?
5   What do you understand by the term child health promotion?

Social services systems and support

Social services departments (SSDs) are part of local authority provision. At central government level they are responsible to the Social Services Inspectorate and the Department of Health.

SOCIAL SERVICES DEPARTMENTS' DUTIES

In respect of children with special needs, SSDs have a duty under the Children Act 1989 to:

■   provide a range of support services, which will promote and safeguard their welfare, minimise the effect of the special need and allow children to be cared for within their family
■   work closely with local health services, including the primary health care team, and be aware of local policy and practice in child health promotion
■   work closely with the local education authority and offer information or advice about a child known to them when a statutory assessment or a statement of special educational needs is being prepared.

Services should:

■ be flexible, locally accessible, culturally and racially appropriate
■ provide information and choice
■ recognise the importance of partnership with parents.

SOCIAL SERVICE SUPPORT AND PROVISION

Through their social services departments, local authorities provide particular non-medical care and support for children with special needs and their families. Some of this is detailed ON pages 129–38.

Social service professionals
See Chapter 1, pages 30–1.

All Early Years settings should promote inclusion and welcome children with special needs. Some settings, such as Opportunity Playgroups, are specifically intended to meet the needs of disabled children and to offer support to their parents, although some non-disabled children may also attend. A specialist setting for early intervention care may be of greater help to children with profound and complex special needs and may be the preferred choice for some

A day care session in a family centre

parents. It is unlikely that a specialist setting would be available in every neighbourhood and travelling to another area each day may mean a child and his parents have little social contact with other local children and their families.

Social services can help to arrange access to appropriate Early Years provision for children with special needs and offer a range of services to the family to support and improve their strengths and skills. Some Early Years and family support provision is identified in the table below. A statement of special educational needs for children under five years may recommend day care provision in a day nursery, pre-school, playgroup or parent/carer and toddler group. Although acceptance of this provision is not obligatory, most families recognise its value in the overall development of their child. The role of a key worker in a day care setting is described in Chapter 5, pages 170–5.

Setting/Provider	Provision offered *
Day nurseries	Provide childcare throughout the day to suit the needs of working parents. Usually open from 8am–6pm, Monday to Friday, closing only during the Christmas period. Nurseries often care for babies and children from twelve weeks to five years. There will usually be a separate baby room. The Early Years Foundation Stage applies. Some workplaces set up their own nursery for the children of their staff.
Pre-schools	Pre-schools can vary greatly in terms of opening times. Many open the same hours as schools, closing for holidays. Some have hours similar to day nurseries. Some open every weekday, others just on two or three days a week. Most cater for children aged three to five years. The Early Years Foundation Stage applies.
Childminders	Provide childcare in their own home, caring for children of any age. The Early Years Foundation Stage applies to children aged 0 to five years.
Nannies	Provide childcare in the child's home, caring for children of any age. A nanny may live in or live out of the family home.
Crèches	Provide childcare for a period of time (usually only up to two hours) while parents do another activity such as shopping, attending a short course or going to a leisure centre. The Early Years Foundation Stage may apply to some settings.

Setting/Provider	Provision offered *
Children's centres	(Including Sure Start Centres and Family Centres.) These are known as multi-agency settings because professionals from different sectors will work there. Provision may include a combination of: childcare for children of all ages, child health services, family support services including counselling and help with parenting skills, welfare rights advice, toy libraries, drop-in sessions and special events. (Family centres may operate an 'open door' policy or families can be referred from the local health or education authority as well as social services.)
Nursery schools	Provide education for children from age two upwards during term time. The Early Years Foundation Stage applies.
Infant schools	Provide education for children aged five to seven years during term time. Children follow the Early Years Foundation Stage and the National Curriculum. A nursery class for children aged three upwards may be attached to the school.
Primary schools	Provide education for children aged five to eleven years during term time. Children follow the Early Years Foundation Stage and the National Curriculum.
Out-of-school clubs	These may include before school, after school and school holiday provision. Childcare is combined with a safe place to play for children of school age. Breakfast clubs usually open at 8am. Staff look after children until it is time to escort them to school. After-school clubs collect children from school, usually staying open until 6pm. Holiday clubs often open all day from 8am–6pm. Clubs may be attached to another setting such as a school, day nursery or leisure centre. The Early Years Foundation Stage applies to some settings.

* The provision of the Early Years Foundation Stage and the National Curriculum applies to settings in England.

Activity

If you are caring for a child with special needs either in an inclusive or specialist day care setting, ask his parents what they consider the advantages and disadvantages of the setting are for their child and for the family as a whole.

A typical education scene in a combined nursery centre

KEY POINT

Pre-school care and education services may be maintained by the local authority or provided by the private, voluntary and independent sector.

PROGRESS CHECK

1   How do children's centres support a child with special needs and his family?
2   Why do some children attend Opportunity Playgroups?

Childminding provision
Parents may prefer childminding provision for their child with special needs. Arrangements can be made through social services departments, Ofsted Early Years Directorate or the area Children's Information Service.

Respite care (short-term care and accommodation)
Respite care can be arranged and funded by social services departments (also by the health service and some voluntary organisations) for families with children with special needs. It aims to relieve some of the stress and strain of what is often twenty-four-hour care and can mean the difference between a child remaining

at home or being looked after by a foster carer or in a residential home. However, it is not just a means of giving a family a break – it must always be a positive experience for the child. Regular and emergency respite care is considered essential by most parents and should be included in the care and support package.

KEY POINT

Respite care must meet a child's needs, even very complex needs, and take account of the child's family background and culture.

Planning respite care

Social or health services and voluntary organisations prepare a written care plan for any child they propose to accommodate in respite care. Respite carers receive training and are paid according to individual local authority policy. Young children do not like to be away from their home at night unless their parents are with them or they are staying with relatives. The same applies to children with special needs and it is not unusual for many of them to experience homesickness and distress in respite care settings. Sensitive planning is needed to make sure the child feels secure with the carers.

Types of respite care

There are four types of respite care where children, who normally live with their family, may spend short or sometimes longer periods of time.

1 *Family link care*: the most commonly used type of home care where a child is looked after by an approved family or single person in that family or person's home. The carers are go through the Criminal Records Bureau disclosure process and they are trained in specific caring procedures such as lifting, feeding and giving medication. A child may spend a few hours a week, a weekend, a week or longer away from home. Initially, the families will get to know each other and then go on to make their own arrangements.

KEY POINT

It may be difficult to find family link respite care for children who are disruptive, aggressive or display challenging behaviour or whose physical needs are great. However, with extra training and appropriate back-up support it can be successful.

2 *Approved residential accommodation*: this might be a children's home, or a hospital ward or unit. Families often prefer to use children's wards for short-term care for their children – particularly if there are considerable medical or nursing needs.
3 *'Own home' care*: a child is cared for in his own home by a trained family aide, or other substitute carer, while the family take a break.

4 *Children's holiday schemes*: these schemes are usually provided by voluntary organisations and paid for by the family. Many provide one-to-one key workers. Some voluntary organisations arrange family holidays. While these do not give parents and siblings a total break from childcare, they do offer a change of scene and the opportunity for some relaxation.

PROGRESS CHECK

1 What do you understand by respite care?
2 Describe the types of respite care.
3 Why is sensitive respite care planning always necessary?

A family aide provides 'own home' respite care

Residential settings – foster placements and residential care

Foster placements
More children with special needs, who, for a variety of reasons are unable to live with their natural family, are being successfully fostered. Disabled people themselves are actively encouraged to become foster carers so providing children with positive role models.

KEY POINT

Attempts are always made to provide a cultural and ethnic match between a child and his foster carers.

Foster carers
Social services must be satisfied that foster carers can provide:

- any specific care and management routines, for example, physiotherapy for a child with cystic fibrosis, management of an epileptic seizure or caring for a hearing aid. Appropriate training will be given
- adequate privacy for the child especially in the bedroom and bathroom
- appropriate safety – easy exit from the house in case of fire is important.

Social services provide necessary adaptations to the home such as fixed or moveable ramps, hand rails in the bathroom or widened doorways. They also arrange day care and respite care and offer support, advice and help to the foster parents. Importantly, they advise foster parents of the range of statutory and voluntary provision available for both the child and themselves.

KEY POINT

- Foster carers are involved in the normal range of school activities such as helping a child with school work, attending open evenings and PTA meetings and maintaining the home/school diary. Encouraging their foster child to bring friends home and join clubs such as Rainbows, Beavers and Brownies, where they can make and maintain friendships, lessens the risk of isolation.
- The Foster Placement Regulations require prospective foster carers to agree not to use physical punishment on children they look after. Advice and reassurance about managing difficult behaviour would be offered where necessary.

Activity

1   What are the benefits for a child with special needs being looked after by a disabled foster carer?
2   What might be the advantages of accommodating a child with special needs with foster carers rather than in a residential home?
3   How would you organise a recruitment campaign for foster carers for children with special needs in your local area?

A child looked after by foster carers needs opportunities to make friends in the neighbourhood

Residential care

Some children with special needs may not live at home with their natural or foster family, either because they require long-term medical care in hospital or because, for different reasons, they need to live away from their family for a period of time in a local authority children's home.

Residential care settings include:

- *health care settings* such as hospitals and hospices where medical care and treatments are provided. If a child is in hospital for a long period the hospital social worker will support the family and work closely with the hospital team, the family doctor and the health visitor.
- *residential children's homes* registered by social services departments. The homes should be friendly and welcoming, and offer children access to the recreation, living and garden areas. Where necessary ramps, rails, special facilities and equipment are provided.

GOOD PRACTICE

- Privacy is very important, especially for intimate personal care needs such as incontinence, and adequate bathroom facilities are essential.
- Regular fire practice is important. Procedures enabling children with physical conditions or sensory impairments to respond to fire alarms must be in place.

KEY POINT

Social services try to accommodate young children with special needs with foster carers rather than in a residential home.

PROGRESS CHECK

1   Why are disabled people actively encouraged to become foster carers?
2   How can foster carers ensure the children they look after make friends in the local neighbourhood?
3   Give an example of inter-disciplinary co-operation where a child with special needs is accommodated in a residential setting.

Toy libraries

Toy libraries may be organised by social services, health services or voluntary organisations. They can be set up in an Early Years setting, child development centre, hospital, health centre or other suitable accommodation. Toys made of sturdy materials and suitable for different ages and stages of development are available for the children to play with in a safe setting. Many toys are specifically for use as learning aids for children with special needs. Examples include toys that give an electronic response (flashing lights, buzzer or music) when the toy is manipulated in a particular way by the child. This teaches a child the principle of cause and effect. Toy libraries offer a loan service for a small charge. The library also serves as a meeting place for families where ideas and information can be exchanged in an informal and friendly setting. The Toy Libraries Association gives advice on how to set up and run a toy library and offers guidance on suitable toys. It also runs courses for organisers of toy libraries.

Advocacy

Children and their parents may need an advocate to help them access the support and resources they need (see Advocacy, Chapter 3, pages 114–15).

Family aide service

A family aide provides valuable support and practical help to a family caring for a child with special needs. The aide may live with the family for a short time or visit on a daily basis to assist with the general running of the home. Tasks may include childcare and domestic duties. Training can be given for a family aide to provide 'own home' respite care.

Transport costs

Help with transport costs to visit children living away from home or to attend a hospital appointment may be provided.

Financial advice and cash grants

Social services departments, as well as the health service, advise families on their financial entitlement and make grants for specific aids and adaptations such as handrails, bath hoists, ramps and ground floor extensions. Aids and adaptations may be provided free of charge depending on individual circumstances. Benefit forms are often long and difficult to understand. Families may appreciate help from the social worker or other professional in filling them in.

PROGRESS CHECK

1   What are the benefits of a toy library for children with special needs?
2   What is the function of the Toy Library Association?
3   For what specific equipment might social services departments make a cash grant?

Education authority systems and support

The Department for Children, Schools and Families (DCSF) is the statutory body for controlling and regulating education provision. Education is compulsory in Britain for children between the ages of five and sixteen years. It is also a right to which all children, including those with special needs, are entitled. The goals of education, as stated in the Warnock Report, are:

■   to enlarge a child's knowledge, experience and imaginative understanding, and thus his awareness of moral values and capacity for enjoyment
■   to enable him to enter the world, after formal education is over, as an active participant in society and a responsible contributor to it.

KEY POINT

The goals set out in the Warnock Report are still the same today but the help that individual children need in progressing towards them will be different.

The Education Reform Act 1988 introduced for the first time in England and Wales a national curriculum, which *all* children in state-funded schools were expected to follow. Teaching staff were made responsible for ensuring children have access to, and can make progress in, the subjects they teach.

Teachers are aware of individual differences in children. When some or all of those differences affect a child's learning to the extent that the teacher (or parent) is concerned, the procedures of intervention, action and accessing special educational provision are put in place. Management of a child's education becomes 'special' when his needs are particularly different from his peers.

Activity

Check with Chapter 3 for the definition of special educational needs (page 77) and the procedures to be followed, as set out in the SEN Code of Practice, when there is concern about a child's progress.

THE LOCAL EDUCATION AUTHORITY'S DUTY

A local education authority has a duty to:

- provide education for children of compulsory school age until aged sixteen when necessary
- make a statutory assessment for and write a statement of special educational needs for children aged five years to sixteen years (up to nineteen years if a child is continuing with education in school)

Education service professionals

- make a statutory assessment for children under compulsory school age and over two years
- write a statement of special educational needs for children under compulsory school age and over two years with severe and complex needs
- make an assessment of the special educational needs of children under two years (a) if it is considered necessary and provided the child's parents consent to it, or (b) if the parents request an assessment.

Education service professionals
See Chapter 1, pages 29–30.

Nursery education
For information about Nursery Education Grant Funding and the Early Years Foundation Stage, see pages 52–9.

GOOD PRACTICE

It is essential to monitor progress throughout the Early Years Foundation Stage, identify those children who may have general or particular learning difficulties and provide appropriate levels of help. When necessary, the setting must intervene through Early Years Action and Early Years Action Plus.

CHILDREN AGED THREE TO FIVE YEARS WITH SPECIAL NEEDS IN AN EARLY EDUCATION SETTING

Introducing a child with special needs into an early education setting such as a nursery school or class or a pre-school requires careful planning and co-ordination between the Early Years team, parents, outside specialists already involved with the child and the child himself. The aim is to provide a safe, welcoming environment within which the child feels comfortable and is able to learn, play and socialise.

KEY POINT

Many children with special needs may not necessarily have special *educational* needs, for example, children with controlled diabetes or epilepsy, or children using mobility aids.

Care and education
Before a child attends the setting any difficulties of access to the toilet and washing facilities (including facilities for caring for a child with **incontinence**), and to the play and learning environment, are likely to have been resolved. Provision of special equipment and matching the layout of the setting and use of space to individual needs must also be considered in advance.

A key worker, in particular, needs to know how much help a child requires with toileting, hand washing, managing clothing and footwear, and eating and drinking. Details of medical health needs such as a special diet, physiotherapy and medication routines are also important and should be discussed with the child's parents (see Managing medicines, Chapter 7, pages 270–1). Knowing a child's specific care and health needs beforehand, and having arrangements for these routines already in place when the child first attends, avoids possible uncertainty or stress for the child and his parents.

The setting requires information about a child's previous education provision, for example, day care, Portage and speech and language therapy. Records of past assessments and reviews are important for future planning. For those children with special educational needs it is important for the SENCO and Early Years staff to work closely with the parents and child in planning the curriculum. If a child's learning difficulties require 'graduated action and intervention', as set out in the Code of Practice, the SENCO, key worker and other Early Years staff, together with the child and his parents will plan and implement an individual education plan (IEP).

KEY POINT

Although Early Years workers may care for children who are assessed through the stages of Early Years Action and Early Years Action Plus, it is probable they will have moved on from Early Years provision before a statutory assessment is made and a statement of special educational needs is drawn up.

KEY POINTS

- The key test of how far a child's learning needs are being met is whether they are making adequate progress (the SEN Code of Practice).
- An early years education setting must know how to access information and advice about health matters using the school health service, the child's family doctor or a relevant member of the child development centre team

Differentiated curriculum and individual education plan

All children, including children with special educational needs, follow the curriculum of the setting they attend. The curriculum is 'differentiated' (planned) to meet the learning ability of high, average and low achievers.

Children with SEN who have difficulty following the lowest level of differentiation in any area of learning will require an Individual Education Plan (IEP). An IEP is a planning, teaching and reviewing tool that underpins the process of planning intervention for an individual child's needs. It builds on the

The role of a key worker in an Early Years education setting

Closely monitor the child's progress. Maintain assessment records and observations of development and behaviour.

Maintain the confidentiality rules of the setting, especially with regard to releasing or requesting information about the child.

Good Practice
Help and support the child by:
- enabling him to feel confident and valued
- promoting communication and language skills
- encouraging independence and social skills
- praising and encouraging his efforts and achievements
- being imaginative and creative in finding ways to enable him to make full use of available resources and materials
- caring sensitively for his physical and emotional needs.

Work closely with the child's teachers and parents to deliver the early years curriculum.

Approaches to delivery may be:
- differentiation
- strategies and provision identified in an IEP or statement of special educational needs.

Liaise with outside specialists who may be involved in helping the child, e.g. family doctor, educational psychologist, speech and language therapist, teacher for the hearing or visually impaired.

Familiarise yourself with the special needs and special educational needs policy of your setting.

Study the SEN code of practice. Make sure that you understand:
- Early Years Action
- Early Years Action Plus
- Statutory assessment
- A statement of special educational needs and how these procedures support a child's learning.

Build a trusting, mutually supportive relationship with parents and discuss with them any learning difficulties their child is experiencing. Talk to them about the role of the SENCO.

curriculum that a child with learning difficulties is following (either the EYFS or the National Curriculum).

The SEN Code of Practice states that an IEP should include only what is *additional to*, or *different from*, the differentiated curriculum. An IEP at Early Years Action is planned and drawn up by the SENCO, key worker and the Early Years team, in discussion with the child and his parents. At Early Years Action Plus, the team in the setting is joined by specialists from outside agencies (for example, the educational psychologist, support teachers and speech and language therapist) and, with the parents and child, plan a new IEP. When planning and implementing an IEP:

- set only a few, carefully graded and achievable key targets at a time, starting with what a child *can* do
- make sure targets are neither too simple nor too difficult
- adopt flexible teaching strategies
- allow time for practice and repetition of steps towards the targets
- praise effort as well as achievement
- make sure each target is achieved before a child moves on to the next one
- monitor, record and review progress. Change part or all of the IEP if it is not helping the child.

KEY POINTS

- Similar procedures are followed when devising and implementing an IEP within School Action and School Action Plus in infant and primary schools.
- Most LEAs have a standard IEP form, which settings may use to record essential information about a child's particular learning programme, including areas of difficulty, teaching methods used and date of next review.

PROGRESS CHECK

1   What information about a child's previous care and education provision will be helpful for the Early Years team prior to him attending their setting?
2   What do you understand by the term 'differentiated curriculum'?
3   For what reason would a child require an IEP? What principles would you follow when planning and implementing an IEP?

GOOD PRACTICE

The Early Years team must always remember to care for a child's emotional and social needs as well as his special educational needs.

Communicating with parents
Children's experiences at home, including continuation of learning opportunities provided in the Early Years setting, significantly influence their overall progress. Always make sure parents are involved in planning and implementing their

child's education programme. Parents are an invaluable resource and need to know how best to support their child's learning and to whom they can turn if they have any worries or queries. Telephone calls can often give instant reassurance and parents are usually offered easy access to their child's teacher or key worker.

Regular, effective communication and contact between staff and parents is very important and reduces any sense of isolation parents may feel. Remember to encourage them and let them know how much you appreciate their help and input. Most settings have a shared record-keeping system in which the teacher, key worker and parents make daily comments.

KEY POINT

A child may be unable to tell his parents what he has done during the day. Make sure he takes pictures, craft work or other items home so that his family can enjoy his activities and build up a picture of the school day.

Communicating with parents

PROGRESS CHECK

1   How can you help and support a child with special needs/special educational needs in an Early Years education setting?
2   Why is it important for a key worker to know the details of a child's statement of special educational needs?
3   Describe how would you help parents to feel valued and supported.

CASE STUDY

Early in her pregnancy Aaron's mother (a lone parent) contracted rubella and, although only mildly unwell herself, her son was born with profound vision and hearing impairment and learning delay. Looking after Aaron was exhausting and distressing for his mother whose own family lived abroad and were unable to give practical help and support.

Aaron's development was assessed by a multidisciplinary team during his first year and both Aaron and his mother received appropriate care and support from statutory and voluntary agencies. In particular, they found the Named Person (a 'special needs' health visitor) of great help in enabling them to gain access to the necessary provision.

Aaron is now two-and-a-half years old and currently attends a local authority inclusive day nursery part-time. He will have a statutory assessment of special educational needs when he is three years old.

1   Which statutory service would have been responsible for Aaron's developmental assessment in his first year?
2   Where would Aaron's assessment most probably have taken place?
3   Name the professionals likely to have been involved in the assessment procedure.
4   Which local authority department would have arranged Aaron's admission to the day nursery?
5   Which statutory service will be responsible for Aaron's assessment of special educational needs?
6   What particular provision might be recommended in Aaron's statement of special educational needs?

SPECIAL SCHOOLS

Special schools were first developed in the UK in the eighteenth century when Thomas Braidwood established a school for the deaf in Edinburgh in the early 1760s and Henry Dannett founded a school for the blind in Liverpool in 1791. The first special schools for children with physical handicaps were founded in London – The Cripples Home and Industrial School for Girls in 1851 and the Home for Crippled Boys in 1865. Before the middle of the nineteenth century so-called 'mentally defective' children who were in need of care were placed in workhouses and infirmaries. In 1847 the first specific provision for them, the Asylum for Idiots, was established in Highgate, London. Following the Forster Education Act 1870 (and the corresponding Education (Scotland) Act of 1872) state education was introduced and a small number of school boards, out of social conscience rather than as a result of educational legislation, introduced special classes for deaf and blind children. In 1892 the Leicester School Board opened a special class for selected 'feeble-minded' pupils and in the same year the London Board opened a special school for physically and mentally defective children.

The Warnock Report 1978 states:

New provision continued to be made, much of it by voluntary effort and of a pioneering nature. Open air schools, day and boarding schools for physically handicapped children, schools in hospitals and convalescent homes and trade schools all contributed to more varied facilities available to local education authorities and parents. Examples were the Heritage Craft Schools and Hospital at Chailey, Sussex (1903), the Swinton House School of Recovery at Manchester (1905), the London County Council's Open Air School at Plumstead (1907) and the Lord Mayor Treloar Cripples' Hospital and College at Alton (1908). The Manchester Local Education Authority had opened a residential school for epileptics in 1910: by 1918 there were six such schools throughout the country.

The statutory foundation for special education, conferring powers on local councils to provide education in special schools or classes for blind, deaf, defective and epileptic children, was consolidated in the Education Act 1902 and 1921. The Education Act 1944 increased the number of categories of children with special educational needs from four to eleven and many special schools were built to cater for extra demand, although less seriously handicapped children could be educated in ordinary schools.

Activity
Identify the terminology in the above text that is no longer appropriate or acceptable.

KEY POINT
The Second World War destroyed much school accommodation. Building materials and teachers were in short supply during the immediate post-war years. It was easier to expand the use of special schools, by buying large country houses or mansions (often in isolated areas), than providing special education in ordinary schools.

The Education Act 1976 placed a responsibility on local education authorities to provide special education in ordinary schools where practicable. However, although the new legislation would create a move towards integration, the government of the time felt that special schools would continue to play an important role in educating children with special educational needs.

Special schools versus ordinary schools
Special schools are educational establishments solely for the education of children with special educational needs. Their existence is becoming increasingly controversial with many teachers, parents and disabled people's organisations looking for greater changes in the education system. They believe inclusive education to be a human rights issue but perceive a lack of will to see it implemented nationally. Ideally, they would like special schools phased out and all children educated in inclusive, mainstream school settings.

Both the Centre for Studies on Inclusive Education (CSIE) and the Alliance for Inclusive Education (AIE) believe all children would benefit if those with special needs were brought into mainstream education.

KEY POINTS

- More and more special schools are currently linking with mainstream schools in their area to share facilities, resources such as computers and social activities.
- For many children, particularly those with profound and complex special needs, special schools are seen to provide a safe, protected and adapted environment in which they can develop and gain confidence while receiving individual attention and teaching.

Specialist resources and services are thought to be more efficiently used in a single setting than in a range of different settings. All these factors can be particularly reassuring for parents. Resources such as speech and language therapy are often more readily available in special schools.

Children attending a special school

PROGRESS CHECK

1 Why did special schools develop in large houses in rural areas?
2 Which organisations promote inclusive education?

KEY POINTS

- Education in a special school may be recommended in a child's statement of special educational needs.
- Children with special educational needs, whether in special or mainstream school, are required to follow the National Curriculum differentiated to meet individual needs.

Activity

Prepare a talk for your peer group presenting both the advantages and disadvantages of special schools.

Inclusive education

The move towards including children with special educational needs into mainstream schools started with the Education Act 1981. Schools are required to publish SEN policies and must be open and honest about their plans for inclusion.

Inclusive education means educating children with special educational needs in mainstream settings with relevant and appropriate support networks. For a school to be truly inclusive there has to be a commitment to ending discrimination, removing barriers and welcoming all children. Thought must be given to the curriculum, learning support, funding and the physical environment.

One of the gang

KEY POINT

Local education authorities are required to educate children with special educational needs in mainstream schools providing:
(a) appropriate educational provision is available
(b) the interests of other children in the school will be maintained
(c) there is efficient use of the local education authority's resources.

Hospital schools

Many children spend periods of time (sometimes long periods) in hospital, inevitably missing out on attending school. Hospital schools are run by the local education authority (in co-operation with the health service) for the benefit of children of compulsory school age. The children follow the National Curriculum. Extra help for children with special educational needs is provided. Exams can take place in hospital.

Lessons in a hospital setting

Office for Standards in Education (Ofsted)

Ofsted, a non-ministerial government department and independent from the Department for Education and Skills (DfES), was set up in September 1992. It is responsible for the improvement of achievement and quality in education in England. From September 2001 the Early Years Directorate of Ofsted became the registration and inspection body for all Early Years care and education provision – nurseries, playgroups and pre-schools, crèches, childminders, out of school clubs and holiday play schemes for children under eight years of age.

Benefits

The Department for Work and Pensions (DWP) is the government regulatory body for financial benefits and allowances. The DWP manages most benefits through Job Centre Plus offices, including the benefits for children and families and those for disabled people and carers.

Expenses incurred when providing for a child with special needs can be substantial and reduce the family budget very quickly. Parents are entitled to certain state benefits regardless of income or savings. Some benefits are means tested. Claim forms are available from Job Centre Plus Offices, which also offer benefit advice. Other parents in support groups, social workers, Citizens' Advice Bureau or Sure Start staff can also give advice about particular benefits and help parents, if necessary, to fill in the forms. You can research benefits at www.dwp.gov.uk/lifeevent/benefits.

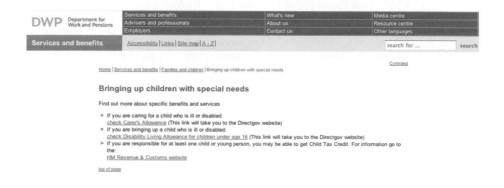

Families of children with special needs may be entitled to a range of allowances

Activity

1 Research the benefits and grants available for a lone, unemployed parent whose seven-year-old child has spina bifida. The child uses a wheelchair for mobility and, as yet, does not have bladder or bowel control.

2 Research as above for a professional couple who are both in well-paid employment. They have a seven-year-old son who is profoundly deaf.

3 Find out about the Family Fund. Who finances it? Who pays out the grants? For what particular provision or help might a grant be given? Are grants means tested?

Financial benefits are constantly changing. It is a good idea to update your knowledge regularly on monies available.

KEY TERMS

You need to know what these words and phrases mean. Go back through the chapter and make sure that you understand:

child and family guidance service
child development centre
combined children's centre
Department for Children, Schools
    and Families (DCSF)
differentiated curriculum
Individual Education Plan (IEP)

National Health Service
Office for Standards in Education
    (Ofsted)
respite care
social services
statutory services

5 CARE AND SUPPORT

This chapter covers:
- **Parents as partners**
- **Community-based support services**
- **Developing independence in physical care routines**
- **Day care – key worker support**
- **Voluntary provision**
- **A multisensory room and soundbeam**

The most important thing that happens when a child is born with disabilities is that a child is born. The most important thing that happens when a couple become parents of a child with disabilities is that the couple become parents. (R. Wills, 1994)

This chapter emphasises the integral role of parents in the delivery and success of any service provision or care plan. Recognition and acknowledgement of the valuable and crucial role of parents as partners with the multidisciplinary team leads to greater improvement for the child and her family.

The value of community-based, integrated care and provision, easily accessible information, link workers for ethnic families, and choice and flexibility of services in meeting the needs of children and their families, are all discussed here.

The role of a day care key worker is explained in the general text and in table form. Attending to children's physical care with sensitivity and respect and helping them towards independence in self-care routines is also included.

Voluntary provision, an important service for children with special needs and their families, is wide ranging. The Portage home visiting service, playgroups and befriending schemes are described here.

Parents as partners

There is general agreement among childcare professionals that parents know their children best and every effort should be made to keep children with special needs at home with their families. This can be achieved only if sustained, flexible and child-centred services are provided, which allow families choice and make it possible for children to be cared for at home. Each family is unique. Considerable extra help may be needed at particular times, while at others a small input of help can make all the difference in keeping the family together. Accessible help and support should be available when needed. This gives families the confidence and control they need to shape their own lives.

Parents know their children best

Professional knowledge and ability in caring for children with special needs and their families will vary according to individual training (including disability awareness and equality training), experience and personal qualities.

The MENCAP publication *Ordinary Everyday Families – A Human Rights Issue* by Jo Cameron and Leonie Sturge-Moore, 1990, states:

> *Through lack of knowledge and experience, mainstream professionals and other workers may find themselves in a difficult position as they are confronted with a child with special needs. Some are able to react constructively and find ways and means of helping the child and his or her family. Others, however, may be deterred from offering this help, so that the family miss out on possible support and the professional may be left feeling dissatisfied.*

KEY POINTS

- Children with severe and complex special needs are very dependent on their parents to meet continuing care and management needs. As children grow and get heavier, caring, lifting and carrying become increasingly difficult and tiring. All young children need help with physical care routines such as washing, dressing, eating and drinking, but for many children with special needs the need for this help does not diminish as they get older.
- Children with special needs may need regular and time-consuming regimes, such as physiotherapy, medication and special diet, several times a day. Some rely on medical equipment, for example, suction or feeding systems, oxygen and pain relief pumps. Initially, parents may be very dependent on the professionals for support and reassurance.

The Children Act 1989, the Education Act 1996 and the Special Educational Needs (SEN) Code of Practice give parents a greater say in what happens to their children with a right to be consulted, informed and involved in all planning and provision (health, education and social care).

MULTIPROFESSIONAL CARE

Effective communication between different agencies and departments needs to work smoothly if it is to benefit the child and her family. Professionals should be sure of their own roles and responsibilities and those of their colleagues. This will result in greater understanding, co-operation and efficiency, facilitate better communication with parents and help to establish 'parents as partners'.

GOOD PRACTICE

A partnership between the professionals, the child and her family, built on mutual trust and respect, and which recognises the value of the child, is essential to the well-being of the child and her family.

KEY POINT

In the past, dependence on professionals often continued for a long time. Today, with the emphasis on a shared and supportive partnership between parents and professionals, the expectation would be for parents to be more informed and involved in all aspects of their child's care and management needs, confident in their parenting skills and able to make independent decisions.

FINDING OUT THEIR CHILD'S SPECIAL NEED

Whether a special need is identified at birth, or later on when a child is not walking, talking or 'catching up', parents have to try and come to terms with the fact that their child is in some way 'different'. Support for them must aim to reduce stress and anxiety and boost their confidence in their own ability to care for the child.

Initially, parents may be confused and bewildered, with the demands of their child's special needs seemingly beyond their ability to cope. They look for an accurate and early diagnosis of what is wrong. Usually, they prefer the truth, however painful and distressing, to not knowing what is wrong. Having a name or 'term' for their child's special need gives them a starting point from which they can begin to understand and adjust. There may not be definite answers to all questions and concerns, but a sensitive assessment of possible problems and likely health and developmental progress should be given.

KEY POINTS

- Parents' concerns about their child's health or development should never be ignored; they are usually right. Sometimes, they may have to insist there is 'something wrong' or 'not quite right' with their child in order to get a second opinion.
- It is often difficult to decide what, if anything, is wrong with children who are not quite achieving their developmental norms. Much depends on their home environment and how their overall needs are met. A child who is not making progress, though, should be assessed to find out the help required.

PROFESSIONAL GOOD PRACTICE

The Scope template of good practice (produced by a working group led by Scope) recognises the *value of the child*, *respect for parents* and *the importance of communication skills among professionals*. These three template principles (taken from *Child Health in the Community: A Guide to Good Practice*, published by the NHS Executive) can be implemented through:

- parents being together when informed of the diagnosis
- keeping the number of professionals to a minimum, ensuring at least one of them is known to the family
- being honest with parents and openly acknowledging the limits of professional knowledge
- ensuring that discussions about the child have a positive focus
- responding to parents supportively and openly – for example, ensuring continuity with primary health care by contacting the family doctor
- providing families with all the information possible about their child's condition and about services and welfare benefits
- following up with written notes of the initial meeting and giving advice about practical help – for example, voluntary organisations providing family support.

KEY POINTS

- More than anything parents want to be listened to and involved in meetings about their child. Helping parents to take part in planning and decisions can ease the transition from distress and sadness to acceptance and adjustment.
- As well as professional offers of appropriate support and provision parents should be asked questions such as: 'How do you think we can best help your child and family?'; 'What particular provision would make life easier, more comfortable/stimulating/enjoyable for your child and for your family?'
- No parents should leave an assessment or follow-up appointment dissatisfied and with questions unasked or unanswered.

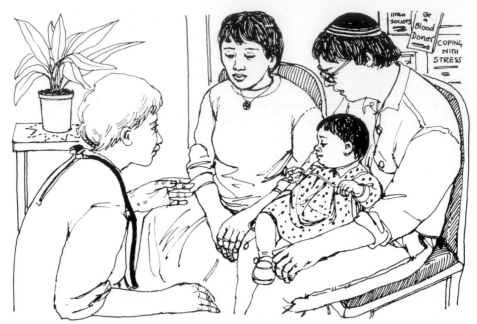

'Is there any other particular help we can offer you and Miriam?'

Activity

Think of an occasion when you listened to what the parents of a child with special needs were saying about their child. Where did the conversation take place? Did the parents share any particular concerns with you? How did you respond to their concerns? How effective do you consider you were in listening and responding to the parents? How did you feel about this conversation?

PROGRESS CHECK

1 Why might some professionals be deterred from offering constructive help to children with special needs and their families?
2 In what ways are children with severe or complex special needs dependent on their families?

At recognition and assessment

When a need is recognised and assessed families should be offered:

■ care and support
■ a Named Person, for example the health visitor or social worker as a key worker and a link between the family, statutory and voluntary agencies
■ professional counselling
■ well co-ordinated service provision

- opportunity to be involved in making decisions that feel right for them (a counsellor or other professional supporters should not try to impose their own solutions).

Sensitivity to cultural and social differences and requirements must be reflected in the total care plan.

CARE AND SUPPORT PROGRAMMES

Care and support programmes need to be flexible and effective to meet the needs of both the child and her family. In the early years the main care providers are likely to be *health and social services*. Later, *educational provision* will be the responsibility of the local education authority.

Early Years day care provision

Through the Named Person, parents have the opportunity to learn about and discuss possible care and management, including goals and long-term objectives. They can be helped to understand their own role as partners and develop skills for managing their child's needs – for example, the best way to hold or position their child for feeding (particularly a child with oral or facial malformations or poor muscle control such as in cerebral palsy), bathing and dressing routines, and ways of communicating and playing with her. As partners with the professionals they are enabled and encouraged to become competent care-givers. Early successes in their child's health or development encourage them towards greater participation in care and management routines.

KEY POINT

Not all parents have the immediate confidence or desire to be actively involved in care and management routines, particularly if they are still grieving for their 'lost' child or there does not appear to be any significant progress.

GOOD PRACTICE

Helping parents to feel confident and find pleasure in their child is an essential part of professional support.

PROGRESS CHECK

1   How can society help children with special needs to remain at home and be cared for by their families?
2   What does current legislation say about the rights of parents of children with special needs?
3   Why do parents prefer a name or 'term' for their child's special need rather than not knowing what is wrong?
4   On what three principles is the Scope template of good practice based?
5   What do you understand by the term 'Named Person'? What are the Named Person's functions?

Community-based support services

An important way of offering support to children with special needs and their families is through community-based family support centres and initiatives, some of which are described below.

HONEYLANDS SPECIALIST CHILDREN'S CENTRE

Honeylands is a well-known and frequently described children's centre and family support unit in Exeter combining local health, education and social services. Honeylands, and other similar units, recognise the need for children with special needs to be cared for in a community rather than a hospital setting. Parents are valued as partners with other care providers and involved with them in all aspects of their child's care, assessments and medical provision. Honeylands provides services according to the needs of the child.

Its aims are:

- to provide parents with support and information about their child's special needs
- to help parents come to terms with their own feelings and acquire the special skills needed to increase their confidence and competence in caring for their child
- to offer flexible day care and short-term residential support
- to relieve family stress, strain and exhaustion by offering the family day or night support.

Services

Services available at Honeylands include:

- respite care
- day care facilities
- carers' groups
- health care including physiotherapy, occupational therapy, speech and language therapy
- counselling
- a weekly boarder scheme.

Children with special needs are vulnerable to abuse. Where there is ready access to a range of co-ordinated services such as at Honeylands their vulnerability is reduced.

WANDSWORTH EARLY YEARS CENTRE

Wandsworth Early Years Centre in London is a multi agency resource centre offering assessment and continuing support for children under eight years with special needs and for their families. A key worker enables families to access appropriate services. Following assessment and identification of needs in the day unit, the centre can offer:

- clinical psychology
- Early Years education
- educational psychology
- EarlyBird and EarlyBird Plus programmes for parents of children on the autistic spectrum
- occupational therapy
- Portage
- paediatric assessment and advice
- social work/case management
- specialist speech therapy.

CHEVIOT'S CHILDREN'S CENTRE

Cheviot's Children's Centre in Enfield is funded by the local social services department. Its aim is to 'Keep children in their families, and make sure that children with disabilities can be included in mainstream life'. Cheviot's provides for the 150 plus families who use its services:

- a social work service
- shared care (family-based respite care)
- a home-sitting service
- home care support
- holiday play schemes
- youth clubs and a range of different clubs
- support groups for parents, carers and siblings
- a toy library
- parent and toddler play mornings.

SURE START

Sure Start is the government's programme to deliver the best start in life for every child by bringing together early education, childcare, health and family support. Some Sure Start initiatives apply universally, while others apply only in targeted local areas and/or to disadvantaged groups in England.

Responsibility for Sure Start lies with the Early Years, Extended Schools and Special Needs Group, which belongs to the Department for Children, Schools and Families (DCSF). Sure Start tells us the following about their service:

Services
- *Sure Start covers children from conception through to age 14, and up to age 16 for those with special educational needs and disabilities. It also aims to help parents and communities across the country.*
- *There are a wide range of services currently available, from Children's Centres and early support programmes to information and advice on health and financial matters. We are helping set and maintain childcare standards.*
- *Sure Start is the cornerstone of the government's drive to tackle child poverty and social exclusion working with parents-to-be, parents/carers and children to promote the physical, intellectual and social development of babies and young children so that they can flourish at home and when they get to school.*
- *All Sure Start local programmes have become children's centres. Local authorities are responsible for Sure Start children's centres, and the services on offer may vary from area to area.*

How do our services work?
Our services bring together universal, free, early education and more and better childcare. Sure Start does this with greater support where there is greater need through children's tax credit, children's centres and Sure Start local programmes.

Integrated Early Years Services

For some time we have been encouraging the delivery of childcare alongside early education and other health and family services.

Sure Start Children's Centres

Sure Start Children's Centres are building on existing successful initiatives like Sure Start Local Programmes, Neighbourhood Nurseries and Early Excellence Centres, and bringing high-quality integrated early years services to the heart of communities.

Our target of 2500 children's centres was reached in early March 2008, and 2911 centres have now been established (October 2008), offering services to over 2.3 million young children and their families.

By 2010, the number of children's centres will increase to 3,500 - so every family has easy access to high-quality integrated services in their community and the benefits of Sure Start can be felt nationwide.

Early Education

All 3- and 4-year-olds are now guaranteed a free, part-time (12½ hours per week, 38 weeks per year, increasing to 15 hours per week in 2010), early-education place. There are over 37,000 settings delivering free, government-funded, early education in the maintained, private, voluntary and independent sectors.

Childcare

In June 2008, the stock of registered childcare stood at approaching 1.3 million places (more than double the 1997 level).

There will be a childcare place for all children aged between 3 and 14, between the hours of 8am and 6pm each weekday by 2010, when there will be over 2 million sustainable childcare places for children up to 14.

For further information, visit www.surestart.gov.uk.

KEY POINT

A key principle of Sure Start is to provide support for children and parents with special needs and help them to access specialist services. In some instances children with special needs will be initially identified through Sure Start programmes.

OUT-OF-SCHOOL CARE

Out-of-school care provides play and learning opportunities in a safe environment for children between the ages of four and twelve (and older) before school opens, at the end of the school day or during school holidays.

The main purpose of this provision is to look after children in the absence of their parents. Typically, services and care offered include: breakfast clubs (may be in school and linked with homework support); after school clubs; holiday clubs; summer camps; and holiday play schemes. Facilities are usually based in or near schools. They are generally organised by school staff or playworkers. Breakfast clubs provide cheap, nutritionally sound meals before the school day starts, and are particularly needed in areas of social deprivation.

Ofsted is responsible for out-of-school registration and the inspection of registered out-of-school clubs. Most childcare providers working with children aged 0 to five years, including out-of-school clubs, will be registered on the Early Years register. This means they will be required to deliver the Early Years Foundation Stage. Most childcare providers working with children aged five to seven years, including out-of-school clubs, will be required to register on the Ofsted Childcare register. There is also a voluntary part of the register for settings that are not required to register but would like to do so.

If a school directly provides their own childcare or supervised activities for children aged three years and over, it must meet the registration requirements and deliver the EYFS where appropriate. However, it will not join either register as the provision will be inspected by Ofsted via the school inspection system.

4Children is the national organisation for out-of-school care and offers advice, practical support and training to the government, EYDCPs, childcare providers and parents. The address and website is on page 408.

PROGRESS CHECK

1 What are the advantages of community-based support services such as those described above?
2 Describe the Sure Start initiative.
3 Identify three services that may be available within a children's centre.

Activity
1 Try to arrange a visit, either individually or in a group, to a Sure Start Children's Centre in your area. Planning the visit will require a considerate approach to the staff of the centre. Find out about the services offered and, if possible, talk to the children and parents using the facilities.
2 Find out about the ways in which your local Sure Start supports (a) children with special needs and their families, and (b) mothers with postnatal depression. If possible, talk to the children and parents about the services offered.

Developing independence in physical care routines

Children with special needs may take longer to achieve independence in physical care routines than other children. A knowledge of child development and the sequence of emerging independence skills is necessary in helping children move from one level to the next. Gross and fine motor skills and hand–eye co-ordination are particularly important for tasks such as eating and drinking, dressing and toileting. The level of help needed will vary acording to the special need. Children with cerebral palsy, Down syndrome, brain injury or complex multiple needs are likely to have difficulties in these areas.

GOOD PRACTICE

Helping children with their physical care routines provides you with the opportunity for close personal contact with them. Do not rush these times. Sensitivity to a child's feelings will be especially important when she is at the age when her peers are able to manage their care without help.

Learning to be independent can be tiring and stressful for a child, especially if you try and rush her into achieving. So remember to:
- allow plenty of time for a child to attempt or complete a task
- remain relaxed and supportive
- break the task down into small, manageable steps and make sure she knows what you want her to practise and achieve.

KEY POINTS

- You may be tempted to take over and dress or wash a child quickly yourself but that will not help her to become independent.
- Repetition is important in helping a child to remember and retain a skill, so give her the opportunity to repeat over and over again what she has learnt. Obviously, there is a limit to the length of time a child can concentrate and remain interested, and sensible breaks are necessary.

GOOD PRACTICE

Give children lots of praise and encouragement and tell them how well they are doing. Remember to praise effort, not just achievement.

The following sections offer suggestions for helping children with special needs to develop independence skills.

Mealtimes

- Offer a child implements similar to those she uses at home. Familiar cutlery and crockery is particularly important for a child with visual impairment.
- Remember that in some cultures eating with fingers is usual.
- Wide-handled spoons and forks, high-edged plates with non-slip bases and non-slip mats to hold cups and plates securely in place are available. Plastic, flexible straws help children who cannot hold or drink from a cup. Make sure clothing is protected.
- Eating or assisted eating may take a long time and patience is needed.

Eating independently

KEY POINT

Children with severe or profound language and communication difficulties can be at risk from under-nutrition and dehydration. They may not be able to indicate they are hungry or thirsty. Until you get to know a child you may be unsure if she has had enough to eat or drink, or you may remove her plate, bowl or cup too soon. Offer regular drinks during the day, also snacks if necessary.

GOOD PRACTICE

Find out from the parents what signs a child uses to indicate she is hungry, thirsty, has had enough or would like some more.

Make sure your practice is safe:

- Check the temperature of feeds and the rate of milk flow.
- Check the temperature of food.
- Check chicken and fish for bones, and fruit for seeds and pips.
- Cut food up into manageable pieces.
- Never 'prop' feed a baby or leave children alone during mealtimes.
- Broken and whole nuts must not be given to young children under four years or to any child over that age who has difficulty in chewing and swallowing.
- Children with cerebral palsy may have difficulty swallowing crumbly foods such as biscuits.

Dressing and undressing

The design of clothing must take account of a child's special need, allowing her

'I can put my coat on by myself.'

as much independence as possible in putting clothes on and taking them off. Clothes may have to fit under, over or around braces, callipers, harnesses and tubes. They need not be dull and drab. It is possible to make, buy, adjust and adapt colourful, fashionable clothes in a variety of fabrics. Some voluntary organisations have a mail order service or give advice in a factsheet or newsletter.

Clothing should be:

- strong, durable, washable, unfussy and appropriate for the weather
- comfortable, allowing a child to move freely. Wide or stretchable neck openings, large armholes and front fastenings are sensible. Velcro fastenings may be preferable to buttons on some items
- suitable for children with restricted mobility who enjoy rolling and crawling around
- easy and quick to put on and take off, especially for toileting needs. Children who are incontinent (unable to control bladder and/or bowel) need frequent nappy or pad changes. Larger size top clothes, a large ring attached to a zip and elasticated waists on trousers and skirts make clothes easier to put on, pull up and take down
- enjoyable to wear. Like any child, a child with special needs will enjoy being given choices and opportunities to wear clothes in a variety of fabrics and colours.

Clothes should be practical and pleasurable to wear

Protective clothing is sometimes required. Extra padding may prevent injury to a child with cerebral palsy. Knee or elbow padding protects a child with haemophilia following a joint bleed. Helmets may be necessary for children with epilepsy and brain trauma in preventing injury from falls or knocks to the head.

Make sure children with severe eczema wear protective gloves in cold weather and when using art and craft materials. This prevents further skin irritation and discomfort. Children with sickle cell condition should wear a tracksuit or extra jumper and gloves when it is cold to lessen the risk of their abnormal blood cells becoming sticky, blocking small blood vessels and impeding the circulation. Children with Down syndrome often have heart and circulatory complications and require similar extra warm clothing in cold weather (see also Part Two for more on the care of children with these conditions).

Unless children with special needs wear prescribed boots or shoes, trainers and shoes with Velcro fastenings are probably the easiest to put on and take off. Children with disorders affecting movement, posture, balance and co-ordination require well-fitting and supportive footwear.

KEY POINT

All footwear (socks, shoes, slippers, wellingtons, etc.) must be comfortable, well fitting and allow adequate ventilation. These principles are especially important for children with diabetes, because damage to the skin from rubbing, blistering or the feet being squashed, can lead to serious infection and even gangrene. Nylon socks and vinyl and plastic shoes and sandals should not be worn by children with diabetes as they prevent good circulation of air around the feet.

Personal hygiene

Personal hygiene routines are an important part of physical care. Keeping a child clean will:

- help to prevent infection
- keep her comfortable
- promote confidence and self-esteem.
  Personal hygiene routines include:
- 'topping and tailing' – washing a baby's face, hands and bottom only
- bathing
- hand-washing
- hair, nail and dental care.

Children usually enjoy these times of close contact and feel reassured by a cuddle or hug from their carer. However, not all children want such closeness. You will need to look for signals and signs from a child, which indicate the level of contact she likes.

KEY POINTS

- Most children enjoy water and water play. You will quickly find out what children can and cannot manage in washing their hands and face and cleaning their teeth. Long-handled taps will be easier for children with poor manipulative skills to manage than the more usual rotating types.
- Special mesh bath seats that protect and support a child are available.

Children will need variable amounts of help with personal hygiene routines

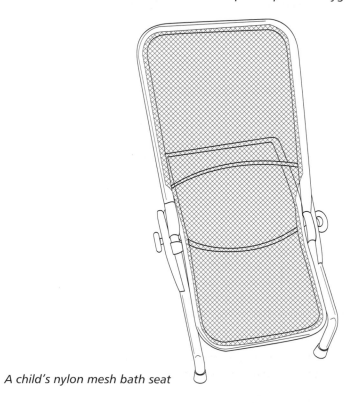

A child's nylon mesh bath seat

Always make sure your practice is safe. Never leave children alone near water and always check the temperature.

Toileting

Control of bladder and bowel is always a major achievement on the road to independence. Many children with special needs are likely to be delayed in this area of development. There are no short cuts towards being potty-trained or toilet-trained. Children will be clean and dry in their own time. The principles of helping children towards control apply equally to children with and without special needs.

Watch for signs that a child might be ready:

- dry when waking up from a sleep
- dry for longer periods during the day
- indicating by words or gestures that she is wet.

Have a potty within easy reach, dress her in simple clothing, remain calm, expect accidents and wet and soiled floors. Special potties and toilet seats are available.

Potty-training is covered in detail in most childcare books.

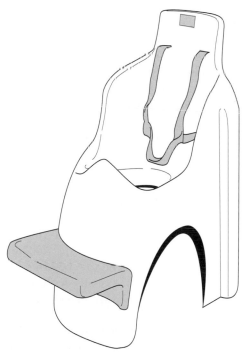

A three-year-old's plastic toilet seat fits over a standard WC, supporting the head and back

KEY POINT

Some children will never learn bladder and bowel control because of their particular condition. Children with spina bifida or those who are paralysed from the waist down may be permanently incontinent (see Chapter 9, page 367).

GOOD PRACTICE

Children who are not yet toilet-trained and those who use nappies, incontinence pads and catheters will need regular care during the day to keep them fresh and dry and prevent soreness.

KEY POINT

Remember to care for children's intimate needs with respect and sensitivity at all times. You will be washing, changing and toileting older children who need a great deal of assistance. Always make sure the children have adequate privacy.

PROGRESS CHECK

1   What principles would you follow when helping children with special needs to develop independence in their physical care routines?
2   What types of cutlery and crockery are particularly beneficial for children with special needs?
3   What important factors do you need to remember about clothing and footwear for children with special needs?
4   For which children might protective clothing be important?
5   What do you understand by 'incontinence'?
6   Which conditions are likely to cause incontinence?
7   What particular good practice must you follow when caring for children with special needs who are not yet toilet-trained or who use incontinence pads, nappies or catheters?

Day care – key worker support

In settings to which the EYFS applies, each child will have a key worker. The role of the key worker is to take special interest in the well-being of their key children, to form close attachments with them and to establish a partnership with their parents. This helps children to feel emotionally settled and secure in the day care environment. Attending to children's care needs is an important part of forming such an attachment. Starting a day care setting may be the first time a child with a special need has mixed with other children outside her family circle. A child with a physical condition may have been unable to exercise, perhaps because of lack of space in the home or because her condition is particularly limiting. Outside the home she may meet people and children who stare and are less sensitive and supportive than her family. So the key worker relationship is particularly important.

Personal needs

- Care sensitively for the child's intimate personal needs.
- Respect the child's right to privacy.

Health needs

- Liaise with parents about their child's health needs.
- Find out details of any special diet, health care routine and medication.
- You may need to carry out postural drainage (physiotherapy), give an insulin injection or care for a child during an epileptic seizure. The parent, senior member of staff, school nurse or physiotherapist will teach you how to carry out these procedures.
- Always record health care and medication routines (see Managing medicines, Chapter 7, pages 270–1).

Liaison with other professionals

Professionals you may liaise, or work closely with, are:

- family doctor
- health visitor
- speech and language therapist
- physiotherapist
- occupational therapist
- support teachers
- clinical psychologist
- SENCO.

ROLE OF THE KEY WORKER IN A DAY CARE SETTING

Pre-visit to the family at home

- Start to get to know the child and observe how she relates to family members.
- Find out what she can do, her particular strengths, likes, dislikes and needs. If she has already been assessed you may know the type of help she requires.
- How will you communicate with her? Ask her parents to help you with this. You may need to learn Makaton or British sign language to support a child with speech, language and communication difficulties.
- Find out if there are any religious or cultural preferences or customs for consideration in any care or education programme.

Settling-in

- Several introductory visits will be needed before the child attends on a regular basis.
- Help the child to settle into the setting at her own pace.

Partnership with parents

- Build up a partnership of respect and trust with parents. This will enable them to feel confident and reassured about leaving their child in your care.
- During regular contact with the parents help them to take pleasure in their child. Listen to what they are saying about their child and talk through any concerns they may have about sleep or eating patterns, toilet-training, behaviour, or involvement in a care or learning programme.
- Maintain a home/nursery diary or record card.

The role of a key worker in a day care setting

KEY POINT

A key worker is a valuable point of contact for both the child and her family and a link with the Early Years staff and other professionals providing care and support both inside and outside the setting.

In some circumstances, a key worker may be employed to work on a one-to-one basis with a child with special needs, or to support a small number of children. When working with older children, in schools or out-of-school clubs for example, the key worker may be known as a Personal Assistant or PA.

THE KEY WORKER AS A TEAM MEMBER

A key worker is an important member of the multidisciplinary team, receiving and sharing information about a particular child. You will be involved in writing observations and reports, and attend meetings both with the staff in your setting and with the wider team. To be an effective team member you need an accurate knowledge of other professional roles. This enables you to understand and draw on their expertise and experience, and to take a more effective part in formulating care plans for a child's overall needs.

A key worker in a day care setting

You may be a key worker for a child in a day care setting whose difficulties require special help through Early Years Action and Early Years Action Plus, or for a child who has received a statutory assessment, or is the subject of a statement of special educational needs. This means you will work closely with the SENCO, external specialists, the child's parents and the child herself. (See Chapter 3, pages 84–7 for Early Years Action and Early Years Action Plus, statutory assessment and writing a statement for children under compulsory school age).

KEY POINTS

- Encourage parents and help them to reinforce efforts in their child.
- Information for parents for whom English is not their first language, or who have communication or sensory difficulties, must be available to them in an appropriate format.
- Information you receive or share must be accurate and up to date. Check carefully whether information is confidential and from whom you require permission before you release it.
- Always make sure the records and reports you make are accurate, clear and objective. They are necessary for professional use and parents have a right to read them. Parents should be invited to attend meetings that directly affect their child.

Activity

Alice is four years old and for the last two years the family (Alice and her parents) have been living in hostel accommodation. Alice displays persistently difficult behaviour including temper tantrums, head-banging, wetting and soiling and disturbed sleep. There has never been any real structure to her daily life, and few opportunities for play and stimulation. Alice's parents finally agreed to an appointment with their family doctor who, in addition to recognising her emotional difficulties, found her to be below her expected weight and height. She was referred to a child and family guidance centre where family therapy has been arranged. A day care place has been secured for Alice and you will be her key worker.

1 Write an overall care and learning plan for Alice that will meet her individual development needs, particularly her emotional needs.
2 Which other professionals would you probably liaise with during your time as Alice's key worker?
3 Why will a variety of observations and accurate record keeping be an important part of your plans?

You may find the section 'Emotional and behavioural difficulties' in Chapter 8, pages 304–15, helpful in carrying out this activity.

- Through observing a child's play, behaviour and interaction with those around her a key worker contributes towards a programme that starts with what the child can already do, extends her learning and supports her individual developmental pattern.
- While activities and learning plans should be designed to promote thinking and independence they must also be enjoyable. Like all children, those with special needs learn more quickly if they are given the right tools.

GOOD PRACTICE

The demands of care and management routines and the focus on developmental progress should not be so excessive as to limit loving and meaningful relationships being established between the child and members of her family and her friends.

A key worker

A key worker is particularly necessary for children with:

- physical conditions or sensory impairments that limit mobility and access to the environment and equipment
- severe or profound learning difficulties limiting play opportunities and experiences
- speech, language or communication difficulties.

CARING FOR PERSONAL EQUIPMENT

Children with special needs may use specific items of equipment. Make sure you know how a child's personal equipment works and that it is clearly marked with her name. As far as possible, encourage children to take care of their own equipment and teach other children in the setting to respect all items. Equipment that is broken or badly damaged is of no use to a child. Battery-operated equipment such as wheelchairs or some types of hearing aids must be recharged as necessary – this is usually done overnight in the home. Spare batteries may be kept in the setting. More sophisticated equipment is discussed in Chapter 2, pages 39–40.

PROGRESS CHECK

1 Explain the importance of a key worker visiting a child with special needs in her own home before she attends a day care setting.
2 For which children with special needs is a day care key worker particularly beneficial?
3 As a member of the multidisciplinary team how could you contribute to the overall care of a child with special needs?
4 How would you build up and maintain a positive relationship with the parents of a child with special needs?

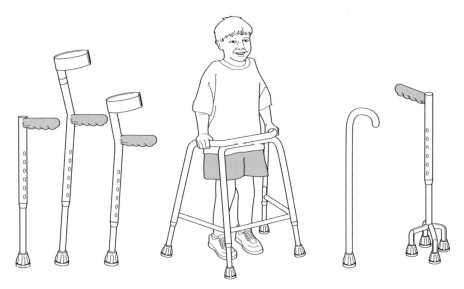

A variety of mobility aids: elbow crutches, walking frame, walking stick and tetrapod

Voluntary provision

VOLUNTARY ORGANISATIONS

Voluntary organisations are a valuable additional source of help for children with disabilities and special needs and their families, supporting the work of health, education and social service departments. Many of their initiatives have arisen out of lack of statutory provision. With continuing limited statutory resources the contribution of voluntary provision is essential.

Parents have always played a major role in voluntary organisations, often setting them up and being involved in their day-to-day running and management. Voluntary organisations recruit staff and volunteers with a wide range of experience and ability who are able to be innovative in a less rigid and structured environment than a statutory agency. The care and support they offer is flexible and positive.

KEY POINT

National organisations frequently have local groups that offer care and support to children with special needs and their families.

Services provided by voluntary organisations

The range of services provided by voluntary organisations includes:

- day care and education facilities
- developmental assessment, care and management programmes
- advice and counselling (including genetic counselling)
- information through seminars, workshops, conferences, leaflets and fact sheets
- home assessment facilities by trained health and social work professionals
- respite care
- financial assistance (such as grants for special equipment) and advice on benefits.

Names, addresses and websites of many voluntary organisations are listed throughout Part Two of this book and in Useful addresses on pages 408–412.

Activity

Choose *one* voluntary organisation from Part Two of this book. Research its history, detail its provision and write up your findings.

PORTAGE HOME VISITING SERVICE

The Portage home visiting service, an early intervention programme, was developed in Wisconsin, USA in the 1960s. It is a valuable early learning resource for children with special needs, providing a home-based daily teaching and learning programme for pre-school children with learning difficulties and physical conditions. For example, a toddler with Down syndrome or cerebral palsy or a pre-school child with language delay could be helped by Portage, including learning Makaton sign language. The National Portage Association UK, a charitable organisation formed in 1983, works with families to provide a carefully structured but flexible programme, building on the abilities a child already has and teaching skills she has yet to achieve. Portage home visitors have wide experience in working with children and come from a variety of backgrounds such as teaching, nursing, health visiting, social work, speech therapy, Early Years and playgroup work, or they may be parents or volunteers with relevant experience. They are usually employed by local health, social services or education departments. Visitors receive appropriate training enabling them to focus on what a child *can* rather than *cannot* do, believing in the principle of 'one step at a time'. Their work with children is closely supervised. The provision of Portage may be patchy in some areas.

KEY POINT

Portage home visitors work closely with parents who are actively encouraged to implement the programme themselves and, in effect, become their child's teachers with the visitor assuming the role of consultant and supporter. Progress and achievement can be enjoyed by parents, siblings and extended members of the family.

The National Portage Association tells us the following about how Portage works.

> Families are visited weekly, at home by their trained Portage Home Visitor. Parents share with the home visitor their understanding of their child's individual gifts, abilities and support needs. Profiles or developmental checklists may help with this process of identifying strengths and goals for future learning when Portage visits begin. The emphasis is on the positive, finding out and building on what a child can do. Parents take the lead in planning their goals ensuring that Portage support is relevant to the needs of their child and family. Goals may focus on developing movement, learning, play, communication and participation in the activities of everyday living.
>
> Usually the aim of each home visit is to decide on an activity which the family can practise and enjoy together. The activities are based on play grounded in everyday situations to provide fun and success for the child. Each activity may represent a small step towards one of the family's planned goals and families using Portage usually choose to practise activities between weekly visits. Parents may use charts or diaries as a reminder of the activity and a record of what happens between visits. In this way a family can build a shared record of their child's involvement with Portage.
>
> Portage offers a framework of support which respects each family and their own individual priorities. It is a model that adapts flexibly to individual child and family needs.

You can find out more at www.portage.org.uk.

The series of photographs on page 178 shows Steven, aged twenty months, with his Portage home visitor who visits once a week. In the first photograph Steven is learning to sign. Two other photographs show Steven developing manipulative and cognitive skills. In addition to Portage, Steven attends day care twice a week.

Steven learning to sign

'Yes! The round object fits in the round hole.'

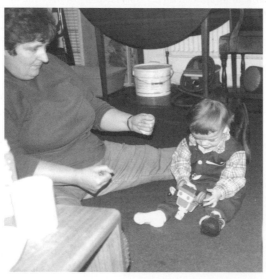

Manipulative skills

PROGRESS CHECK

1   What is the function of the Portage home visiting service?
2   On which developmental skills does Portage particularly concentrate?
3   In what ways are parents involved in the Portage programme?
4   What is the guiding principle of the Portage programme?

PLAYGROUPS

The Pre-school Learning Alliance

The Pre-school Learning Alliance is a national educational charity offering play and learning opportunities for children aged two years and nine months to five years (in some areas three to five years), through its network of community based pre-schools. The Alliance is committed to a policy of inclusive day care.

Pre-schools are validated for their care and educational programme by Ofsted Early Years Directorate and the children follow the Early Years Foundation Stage curriculum. Some pre-schools offer full day care, but most are sessional. Opportunity playgroups and specialist language groups come under the Alliance umbrella. Parents may help the pre-school staff run particular groups. Speech and language therapists, physiotherapists and other health professionals attend the opportunity playgroups to help young children in their care.

Parent/carer and toddler groups

Parent/carer and toddler groups are usually organised and managed by parents/carers and other members of the community. They are often situated in a church or community hall, sometimes in a health centre, and increasingly in children's centres. Babies and young children attend, always accompanied by an adult who stays for the duration of the session. The groups offer play facilities and social contact.

Adventure playgrounds

Article 31 (summarised) of the Convention on the Rights of the Child recognises the right of children *'to engage in play and recreational activities according to their age,'* and encourages *'the provision of appropriate and equal opportunities for leisure and recreation'.*

Play activities in a pre-school

Sadly, many playgrounds are not accessible to children with special needs, although things are improving. There are a number of fully inclusive adventure playgrounds across the country that provide somewhere for all children to play adventurously, giving the opportunities for children to experience freedom, challenge and stimulation in a safe and supervised environment. Age ranges vary, but typically a playground would cater for children aged five to fourteen years.

KEY POINT

Many children with special needs have little access to physical space or opportunities to choose what they would like to do. An adventure playground offers the children both these facilities.

A typical adventure playground would include:
- a large outdoor area with access everywhere for wheelchairs
- handrails and ramps for children with mobility difficulties
- boat, tyre and bed swings – rubber moulded swing seats give good support for children with balance and co-ordination difficulties
- an aerial runway with harnesses
- timber structures with ramps, ladders and poles
- sand and water play equipment
- slides that are wide enough to take a child and accompanying adult or other child

- a garden area for digging and planting activities – a sensory garden with herbs and aromatic plants
- assistance for children with visual impairment through use of bright coloured marker lines around the swings; textured surfaces for different playground areas, changes of level or an obstacle near by (avoid bark chippings surfaces, as they are inaccessible for wheelchair users)
- indoor soft play equipment and facilities for art and craft activities
- perhaps a multisensory room and soundbeam.

GOOD PRACTICE

One-to-one care and support is provided as necessary at the playground and medication and therapy routines are implemented.

KEY POINT

The siblings of children attending the playground are also welcome. Special school groups may use the facilities during the school term. Many adventure playgrounds organise holiday play schemes.

PROGRESS CHECK

What are the advantages of adventure playgrounds for children with special needs?

Activity

Using the information above, plus further research, design and draw a plan, or make a model, of a typical adventure playground. You should include indoor and outdoor facilities. Make a list of all the safety factors you have included.

Adapted swings

A slide for a child and accompanying adult or other child

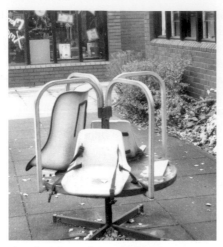

A safe adapted roundabout

A large ball to push and climb on promotes posture and gross motor skills

A variety of outdoor and indoor equipment for children with special needs

BEFRIENDING SCHEMES

Volunteer befrienders are well-informed, experienced parents who have been through their own personal experience of caring for a child with special needs and have faced their own feelings before reaching the stages of acceptance and adjustment. They are not professionals, therapists or counsellors but have received training in listening and counselling skills, and draw on their own experiences to help and support families who feel lonely, isolated or stressed. A one-to-one relationship is built up between the parents and the befriender before they meet with other families, who are facing similar difficulties, in a mutually supportive group setting. Many families value the support they receive from parent befrienders and eventually become befrienders themselves.

Face to Face

Face to Face is jointly funded and managed by Scope and Mencap. It offers a support service for parents or carers who have difficulty in coming to terms with their child's special need.

Homestart

Homestart befriending schemes offer a home visiting support service for families under stress trying to care for very young children. The visitors (parent volunteers) listen to their concerns and offer regular support, friendship and practical help. In addition, they enable families to make use of community resources such as parent/carer and toddler groups, playgroups and toy libraries.

Local social services departments and Early Years Development and Childcare Partnerships can put families in touch with other befriending and support groups. Other befriending schemes are: the Parent Link support service in London; and Parent-to-Parent Befriending set up by Mencap in Wales.

PROGRESS CHECK

1 What is a befriending scheme?
2 What experience and training is necessary to become a befriender?

A multisensory room and soundbeam

A MULTISENSORY ROOM

Relaxation and stimulation in a multisensory, or white room, are particularly beneficial for children with special needs. The room decor is white – floor, walls, hammock and seating. There are no windows. Equipment includes multi-coloured lighting, water-filled bubble tubes, fibre optics, aromatherapy tubes, different textured collages (at a child's handrail height), taped music, wall and ceiling pictures and a wind box. Some rooms have a water bed. All the equipment is specifically designed to offer a range of sensory experiences (sound, highly visible, textured and perfumed clues) to children who find it difficult to explore, discover and understand their environment. The combination of light, sound, touch, smell and movement creates a calm and peaceful learning environment.

Children, accompanied by their parents or carers, are encouraged to use and experience the equipment. Vibrations are felt when touching and holding the bubble tubes. Bright colours are a stimulus for children with visual impairment (although children with albinism tend to be light sensitive), and coloured balls rising and falling in the tubes help to develop vertical tracking skills. Changing the colours, sounds, smells and pictures in the room by pressing different knobs and levers offers children choice and gives them a sense of being in control of their experiences, as well as developing manipulative skills. The wind box and collages help children who are tactile defensive (apprehensive about new tactile experiences). Children with emotional or behavioural difficulties can be calmed by the total experience of the room.

THE SOUNDBEAM

An ultrasonic, adjustable, invisible soundbeam provides music through a cause and effect principle. It can be operated by children who are virtually immobile through the slightest movement of a finger, hand or eye across the beam so activating a keyboard. Children moving through the beam or a child rocking in the beam can produce different sounds of varying tones and intensity. Like the multisensory room it has a pleasurable and peaceful effect on children with special needs.

Multisensory and soundbeam provision is not exclusively for children with special needs. Any child would benefit from the unique learning and calming experience. The equipment is expensive to buy and fundraising projects are often the only way of purchasing it. Special schools and adventure playgrounds may provide these facilities for the children.

PROGRESS CHECK

1   Describe how a 'white room' provides multisensory experiences for children with special needs.
2   In what ways can children with special needs activate a soundbeam?

CASE STUDY

Leonie and her twin sister Petra, now aged two years, were born at thirty-two weeks' gestation and sustained brain injury during a difficult birth. They have severe motor and learning difficulties. The family are very new to the area and are trying to settle in as part of the community.

Caring for Leonie and Petra is exhausting and time-consuming. The children's mother, in particular, is at the end of her tether. She has visited the local health centre, registered with a family doctor and made an appointment to see him tomorrow.

1   How can the family doctor help the family, especially the mother?
2   Which other member of the primary health care team is likely to be immediately involved with the family? What help and support might be offered?
3   What would your role be as key worker for Leonie and Petra in a day care setting?
4   Which voluntary organisations have particular knowledge, facilities and resources that may be supportive for the children and their family?

KEY TERMS

You need to know what these words and phrases mean. Go back through the chapter and make sure that you understand:

adventure playgrounds	Portage
befriending schemes	role of a key worker
community-based services	Scope template of good practice
incontinence	soundbeam
multisensory room	Sure Start
out-of-school care	voluntary provision
parents as partners	

PART 2
Introduction

The second half of this book covers information to ensure good practice in caring for children with the more commonly occurring conditions. Part Two can be used for quick reference either for a specific piece of information or to gain wider knowledge. We hope it will help you to work with young children safely and effectively, meeting any particular needs a child may have, with confidence.

An introduction gives a brief background to each condition, including the frequency of occurrence, severity of the effect and any specific sex or race implications. The following headings give more detailed information about each condition.

What happens: how a condition first shows itself – the signs that something may be amiss – and what to look for if you are worried about a child's development. Patterns of inheritance are described, including a description of how a condition usually progresses and develops.

Diagnosis: which tests or examinations may be used to confirm a child has a certain condition.

Care: immediate care and priorities of management are covered, including all aspects of a child's physical, emotional and social well-being. If applicable specific first aid measures are described and any special medication discussed.

Ongoing management: longer term issues concerned with a child with a chronic or possibly life-limiting condition are described. This section looks at preparation for care in wider settings away from the home, including nursery and primary school.

General implications: wider, possibly ongoing, issues are raised.

Additional developments: any recent, specific developments and thoughts about children and their care and management are discussed – not all sections have recent developments.

At the end of Chapter 7 information is given about the management of medicines in schools, nurseries and playgroups – essential information for safe practice.

Resources: listed at the end of each section are the national addresses and websites of the main voluntary organisations associated with a specific condition. Regional and local contact addresses, together with information in different languages can often be found through the national websites.

Non-specific organisations and websites are listed in the 'Useful addresses' section at the end of the book.

Note: when using the internet, select your material carefully and remember that not all sites supply information that has been supported by wide research and academic scrutiny. Government and established charities, however, are excellent sources and provide comprehensive, current and accurate information.

In Part Two *individual* conditions are explained. However, many children will have a range of disabilities or complex needs. For example, a child with behavioural difficulties could also be deaf or have eczema, and a child with cerebral palsy could also have a visual impairment. To work effectively with children with multiple and complex needs you may need to read several sections of this part of the book.

Different therapies and management techniques discussed may be helpful for children with a range of conditions. For example, speech and language therapy is essential for deaf children but also for some children with cerebral palsy, while conductive education can help children with cerebral palsy and also children with dyspraxia.

KEY POINTS

■ The name of a condition, for example cerebral palsy or Down syndrome, is only a tool to help Early Years workers and parents provide the most suitable, enabling and enriching environment for a child. The names are not an end in themselves and sensitivity in the use of such terms is vital. Always remember that the child, his personality, abilities, hopes and wishes come before any umbrella name that may be given to a particular condition. The child is not 'a condition'.

■ Each child is an individual and will respond to challenges, stress and distress in different ways. The care and management issues discussed in Part Two are for guidance and general principles only.

When a child is born with a special need, parents and, later, children themselves, usually want to know why this has happened. Access to this information is a basic right. Knowledge about the reasons for a disability, and its associated special needs, can sometimes give relief from uncertainty and help families plan and focus on the future. Often, following this information, families wish to take genetic counselling.

Professionals working with families need to work as a cohesive and sensitive team, valuing and understanding the parents' knowledge of their child and the specific anxieties about him and his individual special needs.

KEY POINTS

■ If you have information regarding a child's medical condition this must remain confidential and should not be shared with others without permission from the parent.

■ Medical records should always be stored within a locked cabinet and accessed only by those with parental permission.

■ Some children with these conditions will require a statutory assessment and statement of their special educational needs (see Chapter 3, pages 90–1).

■ All children attending maintained Early Years education settings follow the Early Years Foundation Stage and National Curriculum.

6 PHYSICAL CONDITIONS

In this chapter we look at a range of physical conditions that affect children. These require some medical supervision and the use of medicines to control and minimise the condition's effects. Even though there may be an acknowledged term for a specific condition, remember each child will respond and be affected differently.

Epilepsy

Epilepsy is the most common serious neurological condition, affecting approximately 43,500 children in the UK. The brain is a highly complex structure comprising millions of nerve cells or neurones, which are responsible for a wide range of functions, including consciousness, awareness, movement and posture. In epilepsy there is an interruption in the chemical activity in the nerve cells and a 'fit' or seizure is the result.

Seizures can occur that are not epilepsy. In very young children, under two, these are often triggered by a high temperature and rarely lead to epilepsy.

About six in every thousand children have epilepsy and 80 per cent attend mainstream schools. Slightly more girls than boys have epilepsy.

WHAT HAPPENS

Electrical changes in the brain neurones may occur because of intrinsic factors – something in the brain itself – and the reasons are usually unknown but can include:
- antenatal infections
- family history
- jaundice
- some drugs taken in pregnancy.

Or, external factors – something affecting the brain from outside – may be the reason, including:

- a temporary lack of oxygen, perhaps caused by an injury or birth damage
- susceptibility to flashing or flickering lights (photosensitivity)
- severe infections often with associated brain infections
- certain severe diseases.

There are more than forty types of seizure, usually classified as either generalised seizures or partial seizures. They need to be managed in different ways.

Generalised seizures

Tonic/clonic seizure

The tonic/clonic seizure used to be known as 'grand mal'.

- The start is sudden and may occur at night. About one-third of children experience auras (see coloured lights, taste or smell something specific), which often occur with subsequent seizures.
- The next stage is the tonic or spasm stage. The child's entire body becomes stiff and he falls to the floor, losing consciousness. His face may be pale and distorted, with eyes fixed in one position, often rolled back. The back and neck may arch, with arms flexed and hands clenched. He may utter a piercing cry, be incontinent (pass urine or stool) and bite the inside of his cheek during the first spasm. Frothing at the mouth and difficulty in swallowing the saliva may occur. This stage leads into the clonic phase.
- In the clonic phase the child starts to twitch, sometimes just involving the face, sometimes the whole body, lasting from a few seconds to several minutes. This is followed by the post-convulsive stage.
- In the post-convulsive stage the child is usually sleepy and may complain of a headache, he may appear dazed and have a memory loss of the convulsion.

Absences

Other generalised seizures can occur and are all much less dramatic in presentation. The most significant to be aware of are 'absences'. Here there is a brief interruption of consciousness without any other signs, except perhaps for a fluttering of the eyelids. This type is especially common in children and used to be known as 'petit mal'. It occurs most frequently in children from three years onwards.

Partial seizures

Simple partial seizures

Consciousness is not affected and the seizure is confined to rhythmical twitching of one limb or part of a limb or to unusual tastes in the mouth, or a sensation such as pins and needles in a specific part of the body (this can be similar to the aura that may precede a major tonic/clonic seizure).

Complex partial seizures

Consciousness is affected and the child shows 'semi-purposive' movements such as fiddling with clothes or objects, wandering around or appearing confused. These types of seizure occasionally lead to other forms of general-ised seizures.

DIAGNOSIS

A child is said to have epilepsy if he has repeated fits from a cause triggered inter-nally or externally. Confirmation of the decision is made by looking at the electrical impulses of the brain on an electroencephalogram. Electrodes are attached to the head and a moving record of the brain's activity is recorded – this is a painless and harmless procedure.

CARE

Major seizure

There is little complex treatment required during this time. Basic first aid is all that is required and carers can be reassured that mostly children with seizures need a 'watching brief'. Follow the procedure below.

- Stay calm, remember that a low, quiet voice is reassuring, and keep onlookers away.
- Ensure there is nothing around the child that could damage him, such as hard furniture.
- Remove any spectacles if necessary.
- If possible put something soft under the child's head.

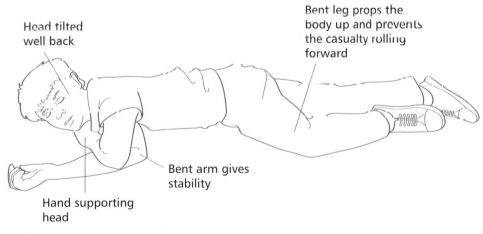

The recovery position

When the spasms have finished proceed with the following.
- Turn the child on to his side and place him in the recovery position.
- Check, with sensitivity, if the child needs his clothes changing.
- Encourage him to return to his usual activities when he feels ready.
- If the child fell during the fit, ensure he hasn't hurt himself.
- Maintain a matter-of-fact approach.

- During a seizure never try to force anything between the teeth – you may push a tooth down the throat and cause choking.
- Do not try to restrain the child.
- Keep a record of how long the seizure lasted.
- Seek medical help if this is a first convulsion.

KEY POINT

Your own responses to a major seizure are important, both to the individual child and other children. Your reactions show the child and his friends how you view epilepsy. Feelings of fear, anxiety and panic are easily transmitted, and you may unconsciously increase a child's feelings of embarrassment and guilt and even make him sad or depressed. Remember, too, he may be upset if his peers saw that he soiled himself. This is more likely if a child has only recently mastered the skill of bladder and bowel control. The child may have no recollection of the seizure, only sensing what happened from the people around him.

Non-convulsive seizures

As these seizures vary in type and intensity the response needed may differ – the main principles are as follows:

- Gently guide a child away from obvious danger.
- Keep onlookers away.
- Speak gently and calmly to the child to help him remember his surroundings as quickly as possible.
- Remember that he may be confused for some time after the seizure and it is better to leave him alone than to overcrowd him – discreetly observe him.
- Stay with the child until he resumes his normal activity.

ONGOING MANAGEMENT

Epilepsy can usually be successfully controlled by medication, but the success in this depends on several factors:

- the type of epilepsy
- the accuracy of diagnosis
- the accuracy of treatment
- the child's response to the medication
- additional problems.

With appropriate drug treatment seizures can be completely controlled in about 80 per cent of children with epilepsy. Occasionally seizures diminish as the child grows, however it is usually recommended that anti-epileptic drugs continue for several years even after seizures stop.

A child needs to become involved in the management of his own treatment and see medication as a positive part of remaining healthy and not as part of an 'illness'. He can be especially affected by negative images of this condition from peers and surrounding adults, which are the results of fear and ignorance.

GOOD PRACTICE

For the young child minor adjustments to routine safe practice will be needed:

- Doors should open outwards and locks be positioned so that they can be operated from inside and out. You would need to reach the child easily if he had a seizure.
- Provide routine supervision at mealtimes, outings and bedtimes – potentially dangerous times for any child.
- Use special anti-smother pillows.
- Check that all your climbing equipment is secure and stable – in case of falls.
- Monitor the condition of toys – check there are no loose pieces to be torn off and inhaled.
- Ensure safety surfaces in playgrounds are in good condition.
- Be aware of any situations that might trigger a seizure.

The disabling effects of epilepsy can be substantially lessened if there is good communication between professionals, parents, the child and his peers. A teacher or other carer must have full information on:

- the type of epilepsy the child has
- the frequency of seizures
- the speed of recovery
- the most appropriate management for the child
- how he feels after a seizure
- how positive he is about his condition
- information about triggering factors, if known
- details of medicines, including any possible side-effects.

KEY POINT

The teacher needs to feel confident and so requires information about the child and his condition.

PROGRESS CHECK

Imagine a child has a major seizure when you are involved in playground supervision in the nursery class.
1   How would you manage the child who is having the seizure?
2   How would you manage the other children?

Telling other people

It is estimated that for every child with epilepsy one in three will experience problems in school with his peers, and a quarter will have difficulty with the teaching staff. Early Years workers must examine their own attitudes and values, and update their personal knowledge of the subject to help address these issues.

The other children in a class may feel fearful if a seizure occurs and they are unprepared. This can result in myths and stereotypes being reinforced. It may be constructive to include information into general classroom planning before the admission of a child with epilepsy and before any seizure happens. The amount of information disclosed to the class about a specific child must be agreed between the parents, teacher and child, and the decision respected.

Consider, too, the importance of sharing information in other childcare situations – playgroups, childminders and with parents and carers or friends.

KEY POINT

Hiding epilepsy does not limit the risk of seizures – but confidentiality must be respected.

Generally the child should develop and grow in as 'normal' an environment as possible. Each child will have different needs depending on the degree of control by his medication. As with any child, normal discipline and risk taking are part of learning and must not be avoided. It is almost unheard of for routine discipline of a child to promote or trigger a seizure.

Children with epilepsy need a normal environment

KEY POINTS

- Over-protection will affect the child's self-esteem, his learning opportunities and eventually his ability to assess danger himself. He should not feel he can never be alone.
- As the child grows he needs appropriate information regarding his condition and its control. Answer questions honestly.

GOOD PRACTICE

- Activities such as swimming or climbing in high places need not be avoided, but care should be taken to ensure supervision is present from someone confident in seizure management.
- An identification bracelet helps provide useful information, especially if a seizure occurs in an unexpected situation or new staff are involved in care.
- If medication is given at school, ensure storage is secure, dosage is always checked and possible side- effects known.

Additional help must be sought in the following situations:
- The child has injured himself badly in a seizure.
- The child has trouble breathing after a seizure.
- One seizure immediately follows another, or the seizure lasts longer than five minutes and the carer is unaware of the usual length.
- The seizure lasts longer than usual (often a card is carried to indicate length of seizure).

GENERAL IMPLICATIONS

Can epilepsy affect progress?
Occasionally teachers, nursery careworkers and other staff have low expectations of children with epilepsy and may unconsciously treat them differently. If the seizures are well controlled and there are no other associated disabilities there is no reason for underachievement or any unacceptable behaviour in such children. Behavioural problems that sometimes occur can often be caused by tension and anxiety from carers causing low self-esteem in the child.

Epilepsy should not be used as an excuse for attention-seeking and unacceptable behaviour, as this can result in isolation and affect the child developing strong peer and social relationships.

The following are some possible causes of the child underachieving:
- Frequent major seizures may lead to poor school or pre-school attendance. This is made worse if the child is unnecessarily removed every time a seizure occurs. In addition, absences from pre-school and school can affect a child's confidence in making social relationships.
- Frequent 'absence' seizures, which may be difficult to detect, can hinder learning.

- Children with especially severe epilepsy may have periods of disorganised brain activity, not enough to cause seizure but which may affect performance and learning.
- Incorrect or excessive drug treatment can cause sleepiness.
- Children who are going through periods of rapid growth may need adjustment of their drugs more frequently.

KEY POINT

Behavioural difficulties should not always be put down to drug effects.

ADDITIONAL DEVELOPMENTS

Epilepsy and surgery

If the epilepsy is caused by a specific structural problem in part of the brain, possibly from a form of head injury or following an infection (e.g. meningitis) and scarring of the brain has occurred, surgery is sometimes undertaken. This may be considered if the child is otherwise fit and medication has proved to be unsuccessful. This is only ever undertaken after extensive investigation involving special brain (MRI) scanning and other procedures to ensure areas responsible for speech, sight, movement or hearing are not close to the affected area.

Specific stimulation, via a nerve in the neck, is offered at present for older children in some hospitals throughout the UK. A small battery-operated device is programmed to send a mild stimulation to the brain. It is only suitable for certain types of epilepsy that do not respond well to medication. This is not yet widely available.

Mostly, however, children manage their epilepsy effectively through medication.

CASE STUDY

Jack was what his mother described as 'dreamy' – he often seemed to disappear into a world of his own. This dreaminess increased when he started infant school and sometimes his teacher complained that he did not appear interested in what was going on in the classroom – he frequently stared blankly ahead and gradually became labelled as 'not interested'. Usually Jack was outgoing and had friends and many interests.

He failed to make the expected academic progress of which he was thought capable. When he started to learn to read he seemed to find it difficult and would often appear to have forgotten several pages of the stories associated with a book he was reading. Even at home when watching television he missed major parts of the 'plot' of a programme.

Jack's mother became worried and took him to the family doctor who referred him to a neurologist for special tests.

Jack was diagnosed as having a type of epilepsy known as 'absences' – he was losing consciousness for very brief spells of time, not long enough to fall or show any obvious signs, but sufficient to affect his continuity of learning. He was missing some of the main teaching points or the essential linking material.

Jack was prescribed medicines to help limit the absences but it was not yet fully effective.

1 How could you, as a childcare worker, help to make up the missing periods for Jack?
2 What knowledge do you need about Jack's medicines?

RESOURCES

British Epilepsy Association
New Anstey House
Gate Way Drive
Yeadon
Leeds LS19 7XY
www.epilepsy.org.uk

F.A.B.L.E (For a Better Life with Epilepsy)
Lower Ground Floor
305 Glossop Road
Sheffield S10 2HL
www.fable.org.uk

National Society for Epilepsy
Chesham Lane
Chalfont St Peter
Bucks SL9 0RJ
www.epilepsynse.org.uk

Asthma and eczema

Asthma, eczema and hay fever are related conditions that often run in families and may be inherited. Two particular sets of genes have been found to influence allergic responses in asthma and eczema. In addition, there is new research to suggest that exposure to infection in early life may protect against the development of asthma and other allergies in later life.

Asthma

Asthma is a recurrent and reversible condition of the lungs, which means that the narrowing of the tubes that happens is temporary and is caused by specific factors. A child with asthma responds to specific triggers and irritants by having breathing difficulties – another child without asthma, exposed to the same triggers, does not react. A genetic susceptibility in a child is now acknowledged as an important factor.

Asthma is thought to be increasing in frequency and severity with one in seven school-age children now having the condition, and approximately six children being daily admitted to hospital in the UK. It is not fully understood why there has been a rise in the incidence of asthma over recent years. Outdoor air pollutants, thought by some to be a factor, have actually decreased in industrial countries, in the last ten years.

Possibilities for the rise in asthma include the increased survival rate of more low birth-weight babies who may be at greater risk. Unknown airborne or environmental factors, and an over-exposure to indoor allergies (children now spend more time inside watching television or playing computer games). A raised awareness, and reporting, of the condition itself is also thought to be a possible cause for the increase in numbers, however research is ongoing. A genetic susceptibility in a child is now acknowledged as an important factor.

Breast-feeding is often encouraged in 'atopic' (allergic) families. It is helpful in delaying the onset of asthma, but not necessarily preventing it. Smoking in pregnancy is considered to increase the chances of a child developing asthma.

WHAT HAPPENS

A 'trigger' or irritation causes a temporary obstruction in the tiny tubes of the lungs – the bronchioles. These bronchioles go into spasm and produce extra secretions and coughing. Because the airways are in spasm the air passages narrow, causing difficulty in breathing in and out. A wheezing noise is produced. The child fights for breath and can become frightened.

Asthma often has no set pattern of occurrence or severity of symptoms. Up to 30 per cent of children under five years wheeze but never have further symptoms. Many children 'grow out of asthma'.

DIAGNOSIS

There is no single cause for asthma. It is usually divided into the following types, depending on what is found to stimulate a child to produce asthmatic signs.

Extrinsic asthma
The trigger factors for extrinsic asthma can be:
- infections, especially coughs and colds
- pollen, feathers, household dust mite, animals, mould and certain foods

- cold and, occasionally, humidity
- chemicals
- pollutants, especially carbon monoxide, cigarette smoke and fuel and paint fumes, sprays from cleaners and perfumes
- exercise – thought to be a trigger in about 50 per cent of asthma
- emotional factors (in a child with an existing allergic response).

Intrinsic asthma
Here no specific sensitivity or trigger can be found.

Very young children often have troublesome coughs, especially at night or following colds or exercise. If these persist over a period of time asthma may be diagnosed. This diagnosis is helpful as a child can then receive effective monitoring and treatment.

Allergy tests may be undertaken to find if a specific allergen can be identified and removed or its contact with the child limited. However, children often have many responses to these tests and it would be impracticable for all the allergens to be eliminated.

KEY POINT

Asthma or wheezing in babies and small children is rarely triggered by allergy, but follows colds and chest infections.

Degrees of asthma
- Severe asthma can result in sleeping difficulties – the child coughs and wheezes more at night – and poor feeding – the child is too breathless to feed effectively and loses weight. General lethargy results, the effort to play and get involved in usual activity is too great – too much energy is spent forcing air in and out through reduced airways. Occasionally the child's lips go blue.
- Moderate asthma is waking at night coughing and, in the day, coughing and difficulty in running around and playing without wheezing.
- Mild asthma means only coughing and wheezing but not to an extent that playing or feeding is disrupted.

KEY POINT

Healthy children rarely cough except with a bad cold. Many young children with dry irritating coughs may have asthma, even though they never wheeze.

CARE

Medicines
Although asthma cannot be cured, with effective management symptoms can be reduced and usually controlled, allowing children to lead full and active lives.

Almost all asthma medicines are given in some form of inhalers, even to very small babies. Given this way means that correct doses of medicine can be sent straight into the lungs.

There are two main types of medicine and it is important to know what they do as they will be needed in different situations.

Preventers (often in brown, white or red inhalers)
Preventers protect the lining of the airways and make them less likely to narrow when triggered by a specific irritant. They reduce the airway's response to allergies and act specifically on the tubes in the lungs. Usually they are taken morning and evening and must be taken regularly, even if the child is well. Many need to be taken for fourteen days before becoming fully effective. A child can remain fit and well and be completely free of symptoms on these types of inhalers. They allow the child to use the whole of his lungs. Unfortunately parents and carers often stop using this type of treatment precisely when it is most effective – the child seems completely well. When these are stopped an attack may occur.

Relievers (often in blue inhalers)
Relievers make breathing easier by relaxing the tiny muscles surrounding the narrowed airways and allowing them to open up; they do not prevent the narrowing occurring again in the future. As well as being effective for symptom relief, they may also be used immediately before exercise (if this is known to be a trigger). A child learns to recognise this type of inhaler, which gives him almost immediate symptom relief.

Other medication
Other medication is used if a child fails to respond to inhalers. Steroid medicine is usually given for a short period of one to five days to counteract a severe attack. The child then continues with his spacers and puffers.

Complementary medicines
Complementary medicines are sometimes used in conjunction with the traditional approach if this is wished by parents and carers.

Using inhalers (puffers) and spacers
Make sure you know how to use the inhaler or spacer – information and demonstrations on how to use one effectively can come from school nurses, pharmacists, family doctor and hospital staff.
    When caring for a child with asthma check the following:
- that the type of inhaler the child uses, whether a preventer or reliever
- that the inhaler is full, and shaken before use, or attached to the spacer
- that the inhaler is cleaned and replaced as necessary.

Check you know how many puffs the child takes and how the inhaler is used (usually the child exhales before taking an inhaler, holds his breath following the inhalation and keep his lips shut for ten seconds after).
    The following are other points to consider:
- Consider how to administer to a child who is not co-operating because he is frightened. (If a child is distressed he will still be able to get this medicine quickly even when crying, through his spacer.)

HOW MEDICINE IS GIVEN IN ASTHMA

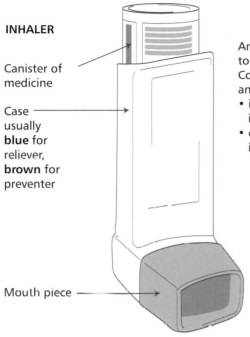

INHALER

Canister of medicine

Case usually **blue** for reliever, **brown** for preventer

Mouth piece

An inhaler allows medicine to be taken directly into the lungs. Coordination in releasing medicine and inhaling means:
- in young children an inhaler is used with a spacer
- children can rarely use an inhaler alone before five years.

SPACER

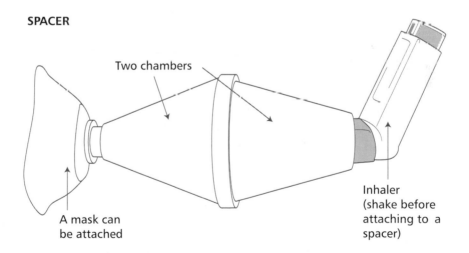

Two chambers

A mask can be attached

Inhaler (shake before attaching to a spacer)

A spacer fits the aerosol inhaler – medicine is puffed into the spacer via the inhaler, one puff at a time. The child breathes via the mask.
This allows the medicine to be directly sent to the lungs to dilate the bronchioles and allow breathing to ease.
Keep spacers clean – wash reguarly and air dry.

- If a young child is having difficulty, show him how by using the inhaler yourself (without filling the spacer with medicine) and try to make taking it into a game.
- Keep in contact with the health visitor or school nurse over new developments in asthma management.
- Know the school or nursery policy regarding children's medicines. Does it take into account the urgency of access to inhalers for children with asthma?
- Is there a special policy for children with asthma in the school?
- Remember to include a general reminder in letters to parents/carers about taking inhalers on school trips and outings.
- Young children can be given medicines via spacers while asleep.

GOOD PRACTICE

Relieving inhalers should be readily to hand and not locked away in cupboards. Preferably they should remain with the child – remember it is his condition for him to manage, so he should feel in control. Obviously very young children will need help in using their spacers.

KEY POINTS

- A recent study of more than 3000 children on the possible effects on children's growth from the regular use of 'preventers', discovered that the vast majority of the children were of normal height, weight and growth rate for their age.
- Research tells us that a significant number of people fail to use their inhalers correctly, making them less effective.

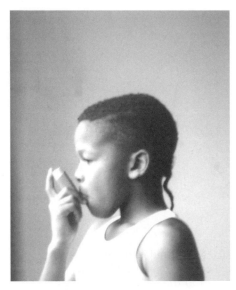

The correct use of an inhaler for an older child

A younger child finds a spacer easier

- Treatment is aimed at the prevention of the appearance of symptoms.
- If another child got hold of an inhaler and used it, it would not cause any damage.
- A child cannot 'induce' an asthma attack – asthma is a physical reaction of the lungs to a variety of triggers, not an emotional reaction. Not being able to breathe easily is frightening and can induce panic in a child, reducing his already limited lung capacity.
- Quick and calm response is important.

ONGOING MANAGEMENT

Childcare workers need to work closely with parents and carers so everyone is aware of known triggers and can try and eliminate them. All involved in care should understand the importance of the management of a child's particular asthma and its special implications for him.

The aim should be to help the child remain symptom free so he can be fully involved in all activities at home, playgroup or school. The child learns to recognise situations that might make him wheeze and develop confidence knowing his symptoms are controlled by his inhalers, so he then can forget his asthma. When very young he may need a reminder to take an inhaler before exercise. Check the child's inhalers are with him when he is on outings and trips.

Making the environment asthma 'friendly'
- Dust mites are a common allergen – rooms will need regular vacuuming, including mattresses and curtains.
- Regularly wash cotton bedding and use non-allergenic pillows.
- Keep good ventilation especially in bedrooms

Asthma may be triggered by a pet with a furry coat, exercise or cold weather

- As a smoky environment makes wheezing worse, a diagnosis of asthma is often the spur families need to give up cigarettes.
- Wash any soft toys regularly. Freezing toys in a plastic bag overnight kills any dust mites. They then need defrosting and washing to remove mites and droppings.
- Check the family, school or nursery pets, as guinea pigs, hamsters, birds and rabbits are often triggers. Try letting the pet have a 'holiday' with a friend and see if the child wheezes less. Perhaps just not handling the animal and certainly stopping the pet sleeping on a bed may be enough. If the pet is the cause try and find an acceptable alternative, perhaps a snake or fish – one without a hairy or feathery coat.
- An air conditioner or air filtration system in the home may be helpful for a child who is severely affected.

Exercise

Moderate exercise is good and each child will have different amounts he can manage and will learn to pace himself. Nearly all children with asthma become wheezy during exercise and a dose of a dilator or reliever prior to starting to run and jump is often very helpful. He may need a gentle reminder to take the inhaler.

It is important for a child to remain fit with all the benefits of lung expansion, prevention of infection and the opportunities of challenge and adventure that outdoor exercise provides. However if the weather is particularly cold or foggy watch that his breathing remains easy. A scarf over the mouth, on cold days, may help by warming the air before it enters the lungs. Try and encourage the child to breathe through his nose. Asthma is often worse during cold, dry days than warm, humid ones. Long spells of exercise are more likely to set wheezing off than short bursts.

Grass pollen during late May and June can be difficult for a child allergic to flowering grasses and he will need to stay away from such places during this time.

Swimming is a particularly valuable form of exercise for children with asthma, rarely provoking wheezing if the water is not too cold or heavily chlorinated.

GOOD PRACTICE

- When joining in school games a child's inhaler should always be near to hand.
- Never force a child to continue to exercise if he is wheezing and uncomfortable.
- Be aware that some children are uncomfortable with taking an inhaler in front of their friends; check if privacy is required.

Diet and asthma

A special diet may be of help for the following children:
- those with clear family histories of food allergy
- those with eczema as well as asthma
- those whose wheezing started when weaning began, or when cows' milk was introduced.

Close liaison with medical personnel is essential before applying a limiting diet to a child. This is especially so for a baby, who is growing and developing and requiring a wide variety of foods to meet his needs.

If it is felt that a special feeding regime is required the following advice is usually given:

- Mothers should breast-feed for as long as possible, while avoiding foods to which they are allergic.
- Especially formulated milks will need to be prescribed by the doctor. Soya milk is almost as likely as cows' milk to cause allergy and sheep and goats' milks are unsuitable for babies.
- Introduce one new food to a baby at a time and watch closely for a few days to assess the results. If the baby becomes snuffly, wheezy, colicky or develops a rash, stop the new food.
- Continue to add new foods one at a time – try and maintain variety.
- Gradually introduce different drinks, one at a time. Avoid fizzy drinks and squashes for at least eighteen months.
- Avoid eggs and cows' milk until the baby is one year old.
- Avoid fish, nuts or wheat flour for at least the first year if there is a family history of allergy.

KEY POINTS

- If a child has a fever it is the result of infection, *not* an adverse food reaction.
- Children who do not have dairy food, or a recognised baby milk after stopping breast-feeding, will need a calcium supplement prescribed by their doctor.

Activity
To help explain asthma to children of infant school age blow up balloons with a pump. Explain to the children the balloons are like lungs. Give them out to the children and, under supervision, ask them to deflate them while restricting the amounts of air released by squeezing and stretching the necks. Tell the children this is how air has problems in leaving the lungs of a child with asthma.

Compare how quickly the air leaves the balloon if the neck is not squeezed. Compare the noises the escaping air makes when restricted and when free. Always closely supervise children with balloons.

Good practice in managing an acute asthma attack
During an asthma attack coughing, wheezing or breathlessness worsens quickly until breathing becomes difficult. Some children become too breathless to talk or feed during an attack. Attacks can take anything from a few hours to a few days to develop. Regular observation is important.

Asthma attacks can occasionally be life-threatening. The following danger signs indicate that routine management is not controlling the condition:

- A reliever needs to be repeated before three hours have passed.
- The child is too breathless to feed or talk and is becoming very distressed.
- The child becomes pale and blue around the lips.

If this happens the following steps should be taken:

- Call for help immediately – it may be quicker to take the child in a car to the nearest accident and emergency department.
- Give the reliever treatment straight away, repeating this treatment every five to ten minutes until the child's breathing improves or help arrives. Check he is taking the reliever treatment correctly.
- Give any other prescribed medicines reserved for such occasions, often steroid tablets.
- Hold or sit the child in a comfortable upright position. He may like his hand held, but do not put an arm around him as this may feel restricting.
- Reassure him and remain calm yourself – the child will be frightened.
- Loosen tight clothing around the neck.
- Sips of tepid fluids can help with a mouth dry from rapid breathing.
- Contact parent/carer.

Often simple breathing exercises are given by physiotherapists to help children with asthma to use their lungs effectively. Generally the emphasis is on fully exhaling rather than trying to increase inhalation, together with the use of additional muscles, i.e. the abdomen to help increase chest capacity. Occasionally these exercises can stop an attack developing and lessen the severity. They also help a child feel more in control.

PROGRESS CHECK

1 Has a child in your care been given such exercises?
2 How can you support and encourage the child in the use of exercises?
3 When and how should the exercises be used?

GENERAL IMPLICATIONS

The number of children with asthma is increasing, doubling in the last twenty years. Luckily, treatments are increasingly effective even in children seriously affected. Most children do eventually grow out of their condition or the intensity of the symptoms settles over time. Research continues and current projects include the development of a test for the respiratory function of young adults, which can be used in the home, a new lung function technique to improve the diagnosis of asthma and analysis of the benefits of the various reliever treatments currently in use.

CASE STUDY

Aaron had been a sturdy four-year-old boy who regularly attended playgroup. Normally he was active and energetic but recently he seemed to have difficulty in shaking off a persistent cough. This was made worse when he was running and climbing in the outdoor area, and seemed to trouble him even more during a particularly cold spell. He began to lack his normal enthusiasm and even fell asleep in the story corner.

After discussion with his mother it was realised that Aaron's cough had persisted since his attack of measles the previous winter. It was worse at night and was causing him sleeplessness.

Aaron had several courses of antibiotic medicine to try and cure the cough but all to no avail. On his next visit to the family doctor he was given further tests. These included measuring his breathing capacity and listening to his chest after he had been running around. The doctor decided he probably had asthma and Aaron's mother confirmed that when she was a child she too had breathing difficulties.

Aaron was prescribed inhaled medication, which gave him immediate relief and made him feel much more comfortable, returning him to his usual energetic self. He will continue with his spacer and be regularly checked.

1 What were the three triggers that could have stimulated Aaron's asthma?
2 What precautions should the nursery take in future to ensure Aaron can be fully involved in playgroup activity?

Eczema

This is sometimes called atopic eczema, infantile and childhood eczema and dermatitis.

KEY POINT

Eczema is not a disease but more a reaction of the skin to certain triggering factors. One person in ten has a degree of eczema at some time. The severity of the symptoms varies widely.

WHAT HAPPENS

Usually the skin is very dry with an overwhelming itchiness. The skin may become inflamed, crack and split, leaving the child vulnerable to infections and with painful areas or limbs.

In babies the areas affected are concentrated on the head and body, but the eczema may spread and cover the whole child. Even on children not severely affected, patches can often remain and be seen, especially in the creases of the body, behind the ears, knees and under the arms. The irritation is made worse when the child is warm, it can disrupt his sleeping, and lead to tiredness and irritability. Different parts of the skin can be at various stages of eczema at the same time. These stages can range from a red rash, to dry scalings or cracks and to bleeding or infected skin with pustules and crusting. Typically of eczema there are times when the skin flares up and is badly affected, yet at other times is completely clear.

DIAGNOSIS

Although a significant number of children come from families with an allergic history the cause is not always known. Diagnosis is made from observing the skin, which may react to certain triggers – setting off lesions or sore and irritating patches.

Triggers can be:
- bacterial, viral or fungal infections
- specific contact irritants such as perfumed soaps, washing powders and paints
- environmental factors, such as temperature (especially heat) and humidity, and inhalants
- certain foods, especially dairy products and foods containing dairy products
- emotional or physical stress
- drugs.

KEY POINT

Each child may have a different trigger or react to a combination of triggers.

CARE

The aim is to keep the skin in good condition, lessening the chances of skin infections and reducing the painful and irritant effects for the child. For the very young child there are several things that can help:
- Emulsifiers or emollient ointments are vital as they help limit dryness and reduce irritation. They are mild, easily obtained and do not contain steroids. They must be used freely and generously. Put them in the bath water and liberally spread on to the skin after washing. A toddler who is distressed and scratching can be helped by having his cream applied. It needs to be easily available, day and night.
- For bathing use only warm water as heat irritates. Try an aqueous soap substitute. Do not use perfumed soaps or bubble baths as they dry and irritate the skin.
- Change the child's nappies frequently and maintain good skin condition. A sore nappy rash will make the eczema much worse, so watch this area especially. Leave the nappy off for part of the day.
- Check the skin creases: underarm, behind the ears, in the groins, etc. Pat the child dry thoroughly. Do not use powders as they cake and dry the skin further and they may be a focus for bacteria to multiply.
- Keep nails short and hands clean to lessen the chances of secondary infection.
- Use non-irritant fabric for clothes – natural cotton is best. Avoid wools, non-absorbent nylons and clothes with 'pile'.
- Use mild, non-biological soap powder in laundering clothes as they may be greasy from the effects of the emulsifying ointments.
- Keep the child cool. Make sure a bedroom doesn't become overheated, as it is at night that scratching is most likely to occur. Use light bedding, with no feather duvets or wool blankets. Cotton cellular blankets are ideal.

- Limit damage to the skin by providing all-in-one sleep suits at night, with cotton mittens and socks. This helps reduce the extent of easily exposed skin.
- Dummies are helpful as night-time pacifiers and can be valuable as a distracter – better than a thumb, which can become sore and cracked, so increasing the child's distress.
- Toddler anger and frustration often sets off intense irritation of the skin. Distraction management is helpful, so try to anticipate his needs.

KEY POINT

A child with eczema can be particularly sensitive to apparently minor infections prevalent in groups of children.

For children with eczema:
- herpes simplex or cold sores can lead to serious viral illness
- impetigo can result in infected eczema needing antibiotic treatment.

Diet

Breast-feeding lessens the severity of eczema and should be encouraged.

Babies who are unable to tolerate cows' milk can be provided with a special replacement formula obtained from their doctor. Goats' and soya milks are found to cause similar skin reactions to cows' milk.

Tests can be undertaken to show which foods produce skin reactions, however they are more likely to show what irritants in the environment make the skin worse, for example animal hair or pollen, rather than a specific food. The most effective way of finding an unacceptable food is by 'exclusion and challenge'.

Here foods are removed from the diet for two to four weeks and the condition of the skin observed carefully. The food is then reintroduced to check if the skin worsens. It is then excluded again, for a second time, to see if any improvement is continued. This is undertaken under the supervision of a specialist paediatric team including a dietician.
- A child from a family with a known family history of food intolerance may well show a reaction.
- The younger the child, the more likely food is to be a trigger.
- A child with eczema who also has other symptoms such as rashes, loose stools and a runny nose may be prone to skin reaction due to food.

Foods possibly likely to provoke a reaction include eggs, cheese, cows' milk, chocolate, nuts, wheat cereal, orange juice and additives.

GOOD PRACTICE

Restricting children's diets must never be undertaken unless in conjunction with qualified registered dieticians. Severely limiting children's food can be dangerous if not carried out correctly and may cause long-term nutritional problems, including delayed growth and development. Excluding cows' milk from a child's diet reduces his calcium intake by 75 per cent.

Also, reintroducing food at home to which a child is strongly intolerant, without medical supervision, may produce asthma attacks.

KEY POINT

If you are working with a child on a restricting diet, emphasise the food he can eat, not the food he cannot.

PROGRESS CHECK

1 What are the most common triggers for eczema?
2 What makes the skin irritation worse?
3 In what circumstances might a special diet be advised?
4 How could you help a toddler whose skin was causing him intense irritation?

Medicines
The condition of the skin is maintained with the moisturising of emulsifying ointments. Local lesions are also treated with very mild steroid creams. These are effective and quickly heal any sores but, unlike the emulsifiers, they must be applied sparingly and only as prescribed.

If a child with eczema has enormous difficulty in sleeping due to constant irritation then antihistamine tablets are sometimes given. Antihistamine creams are not used as they can cause an extra skin reaction. Antihistamine tablets reduce irritation and help the child to sleep; however the effects can make the child sleepy the following day as well and may affect his ability to take full advantage of play and learning. For this reason, correct dosage is important.

If a child's eczema becomes infected then often antibiotic medicines are prescribed to treat this. Very occasionally a child is admitted to hospital, for a short period, if his eczema is not responding to treatment.

Complementary therapies
Complementary therapies, particularly Chinese herbal treatments, are increasing in popularity. However they are not regulated, unlike medicines, and their content may not always be fully known – a recent study found high levels of topical steroids in one preparation. Care must be taken when using these treatments with young children, particularly with those under two years, and with any child who has liver or kidney disease. Remember 'Herbal' does not always mean safe.

Bandaging
Occasionally a child with severe eczema may respond to 'wet wrapping'. Here, bandages impregnated with soothing pastes, such as camomile or tar preparations, are wrapped around the limbs, usually in the evening before bedtime and following an emulsifying bath. The bandages encourage restful sleep, reduce

irritation and restrict opportunities to scratch. However, they are time consuming to apply and require dedication and commitment on behalf of the parent or carer. During the day a child wears the bandages, under their usual clothes.

PROGRESS CHECK

Which creams must be applied liberally and which type sparingly?

Activity
Plan a day's routine for a two-year-old boy with eczema. Include in your plan of activities things that will give him quick release of tension if he is frustrated.

GOOD PRACTICE

- It is unhelpful to tell a child not to scratch a severe itch – try not scratching yourself when you have intense irritation!
- Encourage the child to use pressure on the area or rub gently in a circular movement.
- Always keep the child's nails short and clean.

KEY POINTS

- Eczema is usually controlled and has few long-lasting physical effects, very rarely causing scarring. However, to many parents the good appearance of their child's skin is a sign of being a 'good carer' so great distress can be caused by the condition.
- Ensure everyone knows that eczema is not catching and is not caused by neglect or poor hygiene.

ONGOING MANAGEMENT

The skin dries more quickly in hot, dry atmospheres found in schools or playgroups, so it is important that a child can use his emulsifiers regularly during his school day. An application at breakfast will not last all morning, more will be needed to limit irritation and keep the skin in good condition.

Signs of discomfort in the child include:
- wriggling
- lack of concentration
- red and flushed skin
- irritability.

The table on page 210 gives suggestions on how to cope with the various potential stresses that may occur in children.

ECZEMA

Potential stresses for child	Coping suggestions
Soaps, detergents and paper towels can cause irritation.	Arrange for child to have their own aqueous soap substitute and access to cotton towels. (Parents/carers may wish to bring these in.)
Classroom is hot and dry, making irritation worse.	Position child away from radiators and sunny windows, have damp flannel available to cool down overheated limbs. Tights and woolly trousers increase itching. Keep emollients to hand, remembering younger children may need help applying them.
Seating arrangements can increase irritation, e.g. plastic chairs, storytime on a carpet with pile.	Provide cotton squares for chairs; temporarily cover carpet area with cotton sheet.
Messy activities provoke a skin reaction, e.g. sand, water, paint, dough and clay.	Encourage the use of cotton or even light plastic gloves. In an emergency tape plastic bags around wrists. Try to avoid stopping a child's involvement in an activity if possible. Liaise with parents/carers.
School meals are unsuitable; there is limited choice. Poor nutritional balance of 'allowed' foods.	Liaise with kitchen staff. Check everyone is aware of any dietary restriction. Suggest packed lunches if agreement cannot be reached. Monitor the suitability of any snacks given, e.g orange or milk drinks. Try and offer acceptable alternatives.
Swimming, especially in chlorinated pools, may dry and irritate the skin.	Encourage the use of emollients before swimming. Shower chlorine off after swimming then re-apply emollient. Allow privacy and additional time for this.
Child appears listless, sleepy and lethargic during the day.	Liaise with parents/carers, as this may be the effect of antihistamines. Provision of additional rest facilities might be needed for occasional short-term management.
Child continually scratches.	Try distraction activities: involve the child in small tasks, suggest a brief physical exercise. Remind the child to apply pressure and try not to scratch. Suggest finding a quiet space to apply emollient. Check nails are short and not increasing damage to skin. Is the child wearing too many clothes?
Child appears to be losing confidence, embarrassed about appearance of skin, reluctant to expose body (e.g. changing for games or swimming).	Challenge any teasing or name calling. Give physical contact, e.g. holding hands with child, which publicly reaffirms condition is not infectious. Check you are providing an easily available private area for changing, applying ointment, etc., so child is not singled out. Do not always comment on skin condition with parents/carers. **Key point:** put the child before the eczema.
There is chicken pox, cold sores or impetigo in the nursery/school.	Liaise with parents/carers and the school nurse. These conditions can cause serious complications if contracted by a child with eczema. Maintain routine measures for the prevention of infection, e.g. encourage effective hand washing for staff and children. Ventilate classrooms well. Keep environment clean, especially the furniture, lavatories, toys and teaching materials.
Developing fine manipulative control is painful and difficult with sore hands and fingers. Emollients leave greasy marks on paper and can cause slipping when holding pens, etc. Learning to write or paint activities are not going well.	Eczema is constantly changing and there are often good periods when the skin is clear. So if the skin is sore and cracked leave practising fine manipulative skills and associated activities for a while. Frustration over failure to achieve can make eczema worse. Reintroduce fine skill development when the skin is improved. Offer an alternative new challenge. Keep a calm matter-of-fact response. **Note:** computers and word processors are valuable aids as the child grows.
Handling the hairy or fluffy nursery pet makes the irritation worse.	Unfortunately it may be better to leave that specific animal alone; encourage involvement with other live creatures such as feeding the goldfish or developing a wormery.

The family pet may make eczema worse

PROGRESS CHECK

1   Look through your chosen outline plan of the week for your nursery or playgroup. Identify possible triggers in the chosen activities.
2   How could these activities be adapted?

GENERAL IMPLICATIONS

It is important for a child with eczema to remain positive. Symptoms usually can be controlled, and diminish with age; by thirteen years old 50 per cent of all affected children go into spontaneous remission. Managing his condition himself helps promote the child's own self-esteem, as he learns that he can help control his condition rather than the condition controlling him.

DEVELOPMENTS

New developments in the treatment of severe symptoms include possible forms of phototherapy. Infection control is now seen as important in the reduction of symptoms and increasingly antibiotic creams are being used, often replacing the need for topical steroids.

CASE STUDY

Jonny was four. He had had mild eczema since he was six months old. At times his eczema appeared as only minor with red scaly patches behind his knees and ears, but occasionally there were periods when several areas of his body were affected and bled after being scratched. These patches had sometimes become infected, once requiring admission to hospital.

Jonny used a variety of emollients to control his condition. However, he constantly woke at night with extreme irritation. He disturbed his two-year-old brother who shared his bedroom and woke his mother who slept in the next room. All the family, as a result, were exhausted and were finding it difficult to function effectively the next day.

Jonny attended a dermatology clinic and a meeting was arranged to reassess the effectiveness of his treatments.

As Jonny appeared most distressed at night this problem was discussed. It was suggested that his bathing routine was changed to exclude the use of the bubble baths that both brothers normally enjoyed together, lowering the water temperature and changing to using cotton pyjamas. The temperature of the bedroom was to be reduced and the central heating turned off overnight. Jonny was to stop using a duvet and to sleep under cotton sheets and blankets.

A strict policy of not allowing the family cat to sleep on the bed when Jonny was at nursery was introduced and Jonny was prescribed antihistamine medicine for use when his irritation was especially distressing. However, the procedures introduced for bedtime greatly reduced his night-time scratching and antihistamines were rarely required.

Jonny's mother had recently joined the National Eczema Society, which she found very supportive.

1   How could you ensure Jonny's skin was kept in good condition?
2   How could you reduce the chances of Jonny developing secondary skin infections?

RESOURCES

Kick Asthma
The website for children with asthma
www.kickasthma.org.uk

National Asthma Campaign
Summit House
70 Wilson Street
London EC2A 2DB
www.asthma.org.uk

National Eczema Society
Hill House
Highgate Hill
London N19 5NA
www.eczema.org

Diabetes

Diabetes is a common health condition, affecting about 2 per cent of the UK population. It runs in families and is second only to asthma in prevalence among schoolchildren. The incidence is increasing, particularly in young children aged between one and five years, where there has been an 11 per cent yearly rise since 1985. The reason for this is unknown but is thought possibly to include environmental factors.

Children are most likely to have the insulin-dependent variety of diabetes.

The condition is caused by a failure of the body to manage and control its use of carbohydrate and to a lesser extent fat and protein. Carbohydrates are found in starchy foods, such as bread, potatoes, pasta, cereals, and sweet foods such as cakes and pastries. All types of carbohydrates are broken down, during digestion, into glucose. Glucose is also made in the liver.

Diabetes cannot be cured, but it can be controlled effectively.

WHAT HAPPENS

The pancreas fails to work effectively. This organ, hidden underneath the stomach, has two main jobs:

1 to produce chemical enzymes that are released into the gut to break down food
2 to produce insulin, a hormone that controls the amounts of sugar released into the bloodstream. This sugar, or glucose, usually enters the cells and is used by the body as fuel.

A child with diabetes loses the ability to produce insulin. This is because the cells in the islets of Langerhans in the pancreas (see page 214) have lost their ability to work. Without their beta-producing insulin the child's body cannot use glucose and the blood glucose level rises. The kidneys work hard to get rid of the excess glucose in the urine, losing, in the process, large amounts of fluids. Without insulin the body cannot use the glucose, so the child loses weight and becomes listless. If the situation is not noticed he continues to lose fluids, becoming dehydrated and drowsy. In order to maintain his energy levels his body begins to break down fat causing keytones in the urine, which smell of pear drops. Coma, leading to death, will result if medical aid is not sought.

DIAGNOSIS

Signs that might indicate a child has diabetes are:
- thirst and dry mouth
- frequent trips to the lavatory
- weight loss
- tiredness
- bedwetting, especially in a child who was previously dry at night
- irritation around the genital area
- dry skin

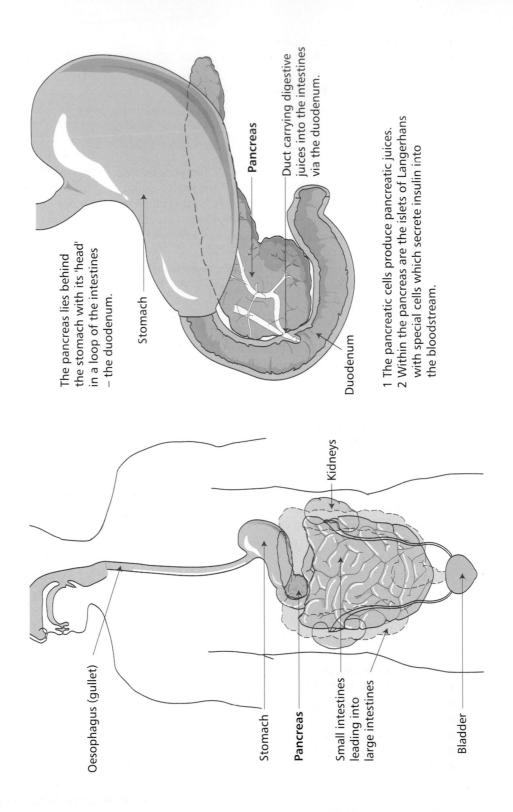

The pancreas lies behind the stomach with its 'head' in a loop of the intestines – the duodenum.

Stomach

Pancreas

Duct carrying digestive juices into the intestines via the duodenum.

Duodenum

1 The pancreatic cells produce pancreatic juices.
2 Within the pancreas are the islets of Langerhans with special cells which secrete insulin into the bloodstream.

Kidneys

Oesophagus (gullet)

Stomach

Pancreas

Small intestines leading into large intestines

Bladder

- frequent urinary tract infections
- in young babies a failure to thrive (remember diabetes is rare in babies under six months).

A final diagnosis is made by blood and urine tests.

CARE

The aim of management is to control the blood glucose level so that it does not rise too high – the term for this is *hyper*glycaemia. (The term for the blood glucose level being too low is *hypo*glycaemia.) Control is achieved by replacing the missing insulin by injections and by a special diet. Managing one of these areas without the other is ineffective; they are interlinked.

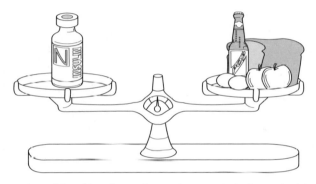

Keeping the scales of food intake and exercise evenly balanced with insulin given is the key to a healthy future for a child with diabetes

Insulin
Children with diabetes need regular insulin injections, usually twice daily, often before breakfast and the evening meal. Injections are needed as insulin is a protein so it cannot be taken by mouth – it is digested and neutralised by the stomach.

From about six years old, a child can be taught to give his own injections with a syringe or pen device. This encourages him to feel in control of his diabetes. These injections are accompanied by testing the blood glucose levels, usually by a simple finger-prick blood test. The blood is put on to a prepared reactive strip, which shows the level of glucose in the blood. The amount of insulin given may then be varied to meet individual need.

Good practice in managing injections
Inevitably the younger the child the more difficult is the idea of the dependence on daily injections, for the maintenance of life. This is true for parents/carers and child. Frequent finger pricks, too, may initially be distressing. How can you help him to adjust and adapt?
- Always tell the child what is going to happen; you will promote trust.
- Never surprise an unprepared child with a syringe or insulin pen.

- Always reward after an injection with a cuddle or praise.
- Understand his distress and encourage him to talk about it if he wishes.

KEY POINTS

- A child will get used to these procedures, especially if managed efficiently, calmly and as a regular part of a daily routine.
- As he grows he will be able to make the link between his injections, his diet and feeling well.
- The child will recognise the signs his body tells him when his insulin or diet are out of balance with each other.

Activity
Let a toddler practise his 'injections' on a teddy.

Practical issues

Insulin should be stored in the fridge, the type and amounts to be given carefully checked prior to each injection. Shake the phial as insulin has crystals that need dispersing.

If a pen device is used the insulin is contained within a cartridge and the dose dialled with a mechanism at one end of the pen so there is no drawing up of the insulin required. Needles are attached to the pen.

Injection technique will be taught at the special diabetic clinic for children and their carers. You may be required to support and help in the home, possibly giving the injections. In school these are mostly organised before or after lessons.

There are areas to consider when giving or supporting children having insulin injections:

- *Timing of injections:* these are arranged with the medical team, but usually happen twenty to forty minutes before a meal so the insulin starts working in the bloodstream at the same time as the carbohydrate from the meal. Too late (less than fifteen minutes) before a meal means that the blood glucose levels may be too high after the meal because the insulin was not available to help use it. But each child is an individual and his schedule will be arranged for his particular needs.
- *Air bubbles in a syringe:* these should be removed (by flicking it with your finger) as bubbles take up insulin space. This can cause inaccuracies in dosage.
- *Safety:* secure a toddler firmly, in your arms, if you are involved in helping another adult.
- *Cleaning the skin at the injection site:* out of a hospital environment normal hygiene measures are usually all that is required. Of course, wash hands before handling any equipment.
- *Injection areas:* usually a child rotates these around the body from upper thighs and arms to tummies and buttocks. Also, moving around within these areas is helpful in limiting 'fatty lumps' at injection areas.

- *Angles and areas:* the small, half-inch needle is inserted under the skin (subcutaneous) at an angle of 90 degrees. Lifting the skin slightly helps this.
- *Bruising or slight bleeding at the injection site:* this only means a small blood vessel has been punctured – it is harmless.
- *Disposal of needles and syringes:* the usual procedure is to keep all used equipment in a strong, plastic box (sometimes provided by the health authority). The hospital or health centre will arrange collection and disposal.

KEY POINTS

- Never put syringes and needles into the dustbin.
- Never use other people's syringes or needles.

PROGRESS CHECK

How would you respond to a four-year-old child who does not wish to have his injection today?

Diet

A specialist dietician will plan a child's diet in liaison with parents and carers, taking into account personal likes and dislikes and cultural and religious preferences.

Each child will have his own diet plan, involving the eating of the correct amounts as well as types of foods. Usually this means a healthy balanced diet that is low in sugar and saturated fat, and high in fibre. The diet should have variety and be designed to meet his growth needs from regular meals and snacks. Snacks are important as they prevent the child's blood sugar falling too low between meals.

Carbohydrate intake is controlled, especially those found in sugary foods – these quickly raise the blood glucose levels. Starchy carbohydrates take longer to digest and help maintain blood sugar levels, so are included more freely in the diet, e.g. bread, pasta, rice, potatoes and cereals.

Fibre-containing foods, especially oranges, lentils and beans, are all valuable in a diet for diabetes.

Foods containing polyunsaturated fats are included (fish, olive oils, etc.), but the amount of animal fats is limited. Trimming meat and removing the skin from chicken helps reduce fat content.

Promoting the habit of healthy eating is important. Encouraging the child not to develop a sweet tooth will be valuable in the long term. Remember, the diet is for life.

KEY POINTS

- If a child is hungry on his diet tell the parents/carers and dietician.
- Sweets and crisps can be eaten occasionally, but not too much or too often and within the overall diet plan.
- It is better to have an occasional treat than regularly to eat 'diabetic' jams, sweets and chocolates. They have no nutritional advantage and are expensive.
- A key factor in good management of the condition is the planning of a diet that a child enjoys – this helps him keep to the regime.

Sweets and crisps should be eaten only occasionally

Food refusal

Any child, especially around two to three years old, will have periods of exerting his independence over food and mealtimes. With diabetes, where regular food intake is essential, this can be an especially challenging time. Mealtimes can easily become a power battlefield if the tension from carers is transmitted to a determined toddler. The following are helpful suggestions:

- Never force a child to eat.
- Try to ensure he eats in company.
- Check his meals are attractive and the environment he eats in is appealing.
- Frequently offer foods the child likes. Keep a list of favourites from his diet. Try to rotate through the most nutritious.
- Only offer foods at snack and mealtimes.
- Do not overload plates in the hope he will eat 'something'.
- Never withhold puddings if a first course is refused; instead offer a second pudding.
- Always give drinks.
- Praise him when he eats, remove uneaten food without comment. Concentrate on the positive. Try to remain in control!
- Ensure all adults involved in his care are following the same policy.
- The dietician will always be available to offer advice on the telephone.

Hypoglycaemic and hyperglycaemic attacks

If the balance between insulin given and food eaten is wrong, in the short term, a hypoglycaemic attack will occur. The causes may be:

- too much insulin
- insufficient food, missed snack or meal

- strenuous physical activity without an adjustment to the carbohydrate intake
- sometimes illness.

The signs of an attack are:
- hunger
- pallor – especially of the face, recognisable in all skin colours
- shaking
- dizziness
- sweating
- tingling around the mouth
- dilated pupils
- mood changes
- irritability
- loss of concentration
- crying easily
- vagueness.

First aid

Immediately give a fast-acting carbohydrate such as a glucose tablet or a carton of sweetened fizzy drink. If the child is uncooperative and this is not possible try rubbing jam or a glucose gel on to his gums. Usually this will be effective in five to ten minutes.

Then follow up with a starchy carbohydrate to make sure the glucose level doesn't fall again – fruit or milk are ideal. Mild 'hypos' can occur often in some children and are easily managed without the need for outside help. However, on-going liaison with the specialist team for diabetes is important in preventing serious hypoglycaemic attacks. These can be especially dangerous in children under eight and can result in seizures as well as coma.

The signs of a hyperglycaemic attack are similar to those the child had when his diabetes was first discovered. The onset of a hyperglycaemic attack is much slower and is generally less common than a 'hypo'. Occasionally these attacks can be triggered by illness.

Check that the child's insulin injection wasn't overlooked and seek advice if you are worried.

PROGRESS CHECK

What are the signs of hyperglycaemia?

GOOD PRACTICE

- If a child shows any symptoms of a 'hypo' and you are unsure if his blood sugar level is low, treat as for a confirmed hypoglycaemic attack. He will not be placed in danger from this.
- Good communication between childcare workers and parents/carers mean a child's individual signs of low blood sugar are familiar to all involved in his care.

ONGOING MANAGEMENT

In the home

Care is the same as for any other child while maintaining his diet and insulin treatment. Allowing diabetes to become an excuse for giving in to all demands and leaving attention-seeking behaviour unresolved is unfair to the child. Although a sensitive approach to possibly unpleasant procedures is important, a child's social and emotional development is helped by the security of understanding the acceptable rules and routines of the family. Learning to live his her diabetes is important.

Physical care

Make sure good skin-care routines develop, as a child with diabetes may heal slowly and become vulnerable to infection. Check he has a daily bath and develops good hand-washing habits.

Watch to make sure clothing does not rub and shoes fit well. Keep nails trimmed regularly and liaise with medical staff if cuts and grazes appear not to be healing. Encourage regular visits to the dentist.

GOOD PRACTICE

Encourage all children with diabetes to wear some identification bracelet or necklace.

Care in the education environment

To help a smooth transition from home to school or playgroup some planning is needed. Remember, parents need to feel confident that you understand their child and his condition.

Before admission

Sharing and exchanging information is important and pre-visits vital. It is helpful for parents/carers to give written information about their particular child on:

- *hypoglycaemia:* the signs and individual symptoms
- *meal and snack times:* what should be eaten, and when
- *exercise and activity:* what preparation is necessary before and during any physical activity
- *emergency contacts:* names and numbers.

Organising the exchange of information before a child is admitted to school or playgroup allows time for the childcare workers to update their own knowledge on diabetes.

Discussion about the following will also be needed:

- where fast-acting sugars are kept and replenished
- how to manage a child with hypoglycaemia
- the importance of full involvement of the child in all activities
- how you will prepare the other children.

Recording information

A child with diabetes will need an individual record card with information on managing his condition. This is essential in any setting where staff are changing and may be unaware of procedures. This card should include medical contact numbers.

Diet

The diet plan from the hospital dietician must be available for staff involved in providing meals. Stress the importance of regular mealtimes.

Arrange facilities for eating any packed lunches. If having school meals he will need to be served first or go to the top of any canteen queue. Check all staff and children understand the reasons for this.

The importance of snacks will need to be reinforced, and these may have to be eaten in class or during a group time. Decide how you will manage this.

Physical activity

In order to fully involve a child with diabetes in all aspects of a school or playgroup, preparation or anticipation about the effects of certain activities will be necessary.

Extra glucose will be needed before vigorous games and occasionally afterwards as well. A younger child may need reminding to take his.

Illness

An unwell child, who is vomiting, may be unable to take his usual solid carbohydrate intake, so offer small, frequent amounts of *fluid* carbohydrates instead, for example glucose drinks. Do not stop or guess his insulin intake, but increase the monitoring of the sugar levels with urine or blood testing. Seek medical advice if the vomiting persists, or other worrying signs such as abdominal pain, breathing difficulties or sleepiness occur.

Trips and outings

On day trips out, remember to take glucose tablets and arrange for 'usual' meal breaks or snack opportunities – plan for any delays with sandwiches etc. Liaise with parents/carers regarding any special arrangements they feel will be necessary.

An older child involved in staying away overnight will need special arrangements for insulin injections and a wider sharing of information regarding food management.

PROGRESS CHECK

How could you give confidence to the mother of a five-year-old child with diabetes, who is to enter your reception class, that her child will be 'safe in your hands'?

Remember, a child with diabetes may need extra glucose after physical exercise

GENERAL IMPLICATIONS

Children with diabetes run greater risks of health problems in later life. These include damage to eyes with cataracts, kidney diseases, increased risks of strokes, heart attacks and gangrene.

These dangers are considerably lessened if a child's diabetes is well controlled when young. So your support, understanding and encouragement in helping him stick to dietary restraint and his insulin regime, is important. All children are resentful and rebellious at times, not wanting to be different from their peers, but with sensible management this is usually short-lived. Children find it difficult to think of themselves as 'old', so telling them they might get ill later if they don't 'follow the rules' will not be helpful. Praise him for being in control of his condition now.

CASE STUDY

Junior was an active, sociable seven-year-old boy who managed his diabetes effectively with insulin injections twice daily, before and after school.

His mother was pregnant and went into labour early one morning before Junior left home. The household was excited and anxious, but even in labour his mother supervised his early insulin injection before asking the neighbour to take him to school. Junior, in all the upheaval, had only a slice of toast, much less than his usual breakfast.

Later at school Junior refused to join in with another group of children and snatched work from his close friend and then sat silently at his table.

The teacher was a supply teacher who commented at breaktime in the staff room upon Junior's 'difficult' behaviour. The permanent staff were surprised as this was out of character, then another colleague casually mentioned Junior had diabetes. The supply teacher immediately gave Junior a drink of sweetened orange juice, followed by a sandwich.

1   What signs of diabetes was Junior displaying?
2   How could this situation be avoided in the future?

RESOURCES

Diabetes UK
Macleod House
10 Parkway
London NW1 7AA
www.diabetes.org.uk

HIV and AIDS

HIV (human immuno-deficiency virus) attacks the human immune system, which is the body's defence system against infection. HIV was first recognised in the US in 1981. Currently, in the UK, no other condition appears to provoke more fear or misunderstanding than HIV or AIDS (acquired immune deficiency syndrome). For children affected there is, in addition, the added distress of possibly having a parent also with the virus. On average two young children are orphaned for every woman killed by AIDS.

It is very difficult to accurately assess the numbers of affected children with the virus. By the end of June 2008, the number of people in the UK under the age of twenty years and known to be HIV positive was 760. Around 90 per cent of the transmission of the virus is from mother to baby, but infected blood products or contaminated needles continue to pose a threat. Approximately 1165 HIV positive women gave birth in the UK in 2007, the highest number ever recorded.

Despite the many research projects under way, and various developments in treatments, there remains no cure for the condition. Once a child is infected the virus cannot be completely eliminated from his system, nevertheless it can be suppressed and the symptoms controlled by current drug treatments.

KEY POINT

In some African countries, where access to expensive drug therapy is limited, children have experienced their whole families die from the effects of the virus.

What is the difference between HIV and AIDS?

A person who has contracted the HIV may feel completely fit and well, with no signs of ill health. In time he may develop a particular rare illness or cancer because his immune system is weakened. When this happens he is said to have AIDS.

At risk in Britain are:

- children who have HIV positive mothers
- babies breast-fed by a mother who is HIV positive
- children of fathers who are HIV positive (often where the father has haemophilia)
- children born in certain areas of Africa and, increasingly, India
- where parental HIV status is unknown
- children who have one, or both, HIV positive parents
- children who have an 'at risk' sibling, e.g. injecting drug user.

WHAT HAPPENS

HIV can affect various parts of the body's immune or defence system. The most important is the damage to special white blood cells known as CD4 or T-helper cells. These are found in the lymphatic system – in the glands and fluids circulating around the body. These cells are designed to trigger the immune system to protect the body when pathogenic or harmful organisms enter to cause disease.

In HIV the CD4 cells mount a defence against the HIV virus, often successfully for many years, but never fully destroying it and it continues to attack the CD4 cells. Eventually the number of these CD4 cells fall and the numbers of the virus rise. This may not happen for up to ten years or longer and one in twenty people affected are thought never to become ill.

When it does happen though, the child becomes vulnerable to a variety of infections, which would not affect someone with a healthy immune system. In a depleted immune system tumours, severe diarrhoea, rare pneumonia, skin cancers, damage to many organs and other serious conditions can occur – these are described as opportunistic infections or tumours.

In addition the virus can attack the cells directly in the brain, affecting its working.

KEY POINT

When a child has one or more of these opportunistic diseases, tumours or brain disease he is said to have AIDS.

Remember, though, a person can just be 'ill' during this period. Not all opportunistic illnesses are part of the AIDS definition – someone may just have a simple cold or flu.

PROGRESS CHECK

What is the difference between having HIV and having AIDS?

How does infection take place?

A sufficient amount of HIV must enter the bloodstream for a child to contract HIV. The virus is significantly contained in only:

- blood
- sperm and seminal fluid
- vaginal fluids, including menstrual fluids
- breast milk.

KEY POINT

Although HIV is present in other body fluids such as saliva, sweat or urine they do not contain enough virus to cause infection.

Even if HIV is present in a person's body fluids it is still difficult for it to enter another person's body easily. In addition, the virus itself is fragile and will not live outside the body. It can enter the body:

- directly into the bloodstream, e.g. through dirty injection needles
- through organ transplant or blood transfusion, but remember this no longer happens in the UK
- transfer through the mucous membrane – the rectum, vagina, etc.
- very rarely through the eyes, mouth or throat.

PROGRESS CHECK

Which body fluids are most likely to cause infection to children?

HIV, pregnancy and birth

Testing and treating HIV positive women with anti-viral drugs, in pregnancy, reduces the rate of transmission of the virus to the baby, to as little as 1 per cent. Without these precautions about 14 per cent of babies with HIV positive mothers will be infected and, if the baby is breast-fed, this rises to 25 per cent. Currently, there is no national routine screening programme. Selected screening does takes place in high-risk areas, particularly in London, where two-thirds of HIV positive births occur.

   Where the mother is known to be HIV positive, delivery of the baby by planned Caesarean section is recommended, in order to lessen the risk of virus transference.

GOOD PRACTICE

Remember, HIV *cannot* be transmitted through:

- intact external skin – so cover all cuts and grazes with a waterproof dressing.
- airborne routes – so coughing, sneezing and kissing are all safe.

DIAGNOSIS

HIV is usually diagnosed by a blood test known as an HIV antibody test. The test looks for antibodies formed by the immune system if HIV is present. However, there is a gap between when infection occurs and when antibodies are formed – this can last from a few weeks to three months.

KEY POINT

If antibodies are present a person is considered 'HIV positive' and although well can transmit the virus.

All babies born to mothers who are HIV positive will have HIV antibodies in their blood. These *maternal* antibodies remain in the child's blood for up to 12–15 months. However, this does not necessarily mean the baby is infected. A diagnosis can usually be made, by the time a baby is 3 to 4 months old, using a polymerase chain reaction (PCR) test, which tests for the presence of the actual virus in the baby's blood.

In Europe:

- Twenty per cent of babies born with HIV develop an AIDS-related illness, and half of these will die.
- Of those children who live for the first two years, 40 per cent will develop an AIDS-related illness before the age of 12 and 25 per cent will die.
- The average current life span of a child with HIV in Europe is ten years.
- Babies born to undiagnosed HIV positive mothers are especially vulnerable to infections, particularly pneumonia.

KEY POINT

- Over the past decade in the West, the use of combination anti-viral drug therapy has greatly enhanced life expectancy and quality of life.
- In the developing world, where treatments are not always readily available, death from AIDs-related illnesses continue. In Africa life expectancy for an untreated child with the virus is just five years.

CARE

The decision about whom to tell about HIV status either for themselves or their child is a major one for parents. This is often influenced by society's ignorance and fear about AIDS and HIV rather than what would be best for the child or family. If you are told a child in your care has the virus confidentiality must be respected.

Normally only childcare workers will have contact with a child with HIV; you are less likely to be caring for a child with AIDS as often specialist nursing care is required.

Breast-feeding

In the UK it is recommended that babies of HIV positive mothers are offered formula milk. This is because of the proven, increased risk of transmission of the virus, through breast-feeding.

In the developing world where water sources may not be clean it is thought that the dangers of HIV transmission are less than the dangers of waterborne illnesses, so breast-feeding remains the recommended method of infant feeding.

GOOD PRACTICE

- A clean environment with good hygiene measures should be routine in all childcare establishments. This is for the benefit of all – staff and children.
- If sensible procedures are followed parents should feel confident their children are safe.
- Consider your own policy regarding health and safety in your childcare establishment.

Good practice for all, with or without HIV, means the following.

- keeping to routine procedures for the disposal of blood and other body fluids such as:
  - clearing up all spills with very hot water or a bleach solution
  - using gloves so you can stand the high temperature
  - disposing of soiled napkins, vomit or urine or faeces accidents, into plastic sealed bags
  - clearly marking mops or cloths for use in mopping floors
  - disposing of cloths used to wipe up body spills.
- keeping your own skin in good condition, cover any sores or cuts with waterproof dressings
- no sharing of toothbrushes
- cleaning toys by regularly washing them, especially if sucked
- encouraging all children to develop healthy habits, especially hand-washing after using the lavatory and using tissues
- making sure everyone knows if there are outbreaks of infection in the establishment – chicken pox and measles might be very serious for a child with a damaged immune system
- excluding obviously infectious children and staff.

In addition a child with the virus will need:

- love, security, stimulation and opportunities to play, develop and learn
- regular medical checks
- routine immunisations but only following discussion with medical staff involved in care ('live' virus immunisations will be avoided, e.g. poliomyelitis)
- good dental care
- observation of any changes in his condition.

Encourage healthy habits

KEY POINT

The HIV virus is fragile and does not live outside the body, when exposed to air.

PROGRESS CHECK

How long may a child with HIV remain symptom-free?

Areas that might need additional consideration

Occasionally a frustrated toddler will bite another child – this really does not pose a risk as blood has to be exchanged for infection to be transmitted.

Ear piercing should always be undertaken by a reputable establishment – do not share children's earrings.

Using public swimming pools is safe – the virus cannot survive in chlorinated water.

GOOD PRACTICE

Demonstrate that a child is not infectious by routine hand holding, kissing and cuddling as with any other child.

ONGOING MANAGEMENT

Unlike those with many other serious conditions children who are HIV positive may also have ill parents, themselves anxious and fearful for the future. Worries they have about their child are to be expected, including what will happen when they die and what care arrangements, permanent or temporary, will be needed if they become ill. This is especially difficult when a very young child is involved. Always be ready to listen and respond to his times of distress, provide plenty of activities for him to release tension or talk about his worries.

A sensitivity and awareness from you, together with a knowledge of support networks and statutory services available, will be essential. Develop effective communication with all involved agencies.

Activity

Design a series of information posters, for the parents in your establishment, on how general infections are spread. Give examples of how specific illnesses may be spread; include HIV as one of your examples. Include a section on myths associated with the spread of ill health.

How can you make your posters catch and hold interest?

GENERAL IMPLICATIONS

Stigma, ignorance and fear regarding HIV and AIDS remain widespread. Parents are often reluctant to seek support from neighbours or friends and cope with the condition in secret. This particularly affects people from African and Indian communities, where the virus is prevalent. In addition they may also face racism and rejection.

For a child to be asked to keep information about HIV and AIDS secret places him under great strain and can isolate him from his peers.

Cultural factors and different child-rearing practices will all influence how parents reach major decisions about how much information to disclose. Support and advice will be available from within the caring specialist team. However, the final decisions made by the parents must be respected and supported.

Consider, too, that you may have to prepare the child for possibly losing a parent, even becoming ill himself, and be ready to answer questions about death.

KEY POINT

For a child in such a situation, the security of a normal routine, in a playgroup, nursery or school will be vital – it may be the only area of stability when many changes and worries are happening in the home. Allow the child to be 'normal' – naughty, active and energetic – but always applying the same rules of managing behaviour as with any child.

ADDITIONAL DEVELOPMENTS

At present there is no cure for HIV. Medical developments are concentrated on producing a vaccine to prevent transmission of the virus. The use of a combination of anti-viral drugs has been effective in prolonging both the quantity and quality of life for children with HIV. This success has, however, also resulted in a lowering of awareness, especially in young people, as to how the virus is transmitted. Care needs to be taken that 'at risk' behaviour does not re-emerge in the mistaken belief that HIV and AIDs can be cured.

Bonnie's Poem
I do not like having HIV
Because sometimes it stings me like a bee.

I do not like it being a secret
But I promised I would keep it.

When I play I want to say I have HIV
But no – it's a secret
And I keep it to myself.

Bonnie died of AIDS at twelve years old, infected after her mother was given a contaminated blood transfusion during her pregnancy. Bonnie's poem appears to show that keeping the secret, for Bonnie, was almost as stressful as being HIV positive.

The poem is printed with the kind permission of Bonnie's brother, Joshua Handel.

RESOURCES

Children with AIDS Charity (CWAC)
Calvert House
5 Calvert Avenue
London E2 7JP
www.cwac.org

Terrence Higgins Trust
314–320 Gray's Inn Road
London WC1X 8DP
www.tht.org.uk

The coeliac condition

This condition has been known under a variety of names for centuries and until the mid-1950s was thought to affect only children. It is now known to occur in both adults and children, happening at any age and affecting one in 1100 to 1500 people.

The condition produces a sensitivity to gluten – a protein found in wheat and rye – and a similar reaction to substances in barley and possibly oats. This means foods such as bread, rolls, buns, biscuits, pastry and pasta must be excluded permanently from the diet.

The coeliac condition can 'run' in families, although a genetic pattern has not yet been identified. It cannot be cured and is life long, but it is effectively controlled by a special diet for life.

WHAT HAPPENS

Gluten, a protein found in certain cereals, damages the lining of the small intestine, so reducing the amount of gut available to absorb nutrients. The signs do not become obvious until gluten has been introduced to a child's diet – usually at the time of weaning at four to six months. Up until that time the child is thriving, alert and interested. Then she:
- begins to refuse food
- fails to gain weight
- is lethargic, irritable and listless
- passes abnormal stools that are usually large, pale and offensive or loose and diarrhoea-like
- may vomit

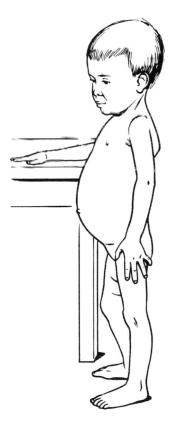

An untreated child with the coeliac condition is typically lethargic with a distended stomach and wasted buttocks

- begins to have increased body-wasting, especially the buttocks, and her stomach protrudes
- has severe illness and dehydration may appear.

In the older child the following may also appear:
- poor appetite
- anaemia – pallor, breathlessness and tiredness
- growth failure
- colicky stomach pains.

DIAGNOSIS

A simple test, not requiring admission to hospital, is undertaken. Under sedation a **biopsy** capsule is passed through the mouth, with X-ray control, into the upper part of the small intestine and a biopsy sample is taken.

The cells will appear abnormal. A second biopsy may be taken later to confirm the diagnosis and if the results are positive then a gluten-free diet for life is recommended.

CARE

The basis of care is to remove all gluten-containing food from the diet for life. After diagnosis the following may also be recommended for a few months:
- a diet with a reduced fat intake, to allow 'healing' of the gut
- extra vitamin D, folic acid and iron
- ocassionally limited sugars, as they can stimulate diarrhoea.

KEY POINT

The three measures listed above are usually only advised for a short period.

In a young baby choosing gluten-free baby foods is simple, since all commercial products are clearly identified. A benefit to introducing this diet early is that a baby will develop tastes for foods that will not damage his health, rather than have to change formed eating patterns later in life.

When following the diet, a baby with coeliac condition will have gradually improved health, growth and weight. Usually by a year, he will no longer have the offensive and bulky stools, have gained weight and will be thriving. There will be no return to the signs of the condition if the diet is maintained.

How do families avoid foods with gluten and also, possibly, barley and oats?
Coeliac UK (see Resources, page 236) produces a yearly list of foods, regularly updated, that contain gluten and so must be avoided – this list should be taken on every shopping trip as products frequently have their ingredients changed.

Gluten-free flours, breads and cakes can be obtained, often on prescription from the family doctor, and traditional recipes can be easily adapted with a little practice. Many foods readily available are also gluten-free.

KEY POINT

Most plainly prepared natural foods, apart from wheat, rye, barley and oats, can be eaten.

Plainly prepared natural foods that can be eaten include the following:
- gluten-free flour, potato, rice and soya flours and arrowroot
- sago, tapioca, maize, buckwheat and rices
- butter, fats and oils, eggs, milks, cheeses (unprocessed) and natural yoghurt
- 'pure' herbs
- pure fruit and vegetable juices, raw or frozen fruits and vegetables
- meat, poultry and fish – care is needed only with products involving processing, stuffing and coatings
- nuts.

In addition, many other foods can be included but their contents must be checked on the packaging against Coeliac UK's list.

KEY POINTS

- Foods containing the following ingredients are unacceptable: cereal binders, starch, food starch, edible starch, modified starch, rusk, stabilisers, cereal fillers and cereal protein.
- Remember, too, that flour is an ingredient in many tinned and processed foods, as well as in ready-prepared meals.

The pre-school child

Useful ways of managing the child's diet within the family can include the following:
- removing all flour from family cooking – gluten-free alternatives may be included if wished
- offering the same food to all the family and visitors
- accepting invitations out, but let the child take his own 'gluten-free' biscuits with him if he wishes
- not blaming every minor stomach upset on the child's 'condition'
- clearly explaining to all involved in the child's care what he can have
- always telling the child why certain foods are not allowed and linking your explanations to his remaining healthy – be matter-of-fact
- not discussing the child's symptoms or his diet routinely before him – he must learn to accept it as an integral part of his life.

It is often easier for a whole family to follow a gluten-free diet rather than isolate a child from sharing family foods, as a gluten-free diet is essentially a healthy diet for all.

PROGRESS CHECK

What are the physical and emotional advantages of cooking gluten-free food meals for all the family rather than producing special foods for the child with coeliac condition?

Are the ingredients gluten-free?

KEY POINT

Many other children are also not offered foods that are harmful to a child with coeliac condition, for example biscuits, ice creams and carbonated drinks. This helpful practice has the benefit of reducing the isolation of the child with the coeliac condition from his peers.

ONGOING MANAGEMENT

A child who is diagnosed with the condition as a baby will have considerable knowledge of his own diet by the time he needs school dinners. He should be empowered to control his own diet and support must be given to allow this.

All involved in his care, including dinner supervisors as well as teaching and care staff, will need to know what is acceptable.

It is always preferable for a child to be the same as his peers, so if they all take packed lunches that will be fine for him, but if school dinners are the norm then he should not be excluded because of his dietary needs. Some authorities cope better than others with special diets, but it must be emphasised that a child with this condition will be healthy, fit and active, providing he adheres to the gluten-free diet. He will have no external signs of his condition.

Special awareness will be needed for:

- parties
- school trips and outings
- changes of staffing at dinner times
- when the child is unwell. He may show signs of intolerance, by fatty stools or diarrhoea, but this does not necessarily mean he has been given gluten.

GOOD PRACTICE

If the child inadvertently takes gluten he may have diarrhoea or stool abnormalities – this may happen within twenty-four hours or up to two or three weeks. No long-term harm occurs, providing the incident is an isolated one.

Activity

Plan a cake baking session for a group of five-year-olds. Identify all your usual learning outcomes for a cookery activity. Ensure your recipe is gluten-free – what 'flour' could you use instead? Research any changes needed to the method for the cake to rise successfully.

Take a group of children with you to buy the ingredients. Look for the contents of the packages in your supermarket visit – how easy did you find it to discover if gluten was included?

GENERAL IMPLICATIONS

While a matter-of-fact approach to the coeliac condition is helpful, it must be remembered there is no cure, only management. Failure to consistently maintain a gluten-free diet can result in health problems in adulthood. These include, in women, an increased risk of miscarriage, low birthweight babies and osteoporosis, and, in both men and women, a raised incidence of bowel cancers.

ADDITIONAL DEVELOPMENTS

Coeliac UK provide the cross-grain symbol under licence for use on food products and promotional product literature. The symbol, indicating that a product is gluten-free, enables those caring for children with coeliac condition to buy appropriate, safe foods.

A new blood spot test that can be done in a local surgery is currently in development, which will help early and quick diagnosis of the coeliac condition.

Conor was a four-year-old boy, the middle child with an older sister and younger toddler brother.

He had always been more demanding than his siblings and was noted to be sickly. He often had periods of stomach upsets and this was the reason his parents gave for his poor appetite, slimness and short stature.

After he started at playgroup he began to have more frequent bouts of diarrhoea, his stools became offensive and he also developed sore buttocks. An infection going around the nursery was blamed. However, Conor continued to appear 'off colour' and eventually the family doctor decided he needed further investigation. A biopsy was taken from his intestine and coeliac condition was clearly identified. He started a gluten-free diet immediately.

Several months later Conor had gained weight, his stools were normal and he was much more outgoing and relaxed. He still remained short in comparison to his peers, but as both his parents are also small this was thought to be related more to their stature, than his coeliac condition.

1   Why do you think discovery of the condition took so long?
2   What other common illnesses may the coeliac condition be confused with?
3   How will Conor's height and weight be measured to monitor his progress?

RESOURCES

Coeliac UK
Suites A–D Octagon Court
High Wycombe
Bucks HP11 2HS
www.coeliac.org.uk

KEY TERMS

You need to know what these words and phrases mean. Go back through the chapter and make sure that you understand:

'absences'
AIDS and the transmission of the
    virus
asthma
atopic
coeliac condition and gluten
    intolerance
diabetes
epilepsy

eczema
gluten
HIV
hypoglycaemia and hyperglycaemia
preventers and relievers
spacers and inhalers
tonic/clonic seizures
trigger factors

7 *INHERITED CONDITIONS*

> ## This chapter covers:
> ■ **Sickle cell and thalassaemia conditions**
> ■ **Cystic fibrosis**
> ■ **Haemophilia**
> ■ **Duchenne muscular dystrophy**
> ■ **Managing medicines in a school, nursery or playgroup**
> ■ **Anaphylaxis**

At the beginning of this chapter we look at certain inherited physical conditions that are transferred genetically from parent to child. In the next part we study the administration and safe storage of medicines in care settings, together with a brief overview of the management of anaphylactic shock in young children.

Sickle cell and thalassaemia conditions

These are the names given to a group of lifelong blood disorders that affect specific racial groups.

Sickle cell

Sickle cell is a genetically inherited condition, commonly found in people of Afro-Caribbean (i.e. African or West Indian) descent. The disease is known in some African languages as 'a state of suffering'. It also occurs in people from the Eastern Mediterranean, the Middle East, India and Pakistan.

Sickle cell is a lifelong condition affecting children from birth. It is thought that one in 500 live births worldwide will have sickle cell condition. Currently there is no cure.

The sickle cell condition is a term given to a group of blood disorders in which abnormal haemoglobin is produced. Haemoglobin is a special protein found in the red blood cells and is responsible for carrying oxygen around the body. Sickle haemoglobin is one of a number of types of haemoglobin. Under certain conditions called 'crisis' the red blood cells in the body change shape. Children with sickle cell condition have low haemoglobin levels because the red blood cells do not last as long as normal blood cells.

WHAT HAPPENS

The sickle cell condition can affect children in two main ways: they may have the sickle cell trait, which means that they are carriers, but healthy, or they may have the condition of sickle cell anaemia.

Sickle cell trait

Genes come in pairs. Each characteristic will have a gene from both mother and father, e.g. colour of hair and physical features. One of these pairs of genes determines haemoglobin – sickle cell trait means that one haemoglobin gene from one parent carries the sickle cell gene, which is HB AS (see opposite).

If a child has the trait it means that she is a healthy carrier and will never develop the condition.

However, it may have implications for her own children. If her partner does not have the trait then all her children will never have the condition. One in ten Afro-Caribbeans have sickle cell trait, which means although perfectly healthy they are carriers of the condition.

Sickle cell condition

If two carriers have a child, there is a one-in-four chance that the child will have sickle cell anaemia. A baby initially appears fit and well with no apparent problems often until four to six months of age. The baby then shows signs of being anaemic including:

- a lack of energy
- listlessness
- poor circulation to hands and feet
- vulnerability to minor infections such as coughs and colds.

DIAGNOSIS

Pre-natal diagnosis is available if both partners are carriers. Sickle cell condition is easily detected at birth by examining a sample of the umbilical cord blood. This allows important preventive measures to start early. These can limit the triggers that promote crisis.

A crisis causes:

- pain
- possible damage to vital organs.

Children in the steady state (between crises) are anaemic due to rapid destruction of the red blood cells, but not from lack of iron. Iron tablets are not recommended and may in fact be harmful. Occasionally the anaemia can deteriorate rapidly and then urgent blood transfusion may be required.

Sometimes parents find it difficult to accept their baby has a life-threatening condition when the baby appears so well.

SICKLE CELL TRAIT - HOW INHERITANCE IS PASSED

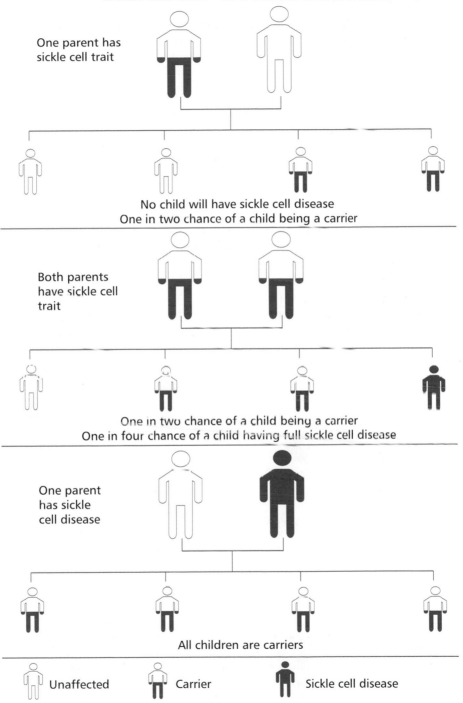

One parent has sickle cell trait

No child will have sickle cell disease
One in two chance of a child being a carrier

Both parents have sickle cell trait

One in two chance of a child being a carrier
One in four chance of a child having full sickle cell disease

One parent has sickle cell disease

All children are carriers

Unaffected   Carrier   Sickle cell disease

NOTE: In each of these examples these chances happen with <u>every</u> pregnancy.

CARE

Sickle cell is characterised by crises in the condition. These happen when the abnormal haemoglobin changes shape from the usual round one to that of a sickled or crescent moon. The cells become rigid and 'sickling' – clumping together. These sickled cells then get stuck in the small blood vessels, often blocking the blood supply to tissues. This can happen anywhere in the body causing severe pain and often slight fever and damaging the affected area. The severe pain associated with crises is frequently in the limbs, back and abdomen. Sometimes these crises happen often and sometimes only once in several years.

What can trigger a crisis?
The following may promote a crisis:

- infection from minor coughs and colds, to common childhood infections such as measles, chicken pox, etc
- dehydration (lack of fluid) such as inadequate fluids in sudden heatwaves
- extremes of cold such as cold swimming pools, unheated classrooms and bedrooms
- stress or distress such as starting a new school, divorce in the family or worries over academic success
- strenuous physical exercises: even normal school games or energetic games with peers

However, there may be no obvious cause.

Strenuous activity may trigger a crisis

KEY POINT

Pain can be exceptionally severe during a crisis.

GOOD PRACTICE

While waiting for medical advice the following may be helpful:
- Support painful limbs and position carefully.
- Local heat or massage may be comforting.
- Give medication if prescribed.
- Songs and stories may give useful distraction.

Children in crisis are initially treated in hospital with oxygen, fluids, blood transfusions, painkillers and often antibiotics.

ONGOING MANAGEMENT

- Maintain good health with freedom from as many infections as possible.
- Protect by routine courses of immunisation.
- Provide a balanced diet, love, security, stimulation and association, as with any child.
- Check that you are using positive images of children from a variety of backgrounds in your displays and educational material.
- Assess the cleanliness of your environment (see Cystic fibrosis, page 251 and follow the Progress check on page 242).
- Consider that children will need frequent drinks and as a result may need more changes of nappies or visits to the toilet.
- Check that the skin remains in good condition.
- Bedwetting or **enuresis** is more likely for a child with sickle cell. It is due to a delay in the ability of the kidney to concentrate large quantities of dilute urine. Stigma related to enuresis can affect a child's peer relationships and make her reluctant to sleep away from home and for older children school visits can be particularly daunting. Liaison with parents and carers is essential, together with careful planning, sensitivity and understanding, to help lessen the stress for the child.
- Strenuous sports and playtimes in wet or cold playgrounds are best avoided.

GOOD PRACTICE

- Check that all staff are aware of the potentially serious nature of the condition and sensitive to the particular anxieties of the parents.
- As the condition affects the blood, ensure everyone is aware that the condition is not infectious and cannot be transmitted.
- Ensure your knowledge of sickle cell is accurate and current.
- Can you answer children's questions honestly, with knowledge and in accordance with parental wishes?
- Maintain good liaison with all the care team including parents/carers.

If a child has only rare crises then normal play, schooling and peer relationships should not be affected.

A child who is more seriously ill, however, may feel isolated, especially if there is no other child with the condition in her family or school. She may feel frightened, especially as she grows and becomes more aware that severe complications and possible early death may occur. Previous experiences of severe pain are not easily forgotten and can affect a child's confidence. Frequent absences from school or playgroup may affect developing relationships or academic progress, possibly leading to low self-esteem.

Staff can help by listening, understanding, acknowledging fears and by developing positive relationships with parents.

PROGRESS CHECK

1 What playgroup or school situations might trigger a crisis?
2 What signs tell you a child is having a crisis?
3 Do you have emergency telephone contact numbers readily available?
4 Are these telephone contact numbers updated regularly?

Activity

For children often away from school involve your infant class in making a Class Diary to keep absent friends involved. This can be given or sent to the child at home or in hospital and could provide a useful link to limit feelings of isolation. Include drawings, examples of work, personal messages, tapes and photographs.

GENERAL IMPLICATIONS

Additional health complications

Children with the condition are especially vulnerable to the following illnesses:

- infections, especially severe ones such as meningitis and pneumonia
- strokes (clots in the brain that can deprive vital areas of the brain of blood). About 6–9 per cent of young children are at risk of sickling episodes that can result in transient or permanent strokes. Signs of these are weakness in limbs, slurred speech and severe headaches. They are a major cause of disability
- jaundice – yellowing in the whites of the eyes. This is not infectious.

KEY POINTS

■ Various counselling agencies are being developed in areas with high incidence of sickle cell. They offer information, advice and support by post and in person. These information sources are especially important when sickle cell affects a child in an area where it has previously been uncommon.

■ Remember, too, that more than one child in a family may be affected.

ADDITIONAL DEVELOPMENTS

Scientists are currently concentrating on two new aspects of developments. The first is attempting to modify the affects of the condition by investigating various techniques to reduce the damage to the red cells. The second is in research for a cure by using bone marrow transplantation and **gene therapy**.

Improved management of sickle cell condition means that while, as recently as the 1960s, most children did not survive their childhood, by 1997 a study found that, depending on the severity, between 85 and 95 per cent of affected children now live into adulthood.

Thalassaemia

Thalassaemia is a general term for a number of inherited blood disorders in which there is insufficient haemoglobin. Specific racial groups at risk are children from southern Mediterranean countries and the Middle East. Occasionally children from Asia and Africa are affected but rarely those from northern European parentage. As with sickle cell this is a **genetic** condition, passed from parent to child. It cannot be contracted in other ways.

WHAT HAPPENS

Thalassaemia trait
Children carrying the trait are normally healthy but may have mild anaemia shown by occasional tiredness, breathlessness and pallor. Their life is not shortened.

Thalassaemia major
In thalassaemia major a child appears well at birth but within months becomes pale and irritable, has a poor appetite and fails to thrive. There is no cure for the condition and without treatment a child would die in infancy.

DIAGNOSIS

Diagnosis can be made before birth either by chorionic villus sampling (looking at a small piece of placental tissue through the cervix at ten to twelve weeks), by foetal blood sampling at eighteen to twenty weeks of pregnancy or, after birth, by a blood test of the baby.

THALASSAEMIA - HOW INHERITANCE IS PASSED

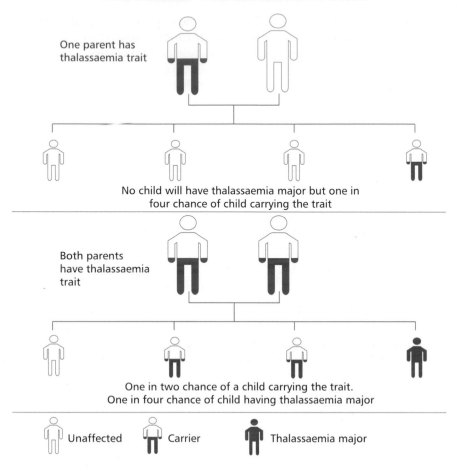

One parent has thalassaemia trait

No child will have thalassaemia major but one in four chance of child carrying the trait

Both parents have thalassaemia trait

One in two chance of a child carrying the trait.
One in four chance of child having thalassaemia major

Unaffected   Carrier   Thalassaemia major

CARE

Symptoms are controlled by regular blood transfusions. However, as a result of these, too many iron-rich red blood cells can accumulate in the body with possible damage to vital organs like the heart and liver. Regular, often daily drugs, given by injections under the skin, are essential to help reduce this. Children are usually given these drugs at night via a portable pump attached to a needle. This allows the treatment to be given over many hours. This treatment can be unpleasant and difficult for a child to live with. Unfortunately, without such treatment a child would die in infancy and so it must be maintained and continued for life. Support for parents and the child may be available, if requested, from one of the specialist counselling agencies.

ONGOING MANAGEMENT

With effective treatment a child can attend and thrive in any childcare setting from playgroup to mainstream school. Check, however, if a child is tired and needs extra rest during a busy school or playgroup session.

GENERAL IMPLICATIONS

In sickle cell and thalassaemia the conditions can be passed on to future generations from carriers who are well in themselves. Genetic counselling regarding the risk for future pregnancies is usually offered.

Points to consider
- Why do you think both sickle cell and thalassaemia, which are genetically passed blood disorders, are relatively poorly understood by the population?
- How can knowledge of these conditions be increased?

ADDITIONAL DEVELOPMENTS

Researchers think that it may be possible in the future to 'reverse the foetal switch' whereby children with thalassaemia can make foetal haemoglobin again as they did in the womb. They would then be able to make their own blood and would not require transfusion. It may also be possible at some stage in the future to replace the thalassaemia gene with a normal gene to cure the disease completely.

CASE STUDY

Daisy was a six-month-old baby brought to England, on holiday, from Jamaica by her mother, to meet her aunts and uncles. The weather was cold and Daisy appeared generally off-colour, unhappy and with a runny nose. She deteriorated and became inconsolable, screaming and crying. Her hands and feet became inflamed.

Her mother took her to the local hospital and she was admitted for investigation and tests. She was fed by a 'drip' and sedated. Her mother was told that Daisy was having a sickle cell crisis. She was unaware that Daisy had the condition and was greatly upset as one of her brothers had died of the condition a few years previously. She was referred for genetic counselling and support.

1 Would Daisy be better returning with her mother to Jamaica? If you think so, explain why.
2 What special precautions should her mother take during the next few years with her physical health?

RESOURCES

Sickle Cell Society
54 Station Road
London NW10 4UA
www.sicklecellsociety.org

UK Thalassaemia Society
19 The Broadway
Southgate Circus
London N14 6PH
www.ukts.org

Cystic fibrosis

Cystic fibrosis (CF) is the UK's most common, life-threatening, inherited disease. The abnormal gene responsible makes secretions that are thicker and stickier than usual, and contain a high proportion of salt. This results in damage to the lungs and digestive system.

Research from the Cystic Fibrosis Trust has found that in 1964 life expectancy for a child with CF was 5 years, today this has risen to 31 years. One person in 25 is a carrier of the CF gene (more than 2.3 million people in the UK) and of the 75,000 people in the UK with CF, 6000 are aged 25 or under. Five babies are born weekly with CF.

CF remains incurable but early diagnosis and treatment limits both the amounts of ill health a child experiences and the damaging effects to the vital organs. People with the abnormal gene are healthy but are 'carriers' of the condition. A child will have a one-in-four chance of being affected if both parents have the carrier gene.

WHAT HAPPENS

Although any organ can be affected by the thicker secretions produced by the abnormal gene the most likely to be affected are the respiratory and digestive systems.

Respiratory system
Damage to the lungs is the most serious worry. The sticky mucus the condition produces is difficult to move to the top of the lungs where, usually, it would be coughed up or swallowed. As a result bacteria build up in the smaller airways, making the lungs liable to infection. The linings of the airways become swollen, and produce more mucus to try and get rid of the increased bacteria.

CYSTIC FIBROSIS INHERITANCE

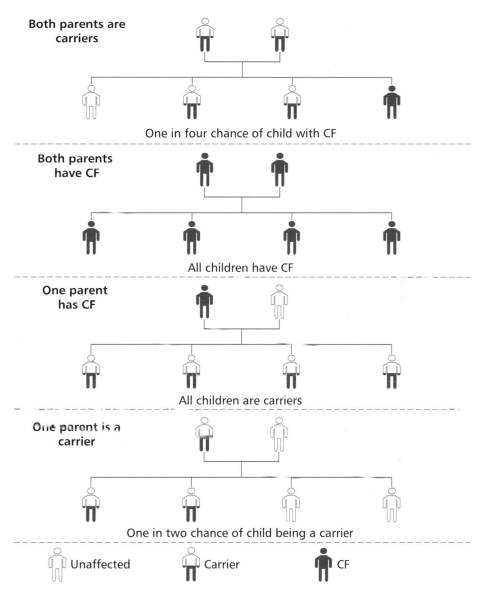

Both parents are carriers

One in four chance of child with CF

Both parents have CF

All children have CF

One parent has CF

All children are carriers

One parent is a carrier

One in two chance of child being a carrier

Unaffected   Carrier   CF

KEY POINT

Repeated infections can cause scarring of the lungs.

Digestive system

The pancreas, the organ that produces insulin and digestive juices, is affected. In cystic fibrosis the digestive juices are thick and can block the duct system where the juices are secreted into the intestines (see the diagram on page 214).

Sometimes this effect takes several months to become apparent. The lack of digestive juices inhibits a child's ability to use her food, especially fats and, to a lesser extent, protein. These nutrients are lost and excreted in the stools.

Meconium ileus

In about 10 per cent of children with cystic fibrosis the baby is born with a meconium ileus. Here the duct from the pancreas is already blocked and the baby has a severe obstruction. She is unable to pass her meconium or first stool. This must be cleared to allow the baby to feed and excrete normally.

DIAGNOSIS

It is not always obvious that a baby has the condition. If she has a meconium ileus this is a dramatic and obvious sign of something seriously amiss.

Other signs in the young baby can occur:

- The mother notices her baby's skin tastes salty when kissed.
- The baby coughs and wheezes.
- The baby fails to gain weight, even though she eats well, in sufficient amounts and appears hungry.
- The baby's stools are bulky, passed often and unpleasantly smelly – this may result in a sore nappy area.
- The baby often vomits when coughing.

Sometimes very few signs are evident and a child may just have a cough and fail to gain weight during her first year.

Confirmation that a child has the condition is made by a 'sweat test' at the hospital. She will also have a chest X-ray to assess if any lung damage has occurred. In Scotland, every new baby is screened at birth by a simple heel-prick blood test.

Recent developments have shown that the abnormal gene can be identified during pregnancy.

KEY POINT

Early diagnosis is important in order that treatment can start immediately to limit the damage to important organs, especially the lungs.

CARE

The prime aims of management are threefold:

- maintenance of nutrition
- prevention and control of lung infections
- physiotherapy and exercises to keep the airways clear.

Nutrition

Even though a child may be eating well her body will be unable to use the food without replacing the pancreatic enzymes. The enzyme is given usually, approximately fifteen minutes before every meal. This replacement has to be continued for life. If not, the child will lose weight, fail to grow and be vulnerable to increased and possibly dangerous, lung infections.

- The diet itself will be high in calories – it is estimated that the child will need a minimum of 20 per cent extra calories than her peers and possibly as much as 100 per cent more.
- The child will require at least three meals daily with two extra snacks.
- The diet will be devised by the paediatric dietician and the paediatrician in conjunction with the parents, carers and the child herself when older.
- The balance between pancreatic replacement and the calorie intake is important.
- Even with enzyme replacement food absorption is not perfect and so the quality of the diet will be important. The child cannot afford to fill up regularly on junk foods or foods with only limited nutritional content. This would leave no room for important body-building nutrients such as proteins. The child needs stores of body fat as an insurance policy for when she may have infections and lose appetite and suffer temporary weight loss.
- Usually the child will be given vitamin A, D, E and K replacements to compensate for those lost because of her difficulty in absorbing fat.
- Fat as part of the child's diet is limited only if she continues to have trouble with digestion. This is shown by continuing, bulky, greasy stools, abdominal pain and failure to gain expected weight.

Diet management for particular developmental stages

Babies
- Although breast milk is the ideal milk for babies, in cystic fibrosis it is important that feeds are frequent.
- Small amounts of pancreatic enzyme will be needed.
- If babies are artificially fed, a modified milk higher in energy and protein than the usual formula milks is recommended for up to one year of age.

GOOD PRACTICE

Never mix medicine into a baby's bottle as you may find the baby rejects her milk. If this happened you would not be able to tell how much medicine had been taken.

Weaning
- A baby with cystic fibrosis may be especially hungry and often will need solids from three months.
- The usual weaning practice is followed, with the pancreatic enzyme increasing with the food.

The toddler

The normal food refusal that can occur at this age may make mealtimes testing for parents and carers. Pancreatic enzymes can be unpalatable and will need to be mixed with an acceptable food such as teaspoons of apple purée or yoghurt – whatever the child prefers.

Food fads normally resolve of their own accord if calmly managed – never withhold food if something is refused. Offer an acceptable 'nutritious' alternative.

Schoolchildren

Eating away from home means the child is controlling her own diet. All carers need to know:

- the child's special nutritional needs
- the child's need to take enzyme replacement at every meal
- where her medicines will be stored and that there are sufficient supplies
- if the daily snacks – which the child will need – can take place in the classroom
- how her dietary choice and intake will be monitored
- extra food will be needed if the child is involved in physical activity
- extra salt will be necessary in very hot weather or after strenuous activity.

GOOD PRACTICE

A child may feel embarrassed at needing medication at every meal – she may feel the need to be the same as her peers. Try to ensure she has privacy to take the medication.

PROGRESS CHECK

Why does a child with cystic fibrosis need extra calories?

Prevention and control of lung infection

The main aim is to keep the lungs as free from damage by infection as possible. This is important in extending both life and its quality.

Often children are maintained on continuing antibiotic medicine. Any new infection needs prompt attention. Some children are given medication via a nebuliser or spacer (see page 198–9). Develop your own observation skills in watching for changes in the child's condition.

You should try to maintain a clean environment by:

- providing good ventilation in the prevention of airborne infections
- the disposal of used tissues into covered bins
- encouraging hand-washing after using tissues
- encouraging covering noses and mouths when sneezing – adults and children!
- trying to stop contact with adults and children who have coughs and colds but without becoming over-protective
- keeping the environment from becoming overcrowded

- ensuring everyone involved with the child with cystic fibrosis, including parents and all carers, have current immunisations
- maintaining good levels of general hygiene
- informing parents and carers when there are outbreaks of infections.

PROGRESS CHECK

1 How can you protect a child, vulnerable to infection, without smothering her?
2 How clean is your childcare environment?
3 How free from infection are the staff?
4 Are all staff protected from transmitting infections, by available immunisation?
5 How effective is the prevention of infection routine in your workplace?
6 How often do you reassess your health practice?
7 Have the staff received recent training?

Physiotherapy and exercises to keep the lungs clear

Even if a child appears symptom-free the importance of measures to help clear her lungs remains vital. These measures are essential in helping to keep the lungs clear and expanded. In children the following methods will be used.

1 *Drainage* – positioning a child to clear different areas of the lungs.
2 *Chest clapping* – a cupped hand is used to clap the chest firmly.
3 *Chest shaking* – place your hands on the chest, tell the child to breathe out and firmly shake the chest, squeezing the air out in short bursts and applying the pressure inwards.
4 *Breathing exercises*.

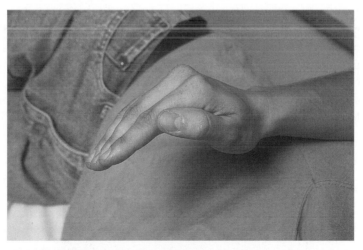

Chest clapping: the chest is 'clapped' firmly to help loosen secretions and encourage the child to cough. Note the cupped position of the hand for chest clapping

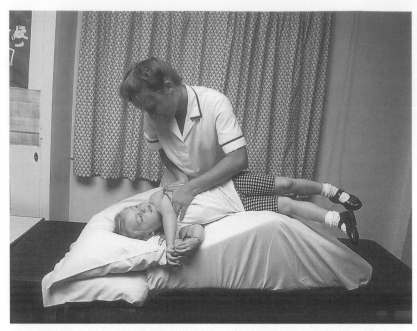

Chest shaking: while the child breathes out, the chest is shaken – pressing and squeezing the air out – so coughing is stimulated and secretions brought up. Note the child is tilted to help drainage

How often and for how long should physiotherapy take place?

- *Length:* this will vary depending on the number and type of secretions a child is producing at any time, but will range from 10–15 minutes to 45–60 minutes.
- *Number of sessions:* usually two per day when she is well, to three or four during times of infections.
- *Changes to the above:* the carer involved in the treatments will learn by experience the need to change the types and amounts of treatment, by looking, feeling the chest and asking the older child.

KEY POINT

Early Years workers involved in caring for a child with cystic fibrosis will need to learn these treatment techniques from the physiotherapist involved in the child's care.

Physiotherapy for a baby

It is often easier to develop treatment routines with babies as a mother and child inevitably spend much time together. Usually the baby will enjoy the physical contact involved.

All areas of the lungs will need to be cleared.

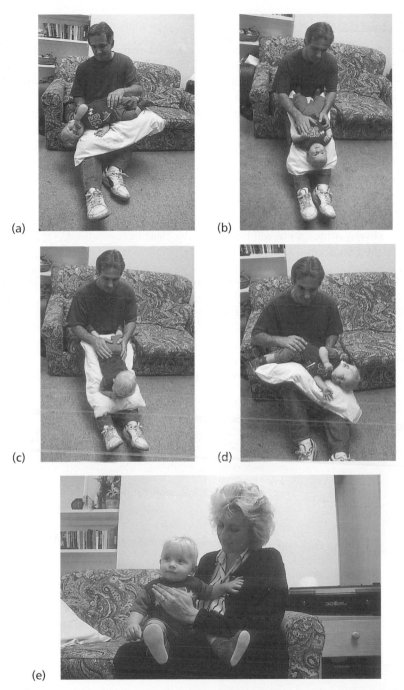

(a)

(b)

(c)

(d)

(e)

All areas of the lungs must be cleared. (a) Right lower lobe, lateral basal segment. (b) Lower lobes, anterior basal segments. (c) Lower lobes, posterior basal segments. (d) Left lower lobe, lateral basal segment. (e) Treatment in sitting for apical (or top) segment of upper lobes

- Treatments take place before or well after a feed as the baby may vomit.
- Check the baby is comfortably dressed.
- Use your knee covered by a pillow for the baby to lie over – she will be comfortable and her head fully supported.
- When clearing the chest by clapping, allow pauses for her to cough and breathe quietly.
- If you are successful she will cough her secretions into the back of her throat – it does not matter if she swallows them.
- Hold young babies who are unable to sit unaided to clear the upper lobes.

KEY POINT

A moist, steamy atmosphere will help the baby clear her secretions – the bathroom may be useful on occasions.

Physiotherapy for toddlers and young children

- When a child is too large to be comfortably placed over the knee, treatment will need to take place over a foam wedge.
- From about two years encourage the child to become more involved in her treatment by introducing breathing exercises such as blowing games with bubbles and steaming mirrors, etc.
- Encourage physical exercise – trampolining is both fun and effective.

Trampolining, huffing and puffing to steam up a mirror and blowing through a cardboard tube are fun ways to help control breathing and clear the chest

Physiotherapy for the young schoolchild

All the above treatments will continue, but the child will increasingly develop an awareness of her own breathing and how to extend her lung capacity. She will be an active participant in treatment.

Breathing exercises

These are an important aspect of managing cystic fibrosis, but they must be taught initially by the physiotherapist. They aim to help the child control her breathing, expand as much of her chest as possible and move secretions. Your role is to encourage and remind.

ONGOING MANAGEMENT

As with other conditions requiring medical supervision, pre-planning before a child starts attending any childcare and education setting will help smooth admission and promote easy transfer. All staff need to be aware of the following:
- the severity of the condition – update your own knowledge
- the importance of the diet and medicine (see page 249)
- reminders that the cough is not infectious
- time and space for physiotherapy – check who will undertake the treatments
- the need for good liaison with the school health service.

Parents and carers may find separating from their child especially difficult, worrying that she may contract additional infections.

KEY POINTS

- The child should be offered full involvement in all activities; let her make her own decisions about how many strenuous games and other activities she can manage.
- Generally, how much participation she can manage will depend on the severity of her condition at any one time.
- The child needs to make friends and develop relationships. It is important too for her to have success in the areas where she can compete equally with her peers, such as in music and creative activities.

Activity

Create a themed interest table on the topic of everyday sounds and noises. Encourage all the children to participate.

- Always be aware and ready to intervene if a child is teased or picked on. This may be because of her coughing or expectorating, her possible underweight and need for regular medicines.
- She may be away from school with infections. You can help by ensuring she is helped to make up work missed and that she is told of classroom or playgroup developments. Keep a Class Diary as for the child with sickle cell anaemia (see Activity, page 242).

KEY POINT

It may be hard for parents and carers to let a child with cystic fibrosis take the normal rough and tumble of a school or playgroup. This is especially so if the child has spent much time in hospital. Both child and parent can lose confidence as a result. You can help by a sensitive and understanding approach.

PROGRESS CHECK

1 What are the two main systems affected in cystic fibrosis?
2 In which system is it more important to prevent damage?
3 Which factors, associated with this condition, do you consider might affect a child's body image?

GENERAL IMPLICATIONS

Increasingly, more and more children with cystic fibrosis are living full and active lives and reaching adulthood. In men with cystic fibrosis the tubes that carry the sperm are blocked, which may cause infertility.

For a childcare worker maintaining the balance of a sensitive approach by demonstrating understanding without over-protecting will help the child take full advantage of the learning opportunities available.

ADDITIONAL DEVELOPMENTS

For some children heart and lung transplants are increasingly being used in treatment for prolonging life. However the condition is not cured by this treatment as the new lungs will continue to be attacked by thick, sticky mucus. Also, the availability of suitable donors means not all children can be offered the treatment.

Scientists are researching at present how to replace the abnormal cystic fibrosis gene.

CASE STUDY

Kirsty was diagnosed immediately following her birth as having cystic fibrosis. She was living in an area where all newborn babies are routinely tested for the condition. As a result she was carefully monitored during her first year to prevent chest infections. She coped well and even enjoyed her chest 'clapping' and physiotherapy and kept healthy. She began attending and enjoying a local playgroup at three years of age.

She developed a faddiness with her food, causing anxiety to her mother. She would only take her enzyme supplement with strawberry yoghurt and seemed to want to eat a diet of only baked beans on toast and yoghurt.

1   Which nutrients, if any, was Kirsty missing in her diet?
2   How would you manage Kirsty's diet?

RESOURCES

The Cystic Fibrosis Trust
11 London Road
Bromley
Kent BR1 1BY
www.cftrust.org.uk

Haemophilia

Haemophilia is a general term used to describe a group of inherited blood disorders in which there is a lifelong defect in the clotting mechanism of the blood. Approximately one in 10,000 men and boys have haemophilia. It affects all racial backgrounds. Although haemophilia is hereditary, up to a third of all occurrences appear in families with no previous history of the disorder.

WHAT HAPPENS

A child with haemophilia does not bleed more heavily or faster than other children, but bleeds for a longer time. If untreated, bleeding will cause pain and swelling, and permanent damage can occur in the area where it is happening, especially the joints. Haemophilia is termed a sex-linked recessive condition. This means that only males have the condition, except in very rare situations, but it is passed through the female line in the family.

DIAGNOSIS

For normal blood clotting a group of agents called factors are involved. The factors all work together to cause a chain reaction and if a factor does not work the chain reaction cannot take place. In haemophilia there are potentially two factors that might be faulty or missing:

■   In haemophilia A factor 8 is missing.
■   In haemophilia B (also known as Christmas disease) factor 9 is missing.

Haemophilia A is five times more common than haemophilia B. The symptoms and inheritance patterns are the same for both types but the medical treatment is different.

HOW HAEMOPHILIA IS INHERITED

Genetic instructions are carried on 46 chromosomes inherited from the mother and father. Two of these decide sex: females have two X chromosomes (XX) and males an X and a Y chromosome (XY).

One chromosome from each parent decides a child's sex.

A normal X chromosome carries the instruction to produce active Factor 8 and 9. If the mother is a haemophilia carrier the defective X chromosome carries no such information.

REMEMBER: the normal Y (male) chromosome has no factor 8 or 9 instruction on it, so if a carrier's defective X chromosome is linked with the father's Y the son will have haemophilia.

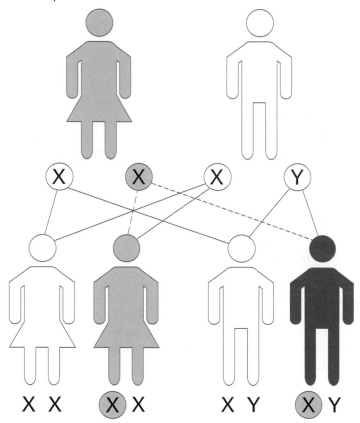

Here the mother is a carrier of the defective X chromosome. This is linked with the father's Y and the son has haemophilia.

Here too the mother has passed her defective X chromosome to her daughter, who will also be a carrier.

NOTE: when the mother is a carrier and the father unaffected, there is a 50% chance for *each child* that a daughter will be a carrier and a son will have haemophilia.

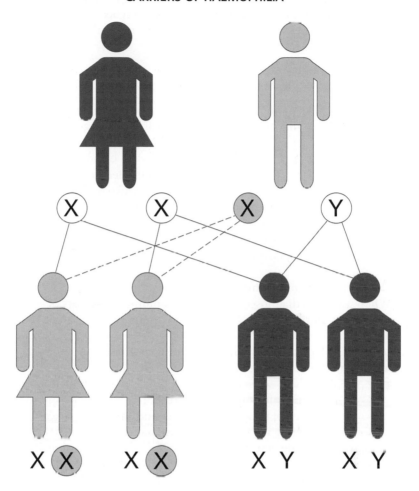

When the father has haemophilia and the mother is not a carrier each daughter *must* inherit the defective X chromosome and will be a carrier.
All sons will be normal because they inherit their father's Y chromosome.
They cannot pass haemophilia on to their children.

What is the range of severity for those affected?

- 1 per cent of haemophiliacs have severe haemophilia where there is frequent bleeding into joints, muscles and tissues. No injury is necessary to set off bleeding.
- From 2 to 5 per cent of haemophiliacs have moderate haemophilia where bleeding is usually related to some injury such as a knock or deep cut.

- From 6 to 25 per cent of haemophiliacs have mild haemophilia where bleeding problems are associated only with tooth extractions, surgery or a severe accident.
- Over 25 per cent of haemophiliacs have a normal range of bleeding for which treatment is rarely required.

CARE

Both types of haemophilia are treated by replacing the missing clotting factor, which is now made in the laboratory. Clotting factors are large molecules and cannot be given by tablets or by injections under the skin. They have to be given into a vein by a nurse or doctor, either as first aid to encourage blood clotting following a bleed – they are effective quickly – or to help prevent bleeding. In the case of helping to prevent bleeding, injections are given routinely two or three times a week.

Quick treatment means permanent damage to joints and muscles is avoided, and the child can return to routine life quickly.

Boys with mild haemophilia are now treated with a drug that stimulates the body to produce a normal factor 8.

Caring for the young child

When a baby is diagnosed as having haemophilia parents need reassurance that the effects on their baby's lifestyle, growth and development should be minimal and that:
- there will be normal growth and life expectancy
- there will not be a life of pain
- normal play and schooling is usual.

Over-protection is sometimes a response to the diagnosis, however, it is important that usual handling, cuddling and play takes place.

Cots and prams do not need extra padding, but when the baby toddles, dungarees provide sensible protection for knees. Occasionally joints will need additional padding, but it should be removed as soon as possible.

Maintain good dental hygiene to reduce the need for treatment that might provoke bleeding.

KEY POINTS

- Bruises often accompany any child learning to walk, and carers will learn when one bruise is more significant than another. Childminders and babysitters all need reassurance and information about what to watch for.
- Toddlers with haemophilia may have more bruises than their peers. False allegations of child abuse have occurred in some situations. Free exchange of information helps stop gossip.

GOOD PRACTICE

- If a toddler or older child falls and hits his head, medical advice should be sought.
- Usual safety precautions, as with any toddler, should be undertaken:

- gates at top and bottom of stairs
- no mats on highly polished floors
- robust toys with no sharp edges
- all heavy ornaments out of reach.

PROGRESS CHECK

1 What are the different levels of haemophilia?
2 How will the different levels of haemophilia affect care?

Caring for the older child

All staff need to update their own knowledge of haemophilia and be aware of the treatments required for the individual child.

GOOD PRACTICE

Procedures for the handling of blood (as discussed in caring for children who are HIV positive, see page 227) need to be implemented and applied for all children who bleed in school, regardless of whether or not they have haemophilia.

A boy usually knows when he is bleeding into a joint or muscle before any obvious signs occur. Listen and believe him, so treatment can then start early.

Following a severe bleed, mobility aids such as crutches, splints or a wheelchair may be needed temporarily (see the mobility aids for muscular dystrophy, page 267). A boy with haemophilia may feel especially vulnerable as he will lack the confidence and skills of the experienced user of crutches or wheelchairs.

If a child needs to rest a limb following a bleed, be creative in providing interesting activities to stimulate and occupy him. Active young children find it difficult to 'rest' and not join in with their friends. Remember he will probably feel well in himself, which may increase his frustration at forced immobility.

At-risk activities

Most primary school games and sporting activities pose no risk. Exercise helps develop strong joints and muscles, better balance and sharper reactions, leading to better avoidance of injury. Swimming is especially valuable, even for a boy with severe haemophilia, as all his joints will be supported. However, physical contact games are not recommended and this may include soccer.

Activities such as woodwork and metalwork are fine, providing supervision means all tools are used correctly.

GOOD PRACTICE

Treatment should be given as soon as possible for the following:
- bleeding into a joint
- bleeding into a muscle, especially in the arm or leg
- injury to the neck, mouth, tongue, face or eye
- Severe knock to the head and unusual headache

Woodwork is fine, but ensure supervision

- heavy or persistent bleeding
- severe pain or swelling
- all open wounds requiring stitches
- following any accident that may result in a bleed.

First aid
The usual first aid measures always apply and the following information may be helpful.
- *Blood in the urine is common, frequent and painless*: increase fluids.
- *Cuts and scratches:* apply waterproof dressings and firm bandaging over cotton dressings.
- *Eye injuries:* seek immediate help.
- *Head injuries:* seek immediate help.
- *Joint bleeds:* never leave untreated, if the child complains of pain or inability to move a joint, a bleed may be happening. This is painful, so handle carefully, support the limb or joint. Firm bandaging, if the child lets you touch, can sometimes help swelling and limit joint damage. Seek help.
- *Mouth, gum and cheek bleeds:* seek advice, offer ice cubes to suck.
- *Neck and throat bleeds:* these sometimes happen after a throat infection or injury. Swelling can obstruct the air passages: seek immediate help.
- *Nose bleeds:* sometimes spontaneous, often from nose picking. Apply firm pressure on the nostril or ice pack to the nose bridge.
- *Bruises:* superficial bruising is common, deep bruising is dangerous. Seek help. If symptoms do not subside following routine first aid, seek help.

KEY POINTS

- Never give aspirin to children.
- Have medical contact numbers readily available.

- Encourage boys with severe haemophilia to wear a 'Medi-alert' identification bracelet.

It is strongly recommended that, as an Early Years worker, you gain a first aid certificate and update your skills regularly. Ensure you are aware of who manages the first aid box, what its contents are and how the checking procedure is recorded.

Activity
1 Design a first aid box for use with a child with haemophilia. What additions to the usual first aid box do you think might be required?
2 How would you record and assess the range of bumps and bruises that are often gained at school?

ONGOING MANAGEMENT

Boys with haemophilia should be regarded as normal children with a chronic, variable problem that sometimes interferes with their education.

ADDITIONAL DEVELOPMENTS

In the past children have been treated with infected blood clotting factors. This resulted in their contracting the HIV virus (see page 223). However, since 1998 all children under 16 years of age have been treated with a man-made 'recombinant' clotting factor where the missing factor is produced synthetically by genetic engineering.

CASE STUDY

Kevin and his father were both well known as haemophiliacs in their local neighbourhood. Kevin was fit and well and, having only minor haemophilia, he was not restricted in his reception class activities. However he became upset and anxious, refusing to go to school, complaining of tummy aches and showing sleep disturbance. His mother visited the school to discuss the situation and try to discover the reason. After discussion it transpired that two other children had been teasing him that his dad had AIDS and was going to die. They had overheard mothers talking at the school gate.

1 How would you help Kevin?
2 How could you counter the rumours?

Duchenne muscular dystrophy

Duchenne is one of over twenty types of muscular dystrophy. They all cause progressive and relentless weakness as there is a gradual breakdown in muscle cells. All muscular dystrophies are thought to be genetic in origin.

Duchenne muscular dystrophy was first identified by a French doctor in the mid-nineteenth century. It is one of the most common and serious muscular dystrophies, and is caused by an X chromosome-linked genetic condition. Mothers carry the condition and pass it to their sons. It results from a fault in a single important protein in muscle fibres called dystrophin. About a hundred boys with the condition are born each year in the UK – one in every 3500 male births.

At present there is no cure for the condition, with the weakness increasing as the child grows and often causing death between twenty and thirty.

Treatment is aimed at limiting the effects of the condition and providing a full quality of life for the child.

WHAT HAPPENS

- A child appears as any other baby at birth; the first signs of the condition may be a delay in walking between one and three years.
- His gait then, typically, will be wide-based and he will have an increased curve in his lower back – lordosis.
- Climbing stairs may be easier on all fours; however, coming down is usually not difficult.
- He may fall more frequently than other children.
- His difficulties will increase, leading to problems in walking any distance.
- He may need support to stand, be unable to sit up in bed or turn over without help.
- His lower legs appear well formed and muscular, but this is due to an increase of fibrous and fatty tissue, while his underlying muscles are small and weak.
- About one-third of boys with the condition will also have learning difficulties, although these will vary enormously in severity and, unlike the weakness, do not increase as the child grows.

KEY POINT

Progress of this condition can often be likened to climbing stairs with steep acceleration and then periods when little changes. Frequently by the age of ten to twelve years a boy will need a wheelchair for mobility.

DIAGNOSIS

As Duchenne muscular dystrophy is inherited families will often be aware of other relatives with the condition. However, in almost half of all affected boys the faulty gene has occurred by a change or mutation in the boy himself – skilled genetic examination is required. In the remaining half it is the mother who carries the gene but is unaffected.

Each subsequent son of a carrier has a 50:50 chance of being affected and each daughter has a 50:50 chance of being a carrier. Daughters will usually be completely unaffected although a very small number have a mild degree of muscle weakness.

PATTERNS OF INHERITANCE FOR DUCHENNE MUSCULAR DYSTROPHY

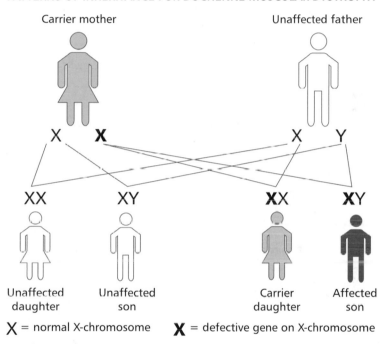

Diagnosis is best made in centres with specific expertise. An initial blood test for levels of serum creatinine kinase (CK) is undertaken and the level will be raised in an affected child. A sample of muscle tissue is usually taken for biopsy to confirm the diagnosis.

KEY POINTS

- Remember, these tests are important as there are many other, more common and less serious reasons why a child may be late to walk.
- Confirmation of a diagnosis of Duchenne muscular dystrophy is obviously devastating for families and they will need much support at that time. Worries about other carriers, the effects on future pregnancies and siblings, are all very real and will need addressing.

What to tell the growing child with muscular dystrophy as he grows is difficult for many parents.

- Information needs to be appropriate to his age and developmental stage.
- Try and answer the child's questions honestly when he wants more information. If you are unsure or his parents do not wish information to be divulged, you will need to seek advice.
- Never force him into difficult truths, but let him set the pace for more information.
- Remember you cannot make him 'better' but you can prevent additional distress. Consider too that the immediate situation is often more important to a young child than weeks or months ahead.
- Always check what parents have told a child and what they wish him to know – there is no right or wrong way to manage such a situation.

PROGRESS CHECK

What might be the first indication that a boy may have muscular dystrophy?

CARE

No specific medicines or treatment can halt the progress of the condition but good management can ensure good quality of life for the child and limit associated problems.

- The child needs to develop wide social relationships, so involve him in as many experiences as possible.
- Help him to develop hobbies and interests that he can continue long term, even when he may have reduced mobility, such as using computers, collecting stamps, reading and listening to music.
- Support and encourage him in all his academic activities; as his physical strength decreases remember his education will be especially important.
- Physical fitness and good general health should be part of a fun routine and pleasurable for its own sake, not forced on him. Swimming, ballet, gym clubs and horseriding can all be included in his overall care plan, giving his muscles valuable exercise.
- Try to ensure he does not become overweight. This can easily occur when he becomes less mobile and so needs fewer calories. Additional health problems can happen if he gains too much weight, so offer a carefully balanced diet. Promote healthy eating habits with not too many fatty, sugary foods.
- A smoke-free environment is important if his chest muscles weaken, making him vulnerable to respiratory infections.

Activity
For pre-school children, help the group create a set of puppets – these need not be complicated. Encourage the children to develop their own puppets' characters in games, stories and songs.

This may be a useful way of helping a child express anxieties about his condition.

Physiotherapy

The physiotherapist will plan a programme of care and you must maintain good liaison with her. The child may require up to four hours of planned exercises a day, which you may have to help him implement. Aim to keep him enthusiastic, co-operative and as independent as possible.

Physiotherapy may involve passive movement of limbs – careful positioning to prevent **contracture** (shortening of muscles) and stretching of any of these already shortened muscles.

Hydrotherapy is often used as valuable and enjoyable exercise – muscles move more freely in water and are less likely to overstrain.

KEY POINT

Use your observation skills to spot any developing weakness or abnormality of the position of limbs or the body, especially the spine.

The following various aids may be required to help the child's posture and mobility:
- callipers – frames around the legs to support, balance and help him to stand
- frames to hold him upright so he can involve himself in activities such as cooking, sewing, drawing and painting, and eating his meals with family and friends
- crutches to continue mobility
- wheelchairs.

GOOD PRACTICE

Always check that aids are comfortable, not rubbing or causing soreness of the skin, in good condition, no parts or bits missing, and no other child is using them inappropriately. Remember as the child grows he may need larger aids.

Environmental considerations – a checklist for mobility and good practice
- Are doors wide enough, handles not too high?
- Is the environment clutter-free? Encourage other children to all pick up debris from floors.
- Are spills from water trays, bathrooms, etc. cleared up immediately and are floors non-slip?
- Are floors in good condition, even, with no mats or loose carpets?
- Are extra handrails needed?
- Are wide ramps installed, with gentle slopes?
- Are the desks or tables at a comfortable height for the child, with a good light?
- Can he move easily around with crutches or wheelchair?
- Will a wheelchair go easily into the lavatory, and can he reach the taps and towels?
- Do the displays and play materials represent other children in wheelchairs, or with callipers or crutches?

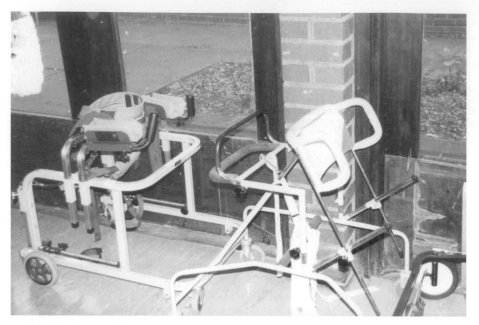

Aids to prolong mobility

- Are wedges and bean bags available for temporary, additional support if necessary?
- Can the child easily use the equipment in the playground – will additional ramps and rails be needed? Is there a safety surface? Are some bikes fitted with hand pedals and are there some trucks he can sit in?
- Can one of the flower beds be raised for him to garden, touch and smell the flowers?
- Can you organise space for an additional adult helper?
- Can a parent park a car with good access to the nursery or school for taking and fetching him?

Good practice is essential in lifting and carrying children
Skills are important not only to protect your own back, but also to ensure a child feels secure and safe:
- Always wear comfortable, non-restricting clothes and flat shoes.
- Do not wear jewellery that could scratch and catch.
- Organise the room so you do not have to carry a child far or twist your body around objects.
- Always lift in pairs if a child is too heavy for you.
- Tell the child what you are doing, how you are doing it and what you want him to do. (It can be useful to say 'One, two, three, up we go'.)
- Bend your knees to the same level as the child you are lifting.
- Keep your own back straight throughout the whole lift.
- Keep one of your feet well forward and the other foot comfortably behind you.

Is your environment wheelchair-friendly?

- Transfer your body weight from one foot to the other during the lift.
- Grasp the child firmly and comfortably using the whole of your hand, not just your fingers, holding him close to your body.
- Always leave him safe, secure and comfortable.

KEY POINT

Encourage the child to help himself as much as possible.

ONGOING MANAGEMENT

As he becomes increasingly affected by the condition and his mobility and strength decrease, remember he will still be growing and becoming heavier.

Electric beds and wheelchairs can be operated with minimal physical strength. They allow him to sit and lie, as he wants, and move around freely, with little adult interference. Computer technology is increasing in sophistication (see the use of microtechnology in cerebral palsy, page 392).

If other muscles weaken, bladder and bowel control may be lost (see bladder and bowel control in spina bifida, pages 370–1).

The child will become increasingly vulnerable to chest and other infections.

Additional family support and help may be needed. Consider the effects on any siblings and remember they need time and attention too.

PROGRESS CHECK

What are the main principles in safe lifting procedures?

ADDITIONAL DEVELOPMENTS

The voluntary organisation involved with muscular dystrophy has developed 'muscle centres', which provide comprehensive medical care, advice and support for some families.

New developments are happening all the time, holding out great hope for a possible cure of the condition in the future. Recently a specific virus has been found, which, it is thought, might carry dystropin genes into muscles and prevent further deterioration. Research is continuing with their development.

CASE STUDY

James was diagnosed as having muscular dystrophy from birth. Now four, he is still unable to walk unaided, but can stand with the help of callipers and has recently been allocated an electric wheelchair from funds from the Muscular Dystrophy Group. He attends and enjoys a local playgroup, which is easily accessible to the family home and is all on one level.

The Early Years workers from the infant school that James is hoping to attend are coming to his home to meet James and his family.

1   What information should James and his family give the Early Years workers about his condition?
2   What changes may be needed to make access to the old Victorian school possible for James and his wheelchair?

RESOURCES

Duchenne Family Support Group
78 York Street
London W1H 1DP
www.dfsg.org.uk

The Muscular Dystrophy Group of Great Britain and Northern Ireland
61 Southwark Street
London SE1 0HL
www.muscular-dystrophy.org

Managing medicines in a school, nursery or playgroup

For a child with a condition that requires vital medicines during the school, nursery or playgroup day, planning and co-operation of the staff will be needed.

Some establishments feel happier about this area than others, but if a child who needs regular and essential medicine is to learn and develop equally with other children, the following points must be considered:

- Who will be in charge of the medicine and take responsibility?
- Has the parent/carer given written consent for the administration?
- When and where will medicines be given?
- Who will check that the dosage is correct and that it is being given to the right child?
- How will the dose be recorded – where will this record be held?
- Where will the medicines be safely stored?
- Is the temperature correct (e.g. antibiotic medicines may need storage in the fridge)?
- What side-effects might occur?
- Is there a current contact telephone number available for queries about the condition and the medicine required?
- Which medicines will the child need to access freely, e.g. inhalers, powders for cystic fibrosis and when will the child take responsibility for this herself?

GOOD PRACTICE

Find out the policy regarding giving medicines to children with special needs in your work setting.

Anaphylaxis

Anaphylaxis is an extreme, life-threatening, rare allergic reaction, which can occur in any child.

A child with special needs, who may have many areas of care requiring attention, is not immune from this additional threat. If a child is very young or has communication difficulties she may be unable to indicate if a food, drug or situation is dangerous for her.

Triggers for an anaphylactic reaction are commonly nuts, eggs, fish, especially shellfish, bee and wasp stings and occasionally some antibiotic medicines. Children should wear identification bracelets if they are known to have this reaction.

Symptoms develop rapidly starting with:

- rash and tingling of the skin
- swelling of the face and throat leading to airway restriction
- increasing difficulty in breathing
- shock and death.

This is a major emergency requiring an immediate response. Seek help and call an emergency ambulance.

Children who have had a diagnosed episode of anaphylaxis will have two pre-loaded syringes of adrenalin (EpiPen or Anapen) that should be readily available at all times. Carers, school and Early Years workers should all know where they are kept. The small, fine needle of the syringe is inserted into a fleshy part of the outer arm or thigh and the drug given. The effect should be immediate. A second dose can be given after five minutes if necessary.

GOOD PRACTICE

In any setting where it is known a child is vulnerable to anaphylaxis, everyone should know how to respond to this potential life-threatening emergency. All carers involved need to know how to protect the child and individual workers should receive training in giving adrenalin, which may be life saving.

RESOURCES

British Red Cross Society
44 Moorfields
London EC2Y 9AL
www.redcross.org.uk

KEY TERMS

You need to know what these words and phrases mean. Go back through the chapter and make sure that you understand:

anaemia	hydrotherapy
anaphylaxis	muscular dystrophy and Duchenne
callipers and frames	muscular dystrophy
cystic fibrosis	pancreatic enzymes
digestive juices	passive movement of limbs
epipen	physiotherapy
factor 8	respiratory system
genes	sickle cell and thalassaemia
haemoglobin	sickled cells
haemophilia	trait

8 CONDITIONS AFFECTING COMMUNICATION AND CONTROL

> **This chapter covers:**
> - Dyslexia
> - Dyspraxia
> - Autistic spectrum disorders
> - Speech, language and communication impairment
> - Emotional and behavioural difficulties

In this chapter we look at a variety of conditions where children find difficulty in controlling and directing a variety of their functions. These include difficulties with speech, behaviour, relationships and physical movement. Many of these conditions do not have an agreed cause.

Dyslexia

Dyslexia is often included under the term 'specific learning difficulty'. It is sometimes subdivided further into specific types of dyslexia, but we will refer to them all under the umbrella term of dyslexia: *dys* meaning difficulty, *lexicon* meaning words or symbols together.

Dyslexia mainly affects one or more areas of reading, spelling and written language. In addition it can affect other skills including:
- short-term memory
- sequencing
- auditory and/or visual perception motor skills
- oral language
- occasionally dexterity – a degree of clumsiness can be present.

KEY POINT

In the past, failure to recognise this specific difficulty has resulted in children being perceived as lazy, uncooperative or stupid. Occasionally these difficulties have been put down to late development. It also has been used as a handy cover-all label for children with minor problems of reading and writing. These assumptions can undermine the serious nature of dyslexia.

True dyslexia is thought to affect between 1 and 4 per cent of all children, with boys outnumbering girls one to four. It occurs despite normal teaching and ability, and affects all social and racial groups. Affected children are often 'quick thinkers and doers' on their own terms – following instructions is more difficult.

WHAT HAPPENS

The condition is not fully understood. Some consider it a brain disorder that happens because there is an immaturity in the neurological system. The processing and transmitting of sensory stimuli – visual and auditory – have been affected, possibly following damage, or as a result of inheritance. Although no genetic patterns of inheritance – faulty genes – have been identified, children with dyslexia often come from families where their parents have had similar difficulties with reading and organising words.

Premature babies and those who have had a difficult period immediately after birth, are all thought to have an increased risk of dyslexia.

Whatever the cause, if a child is not helped to cope with his condition he will suffer stress and anxiety and fall behind in his academic work, failing to reach his potential. His social and emotional development may also be affected as a result of frustration and low self-esteem. He may learn to view school with horror as a place where he never achieves success.

DIAGNOSIS

There is no single test to confirm dyslexia. A combination of signs and events may be used to confirm the diagnosis.

Early indications
Some, or all, of the following may be present in one or more of the following areas:

Speech
- Delayed clear speech development
- Jumbled words and phrases
- Consistent problems at correctly naming colours
- Confusion over directional words – right and left, up and down, in and out, etc.
- Pronunciation difficulties, e.g. lisping.

Movement control
- Delayed fine motor skills in dressing, e.g. tying laces, buttoning, fastening, etc.
- Difficulties in controlling a pencil, crayon, paintbrush, etc.
- Problems over dressing independently, e.g. clothes inside out, shoes not on correct feet
- Frequent tripping, bumping and falling over – general clumsiness
- Difficulty in games requiring co-ordination such as catching and throwing or hopping and skipping; problems over learning to ride a bike, etc.

The slightly older child will reverse and invert letters and handwriting will be poor.

- Delayed development of hand preference (he appears to have no dominant hand)
- Rhythm problems in beating time or clapping to a simple tune.

Rhythm may be difficult

Memory and sequencing
- Difficulty in remembering rhymes, the names of everyday objects, etc.
- Problems remembering time: the routines of a day – when lunch or playtime is – and days of the week, months, years, etc.
- Difficulty in learning and remembering patterns and sequences of coloured beads, finding an odd one out, etc.
- Problems over remembering times tables and the alphabet.
- Bizarre spelling as he gets older.
- Inability to develop reading skills or very late achieving them.

Other areas
- He appears bored and lacking attention, especially in reading and reading preparation.
- He appears uncooperative and doesn't follow instructions.
- He may have great pleasure in creative activities.
- He will be alert and interested when personally engaged and talking with others, whether adults or children.
- He may show anti-social behaviour and frustration if he is unable to complete tasks or is constantly 'failing'.
- He may be shy and withdrawn.

Do not make assumptions that a child is dyslexic from only one or two of the above signs being present in an individual child. Most children will, at some stage, show some of these areas of difficulties – they will also usually disappear with maturity. However a child with dyslexia will have marked and persistent difficulties in several areas.

Who makes the decision that a child has dyslexia?
Often a parent or carer will feel anxiety about their child's progress – always listen and take their concerns seriously. Following a special assessment by an educational psychologist, a multidisciplinary team will assess the child's signs, including, depending on the age of the child, the child's GP or school medical officer, the health visitor, school teacher, care workers and other professionals. Hearing and sight tests are always undertaken to exclude any other possible causes.

PROGRESS CHECK

1   What are the main developmental areas in a child, that are affected by dyslexia?
2   Why is dyslexia difficult to diagnose?

CARE

There are two separate schools of thought about the desirability of discovering and helping the child of pre-school age with dyslexia. Some people think that the younger the child the less certain can be the diagnosis, and an incorrect diagnosis may result in problems being created where none exist. They also argue that labelling a child as 'at risk' of having problems learning to read and write and so on may actually cause a child to be anxious and lose confidence.

The other school of thought is that early identification is vital. This argues that starting appropriate activities early can help a child build a firm foundation for formal learning.

Helping the younger child – useful for all children
■ Listen carefully to the child, spending time explaining and answering questions. Gently and occasionally (not always) correct errors in pronunciation of words, etc. If you ask him to do certain tasks or jobs get him to repeat any instructions back to you.
■ In your music and singing activities include rhyming songs and use much repetition, reinforced with actions. Help him to clap out rhythms.
■ Read regularly and frequently. You will need to look at your own practice to ensure that you are skilful in holding his attention, making books fun. Show him the way to hold the book, where the words start and the pattern they follow. Have familiar stories he can join in with – reinforce them with tapes and music.

Make books pleasurable and encourage children to choose their own stories

- Use actions to accompany your stories. Include poems, rhymes, jingles and nonsense verse. Repeat them regularly.
- Use drama and action where possible and play finger games.
- Encourage games to develop sequencing skills, such as making lists of items to use in a painting activity or ingredients for cooking; and counting cutlery for laying tables (emphasising left and right).
- Help his memory with games such as picture lotto. Reduce the numbers of pictures to remember and build up as his skill improves.
- Play sorting games to help his sequencing, such as sorting buttons into sizes and colours. Use board games to help in taking turns, counting, etc., such as snakes and ladders and lotto.
- Encourage him to paint, let him use his fingers and short stubby brushes. Explain about the top and bottom of the paper and starting at the left when painting horizontal lines.
- Encourage him in dressing and teach him to manage buttons, ties, buckles, etc. Start with simple 'pull-on' clothes, moving on to more complicated ones when he is confident. Give him time and devise schemes to help him remember inside and outside and right and left shoes (these will need to be visual reminders such as stickers or marks).
- Encourage his co-ordination with large ball games and balancing games. Outside, play action games such as 'Follow my leader' and 'In and out the dusty bluebells'.

- Reinforce time, such as days of the week and months of the year.
- Help him recognise and write his own name in lower case letters and teach him the sounds of the letters. Follow this up with teaching and helping him to write his address.

KEY POINTS

- Always extend your activities with appropriate language and use repetition.
- All instructions must be simple, clear and repeated if necessary.
- Try to give the child plenty of time in undertaking any activity.
- Boost his self-confidence by emphasising his achievements.

GOOD PRACTICE

- In your choice of materials, such as songs, poems and stories, ensure some are familiar to the child.
- Are you adequately reflecting his cultural and ethnic background – do you know his particular culture's rhymes, songs and traditional childhood stories?
- Boost his self-confidence by emphasising his achievements.

Develop your technique to hold children's interest

Ensure a child with dyslexia feels he is achieving success in your establishment. He may be very creative, good at construction – make sure he has the opportunities to display his talents.

Activity

Develop a board game to help a four-year-old boy improve his matching and sorting skills. How can you organise your game to increase the level of difficulty as his skill develops?

KEY POINT

Good practice for a young child with dyslexia is also good practice for other children. However, a child with dyslexia will need more one-to-one attention. He will need time and patience and will need to feel able to talk about problems as they happen.

ONGOING MANAGEMENT

As a child grows his special needs should be formally recognised and additional help provided within the educational environment.

This help should be:

- multisensory – developing to the fullest the senses of hearing, touch, sight and smell
- carefully organised and structured
- systematic, with reinforcement at all stages of his learning from all staff within the establishment – this is a continuing programme.

KEY POINT

Ensure you are confident in supporting a child's special learning programme – update your own knowledge. Liaise with the teaching team.

Sometimes a young child with a specific learning difficulty and unmet needs shows anti-social behaviour in school. This can be demonstrated by:

- tantrums in frustration
- school refusal
- clinging and reluctance to leave parents and carers
- biting and kicking
- bedwetting and sleep disturbance
- becoming the class 'clown'.

Tasks difficult to him seem to be easily achieved by his friends, his words and stories are jumbled and confusing, reading is mechanical not pleasurable and his self-esteem is low. When he is demonstrating some or all of the above behaviour he is showing his distress and anxiety in a very obvious manner.

As the class comedian he is often covering the fact that he is finding some work difficult but, in an attempt to win favour with his peers, he resorts to behaving in a way that both gets attention and makes him popular with his friends.

Consider, too, the child who just withdraws and is good or passive.

To help the child learn the rules of the school you will need to provide him with a framework of acceptable codes of behaviour. Be consistent in what you expect of him. Challenge unacceptable behaviour. However, always acknowledge and reward his efforts and provide opportunities for him to be successful – work to his strengths (see pages 309–10).

Support and understand his individual learning programme, remembering that, like other children, he will have good and bad days.

Be aware that all the extra effort and concentration he uses in learning may make him especially tired at the end of a session.

KEY POINT

A child with dyslexia should feel learning is fun. You will need ongoing liaison with the educational psychologist and teachers to support the structured learning programmes.

GENERAL IMPLICATIONS

A child with dyslexia needs encouragement to practise his skills, otherwise he will lose them. It is an ongoing process where he will learn to compensate for the areas he finds difficult. Often he will take longer to achieve skills and reach goals than his peers. Remember, though, his intelligence is the same and there will be areas in which he can outshine his friends.

ADDITIONAL DEVELOPMENTS

A recent survey undertaken in a variety of childcare establishments found many workers felt the incidence of dyslexia was high. However, the childcare workers said they felt they lacked both knowledge and confidence in identifying and developing helpful strategies for these children.

CASE STUDY

Hasan is a seven-year-old boy attending an inner city primary school. He is articulate with strong verbal logic and effective oral reasoning.

He has difficulty in the three areas expected of a boy with dyslexia – reading, writing and spelling. His problems are marked with an apparent total inability to make sense of any written information – in reading he is still unable to recognise flash cards with more than two written words. He is currently being assessed by the educational psychologist.

Hasan is becoming increasingly anxious over his inability to make progress like his peers and he is reluctant to attempt anything new that he thinks would lead to further failure. He is frequently in tears.

His parents are despairing and worried for him.

1   How could you and Hasan's family help improve his confidence in approaching new challenges?
2   What measures could you take to help his recognition of shapes and letters?

RESOURCES

The British Dyslexia Association
Unit 8, Bracknell Beeches
Old Bracknell Lane
Bracknell RG12 7BW
www.bdadyslexia.org.uk

Dyslexia Action
Park House
Wick Road
Egham
Surrey TW20 0HH
www.dyslexiaaction.org.uk

Dyspraxia

Dyspraxia (or perceptuo-motor dysfunction) is the term given for difficulty or immaturity in the organisation of movement. Sometimes, too, there may be problems over language, perception and thought. It is known under a variety of different terms including developmental co-ordination disorder, the clumsy-child syndrome and motor learning difficulty.

A child with dyspraxia will be within the normal range of intelligence, but may be behaviourally immature. Dyspraxia affects at least 9 per cent of the UK population in varying severity – and 70 per cent of children with the condition are boys.

Although dyspraxia cannot be cured the effects of the condition can be dramatically controlled and reduced. In addition associated problems of low self-esteem and possible behavioural difficulties may be eliminated.

WHAT HAPPENS

A child will primarily have difficulty over fine and gross motor development. Occasionally it will be in one area alone, but more commonly it affects both. Skills in these areas seem hard to learn and retain, and the child appears awkward in his performance. As the child grows and develops, certain warning signs may be noticed, such as:

- lateness in reaching physical milestones – rolling, sitting unaided, crawling and walking
- poor balance and frequent falls, slowness and hesitation in action – hopping, running and jumping are all delayed and difficult
- difficulties in managing dressing, particularly with fasteners, zips, buttons and laces
- difficulty in kicking, catching and throwing balls and games needing co-ordination, such as those with bats and balls

- lateness in achieving bladder and bowel control.
- delay in fine motor development with poor control of tools, immature art work and writing skills delayed and laboured
- motor skills that other children achieve easily and instinctively need to be taught.

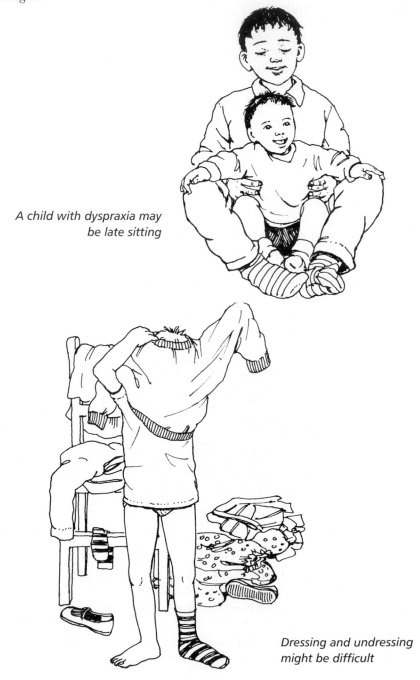

A child with dyspraxia may be late sitting

Dressing and undressing might be difficult

As he grows older the child may avoid physical activity, such as games and PE, and pre-school difficulties remain or even accelerate. His written work appears laboured and immature, and he remains poorly organised.

Other developmental areas that may also be affected

Perception
He may show difficulty in linking the messages his senses convey to his action.

Thought
Planning and organising thoughts may be difficult. This will be especially marked in children who, in addition, have learning difficulties.

Language
Poor articulation, unclear or unintelligible speech may be present and speech development may be delayed.

These difficulties may result in limited attention span, anxiety and distractibility, and confusion over socially acceptable behaviour.

DIAGNOSIS

The condition is thought possibly to be due to immaturity of the nervous system or even damage to the nerve links in the brain that organise the messages received from other parts of the body – the motor sensory system. At present there are no specific tests available to confirm these possible abnormalities.

Diagnosis is made after discussion and assessment from a wide variety of involved adults. The parents and carers are usually the first people to feel something is wrong with their child, and often raise these anxieties with their health visitor or family doctor.

Diagnosis follows an accurate history-taking of a child's particular area of difficulty and a full developmental assessment at a child development centre, where a paediatrician, psychologists and a range of therapists can be involved. Other conditions will have to be excluded before a final diagnosis is made – these include:

- middle ear infections (which can affect balance)
- hearing and vision damage
- cerebral palsy.

GOOD PRACTICE

Remember, a sound knowledge of the range of normal developmental progress in children is essential for all areas of childcare practice. This information allows you to identify easily and early when a child is not reaching his developmental milestones.

KEY POINT

There is agreement by all professionals that the sooner the difficulties associated with dyspraxia are identified the more effective will be the control.

PROGRESS CHECK

1   What are the main areas of development that are affected in a child with dyspraxia?
2   What other secondary areas of development may also be affected?

CARE

All children need to practise emerging physical skills and this is especially important for a child with dyspraxia. As with any child he will need time and encouragement. For the very young child ensure that:

- He is given toys and activities appropriate to his developmental level.
- His clothes are unrestricting.
- He has bare feet as much as possible, when learning to walk.
- He is encouraged and praised for attempting new skills.
- Self-help skills are encouraged, even if it means allowing considerable extra time for putting on shoes, when dressing, cleaning teeth, bathing, etc.
- A flexible yet organised care routine is followed, including a good diet – try not to let him become overweight. Plan for sufficient rest – remember he may use more energy learning physical skills than his peers.
- Encourage speech development, which may be delayed, with stories, rhymes and active listening.

Pre-school activities that will be especially helpful

- Stacking games, using beakers, rings, etc.
- Jigsaws – the size and number of pieces at an achievable level
- Balancing games – swings, seesaws, hopping, skipping, etc.
- Walking heel to toe and along straight lines
- Threading and lacing activities
- Dressing dolls, to include buttons, laces, zips and poppers
- Activities involving turning and screwing lids
- Action rhymes involving body movements and naming body parts
- Any type of painting activity.

Activity

Play a catching game with a group of four-year-old children. Vary the size of the ball or bean bag and the distance. Watch how the children attempt to catch – do they watch you or the ball? How many instructions do you need to give them to help them catch? Do they move their hands and arms or just leave them outstretched? How much complementary activity do they use to concentrate – tongues out, faces screwed up, etc. Compare the skill levels of the group – are you surprised by the results?

Balancing games help develop control

- Encourage walking, not the use of pushchair or car.
- Allow time for skills to be achieved.
- Use distraction when frustration becomes apparent, but acknowledge the child's feelings.
- Break tasks down into small stages, rather than overwhelm him with the whole.
- Always praise effort – never criticise failure.
- If a child is finding an activity exceptionally demanding or difficult, leave it and consolidate a previous skill – this helps self-confidence and makes him keen to try again.
- Ensure success is acknowledged in other unrelated areas in which he has prowess.

KEY POINT

Play and learning should be enjoyable.

Programmes of exercises and activities will be arranged by a variety of involved professionals, including children's occupational and speech and language therapists and physiotherapists.

Check you understand what they ask of the child, how often and when activity schemes need to be undertaken and how you should support their expertise. It is important for any child's security and confidence that all involved in his care have the same approach – ask if you are unsure.

Playing a catching game

ONGOING MANAGEMENT

A child in school, with the condition only recently identified, may have additional behavioural or social problems. Often the playground is the area where children achieve status with their peers. For a child who is clumsy with dyspraxia, however, this may be a place to cause him worry, making playtime distressing.

He may cause irritation by dropping equipment, producing messy work and being slow in dressing, undressing and eating, and his confidence will fall. Check he is not bullied and maintain careful observations.

Try to watch that he is not excluded, that he is learning to make friends and developing social relationships. Remember he may lack confidence and have low self-esteem.

Research tells us the earlier the diagnosis and implementation of a planned programme to help manage the condition, the less is the occurrence of behavioural problems.

KEY POINTS

■ Never label him a 'clumsy' child.
■ Acknowledge what he can do, not what he cannot.

With a planned programme of skill enhancement he is likely to improve the management of his co-ordination and help himself cope with some of his difficulties. However this will need to continue throughout his school life.

GENERAL IMPLICATIONS

Although difficulties associated with motor development have always been present, the recognition of the actual condition is still relatively recent. Many professionals do not have current knowledge of the condition or an awareness of how to manage a child with co-ordination problems. All involved staff will need to update their own knowledge.

ADDITIONAL DEVELOPMENTS

Although controversy continues about the sources and incidence of dyspraxia, there is an agreed feeling about the value of promoting physical skills in management.

Recent practitioners involved in dyspraxia have posited the idea that, as motor sensory skills form the foundation for the later development of abstract and verbal thoughts, improving these motor sensory systems should also allow for higher brain function improvement.

CASE STUDY

Although John appeared as any other baby during the early part of his life he had some minor delay in developing speech. He was an only child with his mother at home as a full-time carer. She identified this as possibly the reason for his delay in gaining the expected skills of independence – feeding and dressing himself and his general clumsiness. Prior to commencing school John was always considered by his mother to be sunny-natured and easy going. Increasingly he had found school difficult. Dressing and undressing for games and swimming lessons took him considerably longer than his peers, he was considered a messy and slow eater, and his peers had begun to avoid sharing the same table with him. John had begun to make excuses for not going to school, he had few friends and was rarely asked to other children's houses.

1 What could you as an Early Years worker do to promote John's self-esteem?
2 Where could John be referred for an accurate assessment of his needs?

RESOURCES

The Dyspraxia Foundation
8 West Alley
Hitchin
Herts SG5 1EG
www.dyspraxiafoundation.org.uk

Autistic spectrum disorders

Autistic spectrum disorders (ASD), or pervasive developmental disorders, first identified in 1943, are a range of complex, lifelong developmental disabilities, which vary in severity. They include autism and Asperger's syndrome.

Autism affects the way a child communicates and relates to those around him, including his parents and carers. His ability to make friends is impaired, as is his capacity to understand other people's feelings. He shows a basic lack of curiosity about his world. He has an inability to understand the meaning and purpose of language and retreats into ritualistic and obsessive behaviour. He cannot make sense of his surroundings and so the world can be frightening.

The exact number of children with autism is unknown but it is now thought to affect around six children in every thousand. There has been a rise in recognition of the condition in recent years and there is an opinion that autism has always been more common than was generally recognised. In one small study a link was made between autism and the MMR (measles, mumps and rubella) vaccine. However, wider national and international research and scrutiny of the evidence consider this link is not proven.

All social and racial groups can have the condition, with boys more affected than girls in a ratio of about one to four.

About 75 per cent of children with autism also have a learning disability.

Asperger's syndrome is part of the autistic spectrum and has features in common with autism. These include difficulty in communicating, problems in social relationships and a lack of imagination and creative play. However a child usually has less difficulty with language and can speak fluently, even if, sometimes, in a formal or stilted fashion. He may appear insensitive, talking regardless of the response or interest of the listener. He is particularly likely to develop obsessive interests or hobbies associated with memorising facts, for example makes of cars, bus routes and numbers.

A child with Asperger's syndrome is often of average or above average intelligence.

KEY POINTS

- There is no cure, currently, for children with autistic spectrum disorders. Careful management strategies with appropriate education and support can help a child improve his communication and social skills to enhance his independence and quality of life.
- Autism and Asperger's syndrome are considered together under the umbrella term ASD.

WHAT HAPPENS

A child will demonstrate difficulties primarily in three areas.

Lack of communication skills

Speech delay may be present and he will often be silent in his play.

However, his communication difficulty is more than his ability to form and use words. He will find it difficult to mix and will appear to prefer his own company. As he grows, making friends becomes problematic and stressful, reinforcing his isolation.

Language seems to develop differently from his peers; he shows constant repetition often of single words and phrases – echolalia. He can remain fixed on a single topic and seem not to listen, constantly interrupting. He often repeats questions back to his questioner – he does not answer. He may avoid eye contact.

He shows inappropriate social behaviour – kissing strangers, asking personal questions of little-known adults. He takes no account of age, status or mood when involved in conversation. He finds interpreting gesture and facial expressions, body language, difficult – often resulting in his making an unsuitable response. He takes words literally.

Feeding the dog – a literal interpretation

Lack of imaginative play

Unlike other young children, a child with autism will be unable to get involved in imaginative or role play, either with objects or other children or adults. Instead, he will spend his time in repetitive activities – arranging and organising objects, even collecting specific items such as bottle tops, leaves, certain containers, etc. He can become obsessive about this and as he grows collections can become a major part of his life. An older child may develop a fascination for certain facts such as types or colours of cars, numbers of buses, and so on.

Obsessive or ritualistic behaviour

Young children usually find security in a degree of ritual and routine. In a child with ASD this need for ritual is obsessive and rigid. It is his attempt to try to impose a degree of control over his sometimes frightening world. Changes in any established routine can make him distressed, anxious or angry, often provoking tantrums. Such routines may be dressing and bathing that must follow a certain plan, routes to nursery or school that must always be the same, the road must be crossed at a certain point or he must always sit in the same chair in the same position.

He may show bizarre repeated forms of behaviour such as hand-flapping, flicking his fingers in front of his eyes or walking on tiptoe.

He often tends to focus his attention on a trivial aspect of his environment, such as excessive interest in someone's jewellery rather than the person wearing it, or the wheel of a toy rather than the whole train.

KEY POINT

As with any special need, the degrees of severity of certain aspects of the condition vary enormously from child to child.

DIAGNOSIS

ASD is now generally considered to be a developmental disorder involving a biological defect in brain functioning. It is no longer thought to be the result of emotional deprivation or misunderstood genius. Although no affected gene has been identified ASD tends to occur in certain families. It also occurs with other brain disorders, e.g. epilepsy, encephalitis (inflammation of the brain) and maternal rubella.

Parents and carers often worry over the lack of response, delay in smiling and dislike of physical contact that a child with this condition will show and they may have discussed this with their health visitor.

There is no simple test for ASD and the diagnosis is made by a multidisciplinary team following a child psychiatric assessment. A child is usually considered to have autism if he shows signs in all of the three areas of poor communication, ritualistic behaviour and lack of imaginative play.

Early diagnosis is important – the onset is thought always to be before three years of age. However, accuracy of diagnosis is difficult under eighteen months. A child is often not identified fully until he begins to attend a care or educational establishment and his particular difficulties over relating and involving himself with peers in usual play and relationships become apparent.

Often a hearing test is undertaken to exclude deafness.

PROGRESS CHECK

Name three significant signs that might lead you to consider that a child of four has ASD and will need specialist assessment.

CARE

Drug therapy is not used in the general management of ASD. A child is helped by a programme of structured activity and response. These programmes are developed through a multidisciplinary team involving psychologists, speech and occupational therapists and, as the child grows, the wider educational team does too, following formal assessment.

The very young child

Often when a diagnosis of ASD is made parents and carers feel a degree of relief that there is some special reason behind their child's challenging behaviour.

KEY POINT

All children with ASD will need considerable one-to-one attention in order to fulfil their potential. This may be demanding and require skill and patience.

Managing communication problems

- Speak clearly and directly, using simple words and language, complemented by gesture.
- Try not to use metaphorical speech or exaggeration – remember he will take your words literally.
- Check he is listening and understanding and repeat if necessary – be aware of your own choice of words.
- Use songs and rhymes, especially those to which he shows response. Encourage him to clap and beat a rhythm. Music is often very helpful in developing oral skills.
- Children with ASD find difficulty in differentiating between objects that are inanimate – toys or furniture – and social, living creatures that are unpredictable and have languages. Consider how confused his world may be as a result.

PROGRESS CHECK

Which professional worker should be able to give expert information and advice on how to develop language skills?

Social interaction

- Encourage him to meet other children regularly, even if he plays passively on his own and doesn't register any emotion – it is part of his learning programme.
- Encourage two-way interaction between child and adult, and later child and child – this is easier than trying to force him into large group involvement before he is ready. Remember the seesaw in the park involves two people, as do blowing bubbles between you, and pouring sand and water over his and your hands.
- Repeat games he enjoys – this rewards him for demonstrating a response.

- Music with a whole group of children is a good way for him to begin to learn interaction with larger numbers of children. Musical instruments that involve banging and shaking can be particularly effective.
- Plan for his development in easy stages; don't overwhelm him.

In group settings it is often helpful to acknowledge to other parents and carers that a child has ASD. This explains any apparent unfriendliness or occasional tantrum following an apparently minor frustration or change of routine. It can prevent the child being labelled as just 'naughty' or 'spoilt'.

Try to encourage single child-to-child involvement

Safety issues and physical care

A child with ASD has a lack of natural caution and this makes him vulnerable.

- Be vigilant. For example, he may consider all water the same, not discriminating between hot and cold and always expect his food to be of the same temperature.
- Remember he may display inappropriate behaviour in public such as approaching strangers and wandering off unsupervised.

Toilet-training, developing healthy food habits and sleep management can all pose challenges when caring for a child with ASD. Try using a routine to extend his interaction: dressing and undressing; laying the table for meals – placing cutlery in expected places. Try to use any obsessional trait to build on rather than see it as only negative.

A firm, caring consistent approach is important, with expected behaviour clearly and simply explained, efforts rewarded and success praised.

He will respond more readily to the expected and familiar (remember he is ritualistic), so if you have chosen a certain plan of action, ensure that this is manageable and keep to it. Do not choose areas of conflict that are unimportant and hard to enforce such as saying 'Please' and 'Thank you', but choose those that are vital to stick to such as safety issues – holding hands when out or on the road, etc. These cannot be compromised.

PROGRESS CHECK

What implications for safe practice does ASD pose for a childcare worker?

KEY POINT

Families can become exhausted with being constantly 'on duty' and will need support and understanding in management issues. Never forget they know their child best. Support groups with families of other children with ASD are often very helpful.

ONGOING MANAGEMENT

The child with ASD in school

It is important to have a sound knowledge of a child's strengths and difficulties to enable you to plan for his schooling. Identifying and listing his special needs and developing action plans for monitoring progress would be helpful.

- Aim to develop his independence and social skills. This may mean watching his developing relationships and intervening if necessary.
- Include him in all activities, but be aware that some team games will be demanding and he may need initially to be involved in one-to-one activities with a specially chosen child. This may help him learn about others' needs and develop his sharing skills.
- Take especial care with your language – both generally and to the class. Avoid sarcasm, innuendo and unclear messages. Always check you have been understood and listened to and be prepared to repeat instructions. Create an environment where a child feels comfortable about asking when he is unsure.
- Always check he is aware that he is part of a group when instructions or requests are made. You may need to identify him by name.
- Develop your story-telling skills and use visual aids and gestures to hold attention. Try to have small quiet groups initially.
- Choose tasks that he can succeed in at the beginning and always break down anything complex you are asking of him into small units. Demonstrate and reinforce, showing him again how you wish something to be undertaken such as in writing, pasting or cutting.

- He may need extra time to complete an activity – he will become anxious if hurried.
- Ensure he knows the school routine and is warned in advance of changes, as things such as fire drills or special visits will make him anxious.
- Check he is not teased or bullied. He may be vulnerable and isolated in the playground. He may laugh at a child who falls or is distressed – remember this is part of his condition and he will need to try to learn acceptable responses. Try to explain to other children the reasons for this.
- Maintain strong liaison with parents and encourage them to help him put into practice at home the skills he is learning in school.

Is the child part of the group?

Activity

Plan a talk at a parents' and carers' evening about the advantages of integrating children with special needs into a mainstream nursery and reception class. Emphasise the benefits there are to the other children in the class in such a situation.

GENERAL IMPLICATIONS

A child with ASD will continue to need considerable support throughout his schooling. Remember the condition can be managed and the effects minimised but not cured – ASD is for life.

ADDITIONAL DEVELOPMENTS

Some other approaches to the management of ASD include other therapies.

Behaviour modification
Behaviour modification means punish bad behaviour and reward good. Success is greater if the emphasis is on the reward rather than the punishment.

Holding
Holding is practised more commonly in the US. The idea is that ASD is primarily a result of the failure of a mother to make an initial, successful bond, for a variety of reasons, with her child, following birth. When the child is distressed he is held close and this is maintained even if the child struggles and resists. In some centres a child is forced into distress by engaging in eye contact or interrupting a ritual so that the 'holding' therapy can take place. This contact can last up to one hour at a time. The aim of this therapy is to try to reduce a child's feelings of isolation.

Some professionals do not advocate this therapy as they feel it reinforces the idea that a parent is somehow to blame for the child's condition.

The treatment has not currently been fully evaluated.

Music therapy
Music is used extensively to break down isolation and reduce disruptive behaviour.

Sometimes parts of the above therapies are used as part of an **eclectic** approach – making management specific for each individual child and his needs.

CASE STUDY

Adam was born prematurely, the third child in the family. His mother became anxious about his progress as he was late in vocalising and seemed to forget to use even the odd word he had learnt, by two years. The suggestion of deafness was raised but dismissed following testing. His mother was told that Adam was a late developer. When Adam became distressed he actively fought against attempts to cuddle or comfort him.

In an attempt to stimulate her son's language and social development Adam's mother took him to a parent/carer and toddler group. Adam showed limited interest in the other children, played alone and did not become involved or demonstrate interest in the group activities of stories, songs and action games. When attempts were made to involve him he had temper tantrums and became distressed. He seemed to prefer to spend his time organising the home corner and lining up the cups and saucers.

Adam's mother persisted in attending the group but her son seemed to make no progress.

Eventually Adam was referred to a local child guidance clinic and, at four years of age, after a full assessment, ASD was diagnosed.

Adam now attends a mainstream nursery class and has additional support from an Early Years worker. His progress remains slow and he has begun to develop severe ritualistic behaviour, especially over dressing for nursery. However he is beginning to demonstrate some affection to his parents and siblings.

1   What other signs might have indicated Adam's ASD earlier?
2   How can you help Adam begin to control his ritualistic behaviour?

RESOURCES

The National Autistic Society
393 City Road
London EC1V 1NG
www.nas.org.uk

Speech, language and communication impairment

Speech, language and communication are complex and complicated areas of child development, and delay in progress and the development of these skills can happen for a variety of reasons. Remember, for a child to gain the maximum benefit from play, education and his social relationships, he will need to communicate effectively. This is usually through speech and language. A child with speech and language impairment needs to be taught the skills that other children learn naturally.

It is thought that one in ten of all school-age children in the UK have a degree of speech and language impairment at some time, with up to one in 500 having a specific longer term difficulty needing specialist help. Remember that learning to speak follows a pattern and some children find the whole process much easier than others – there is a wide range in normal development.

Speech and language impairment can be a condition in its own right or as part of another condition or associated illness. Sometimes the condition is known as aphasia (lack of speech) or dysphasia (difficulty with speech).

WHAT HAPPENS

Any interruption or difficulty in one of the three areas below can cause a child problems with communication. To develop speech a child needs to:
■   listen
■   understand
■   speak.

For speech a child needs:

- ears to hear messages
- an intact nervous system to relay messages to the brain
- an undamaged brain to understand the message, memorise and organise a reply
- a voice to respond
- hands to help support messages with gesture and writing
- tongue and lips to formulate sounds.

Delay or difficulty in developing speech or communication

Primary reasons

- Articulation problems – a child just finds it hard to learn to control his mouth, tongue and lips – sometimes due to prematurity, but often the cause is unknown
- Lack of stimulation
- Shyness
- Emotional or psychological problems, e.g. of the child who has been abused or had trauma in his childhood
- Learning difficulties
- Hearing problems, especially glue ear, frequent coughs and colds
- Delayed or difficult motor development, e.g. dyspraxia or cerebral palsy
- Other associated conditions, e.g. ASD
- Babies born with problems associated with the tongue, mouth or palate.

Secondary reasons

Sometimes specific problems with articulation and control can occur later, after early speech has begun. Examples include:

- 'th' pronounced as 'f'
- 's' giving off a whistling sound
- 'r' pronounced as 'w'
- 'k' pronounced as 't'
- 'g' pronounced as 'd'.

KEY POINT

Speech and language impairment can be either: (a) receptive: a child has difficulty in understanding or receiving what is said to him; or (b) expressive: a child has difficulty with talking and interacting with his peers.

DIAGNOSIS

Various areas must be considered, often to exclude reasons for a child having difficulty in learning to communicate, rather than to provide simple answers.

A full hearing assessment and birth history will be taken. Obvious mechanical difficulties will be excluded, e.g. repair of cleft palate, treatment for adenoids or glue ear, etc. The child will be assessed against the developmental norms for speech for his age.

Terms used in assessing speech impairment

- *Fluency:* the ability to produce a smooth, uninterrupted flow of speech.
- *Dysfluency:* speech that is not fluent.
- *Stammer/stutter:* speech that is interrupted by repetitions, words that are prolonged and non-fluent speech.
- *Prolongations:* a vowel or consonant that is 'stretched out' to sound longer than it normally would, e.g. 'booook'.
- *Blocks:* difficulty in making any sound, especially at the beginning of a word. Muscle tension builds up in the face and neck before the sound is finally pushed out.
- *Avoidance behaviour:* a child feels unable to say words beginning with particular sounds and tries to find alternatives. This can result in an inappropriate use of words or even wrong answers.

Signs to watch for and seek advice on

Birth to 3 months
Mother is not communicating with the child, is seriously ill, depressed or deaf. Severe feeding problems are present with the child.

3–6 months
Child is silent most of the time, even when alone. Eye contact not developing. Little or no response to noise.

6–9 months
Does not respond to play – vocal and non-vocal. Has not babbled or has stopped babbling. Shows lack of rhythm and intonation when babbling. No consistent response to noise.

9–12 months
Not trying to communicate by vocalising or pointing. Not responding to single words and simple commands. Not using a wide range of different sounds and intonation.

12–15 months
Unable to give toy to adult on request, even with gesture. Not trying to copy adult speech. Shows no interest in verbal communication.

15–18 months
Not understanding simple instructions. Not understanding new words. Not getting objects by using voice and gesture.

18–21 months

Not understanding simple questions and instructions, e.g. 'Show me your nose'. Not using words to show meaning. Not attempting to copy words.

21–24 months

Cannot identify objects and pictures of everyday items. Only grunting and pointing, not using recognisable single words. No variety of different speech sounds shown.

2 years–2 years and 6 months

Unable to carry out two-step commands, e.g.' Give dolly a cuddle'. Not linking words, e.g. 'mummy drink'. Speech difficult to understand.

2 years, 6 months–3 years

Not understanding verbs and simple adjectives, e.g. little, big, etc. Not asking questions or using a variety of sentences. Speech unintelligible to prime carer. Symbolic play is not developing.

3–4 years

Speech unintelligible. Poor vocabulary and sentence formation. Difficulty with both answering and asking questions. Lack of fluency in speech.

4–5 years

Unable to relate short sequence of events. Difficulty in understanding complex language. Speech remains unintelligible and with poor fluency. Problems in relating to other children.

PROGRESS CHECK

1 When would you usually expect a child to form simple two-word sentences?
2 When might you expect to understand most of a child's speech?

While it is often helpful to parents to have a well-identified reason as to why their child appears to have difficulty in speech, it is not always possible. Some children may seem to have a combination of factors that are contributing to the impairment. Sometimes, too, professionals are not in agreement as to the reasons for the communication difficulties. Parents can feel anxious about their child being labelled as having a special need when there seems to be no convenient title to cover his individual condition.

However, before any decision is reached, early referral to and the involvement of a speech and language therapist is important. The speech and language therapist is the specialist who will have long-term involvement with the child. He understands each child is a unique individual who will need his own specific treatment programme. You should liaise and involve the speech and language therapist as soon as possible. He will teach the child exercises and develop a programme for him. In addition, parents need to understand how to support and implement therapy at home, as do the staff in the care and education establishment.

CARE

Principles of good practice will help small children develop their speech potential. If you are working with a young child try to include the following opportunities for a child to practise his sounds. This is relevant for all children, but especially helpful for a child with delayed speech.

KEY POINT

Your positive response will make the child want to repeat his noises again – all sounds lead to language development.

Maintain close contact and reinforce his attempts to make sounds

Activities and games to encourage babbling (practising speech)
- Bubble-blowing and any games where excitement can encourage vocalising, e.g. 'pat-a-cake'
- Tongue exercises – licking of chocolate or ice cream from around the lips helps develop the tongue and lips muscles. Let your child copy you and use a mirror so he can see what he is doing. Remember talking and eating use similar muscles so include foods in his diet that encourage chewing, such as carrots and apples.

- Lip shapes – pulling faces in front of a mirror at each other. Try putting on lipstick and making prints on paper.
- Physical games to encourage vocalising such as tickling, action songs, etc.
- Adapting songs – changing familiar songs to include repetition or babbling sounds, e.g. 'John on the bus says b b b' (an adaptation of 'the wheels on the bus'). Be adventurous; now is the time to develop your creativity!
- Noises to complement situations – always try to make noises to match situations, such as 'ah's with cuddles and 'oh's after mishaps
- Noises with toys – complement games with relevant noises such 'brrm brrm' for cars and make farmyard animal noises for toy animals
- Reinforcing his attempts – always copy and extend his sound attempts, such as 'ba' into 'ba ba ba', etc.
- Games to encourage sounds – games where he has to vocalise to continue or extend the game, e.g. 'more' for extra bubbles, ' higher' for the swing
- Everyday situations to encourage him to use his voice to gain items – encouraging him to make sounds for more biscuits, another song, etc. Don't do the talking for him.

Games to practise lip movements

KEY POINT

Always respond when he attempts to communicate with you, verbally or non-verbally. Use short sentences and speak a little slower and louder. Try and use tune in your voice with the child close to you.

When the child makes a sound repeat it back to him to reinforce his learning. It can help too if you emphasise words and sentences when he attempts to have his needs met by non-verbal gestures. For example, if he pulls you to his coat, say 'Do you want your coat?' Hold and show him the coat and ask 'What do you want your coat for? Do you want your coat to wear for a walk?' Continue with 'What a lovely red coat you have. Your coat will keep you warm,' and so on.

GOOD PRACTICE

- Learning language should be part of a fun routine that would benefit every young child.
- If a child is having difficulty do not pressure him and make him distressed. Keep your plans short and fun.
- Repeat successful activities and leave less popular ones for a later date.

ONGOING MANAGEMENT

Remember that many children have delayed or less fluent speech, that often it is only temporary and that speech development is not a competition.

Organise your routine so that every day there is time and quiet space to enjoy books with the child. Encourage him to point and then ask questions when he is able. Make sure this is a fun time.

Never leave television or radio on as 'wallpaper' as it will distract the child and smother his developing attempts at words. In school and nursery try to keep noise levels down.

Always respond to the child's attempts at communication but do not insist he tries to speak clearly, just repeat the correct words or sounds back. Use every opportunity to include speech and communication in all activities, from bathing and dressing and practical activities, to watching television together.

The child may become frustrated if his attempts are not fully understood, so concentrate to understand when he is talking to you.

Management tips for the child in school
- Maintain good liaison with parents, and speech and language therapists.
- Try to limit questions directed specifically to the child.
- Give him full attention when he is speaking.
- Encourage, but do not force participation in a group situation.
- Do not complete sentences for him – encourage other children not to either.

- Use short sentences with him.
- Never ask a child to 'stop and start again'.
- A child may become frustrated if his attempts are not fully understood. Always concentrate when he talks to you to make sure you understand him. Slow down your own speech in response, this will help him follow what you are saying and make it easier for him to understand. It also gives him a lead to speak slowly back to you and so lessen the pressure on him.
- Try not to correct grammar or pronunciation – repeat the correct form back to him.
- Be calm – this will convey a relaxed feeling to the child.
- Use open-ended questions.

KEY POINT

- The child's self-esteem may be low so support all areas of his development to promote his confidence.
- Parents who are worried about their child can contact a NHS speech and language therapist direct. A referral from a general practitioner is not needed.

GOOD PRACTICE

- You are a role model so speak clearly and use language wisely.
- If the child's first language is not English, consider that he is possibly having to master two skills at one time.

GENERAL IMPLICATIONS

Often childcare workers do not feel confident in helping a child who is dysfluent. Sometimes stammering occurs because a child is very eager and is learning new words quickly – this often settles.

About five in every hundred children stammer for a time when they are learning to talk, most of whom will gain fluency, as they become older.

If stammering persists it may cause embarrassment, possibly resulting in teasing and bullying.

Consider if you are embarrassed by a child who stammers – check that you are not avoiding asking him to participate. If you lack skills or confidence, seek guidance from a speech and language therapist on how best to meet a specific child's individual needs.

PROGRESS CHECK

1 How can you help a child at infant school whose speech is not clear and is causing him frustration and affecting his social relationships?
2 What activities could you plan to offer him equality of opportunity?

Habib was four when he started school, coming from a part of the city with high concentrations of families from the Bangladesh community. He had never attended any pre-school playgroup or nursery.

Habib was strangely silent from his admission. He played alone in a rather aimless fashion, rarely completing the tasks requested, but he did not appear distressed. His mother spoke no English and all communication between his family and the school was carried out with interpretation from his outgoing eight-year-old brother.

The staff were not unduly anxious about Habib, feeling that his limited communication was probably caused by his separation from his family and limited access to English before he started school. They thought he would soon catch up with his peers, as did other children with similar experiences from comparable ethnic backgrounds.

After a term, however, Habib was making only incomprehensible sounds and a speech and language therapy assessment was sought. The local therapist, herself Bangladeshi, found Habib's understanding and perceptual levels were considerably below what would be expected of a child of his age. He was referred further for educational psychology and hearing assessments.

Following this it was decided that Habib had learning difficulties. An action programme was developed including speech and language therapy support.

1   What factors contributed to the delay in discovering Habib's particular needs?
2   What simple, routine language development activities might you provide as part of his action plan?

RESOURCES

Afasic
1st Floor, 20 Bowling Green Lane
London EC1R 0BD
www.afasic.org.uk

British Stammering Association
15 Old Ford Road
London E2 9PJ
www.stammering.org

Emotional and behavioural difficulties

Children can demonstrate difficult and unhappy behaviour for a wide variety of reasons. Some causes are easily identified but others are more complex. All children will have periods when they are difficult and disruptive – this is part of normal development. The two-year-old child is expected to have temper tantrums when thwarted, but by five years a child should have developed other skills to cope with frustration. It is essential good practice that Early Years workers have a sound knowledge of the range of normal behaviour. It is important to remember that children coming from similar backgrounds or even within one family may cope with difficult situations with a wide variety of response – not all children will develop emotional or behavioural difficulties even when under considerable stress. Children with behavioural and emotional problems will have the same ability range as other children.

Generally, children whose persistently difficult behaviour causes severe disruption, affects their ability to learn and to develop, and make and maintain relationships, must be considered to have special needs.

This behaviour can result from a wide variety of different causes.

Common causes of emotional and behavioural difficulties

Some of the more common causes of emotional and behavioural difficulties include:

- attention deficit hyperactivity disorder – ADHD
- physical or sensory impairment
- autism/ASD
- learning difficulties
- high abilities
- childhood depression
- emotional deprivation including: separation and frequent changes of prime carers; difficulties with parenting, especially in the early years, such as chaotic parenting with limited structure or routine; lack of physical care and affection; limited or inconsistent rule-setting; and personality conflict between parent and child
- child abuse.

WHAT HAPPENS

Types of behaviour

Whatever the fundamental, underlying cause of a child's distress, the types of behaviour displayed are often similar and can include the following:

- withdrawal or passivity
- aggression – biting, scratching, pushing, hitting, bullying, etc.
- inappropriate social behaviour such as indiscriminate signs of affection or uninhibited behaviour
- verbal aggression in the older child and defiance
- sleep disturbance – frequently a child seems to need little sleep or his sleep pattern is very disrupted
- bedwetting (enuresis)
- soiling (**encopresis**)
- breath-holding and temper tantrums beyond those expected for the developmental age.

Passivity can indicate distress

- head-banging and rocking
- short attention span, difficulty with concentration, never involved in any structured or free activity for any lengths of time in all care settings
- extreme restlessness
- phobias or irrational fears
- difficulty in trusting and forming relationships with adults and children.

Behaviour can be subdivided into externalisation and internalisation

Externalisation
Here the behaviour is directed outwards to the world in general and there is a disturbance of conduct.

Internalisation
Here the behaviour is largely directed internally.

PROGRESS CHECK

Which of the listed types of behaviour would you consider externalised and which internalised?

DIAGNOSIS

A child can present with behavioural or emotional distress causing concern early in life. The signs will be different depending on the age.

Remember, a child who has limited language will show his distress through his behaviour – hitting his toys, demanding affection from strangers, sleep disturbance, bedwetting, persistent biting, etc.

Young children will usually see their family doctor or health visitor in the first step towards assessment. Referral can be through a range of professionals, depending on the age of the child, but most commonly will be the paediatric, psychiatric and child psychology teams and the child guidance clinic. A multidisciplinary approach is followed.

Although some types of behaviour will be common to all conditions additional signs can help the team provide a more specific diagnosis. This is often eagerly requested by parents.

Additional indicators that can occur with specific conditions

ADHD

This condition (see page 313) is thought to be the result of a dysfunction of the brain's filtering system. The diagnosis is made after observations of a child's behaviour, as there are no specific tests. ADHD may affect up to 5 per cent of school-age children and is more common in boys than girls. The symptoms must be frequent, severe and long lasting for confirmation of the condition. Indicators that a child may have ADHD include:

- poor concentration, particularly with tasks requiring long-term effort, easily distracted
- overactivity – often requiring minimal sleep
- inability to curb immediate reactions and impulsivity
- poor physical co-ordination
- rigidity in response to problem solving, disorganisation
- mood swings and tantrums
- frequently low self-esteem.

Giftedness and high ability

A child who has high ability may walk and talk early, developing a wide vocabulary and vivid imagination, constantly questioning and curious. He may pay great attention to detail, and have sophisticated problem-solving ability. Although he may set himself high standards, he might have strong feelings and fixed opinions, but he is likely to lose interest when asked to repeat tasks.

A child whose needs are not recognised can be:

- verbally cheeky
- constantly questioning
- appearing to lack concentration and finishing tasks quickly
- disruptive, becoming the class comic or clown
- intolerant of the less able
- limitless in physical energy
- requiring little sleep.

KEY POINT

Not all children who are gifted and have high ability will present with behavioural difficulties. Many settle well into schools and playgroups, developing good relationships with peers and adults, and having their talents recognised and channelled constructively.

Childhood depression
This is relatively recently recognised as occurring in quite young children. Specific life events such as divorce and separation of prime carers, death and bereavement, or reaction to a parent who is depressed or seriously ill may trigger excessive responses of:
- guilt and fear, denial, aggression, terrors at parting from carers, sleep disturbance, enuresis, concentration difficulties and labile emotions or extreme mood changes.

KEY POINT

Mourning following bereavement and loss must be considered part of the usual process of healing. Although distressing, it should be temporary if the child is supported. It should only be considered as depression if this process is extended.

Emotional deprivation
Children who fail to have their growing needs met will show this physically and in behaviour. Specific signs include:
- altered growth, delay in meeting all developmental milestones, enuresis and encopresis, inappropriate social responses, volatile emotions, limited differentiation between carers and unfamiliar adults, aggression in play with toys and peers, constant need for approval and attention and difficulties in making and maintaining relationships.

Child abuse
A child who is suffering sexual abuse is the most likely to display overtly distressed behaviour. Specific signs include:
- sexual behaviour displaying inconsistent knowledge for age, sexual advances to adults, sexual play with toys, aggression, fears or phobias, biting, food refusal, constipation or encopresis and bedwetting.

However, a child suffering physical abuse may also show signs of:
- aggression, fear and delay in reaching developmental milestones, 'acting out' hurt in play, passivity.

Other specific behavioural signs in ASD, sensory deprivation and learning difficulties are covered on pages 275, 279 and 290.

CARE

Parents and carers often blame themselves and feel blamed by a variety of professionals for failure to manage their children. Living with a child with behavioural and emotional difficulties is exhausting, demanding and isolating for both child and family. The effects on peers, other siblings and the extended family can be enormous. Families will need as much care and attention as the child himself.

Whatever the underlying reason for a child having difficulty in managing his behaviour it is universally agreed that early recognition and intervention will help to limit damage to social relationships and learning and lessen long-term implications.

Any child with challenging behaviour will have low self-esteem. The child has difficulty controlling and directing his behaviour and is constantly receiving negative messages about it and himself, and he may well have guilt feelings. He may be using his behaviour, consciously or unconsciously, in a way to draw attention to his unmet needs. He will be frightened if his world is out of his control and the adults surrounding him also seem unable to organise it for him.

GOOD PRACTICE

- Always consider your own attitude to working with children who have behavioural and emotional difficulties, and to their parents and carers.
- Does your body language give off negative or judgemental messages?

KEY POINT

A child with behavioural difficulties needs structure and consistency in management and a routine developed to meet his individual and developmental needs.

Provide help

There are many ways in which you can aim to help with behavioural difficulties:
- learning about the specific difficulty that may be provoking the behaviour
- developing positive working relationships with parents – joint and consistent approaches with home and educational establishments are most likely to be successful. Remember the parent is in a unique position with very specific knowledge of the child
- understanding the aims and helping to implement any procedures that may have been developed as a programme for any specific child
- understanding the roles of the professionals involved in advice and care
- providing all opportunities to enhance a child's self-esteem
- being aware of the effects of difficult behaviour upon other children – peers and siblings
- always being constructive, challenging the unacceptable behaviour, not labelling the child
- learning and implementing policies developed for the management of unacceptable behaviour and bullying
- learning and implementing policies developed for the management of problems caused by child abuse
- ensuring learning is structured at a level suitable for the individual child and providing opportunities for stimulation and success
- constantly reviewing and evaluating your own effectiveness in management issues
- keeping accurate current records of the child
- Observations of times and events of incidents of unacceptable behaviour, together with extended observations, will be particularly useful (see page 310).

- Be objective in your assessment, use factual words and avoid subjective terms such as 'naughty', 'rude', etc.
- If there is a suspicion of abuse remember observations are an important, objective part of monitoring a child at risk.

Practical care

Changing behaviour will take time and sometimes only small modifications may be achieved. A child will not alter overnight. Issues in very young children such as delayed toilet-training, encopresis, ongoing and persistent temper tantrums and problems over food refusal are best discussed with the local health visitor and at the referral clinic so all involved in the child's care are not causing the child further confusion with different demands.

A child's poor sleeping patterns can affect a whole family – however a child who genuinely needs little sleep should not be made to feel guilty. Families can be helped in such a situation by following a 'maximum rest' for the whole family approach. This can be taught by a member of the multidisciplinary team.

From studies of the child a behaviour management plan will be devised.

Observations of children are an integral part of the work of an Early Years worker. They may have a special use in helping to provide a picture of a child who is distressed and showing challenging behaviour.

Arrange for the child to play or work alongside you

Goals set for changing the child's behaviour must be realistic and achievable. Select specific areas for improvement on which he can concentrate and try not to overwhelm him with everything at once, as this will reinforce his feelings of failure, his behaviour will worsen and a vicious circle commence.

Ensure that each day the child is receiving praise for his efforts. Try to concentrate on the positives in the child's behaviour with smiles, eye contact, gestures and open body language to reinforce your positive approach.

The child may constantly demand attention and probably really needs this, even though it can place additional strain within a group. Get him started on a piece of work or an activity and check he understands what is required. Then arrange for him to work or play alongside you. Ensure you observe his attention levels by eye contact or speaking his name.

OBSERVING AND RECORDING EVENTS

Specific observations can be an important tool in the objective assessment of a child's behaviour, especially when the child first joins a group.

Recording specific incidents of unacceptable behaviour can help staff identify the following:

(a) whether incidents have a clearly identified pattern – time of day, part of week, following certain activities/routines, when a child is tired, etc.

(b) whether incidents follow an identified trigger – a specific activity, working with particular groups of children or a child.

(c) progress or regression.

Records of specific events can provide information for other team members and for parents, and they can help in the development of a care plan to include rewards for periods when incidents do not happen or are lessening in frequency.

Example of an observation record of unacceptable events/behaviour
Event sample and frequency count

Day of week	No.	Duration	Provoked/ Unprovoked	Comments on seriousness

Break formal activities down into small chunks, using a variety of activities and techniques, and space them carefully throughout the day. Learn to distinguish between things the child can do and things he won't.

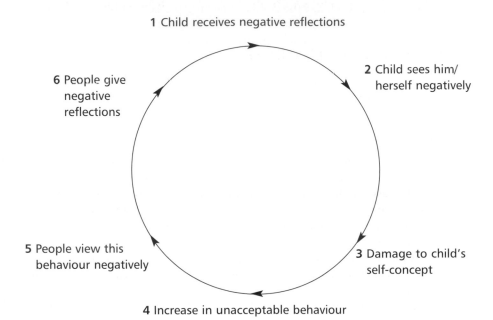

1 Child receives negative reflections

2 Child sees him/herself negatively

3 Damage to child's self-concept

4 Increase in unacceptable behaviour

5 People view this behaviour negatively

6 People give negative reflections

The circle of negative image

PROGRESS CHECK

1   How many ways can you indicate you are pleased with a child's efforts?
2   Refer to the 'circle of negative image' diagram above. How could you
    (a) break the circle; or (b) reverse the direction of the circle?

KEY POINT

Any vibrant classroom or play setting can be noisy and exciting. Are you sure that you are not expecting a child with limited concentration to compete with too much excitement? Make sure the child's table or desk is not by a door or facing a window.

How a child feels about himself is largely dependent on the way he is valued in the early years. Part of managing a child with behavioural difficulties is helping him to develop social relationships, which will promote his self-esteem and feelings of self-worth and teach him skills. A child who is fidgety, impulsive, distracting and sometimes aggressive within a group is often a child with few friends. Consider how you can involve a child who appears on the outskirts of a group.

Activity

One of the uses of creative activities is to provide a release of tension. Arrange a week's programme within the usual classroom plan, where you can provide easily organised activities for a child who needs to use them for this reason.

ONGOING MANAGEMENT

Although the general principles of helping any child develop control and constructive relationships are similar, there are some additional specific measures for identified conditions.

ADHD

Controversy over the management of this specific condition continues. Many children have been treated with drug therapy – usually methylphenidate (Ritalin) – to improve attention and reduce impulsiveness. Parents and carers have often been pleased with the success of this treatment. Drug treatment is commonly used in conjunction with behavioural or family therapies.

There is, however, a strongly held body of opinion that overuse of stimulant drugs for young children, including some children who may not need them, is a cause for concern and some experts feel that intensive behavioural therapy alone may be more effective.

Against this view extensive research into the topic of drug therapy has supported the belief that methylphenidate is helpful for children, for short periods of time. More research is needed on the efficacy of longer term use and the effects of continued use of medication on a child's education and social functioning.

Food additives have been blamed for hyperactive behaviour and research suggests that in a few children removing these from a diet will help a child's control. However they are not the sole cause of the behaviour.

High ability

The identification of children with high ability allows for planning to meet their specific needs and this is a key issue. When this happens, unacceptable behaviour is less likely to occur. Meeting and valuing these special needs, within mainstream schooling, is thought to be most beneficial. Allowing opportunities to stretch an individual child within the curriculum and developing a full programme of extra-curricular activities is valuable. Children of all ages benefit from contact with their peers. Mixing children of high ability with an older age-range is not always helpful as, although these children may be exceptionally able, they are not necessarily socially skilled.

KEY POINT

As part of an international programme to recognise and challenge a gifted child's mathematical and problem-solving abilities, schools can offer children the opportunity to undertake optional World Class Tests. The tests are supported by a package of innovative teaching resources that aim to improve the teaching and learning of gifted and talented students. The tests are targeted at children aged eight upwards, but younger children may take them if they are considered ready.

Childhood depression

Intractable depression will need skilled medical help. A child going through a bereavement, whether through death, separation or divorce from close family members, will need encouragement to discuss his feelings in a one-to-one trusting situation. His fears and anxieties need acknowledgement. The use of creative activities and imaginative play will be valuable in helping him express his feelings. Remember he is already upset and if he cries you have not made things worse, but perhaps allowed him to release some of his painful feelings. Choose words and language carefully: saying 'cheer up' usually only makes the speaker feel better, not the child.

Child abuse

If the abuse is known and formal procedures are already in motion for assessing the safety of the child, then the role of the Early Years worker is to record worrying signs, report them if they arise and support the child. Never force a child to disclose information to you, but be available if he wishes to talk. Always maintain complete confidentiality, but tell a child if you are going to relay this information to other workers – never make promises you cannot keep.

Overt sexual advances that sometimes occur when a child has been abused need to be handled firmly but with a matter-of-fact approach. You must indicate that, although such behaviour is not acceptable, the child is not dirty or disgusting. Be careful in your own responses.

Children may need encouragement to discuss their feelings

Again, allow maximum opportunities for the child to relieve painful feelings through creative and imaginative play.

See also Chapter 9, pages 394–5.

GENERAL IMPLICATIONS

Changing behaviour is demanding and exhausting for all concerned. Perhaps with more than any other condition, a child with severe behaviour problems can dominate his total environment in school and at home. Developing consistent coping strategies that all concerned feel confident in managing, continue to be the underpinning principles of management.

CASE STUDY

Jem's mother had been pressing the school to take her highly active four-year-old son into their nursery class as soon as possible, as he was causing considerable family stress.

Jem slept little, often requiring only two hours a night – this caused worries, especially about safety. He had been discovered recently trying to cook at 3 a.m., while the family slept. Not being able to light the gas he had left the taps turned on.

Jem did not appear to understand the implications of his actions and as a result was constantly in trouble and being told off. He was easily frustrated and with fleeting levels of concentration, starting one activity and moving on if a difficulty arose. He had regular temper tantrums and showed aggressive behaviour towards his eighteen month old sister, hitting and biting her. His family did everything they could to placate him in an attempt to avoid conflict but were beginning to despair.

A home visit by the teacher and Early Years worker was arranged to discuss Jem's needs.

1   What advice might help Jem's family prepare him for school?
2   What preparation will the school staff need to make to ensure both Jem and the group's needs are met as fully as possible?

RESOURCES

The ADHD Family Support Group UK
1a The High Street
Dilton Marsh
Westbury
Wiltshire BA13 4DL
www.pavilion.co.uk/add/english.html

The Compassionate Friends
53 North Street
Bristol BS3 1EN
www.tcf.org.uk

The National Association for Gifted Children
Suite 14
Challenge House
Sherwood Drive
Bletchley
Milton Keynes MK3 6DP
www.nagcbritain.org.uk

NSPCC
National Centre
42 Curtain Road
London EC2A 3NH
www.nspcc.org.uk

KEY TERMS

You need to know what these words and phrases mean. Go back through the chapter and make sure that you understand:

articulation	encopresis
Asperger's syndrome	enuresis
attention deficit	externalised and internalised
autistic spectrum disorders	behaviours
avoidance	'holding' therapy
behaviour modification	hyperactivity disorder
blocks	perception
child abuse	processing and transmitting of
childhood depression	sensory stimuli
children with high abilities	prolongations
dysfluency	ritualistic behaviour
dyslexia	speech, language and
dyspraxia	communication impairment
echolalia	stammer/stutter
emotional and behavioural	tongue exercises
difficulties	

9 COMPLEX CONDITIONS

> ## This chapter covers:
> - **Down syndrome**
> - **Fragile X syndrome**
> - **Hearing impairment**
> - **Vision impairment**
> - **Spina bifida**
> - **Hydrocephalus**
> - **Cerebral palsy**
> - **Child abuse**

The conditions covered in this chapter are major and complex, frequently influencing several developmental areas. Early Years workers are likely to meet children with these conditions in many care settings.

Down syndrome

This particular syndrome was first described in 1866. It is a genetic condition that happens because of the presence of an extra **chromosome**. Children with Down syndrome will have some specific physical characteristics but there will be more differences than similarities among children with Down syndrome, because each child inherits characteristics from her own particular family background.

The child with Down syndrome will have a learning disability and may also have associated physical difficulties such as heart problems, thyroid diseases, extra coughs and colds, and hearing or visual impairment.

The number of babies born with Down syndrome is about one in every 700 births – about 1000 babies each year in the UK. It occurs in all social, economic, cultural, religious and racial backgrounds. It is not a disease and children do not *suffer* from Down syndrome.

WHAT HAPPENS

There are three different types of Down syndrome but the effects on the child are similar.

Standard trisomy

Ninety-five per cent of children with Down syndrome have this type, which is always an accident of nature. Usually a child has forty-six chromosomes in twenty-three pairs, which carry the child's inherited characteristics. Half of these chromosomes come from the mother and half from the father. A child with Down syndrome has an extra chromosome from either the mother or the father, making forty-seven in total. The extra chromosome is produced either during the making of the egg or sperm or during the initial cell division at conception.

Translocation

This is a rare inherited condition occurring in about 2 per cent of children with Down syndrome. Parents pass on an abnormal chromosome 21, which contains extra material, as well as the normal chromosome 21, so the child has the usual total of forty-six chromosomes in all.

Mosaic Down syndrome

This is also extremely rare, occurring in 2 to 5 per cent of children with Down syndrome. Here, some of the child's cells will have the usual forty-six chromosomes and some abnormal cells will have forty-seven. The effects of this condition are less severe, with fewer characteristic facial features and disproportionately less learning disability.

Indications at birth that a baby may have Down syndrome

- The baby is very floppy with poor muscle tone; the joints can be overextended and are highly flexible.
- The mouth is small and often kept open with the tongue protruding; and the palate is high and arched.
- The face and head appear flat; the nasal bridge, too, is flattened; and the hair-line is low with extra folds of skin.
- The eyes slant slightly upwards and outwards, with a fold of skin running vertically between the two lids at the inner corner of the eye.
- The ears are small and low set.
- The hands are broad with short fingers and the little fingers curve inwards. There may be only one crease across the palm.
- The feet are short and broad with a deep cleft between the first and second toe, extending as a long crease on the side of the foot.

KEY POINT

Shared physical characteristics are not an indication of future ability or capacity to learn.

Possible additional health difficulties

The chromosomal abnormalities cause disruption to the growth of the developing baby and additional health problems may occur:

- Hearing may be affected due to the child's vulnerability to catch frequent coughs and colds, causing glue ear.

- Vision may be affected; there is often a squint or other associated difficulties.
- Physical development may be affected; the child will be smaller than her peers.
- Due to her floppiness and general poor muscle tone initially, delay may occur in developing gross motor skills. She will have a tendency to gain weight.
- The immune system may be underdeveloped, leaving her more vulnerable to illnesses, especially in her early years.
- Heart problems may occur. Around 40 per cent of children with Down syndrome have a heart problem, of which half will be serious and require surgery.

KEY POINT

Not all children with Down syndrome will have all these health problems and even if some are present they will vary in severity.

DIAGNOSIS

The risk of having a child with Down syndrome increases with maternal age (see below).

Maternal age	Risk
15–19 years	1 in 1850
25 years	1 in 1400
30 years	1 in 800
35 years	1 in 380
38 years	1 in 190
40 years	1 in 110
45 years	1 in 30

- The reason why the rate increases with maternal age is unknown.
- The risk of a subsequent baby having Down syndrome is increased.
- Genetic counselling is often advised.
- Tests – amniocentesis or chorionic villus sampling – during pregnancy can confirm whether a baby has the condition.

When a baby is born with this condition a mother may recognise she is physically different from other babies, although this does not always happen. A blood test will confirm that a baby has the condition.

While waiting for this information parents will require understanding and support. The process of giving birth is emotionally and physically demanding, and any additional anxieties must cause much shock and distress. How the news of the diagnosis is given can often affect the new and developing relationship between mother and child. Both parents should be present and the positive aspects of what a child can do rather than cannot do need to be discussed. Informative and constructive literature needs to be made available for parents to read at their leisure. The voluntary bodies often provide support and 'enablers' at this time of diagnosis.

KEY POINTS

- There is no right or wrong way for a family to react. Families will have differing responses to the news.
- Telling other family members and friends may be stressful.

PROGRESS CHECK

How would you reply to someone who asked if Down syndrome was inherited?

CARE

The young child

Physical care and prevention of infection

The child's skin may be dry and fragile so use gentle emollient skin care products in your daily hygiene routines. Maintain a hygienic environment (see Chapter 6, pages 206 and 227). While she is very young keep her away from obviously infectious areas such as overcrowded and overheated situations in order to try to limit the number of upper respiratory chest infections she may get. This is important if the child has associated serious heart complications. Routine immunisations will be necessary.

As the child is floppy she will need additional physical support, so hold her firmly with a good grasp. Encourage her to play on the floor on a firm surface to develop her muscles and strength.

Promote her self-help skills, such as washing, brushing her teeth and dressing, as she grows, even if it takes longer.

Toilet-training management means following a consistent approach when she demonstrates her readiness to learn. Watch for non-verbal signs such as taking off a wet nappy or pulling at a soiled one, as she may not yet be able to use words to indicate sensations. The principles of how control is learnt will not differ from the learning of other children.

Stimulation and development

She will need all the usual stimulation of any baby, with handling, talking, singing and, in the early days, cot and pram toys to encourage her development. The mother will learn to interpret her needs. Choose ongoing toys carefully to help her develop skills, remembering her hands and fingers may be small and with less strength. Try to choose toys and activities that stimulate all her senses. Remember to allow a little longer for skills to develop – try not to hurry or interrupt her when she is involved. Break down any activity into small units and show her often how something works. Allow her freedom to explore her surroundings and everyday world.

Break down activities into small units and show the child often

KEY POINTS

- All research tells us that early stimulation and encouragement is vital in helping a child with Down syndrome to develop to her full potential.
- A baby with Down syndrome has all the needs of any new baby, such as love and security, time to develop relationships and opportunities to learn. She just needs a little extra attention in certain areas.
- The baby's first responsive smile will be later than other babies – always reward her attempts at communication with smiles, cuddles, etc.

Activity
Create a sensory area. Make sure you are including visual, auditory and tactile experiences. Design this to meet the needs and interests of all children of pre-school age, regardless of ability.

Developing speech and language

A child with Down syndrome will have small nasal passages and sinuses and the roof of the mouth is small and high, which reduces the mouth cavity. The tongue is often thicker, which leads to her having difficulty keeping it inside her mouth. All this can lead to breathing and articulation difficulties.

Always remain in good visual contact when you are talking to the child and hold her close so she can watch your face and mouth. Be patient when she begins to develop speech.

Some children with Down syndrome are helped by the use of Makaton (see page opposite), which is a structured signing system used to complement speech development.

Makaton is used to help speech development

Early language support is important. See Chapter 8, pages 300–302, for advice on encouraging speech development, and pages 342–3, for promoting oral speech and communicating in hearing impairment.

KEY POINT

A child with Down syndrome can be taught, with encouragement, to keep her tongue inside her mouth. This helps appearance – important for self-esteem – and reduces mouth breathing and its associated problems.

A child with Down syndrome will achieve and continue to develop throughout her life, but her rate of progress will be slower than for ordinary children (see below). The pattern and stages of development are the same as for other children.

KEY POINT

Each child is individual and may achieve more quickly in certain developmental areas than others.

EXAMPLES OF MAKATON SIGNS
■ Always use with speech and complement with facial gestures and body language.
■ Remember it is a staged programme with levels 1 to 8 increasing in complexity.
■ Some specific signs will be especially important to certain children.

Stage one

MUMMY/MOTHER
tap twice

BROTHER
rub knuckles

CUP
DRINK
TO DRINK

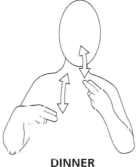

DINNER
move hands alternately to mouth

CHAIR

TEA
drinking from
cup, holding saucer

Stage two

BABY
DOLL
same sign but
without movement

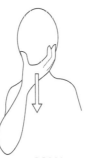

MAN
stroke
beard

BED
eyes open
TO SLEEP
eyes closed

EGG

GOOD PRACTICE

Update your skills – learn Makaton. Courses are often available at evening classes.

Developmental stage	The ordinary baby	The baby with Down syndrome
Sits unsupported	5–9 months	7 + months
Walks	9–18 months	1–4 years
First words	10–23 months	1–3 years
Toilet-training achieved	1–3 years	2–7 years

Babies' stages of development

Feeding

Breast-feeding a baby with Down syndrome can be helped by the advice and support of a lactation sister and health visitor. This may be required as the baby's small mouth, weaker muscle tone and rooting reflex, accompanied by a possibly protruding tongue, may make latching on difficult. The result can be under-stimulation of the breast and reduced milk production. If so the baby may tire before she has received enough milk. Perseverance and maternal motivation usually overcome such initial difficulties.

If the baby is artificially fed ensure that the teats are both soft and large enough to allow an easy flow of milk.

GOOD PRACTICE

- Always hold the baby closely during feeds and consider it a special time for one-to-one interaction.
- If the baby has an associated heart problem her tiredness may be increased during feeding, so do not hurry her and check the teat is not too small.

Weaning

Always supervise well, as the baby's cough reflex may be lessened, increasing the chances of choking.

Tongue thrusting may persist, so do not assume a food is disliked just because it appears rejected. Remember that coping with a spoon may just require patience and persistence.

Do not continue with puréed foods for longer than necessary as the baby will need the practise of coping with lumps and the need to develop chewing as any other baby. Introduce foods carefully and slowly one at a time.

Use trial and error to find a comfortable spoon for this new skill. As she develops the baby may find using cutlery difficult, and although finger feeding is acceptable when a toddler, encourage the use of cutlery in preparation for nursery or school.

Aim for a diet not excessively high in calories, in view of the tendency to gain weight easily. It is much simpler to avoid putting too much weight on, rather than attempting to reduce calorie intake later. Developing healthy food habits when the baby is young will be helpful.

Social and emotional development

It is detrimental to any child not to have acceptable social behaviour, so it is also essential for a child with Down syndrome. She needs to learn to be part of a wider group, share and take turns, and understand the difference between right and wrong. She may become cross and frustrated, and have periods of regression, but such skills are essential to her becoming a valued member of a wider society and making friends.

She needs to develop an awareness of when displays of affection are acceptable, and when they are not, and learn who to respond to and trust.

Lauren enjoys her doll

GOOD PRACTICE

- Always praise and acknowledge good behaviour – do not constantly criticise failings.
- Be realistic in your expectations. The pattern of development will be the same as an ordinary child but she will take longer to reach her milestones.
- Always explain simply and clearly what you expect.
- Remain consistent in your approach.
- Remember that you are an important role model.

KEY POINT

Children with Down syndrome are all different. They will have preferences and likes and dislikes, some will be easygoing, some will be forceful, some compliant and some disobedient – but all will be different.

Safety issues

- Double check that your environment is safe. Remember the child's control and power may be affected with weaker muscles, making her vulnerable to falls. Make sure you always use straps in highchairs, pushchairs, car seats, etc.
- Use non-slip mats in baths, clear toys and debris from floors, and keep stairs clear.
- Always check the temperature of food when she is a baby and as a toddler – she may be less sensitive to extremes of temperature.
- Never leave her alone when she is learning to manage solid foods.
- Teach her how to use equipment and undertake any activity safely. Repeat instructions regularly, but best of all show her.
- She may forget safety instructions so do not rely on her always to remember them. When she is excited, hungry, tired or a routine is changed she is even more likely to forget.

A Portage scheme is often used for children with Down syndrome prior to their entry to care and educational establishments (see pages 176–9).

ONGOING MANAGEMENT

The aim for a child with Down syndrome is for her to reach her potential without being pushed beyond her capacity. So as an Early Years worker it is essential that you motivate and encourage her to regard learning as fun and pleasurable.

Playgroups and opportunities to mix with groups of children are important.

When joining a group of children, sometimes a child with Down syndrome is over-protected by the rest of the children, keen to be caring. This can usually be resolved if handled sensitively and she is encouraged to interact and behave normally within the group. Do not make excuses if she displays unacceptable behaviour – this may reinforce it and make it difficult for her to know what is expected of her.

Always keep watch in a playground for any bullying or teasing.

Factors to consider for the child in a learning environment

- Check you are not asking the child for two things at once, e.g. to draw a picture and then go and place it on the wall – especially in the beginning.
- Break down every task into the smallest unit.
- Check the child understands what you want – she may say 'yes', but this does not always mean 'yes'. She may repeat your instructions or question back, again this does not necessarily imply understanding. Demonstrations accompanied by simple instructions are often most effective. Check understanding at each stage of a task.
- Do not assume the child understands basic terms such as 'over and under', 'top and bottom', etc.
- Do not hurry or rush the child; always allow her sufficient time.
- With small hands the child may find pens, pencils and scissors difficult at first. What adaptations might help?
- If you are teaching a new task or developing the child's concentration levels, check the room or area is quiet and not offering competing stimulation.

- Baby or toddler gym clubs, ballet classes and swimming will all be helpful in encouraging gross motor control and development.
- The child needs much encouragement and positive feedback for her efforts.

Carefully supervised gym sessions can promote physical development

Horse-riding is enjoyable for all children

Medical difficulties

Heart lesions
There is a range of severity of the heart lesions. Often surgery is required early in life and liaison with the medical team will be necessary. Hospitalisation means a child will have to undergo the additional trauma of a change in routine, possibly distressing procedures and increased parental anxiety. Inevitably a change in routine may mean a temporary interruption in her general progress. However, successful surgical intervention means she will be able to participate fully in all activities, without breathlessness and tiredness.

Some cardiac difficulties are such that surgery is not possible.

Respiratory infections

Coughs, colds and chest infections will be more common. Parents and carers need reassurance that it is important to seek prompt treatment for such infections – they are not being over-protective. The effects of persistent infections on general health, and especially hearing and associated heart difficulties may be considerable if not treated.

Auditory problems

Most hearing problems result from a conductive loss, as a result of persistent middle ear infections. Treatment before speech development is affected is important. Remember, too, that such infections can occur at any time and an awareness of any child who is failing to respond to sounds should always be investigated – hearing should be checked after colds. (See the discussion on managing hearing impairment on page 347.)

Visual problems

A variety of different visual problems may occur but the most common are squints and short-sightedness. A child needing glasses will need special attention from the optician to ensure they fit well – if not they may fall off the nose more easily due to the child's flat nasal bridge.

If a child in your care is wearing spectacles check they are:

- comfortable
- clean and unbroken
- worn when they should be.

Other difficulties

A range of congenital conditions can occur in a child with Down syndrome and is more likely than in a baby who does not have the syndrome. Routine health promotion means that any problems identified can be remedied early. No child should endure an illness that can be prevented or successfully treated.

KEY POINT

Many children with Down syndrome have no associated health problems and others will be affected in only a minor way.

PROGRESS CHECK

1 What percentage of babies born with Down syndrome are likely to have associated cardiac problems?
2 Why are respiratory infections more common?

GENERAL IMPLICATIONS

Society continues to have a stereotyped view of children with Down syndrome: they are considered physically similar, often even with haircuts alike, pliant and good-natured and with limited potential. With the advance of integration this view is at last being challenged.

It is important that you, as a professional, care for every child as an individual, balancing all her needs, and valuing and understanding her differences. Check that you do not reinforce stereotypes.

As children with Down syndrome grow into adulthood, they are, increasingly, leading full and independent lives and making positive contributions to society. Sometimes this is from within a sheltered community. Long-term institutional care is no longer acceptable.

ADDITIONAL DEVELOPMENTS

At present confirmation of Down syndrome is possible by about eighteen to twenty weeks of a pregnancy. However a new technique has been discovered, which will allow detection within three months of conception. This tests for the absence of a nasal bone in the foetus, which indicates Down syndrome. Earlier diagnosis would give parents additional time to make a decision about the pregnancy. Currently this screening is only available in a handful of NHS centres.

In some countries, especially the US and increasingly in Germany, Australia, Israel and Canada, cosmetic surgery is being offered to make the physical appearance of a child with Down syndrome similar to that of her peers. This includes reducing tongue size and altering eye and nose contours. Some people argue this is justified in that changing outward appearance alters people's expectations of children with Down syndrome. Others, especially in the UK, reply that we should change society's attitudes and not the child with Down syndrome.

CASE STUDY

Chloe was a keenly awaited first baby, born by Caesarean section, to older parents. Her Down syndrome was obvious at birth and although she was immediately loved and cherished by her mother, her father found her condition distressing and did not visit his wife or daughter during the week they were in hospital.

On discharge home Chloe had difficulties feeding. She had a poor suck and her mother was unable to continue breast-feeding, much to her disappointment. Chloe's mother was tired following both the birth and the additional emotions surrounding the event, but she felt unable to leave Chloe with her husband as he was still refusing to hold or even look at his daughter.

Despite visits from the health visitor and support from the voluntary association the situation did not improve and the parents' relationship was in danger of breaking up.

Chloe progressed, but a heart defect was identified during routine health examination and she was admitted for repair of the lesion at eight months old. On this occasion her father did go to hospital to see both his wife and daughter, and he began to make the first attempts to acknowledge and learn about Chloe as his daughter.

When Chloe was eighteen months old a Portage worker began to visit the home and encouraged both parents to work together with their daughter. Chloe's father later said that having something he could actually do greatly improved how he felt about Chloe – they began learning together. He felt more an integral part of the family with something specific to contribute. The family stayed together as a unit and Chloe blossomed, eventually attending her local primary school. Both her parents are now campaigners for equal access to education for children with Down syndrome.

1 Why do you think society seems to fail to understand that the father may need support adjusting to the birth of a baby with special needs, in addition to the mother?
2 Why do you consider men sometimes feel threatened by the birth of a baby with obvious special needs?

RESOURCES

The Down Syndrome Association
The Langdon Down Centre
2A Langdon Park
Teddington
MiddlesexTW11 9PS
www.downs-syndrome.org.uk

Fragile X syndrome

Fragile X is a relatively recently recognised condition of genetic origin. It is the most common inherited cause of learning disabilities affecting one in 4000 boys and one in 8000 girls. Primarily the effects are on a child's learning abilities, but there are also some physical characteristics.

The specific chromosomal fragility was discovered in 1969. Sophisticated testing mechanisms were developed to confirm the occurrence of this condition, but the associated developmental problems and behavioural difficulties were not fully associated with the chromosomal abnormality until 1977.

WHAT HAPPENS

The condition is passed on by the X chromosome, which is one of the pair that decides a child's sex. A boy has an X and a Y and a girl has two Xs. If a girl has a 'fragile' X chromosome she also will have an undamaged one, which can sometimes overcome the effects of the fragile chromosome. A damaged or fragile X chromosome appears different under a microscope, with an abnormality at the tip and appearing partially separated.

The condition can be passed on by unaffected male and female carriers.

Developmental difficulties

Learning difficulties

Learning difficulties are usually present in both boys and girls, with boys being more severely affected. Severity ranges from mild educational delay to severe difficulties.

Speech and language

Speech and language difficulties are usually present in all children with the condition. Language delay may be the first worrying sign of the condition. The following are difficulties that may occur:

- word and phrase repetition, accompanied by up and down swings of pitch
- echolalia – repetition of last phrase or word
- palilalia – repetition of words or phrases a child has spoken himself
- dysrhythmia – poor control of rhythm and inappropriate use of pauses
- comprehension difficulties of the spoken word.

Behaviour and attention

KEY POINTS

Often some of the characteristics below are present.

- tantrums continuing after the expected developmental stage
- excessive response to stimulation, especially by inappropriate behaviour
- overactivity/hyperactivity – limited sleep requirements, always on the go and difficulty in sitting still
- impulsive – difficulty in waiting and a need for immediate gratification
- concentration problems
- anxiety – avoiding eye contact, gaze avoidance
- short-term memory difficulties but long-term memory is much better
- mimicry, especially specific words
- ritualistic behaviour – having a strong need for routine and is distressed by changes
- repetitive behaviour – finger-flicking, hand-flapping and hand-biting can occur.

The severity may lessen as the child grows.

- The older undiagnosed child may not be noticed as 'badly behaved' – just lacking in concentration or appearing uncooperative at times.

Physical characteristics and health implications

These physical characteristics may not be present in all children and the specific facial appearance may not be noticeable until the child is older

- laxity of joints and muscles: late sitting, walking, etc.
- recurrent middle-ear infections
- a long, narrow face with prominent jaw bone
- epilepsy (twenty per cent of children)
- large testes in adult males.

DIAGNOSIS

A child may cause anxiety to parents, perhaps by delay in responsive smiling, sleep disruption, lateness in sitting or walking, delay in language development or behavioural problems.

Confirmation of the condition is by blood test. The severity of the effect of the condition is variable and not easily predicted.

KEY POINT

The term 'fragile' in the condition does not mean a child is sickly or ill.

CARE

As with a child with Down syndrome, early development and implementation of a multidisciplinary management plan can lessen the long-term effects of the condition, allowing for the development of the child's full potential and promotion of self-esteem.

Support from a wide variety of specialists will be required with emphasis on early speech therapy. The earlier a parent can understand and respond to the child's speech the better. (See Chapter 8, pages 300–302 on helping speech development, and pages 342–3 on promoting oral speech.)

GOOD PRACTICE

- As an Early Years worker helping a child with a learning disability, check you know the norms of development so you can plan for the child's progress. Remember, his development will follow a similar pattern to any other child's, but he may take longer to achieve his milestones.
- A child with fragile X can be 'routine dependent' so a flexible and realistic care plan should be developed.

Health problems are unlikely to be any different from any other child's. However, strain on families where a child needs little sleep can be great, so liaison with the health visitor will be necessary.

Remember the child may use mimicry in his behaviour, so turn it to constructive use by ensuring you always present as a positive role model – especially important in safety practices.

The child needs to learn to be part of a group, whether at home, or in a care and education establishment. This will be by helping the child to moderate his behaviour with verbal reinforcement, praise and example. Understanding his difficulties should not affect your efforts to help him change. Always make sure you are realistic in your demands of him. Remember his cognitive stage of development; for example do not expect him to take turns, before he has learnt to share.

Help the child develop concentration by breaking down games and activities into small, achievable units.

He may benefit from Makaton and Portage schemes carried out in the home by peripatetic workers.

PROGRESS CHECK

Which area of development is the most likely to show signs of delay in a child with fragile X syndrome?

ONGOING MANAGEMENT

When he is involved in more formal pre-school or school settings you can help the child by using the following approaches:

- providing a distraction-free area and keeping noise levels low to allow the child to concentrate on the task in hand
- keeping a calm environment, which the child will find reassuring
- keeping the child close when he is working, having him alongside rather than facing you, as he may find eye contact threatening
- giving the child short sessions if you are expecting concentration – 10–15 minutes at one time, and a little and often is most valuable.

Frequent short sessions are best for maximum concentration

- alternating quiet and energetic activities
- giving the child 'time out'
- keeping your expectations clear and consistent – be realistic in your demands
- telling the child what behaviour is unacceptable and rewarding positive behaviour
- being prepared to repeat instructions and checking the child understands
- developing your skills in storytelling and reading – the child will find a visual-based approach easier
- checking the child's hearing has been re-tested following any colds
- building the child's self-esteem with praise and encouragement for effort
- working to the child's strengths.

KEY POINTS

- All staff involved in the child's care should follow similar management approaches.
- Maintain good home liaison. A child needs the security of routines and will become distressed by changes whether at home or in a playgroup or school. A key worker will be important.

Activity
Make a story prop, which would help hold the attention of a four-year-old child with fragile X syndrome, during storytime.

Special areas of difficulty
It is thought that reasoning and sequential thinking are areas that can prove difficult for a child with fragile X. The child tends to get waylaid and become sidetracked with irrelevancies. Number work can be demanding. Provide structured well-presented activities to gain his attention. Avoid using generalities as he will be confused.

The use of computers, which are non-threatening, consistent and allow for constant task repetition, is often valuable.

GENERAL IMPLICATIONS

Effective communication and sharing of knowledge of the child and the condition is important. Remember he will look similar to his peers and the realisation that he has special needs may sometimes occur after his self-esteem and confidence have been affected.

ADDITIONAL DEVELOPMENTS

Genetic counselling may be offered to families who have a child with fragile X syndrome. Improving public awareness of the condition and its effects is happening mainly due to the efforts of the Fragile X Society.

RESOURCES

Fragile X Society
Rood End House
6 Stortford Road
Great Dunmow
Essex CM6 1DA
www.fragilex.org.uk

Hearing impairment

Up to 65,000 children in Britain have a degree of hearing impairment and about 840 babies each year will be born with a permanent childhood hearing impairment (PCHI). The severity of childhood deafness ranges from mild to moderated and can be either permanent or fluctuating. Nine out of ten deaf children will have hearing parents, often with no experience of deafness.

The development of language, communication and understanding of the spoken word has a direct impact on a child's access to the wider world. The use of English language and education is designed for a hearing child. Late diagnoses of hearing difficulties directly affect a child's ability to gain spoken language. Half of all deaf children are undiagnosed by eighteen months and one-quarter remain undiagnosed by three years. Behaviour and social and emotional development are often affected by a failure to discover an impairment early.

KEY POINT

The major effects of hearing impairment are on the development of language, communication and understanding of the spoken word and deaf children face tremendous difficulties in these areas.

WHAT HAPPENS

Types of hearing impairment

Sensorineural hearing impairment

In this impairment, damage to the nervous system and the hearing apparatus occurs. This can be one-sided (unilateral) or affect both ears (bilateral). It is usually permanent.

The cause of the impairment may be one of the following:

- genetic/unknown/family history of deafness
- maternal rubella (German measles) during pregnancy
- certain drugs, especially during pregnancy
- severe jaundice at birth
- prematurity
- lack of oxygen at birth
- brain damage at birth/brain injury later in life
- some chromosomal disorders
- meningitis – thought to be the cause of one-third of cases of acquired deafness
- some infections, particularly:
  - measles
  - mumps
  - viral infections.

KEY POINT

Some of the causes of sensorineural hearing impairment are congenital – the child is born with the condition. Others are acquired after birth.

Conductive hearing impairment

In this impairment the sound waves are unable to pass through the eardrum, or the eardrum is prevented from vibrating through the middle ear (see page opposite).

The cause of the impairment may be one of the following:

- Blockage of the outer ear, external canal or middle ear by wax or foreign bodies such as beads, peanuts, etc.
- Swollen adenoids at the back of the nose, often following recurrent coughs and colds.
- Middle-ear infections – otitis media. Infections enter via the Eustachian tube.
- Otitis media with effusion – OME or 'glue ear'. After an infection of the middle ear or because of an allergy, fluid remains in the middle ear and becomes thick. As a result the sound waves are stopped from travelling along the ear and the drum from vibrating.

KEY POINTS

- Conductive hearing impairment is usually temporary and often fluctuating – the degree of loss will vary from day to day. As a result a child with a conductive impairment is often unacknowledged.
- A child typically says 'what' and 'pardon' a lot, may speak loudly and appear to ignore other adults and children.

Mixed impairment

Here a child may have a combination of sensory and conductive deafness.

HOW SOUND WAVES TRAVEL IN THE EAR

Sound waves are collected by the outer ear (**1**) and directed into the ear canal (**2**) where they meet the eardrum, which is a tightly stretched membrane (**3**). When the sound strikes this drum it starts vibrating. The vibrations pass into the middle ear (**5**) by three tiny bones linked together (**4**). The first is attached to the eardrum and the last embedded into a second membrane called the oval window (**10**). Behind this second membrane is the cochlea (**6**). This is filled with fluid and contains the hearing nerves (**9**). When the vibration is passed to the fluid it stimulates the nerves, which pass the sound signals to the hearing area of the brain.

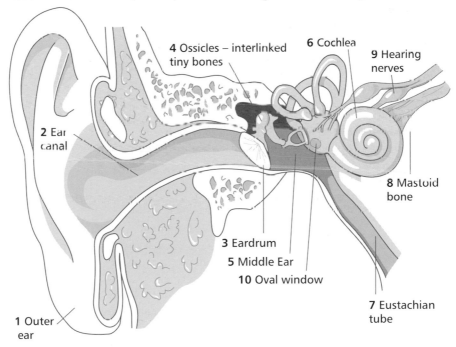

4 Ossicles – interlinked tiny bones

6 Cochlea

9 Hearing nerves

2 Ear canal

8 Mastoid bone

3 Eardrum

5 Middle Ear

10 Oval window

7 Eustachian tube

1 Outer ear

Hearing assessment

Hearing assessment also measures frequencies. Sound varies in loudness and pitch and is divided, for assessment purposes, into high, middle or low frequency, or pitch. The frequency of sound is measured in kilohertz and 1 kilohertz is 1000 hertz. Low frequency is up to 500 hertz; middle frequency is from 500 hertz to 1 kilohertz; and high frequency is above 1 kilohertz.

The lower and middle frequencies tend to convey the louder and vowel sounds in speech; and the high frequency the consonant sounds and is responsible for the intelligibility of speech.

A child with high-frequency impairment will respond to sound, as she hears low and middle frequencies in speech, but she will have great problems in learning and understanding speech. She will be hearing indistinct speech.

DIAGNOSIS

Parents, following the birth of their new baby, are often given checklists and leaflets to help them identify worrying and significant signs, in the early months.

Early signs that might indicate a child is not hearing

Infant to six months
The child:
- does not blink or startle at loud noise
- does not notice household noises such as vacuum cleaner, telephone, either by 'stilling' or appearing to listen when they start
- may not smile responsively by six weeks.

KEY POINT

A baby profoundly deaf from birth may coo and gurgle initially as a hearing baby.

6–12 months
The child:
- does not turn to mother's voice across the room
- does not babble in conversation – vocalising begins to decrease
- does not respond to own name.

Pre-school and infant school
The child:
- may have little or no vocalisation
- sounds indistinct/limited speech
- may have monotone quality of speech
- is active and inattentive
- suffers repeated respiratory or ear infections; sounds 'adenoidal'
- has temper tantrums or behaviour problems, and may seem to daydream
- sits close to television with sound loud
- does not respond to instructions or answer when called
- asks for questions to be repeated or copies other children
- experiences difficulty in listening to stories in a group, and may be disruptive
- may watch adult's face intently
- may complain of earache or have a discharge from the ear
- may begin to lose confidence, or not wish to go to school.

Not all signs will apply to all types of hearing impairment

KEY POINTS

- A child who is born deaf will have the usual capacity to develop language and communication, but is prevented from doing so by not having access to the speech of others. She cannot hear all the necessary sounds.
- Helping the child access speech, from a variety of methods such as lip reading and signing gives her the opportunity to learn and develop as her hearing peers, from all aspects of her environment. As with all children the early years are important in the development of communication skills, so early detection is vital.

PROGRESS CHECK

1 When does a profoundly deaf baby show the first difference in the sounds she makes in comparison with a baby of similar age?
2 After what common childhood infections is it advised a child should have her hearing checked when she recovers?
3 Why is early detection of a hearing impairment so important?

Formal testing

When PCHI is detected research suggests significant benefits can be achieved from early intervention in promoting language development. Studies show that a baby takes note of her family language well before she is able to use it herself. Late diagnosis can severely affect a child's ability to acquire language and communication skills. Advances in technology using automated tests have made universal *newborn* hearing screening practicable and more accurate. The government has launched a pilot scheme to replace the current distraction test with these new, more accurate, tests.

Otoacoustic emissions test (OAE)

This will take place between one to four weeks after birth. A probe is inserted into the baby's ear, fixed by a disposable rubber tip. The probe gives out stimuli, which are detected by the normal cochlea. A receiver within the probe detects the tiny sound signal given by the cochlea in response and the results are analysed by the machine to give an automatic 'pass/fail' result.

Automated auditory brainstem response (AABR)

Shortly after birth electrodes are attached to the sleeping baby's head to detect electrical activity. Sounds, at a level to stimulate normal hearing, are then fed into her ear to stimulate the nerves involved in hearing and the brain's response is monitored.

Distraction tests

All babies are, at present, assessed at around eight months of age, either in the family home or child health clinic, usually by the health visitor, however, the accuracy of these types of tests is now questioned. They will eventually be phased out and, soon after birth, replaced by the tests described above.

In distraction tests the baby's attention is gained by a tester playing with a toy in front of her. A second tester then plays sounds of different volumes and frequencies to the child whose response is noted. If the child 'fails' this test it is then repeated within a month.

Possible causes for a baby failing to respond include:

- poor technique of the tester
- tester with poor hearing herself
- additional noise in the testing area
- a tired or unwell baby
- current cough or cold.

Wider use of universal screening will increase detection of children who are born with a hearing impairment, but other tests remain important for children who become deaf later or for whom there are worries over the progress of their language development or hearing.

Co-operative and performance tests

From about eighteen months of age children can be involved in testing that requires a response to a specific instruction. These include requests in play situations using measured speech volumes, for example 'Put the dolly in the pram'.

A slightly older child can have frequency levels tested by being asked to wait for certain sounds before finishing a task, such as building a tower of bricks in stages.

Pure tone audiometry

This measures a child's ability to hear pure tones produced by a machine known as an audiometer. The intensity and frequency of the tones are adjustable and the child wears headphones and indicates when a sound is heard.

The child must be of an age to understand what is requested and be able to co-operate.

The sweep test

This is a system designed to test large numbers of children, often on school entry. Pure tone audiometry is used and various ranges of frequencies are tested, at fixed levels of intensity. Each ear is tested individually and the child asked to indicate when a sound is heard.

Despite the attempts to screen all children for hearing impairment many still remain incorrectly diagnosed. Referral to a specialist in audiometry should be undertaken in the following cases:

- a child who has significantly impaired language development
- a child with a history of chronic or repeated middle-ear disease, or upper airway obstruction such as adenoids
- a child with developmental or behavioural problems
- any child who does not appear to respond at routine hearing testing such as sweep or distraction testing.

CARE

Conductive hearing impairment, where the effects are fluctuating, can easily be overlooked. Remember, at times a child will hear fairly well. She does not live in a quiet world; she will respond to some sounds. However, her sounds are muffled and cause her confusion. To an uninformed observer she may appear lacking in concentration or attention.

KEY POINT

A child may give the impression, by not turning readily to sound, that she is difficult or naughty.

Types of hearing impairment

Otitis media
Treatment is usually with antibiotic medicine to treat the infection.

KEY POINT

Research tells us that passive smoking greatly increases the chances of otitis media.

Otitis media with effusion – OME – 'glue ear'
If the otitis media persists it may lead to glue ear. These infections are significant as they result in 80 per cent of children under eight years experiencing temporary deafness. 'Glue ear' is sometimes treated by using grommets – tiny plastic tubes that are inserted into the eardrums. These allow the air to circulate within the middle ear and the thick fluid to disperse, the cycle of infection is broken and hearing improves.

Sometimes the child is left to grow out of the condition – the Eustachian tube will change shape, making it less likely as a focus for ascending infections. During this period of growth, concentrating on what a child *can* hear is important.

Ear wax and foreign bodies
When this reason for a child's difficulty in hearing is found the solution is simple and usually easily managed by the family doctor.

GOOD PRACTICE

Never poke around in a child's inner ear as you may push any object further in and cause additional damage. Never use cotton buds to clean a child's ears.

Communicating with a child with hearing impairment
There are different views on the most effective way of developing communication with a child with a hearing impairment.

The three main approaches being used at present are:

- the auditory–oral approach
- total communication (sometimes called a flexible approach)
- bilingualism.

Management of deafness can depend on whether it occurred before, or after the child has gained significant language. It is described as pre-lingual or post-lingual deafness.

The auditory–oral approach

The central principle in this approach is the development of a child's spoken language and understanding of speech by the maximum use of a child's residual hearing. Hearing aids (see pages 348–9) are used extensively, signing is not. The key to success is felt to be early diagnosis, and the consistent use of aids.

A child is taught to listen to help her brain make sense of the meaning of spoken language that surrounds her, however indistinct. A child is flooded with language in her early years in a variety of environments – playgroups, nursery and school. This approach is reinforced by lip reading – helping a child recognise word and sound patterns from lips and sometimes also by cued speech (see page 344).

Whether all deaf children will be able to communicate through speech is controversial. However, recent research indicates the majority of even profoundly deaf children who have been given a true auditory–oral approach can achieve fluent and comfortable communication through speech and with good standards of fluency.

The gaining of such skills in a child with a severe impairment will take considerable time and commitment.

GOOD PRACTICE

- Remember communication is two-way. You must develop active listening skills yourself and show attention and response.
- A child will understand more than she will be able to communicate with you.
- Do not teach a child to talk – surround her with language that interests her and stimulates her and make communication fun.

Promoting oral speech

- Play and spend time with the child just like any other – she needs to hear your voice.
- Always respond to her sounds with a positive response such as a cuddle or clap.
- Talk meaningfully to her; talk her through routines and describe her clothes, meals, etc.
- Make sure you have her full attention using eye contact, touching or pointing as necessary.
- Keep at face level to her, sit in front and keep close.

Have full attention and sit in front so the child can see your face and lips

- Have the light in front of you and not behind.
- Keep background noise low.
- In the home, turn off the radio and television. Do not have permanent background music.
- Do not shout in order to make a child hear you as you will frighten her and may make her fearful – she will feel you are angry with her.
- Maintain normal speech rhythms – do not exaggerate your mouth patterns, but speak slower.
- Accompany words with visual clues, especially for a young child – show her a teddy when you are naming one, and remember she will use gestures before she uses words.
- In the older child, sentences are easier to understand than single words – extra words give a child context clues.
- Be careful with the words you choose and use; if they are unfamiliar this will be especially difficult for a deaf child.
- Check the child is understanding you as you talk.
- Use gestures and other visual clues to help her and always use expression to show pleasure, joy, questions, etc.
- Use your hands to help complement the meaning of words.
- Do not cover your face when talking – and remember the shape of your mouth will change when you are eating and this will confuse her lip-reading attempts.

- Remember moustaches and beards that partially cover the face can hide the lips.
- Large earrings are a distraction to a child who is trying to lip read.
- Never talk over her to a hearing child or adult – always include her in conversations.
- Allow pauses between changes in topics to allow her time to adjust.
- If an older child is frustrated try writing things down – increase mime and demonstration with the younger child.
- Try not to correct her efforts at speech; you may undermine her confidence.
- Give her plenty of time to attempt speech.

KEY POINTS

- Lip reading requires considerable concentration, which may be difficult for a young child.
- Always keep sessions short and check she is understanding as, inevitably, some lip reading is guesswork.
- Remember she may tire easily.
- Always give praise and encouragement for her efforts.

Total communication

This approach follows a combination of systems, involving the development of speech, as above, complemented by an adapted signing system.

In total communication (TC) the signs are arranged so that they are in English word order. TC aims to use a deaf child's hearing and supplement her imperfectly heard speech with visual signs. Remember visual signs are accessible to all hearing impaired children with usual sight.

It is thought this TC approach is especially helpful in the early years and makes the development of oral language easier, limiting delay.

In TC it is therefore vital that all carers can sign competently, confidently and with a depth of vocabulary, and combine this with the spoken word. This will have to be learnt for this system to be successful.

Other techniques

Other techniques sometimes used to supplement residual hearing include the following:

- *Cued speech:* some words appear to have a similar pattern when lip read, e.g 'cat and cut', so a hand is placed near the mouth with a variety of hand shapes to highlight differences.
- *Finger spelling:* each letter of the alphabet is represented by a different hand position – in Britain with two hands. Words are spelt out.
- *Signed English:* signs are taken from British Sign Language (BSL) and used with additionally developed signs, which are only used in signed English. It is used with two-handed finger spelling to give an exact manual representation of spoken English. Unlike BSL it is designed to be used at the same time as spoken English.
- *Makaton:* see page 323.

Bilingualism

Sign language is regarded as a language in its own right and used solely. Here oral language is not developed and signs do not supplement speech. Communication is solely through BSL, *which is considered to be the main language of deaf people.* BSL is another independent language such as French or Swahili – it is not just gesture or mime but a combination of these, including using the face and whole body. It is a visual language both in the way it is used and understood. It has the richness, depth of vocabulary and grammatical rules of any spoken language. The signing is three-dimensional, so complex, simple gesture, or a minute change in movement or facial expression can change a meaning. It cannot be used at the same time as speech.

Using BSL solely as a communication method, it is argued, allows a child to develop a full language in the important early years and so access the curriculum easily. This approach is primarily for the profoundly deaf child. Deaf children are considered to have a right to their own signing language, in which they can communicate easily with other deaf children and adults, and gain access to their own culture. Pride and self-esteem are raised by helping a child feel part of her own group whose traditions are special, valued and promoted, a distinct deaf identity can develop.

Once sign language is established as a first language it is thought to be a good basis for learning English, in its written form, as a second language.

KEY POINTS

- This approach demands high-quality signing skills from all involved in a child's care – learning just a few signs will not help a child develop communication at a sufficient depth.
- Parents and hearing siblings usually learn easily alongside a deaf baby.
- The involvement and training of deaf Early Years workers, teachers and other carers as experienced, positive role models is needed to extend this approach.

Cochlear implants

Since the late 1980s there has been a steady growth in the number of children who have undergone cochlear implants. By the end of 2000 some 1500 children had received implants and now about 200 take place yearly. Generally they are offered to children who are severely or profoundly deaf. There is evidence that implantation can lead to greater improvement in the use of spoken language than is attained by children with similar impairment using hearing aids.

Tiny hair cells in the cochlea (see page 337) convert sound waves into electrical signals that travel along the auditory nerve to the brain. When these hairs are absent or damaged these signals are not transmitted. An implant stimulates the auditory nerve directly, bypassing the damaged cells, to provide a sensation of hearing.

The implant consists of two parts:

1 *External:* a lead, transmitter and microphone worn on the body or, occasionally, behind the ear.
2 *Internal:* a number of electrodes, surgically implanted under the skin behind the ear, that directly stimulate the auditory nerve.

When the child has recovered from the surgery, the microphone and speech processors are provided and tuned over a period of time to meet the child's particular needs. The child, and her family, will have ongoing, long-term therapy and support to learn to listen and understand the new signals.

Currently, the average age for a cochlear implant, is three years. However, they are increasingly being offered to children who are younger, or who may have residual hearing and complex needs. Decisions about suitability for implants involve a multidisciplinary approach when the total needs of the child are assessed.

Follow-up studies indicate a marked increase in intelligible speech *without* lip reading within three to five years.

Controversy and cochlear implants

The British Deaf Association (BDA), the voluntary organisation run by the deaf for the deaf, while supporting the right for parents to make informed choices for their children, does not recommend implants for children. They would prefer resources to be spent on promoting deaf culture and awareness and increasing access, and opportunities for the recognition of sign language (see above). The BDA does not recognise the medical approach, which seeks to 'cure' deafness. However, the National Deaf Children's Society (NDCS), the UK charity dedicated solely to deaf children and their families, has a different policy recognising that decisions over this issue are complex, and that all informed parental choices are valid. To help in decision-making the NCDS produces a variety of materials for parents, including information on aids, implants and communication methods.

Currently a national research project is under way to assess aspects of cochlear implants. These will include scrutiny of the rising cost of implants – annually about £12 million – assessment over the long-term material and educational benefits to the child and her family, and monitoring of access to implants.

Which approach?

No system will be the complete answer for every child; the degree and type of impairment a child has will be one of many factors in the final choice.

All approaches have advantages and disadvantages, and parents should be offered advice and information, from a wide variety of sources. Every child is an individual whose needs, when very young, are best understood by her family. Whatever decisions parents make must be respected by all involved in her care.

KEY POINT

In any approach the quality and depth of communication, whether in signing or speech, is important in helping a child achieve her potential.

Activity
Prepare a talk for your peers describing the different ways available for developing communication and language for children who are deaf. Prepare arguments for and against each main approach. You will need to undertake additional research.

ONGOING MANAGEMENT

- Carers must learn the skills and knowledge needed for implementing the chosen choice of communication.
- Good practice started at home must continue in any care and educational establishment (see Promoting oral speech, pages 342–4).
- You must understand the specific type of impairment a child has and be particularly aware of a child with a fluctuating loss.
- Develop 'listening' activities in the curriculum – helping her discriminate between different non-speech sounds such as animal noises or musical instruments.
- Develop music and sound-making activities and use different types of sounds and vibration.
- Be aware that changes in routine may be confusing to a child who is deaf.
- Understand why behaviour is sometimes demanding – her world may at times be frustrating.
- Use visual aids freely and imaginatively.
- Discuss in advance how you will manage emergency procedures such as fire drills and other safety procedures.
- Be vigilant in looking for non-verbal clues a child may give that she is not understanding, is bored, confused or unhappy.
- Investigate areas of modern technology that will enrich her world:
  - doorbells can be extra loud, or accompanied with flashing lights
  - telephones can have different tones on their rings and lights can be fitted to flash when the telephone rings
  - loop systems are microphones placed on the speaker of the television. A loop amplifier feeds the signal through a piece of thin cable, running around a skirting board. A magnetic field is created within this loop and a hearing aid can be programmed to pick this up and change it back into sound. A child can then listen to television at a level comfortable to both her and her hearing parents and friends.

Supporting a child with a hearing aid
- Always be positive about a hearing aid – encourage the child to value it.
- Check a hearing aid daily (use a stetoclip, which allows you to listen at a comfortable level yourself).
- Change batteries regularly.
- Check the condition and comfort of any ear-pieces. Earmoulds need replacing regularly, often every four to six weeks.
- Check leads are not loose, chewed or punctured.
- Switch the aid on and off.
- Check any microphone grilles are not blocked (perhaps covered with rusk or food!).
- Encourage the child to learn to care for and check her hearing aid herself.

HEARING AIDS

Post-aural (behind the ear) hearing aids
Mini ones are available and are suitable for babies and for certain types of hearing impairments.

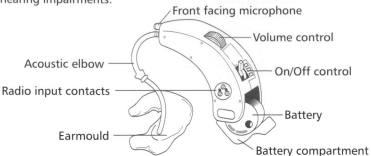

- Front facing microphone
- Volume control
- Acoustic elbow
- On/Off control
- Radio input contacts
- Battery
- Earmould
- Battery compartment

Body-worn hearing aids
Used mostly for profoundly deaf children and especially in very young children. They can produce high levels of volume, with less sound distortion, especially at low frequencies. They are less prone to whistling. They are often worn with an accompanying harness – **check the microphone is not covered.**

Microphone – do not cover

In-the-ear hearing aids
These types are becoming more widely used. They are often most suitable for children with a less severe impairment.

Remember
- Hearing aids cannot make a child hear normally; they amplify **all** sounds.
- New developments have produced high-powered aids to help profoundly deaf children.
- As soon as possible after they are fitted a child should wear them all day.
- Your attitudes to hearing aids will influence how a child feels about hers.

Hearing aids for children

- If you think the aid is not working, do not leave the situation. The parents will have access to advice and maintenance support.
- *Remember*, hearing aids amplify sounds, but they do not make them 'normal'. In amplifying all sounds they may mask speech.

A radio hearing aid

Some children are given radio hearing aids as well as their own hearing aid. Someone else wears the transmitter and can switch it on and alter the setting of a child's hearing aid if necessary. When the radio aid is switched on the child hears the voice of the person wearing the transmitter as if the person was standing next to her. This is especially useful in playgroups, busy classrooms, outside or in playgrounds or in a class itself where the teacher may be across the room. These also help limit the background noise with which a child may have to cope.

A carer and child using radio aids

GENERAL IMPLICATIONS

Deafness is a condition for which children have additional needs. How to identify and meet these needs most effectively is not universally agreed within the deaf community.

One school of thought thinks a child's communication needs are best met by a variety of combinations. This might include use of BSL language or other signing systems, and/or a combination of spoken and written English supported by the use of aids. Above all the choice should be flexible and make best use of the resources and skills available.

However, a second school believe only through the medium of spoken communication can a child truly have the freedom to access the wide social community.

The bilingual school feel children who use their own sign language are freed from disability and able to develop a proud self-identity, without the inbuilt disadvantage of producing speech. They argue that the hearing society should not impose their norms on the deaf community.

ADDITIONAL DEVELOPMENTS

For children who are following a flexible approach to hearing impairment increasingly sophisticated hearing aids are being developed, both smaller and more powerful.

Controversy within the deaf community over the development of new techniques to aid communication continues. In addition to this debate, it is important to remember that six in 1000 children require support because of deafness and deaf children are more vulnerable to neglect, and physical and sexual abuse, than children who have hearing.

Following the introduction of the SEN Code of Practice, local education authorities must now obtain education advice from a teacher qualified to teach children who are hearing impaired, when undertaking a Statutory Assessment of Special Educational needs.

CASE STUDY

Jenny's teacher noted that at five Jenny was constantly saying 'What?' Often Jenny ignored instructions and she shouted loudly when involved in group work. Her voice could always be heard across the classroom. She began to get a reputation as being noisy and difficult.

When this was brought to her mother's attention she said it was what the family described as Jenny's 'domestic deafness' – ignoring what she did not want to hear, but always making sure she was heard when she wanted something.

The teacher felt it was more than this and a hearing test was arranged through the school health service. Jenny was discovered to have quite a marked but fluctuating hearing loss caused, it was thought, by unresolved glue ear. She was treated with antibiotics and the school developed a management plan. This included encouraging Jenny to sit at the front of the class and in the teacher's vision so her lips could be read. At any apparent signs of ignoring instructions, the staff immediately repeated them clearly and plainly.

1   What other measures would help Jenny?
2   What preventive health measures might have avoided the difficulty in the first place?

RESOURCES

British Deaf Association
http://bda.org.uk

The National Deaf Children's Society
15 Dufferin Street
London EC1V 8UR
www.ndcs.org.uk

Vision impairment

Impaired vision or blindness means a child has insufficient or inadequate vision for certain everyday activities. The World Health Organisation (WHO) definition of blindness is the inability to count fingers at 6 metres (20 feet) or less.

KEY POINT

Total blindness is rare. Most children can see something even if only the difference between light and darkness.

Sight continues to develop after birth and vision must be stimulated to allow it to reach its full potential. Seeing also requires perception to make sense of the images sent from the eye to the brain and complex language and communication skills to describe what is perceived. As a result it may be many months before a final decision on the full extent of a visual impairment is made. It is thought that 20,000 children in the UK have a visual impairment.

About half of all children with impaired vision will have associated additional special needs – hearing or learning disabilities being the most common.

WHAT HAPPENS

THE EYE AND HOW IT WORKS

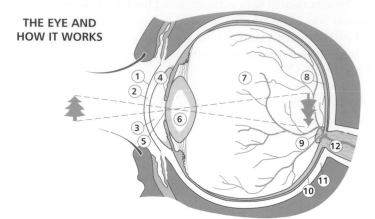

1 Conjunctiva: the delicate thin outer covering of the eye and lining of the eyelids.
2 Cornea: the window of the eye which allows light through to fall on the retina.
3 Aqueous humor: a clear, jelly-like substance.
4 Iris: the area that gives the eyes their individual colour, in front of the lens and behind the cornea.
5 Pupil: the central hole in the eye that varies in size to allow different amounts of light through.
6 Lens: a capsule containing clear fluid which focuses images upon the retina.
7 Vitreous humor: clear jelly-like substance.
8 Retina: the inner lining of the eye which receives and transmits the images via the optic nerve to the brain.
9 Macula: a small circle of cells on the retina, which forms the area of fine sight.
10 Choroid: the layer between the retina and the sclera, which contains the blood vessels in the eye.
11 Sclera: the white, tough, protective covering of the eye.
12 Optic nerve: the main nerve of the eye along which messages are sent from the retina to the brain.

The eye

Damage to the development of the eye or the nervous system that sends and translates visual messages to the brain can occur at any time.

Causes of visual impairment
The following are the main causes of visual impairment:

Before birth
■ Family history of blindness
■ Rubella or other infections such as syphilis or toxoplasmosis in pregnancy.

Around birth
■ Prematurity
■ Infections
■ Oxygen poisoning.

After birth

- Injury
- Infections
- Severe inflammatory disease.

Types of visual impairment

Types of visual impairment vary and will depend on which part of the eye or nervous system is affected. The following are some of the more usual problems:

- *Albinism*: too little coloured pigment is present in skin, hair and eyes resulting in too much light being admitted to the eye.
- *Astigmatism*: the eyeball is unevenly shaped and the light fails to fall on the most effective part of the retina, for focusing. Vision is blurred and distorted.
- *Cataracts*: part of the lens becomes cloudy and the images the child receives are blurred and unclear and vision is lost.
- *Conjunctivitis*: the conjunctiva is inflamed or infected.
- *Hypermetropia*: long sight – only distant vision is clear.
- *Keratitis*: infection or inflammation of the cornea and conjunctiva – if severely affected a child will only see light and the definition of objects will be limited.
- *Microphthalmos*: unusually small eyeballs, sometimes unable to function for sight.
- *Myopia*: short sight – only near vision is clear.
- *Nystagmus*: involuntary flickering of the eyes.
- *Optic atrophy*: the optic nerve fails to send sight messages to the brain.
- *Strabismus (squint)*: weak muscles allow the eye to 'wander' – the eyes appear to look in different directions. It affects three in every 100 children. Common in the newborn, it should disappear by three months of age.
- *Tunnel vision*: only part of an image is seen; vision appears as if looking down a tube.

KEY POINT

Strabismus can cause blindness in the affected eye if untreated.

DIAGNOSIS

Any obvious difficulty will be identified during the routine examinations given to all newborn babies.

Additional signs to watch for will depend on the age of the child. The mother or closest carer is the best person to notice early difficulties and can be guided on what to look for by the use of an ongoing checklist. This is given to some parents to monitor the sight development of their baby.

What should you watch for?

Babies

- There is no eye-to-eye contact, especially with the mother.
- The baby does not react to light.

- There are 'abnormal' eye movements.
- Eyes do not follow objects at two months.
- There is a failure to locate objects at 6–12 months of age.
- A parent expresses worries.

The older child

- The child has cloudy or bloodshot eyes, unusual eye movements, excessive rubbing or blinking of eyes.
- The child is clumsy and has poor hand–eye co-ordination.
- The child moves her head rather than eyes when involved in looking at pictures or stories.
- She holds objects close to the face.
- She loses interest quickly in activities needing the use of near vision.
- She has difficulty in matching or naming colours.
- She sometimes walks with head down and is reluctant to join in physical activities.

Vision screening tests

Vision screening tests for all children are undertaken from six weeks of age by the family or clinic doctor. A baby's emerging ability is assessed in:

- following moving objects
- locating small objects
- more refined testing undertaken during the toddler stage by asking a child to:
  - identify miniature toys at distances
  - match shapes and letters of different sizes
  - pick up minute particles, e.g. 'hundreds and thousands' – a near vision test.

KEY POINTS

- Each health area will have different time schedules for routine screening.
- Specific tests to exclude squint are undertaken if there are worries.
- Referral to a consultant ophthalmology unit, for full assessment, will be made if a child's vision is causing concern.

PROGRESS CHECK

Why is it important to detect any squint early?

KEY POINT

Levels of vision may not be constant and will change from day to day and often within a day. Factors affecting this include:

- lighting
- mood/tension
- tiredness
- illness.

CARE

Part of the initial important bonding process between mother and child is built upon their emerging communication. Eye-to-eye contact is absent in a blind baby and first smiles may be late. Parents will need to learn to respond physically to a baby's smiles, by touch or voice, to encourage her to repeat this action. Apparent lack of response can cause a parent frustration and undermine confidence, even affecting the initial pleasure gained from their child. Early involvement for parents with a support agency or group, who have personal experience of such feelings, is often helpful.

KEY POINT

It is thought that sight contributes to 80 per cent of a child's learning.

For compensation, a baby who is blind or visually impaired will need to learn to develop her other four senses – touch, hearing, smell and taste – to their maximum, as well as using any residual sight. She needs these senses to gather as much information about her surroundings as possible and then learn to make sense of the images she receives or 'sees'.

Your role is to teach her how to use fully these four remaining senses. The following are suggestions on how to do this.

Encouragement
Help the baby use her hands, fingers, feet and mouth – these will eventually tell her about touch, smell, taste and the direction and types of sounds that she hears.

There are many things you can encourage her to do:

- Reach and touch – put toys into her hands.
- Learn about her body and how to move and control it – keep her early clothing free and unrestricted and feet bare.
- Link gesture and touch to actions and words – tell her before you touch her, even when she is a baby – she can't see your hand or know whose hand it is she feels. Always respond to her by word or touch, remembering how much sighted people show feelings such as pleasure, by visual gestures.
- Develop her confidence when she is surrounded by unfamiliar noises, which may cause her concern, by telling her you are there and explaining the unknown to her.
- Teach her to discriminate between types of sounds, noises, smells and taste.
- Develop self-help skills such as washing, cleaning teeth, dressing and undressing as early as possible. Use easy to get on and off clothes with Velcro fastenings. Remove her clothes in the same order coming off so she will learn how to put them on again in the correct order. Choose clothes that will give her positional clues such as buttons at the front, pockets at the sides.
- Help her gain bladder and bowel control. Choose a firm potty that will make her feel secure. Reinforce what you expect her to do with words and by familiar noises – the flushing of the lavatory, the taps running, even a musical potty.
- Exploration and experimentation are important and to do this she needs protection but not smothering. Check fireguards are fixed and secure, electrical sockets covered, loose dangerous ornaments out of reach, always use stair-gates and initially a wooden playpen may be helpful (this would allow her to pull to stand). Discuss safety with her, explaining words such as 'sharp', 'steep' and 'slippery'.
- Teach her to feed herself. Encourage her to hold her bottle, give her a spoon when weaning. Expect mess and plan for it, but help with experimenting with different types of spoons and suction dishes. Choose bright colours to supplement any vision. Let her use her fingers to feel the position of her food as well as enjoy the sensation. Introduce one food at a time – do not overwhelm her. It is helpful for her to take cutlery, beakers or mugs from a firm surface and return them to the same surface – otherwise she may drop them into mid-air.
- Always tell her what you are giving her and expand the range, such as sweet, savoury, hot, cold, warm, etc. and as she grows give her choices.
- Make mealtimes learning, relaxed and fun opportunities.

KEY POINT

The baby needs total experience – to feel her food, hear it being prepared, perhaps in a kitchen away from where she is, smell it and taste it and have you describe it to her.

Stories are important to describe the world

Verbal communication

Every aspect of the child's life will need to be explained and talked through so she can learn the association of words to objects, shapes, and sounds. This will extend her world. The following will encourage her:

- describing everyday events, for example how you run the bath, what clothes you are collecting, what bubbles you put in the water, confirm if they or the soap are the source of the perfumes she smells, show her the difference between warm and hot. Tell her you are rubbing her dry, patting her delicate face, massaging her skin with creams, blowing on her tummy to make her giggle, etc.
- linking sounds to noises – 'This is a rattle'.
- using an exaggerated sound for key words such as 'up' or 'down'
- developing conversations as she begins to learn to imitate. Always listen – she may copy whole sentences but have little idea of what it really means. Reinforce with complementary sounds, for example 'Johnny went in the car' – let her touch the car, feel her seat, toot the horn, etc.
- not anticipating or answering her speech before it is complete
- using books and stories freely, showing clear bright pictures or having 'feely' books
- using rhymes and action songs
- using simple, clear language.

Never talk over or about the child, always to her. Encourage relatives, peers and friends to direct questions to her.

Initiation

Most learning takes place, by imitation, copying and discovery. Exciting activities and objects are not as readily available to the child as a sighted child and so she may be unaware of their existence. Help her by using everyday routines as learning times. Encourage her by using the familiar:

- In the home and garden use opportunities to open drawers, turn water taps, empty cupboards full of interesting and safe objects such as saucepans, ladles, jugs, sieves, etc. Involve her in make-believe activities such as showing her how to 'vacuum' the carpet, knead dough for baking or wash up.
- Bathtime provides opportunities for water play and relaxation.
- Outdoors, a well-fenced garden is ideal for exploration, digging, getting dirty, smelling flowers and growing plants. On park visits she will be using swings, collecting leaves, feeling wind and rain, learning to pedal a tricycle and developing spatial awareness. Use shopping trips for discriminating about traffic sounds, shopkeepers' voices and so on. Well-supervised visits to the swimming pool are fun, developing motor skills and body awareness.
- Visits to and from friends and relatives provide opportunities to socialise and develop acceptable behaviour, sharing and taking turns. They should begin with a single child, then a small group increasing in numbers in preparation for playgroup or nursery.

Toys and activities

Toys and activities chosen need to be big, bright and colourful:

- *Big:* the larger the object, or the closer to the eye, the easier it is to see.
- *Bright:* the more light there is, the better, so ensure play areas are well lit. Use additional lighting if necessary and use reflective or fluorescent lights. Choose matt, light surfaces for reflection and visual comfort, as shiny surfaces can produce unwanted glare.
- *Colourful:* eyes work best with contrasts so develop this with colourful toys against contrasting backgrounds and spread a sheet on the floor as a setting for toys.

Keep toys within the child's reach when she is very young, but gradually move them away to encourage her to move. Use noises from the toys as clues for her such as squeaking, rattling, banging, etc.

Toys chosen should have different textures, colours, sizes, shapes, weights, smells and sounds.

Identification

Interpret the child's world, explaining the nature of objects and the meaning of sounds. Keep her informed of routines, events and everyday happenings.

Remember her ears are especially important so leave them uncovered even on cold days outside.

PROGRESS CHECK

What are the three main points to consider when choosing toys for a child who is blind?

Activity

To develop identification of sounds: make a tape recording of some the sounds of the child's day – doors opening and shutting, introductory music to television programmes, the sound of the toaster popping, taps running, the washing machine working, the dog barking, birdsong, letters dropping through the letter box, and so on.

Talk her through her day, asking her about the sounds and what they tell her. This will help her memory too.

Mobility

Help the child learn about the position of her own body, how it moves, how it changes position and about influences affecting it.

Tell her the names of her body parts and repeat them in rhymes, songs and games.

Support her mobility in line with her developmental progress:

- Place her to kick and move on the floor, on her back and her tummy.
- Use baby chairs so she can be with you in different parts of the house and be near your voice.
- Encourage her to roll and reach, prop her in a sitting position and 'show' her sound toys near.
- Be prepared that she may not crawl, but roll – she cannot see so she will bump her head more readily crawling than rolling.
- Use a wooden playpen, not a mesh-lined lobster pot, as she will find pulling to stand easier on the strong frame – show her where the rails are.
- Hold her hands firmly when she starts to toddle, at first by standing behind her. Keep her hands no higher than her shoulders – use push-and-pull toys that are well balanced when she is stable.
- Let her walk alone when she is ready, keep an uncluttered room, and bind sharp corners with foam in the early days of mobility.
- Provide clues to help her know where she is, such as a clock ticking or a window open for the breeze to blow on her. Let her learn by exploring.
- Teach her about stairs and use safety gates so she can develop skills of climbing and descending one at a time.
- As the child learns and develops you can provide further progress.
- Make obstacle courses where she goes over, under and around.
- Develop her running, at first with her holding your arm, then help her to run towards you. Tie string between posts or trees for her to use as a guide.
- Pace out distances for her between objects and encourage her to count them.
- Use trampolines with added bars for her to hold.

Safety

Provide an environment where the child can explore within safe but extending boundaries. Initially use the playpen or cot, then a safe part of the room fenced off by solid furniture, then the whole room, gradually extending her world. Remember, objects will go to her mouth for her to discover shape, texture and size for much longer than her sighted peers.

The safe practice procedures needed in working routinely with children will usually be sufficient. However, you must remain vigilant and careful, always linking the possibility of safety hazards to her emerging development.

KEY POINT

Your role is to ensure the child is neither over-protected nor placed in danger.

GOOD PRACTICE

- Adult involvement is especially important in the early stages for a baby with a visual impairment.
- Reinforce pleasure for the child by touch – she cannot see your facial response.

ONGOING MANAGEMENT

As with any child the opportunities available in a playgroup, nursery and school are important in enriching her quality of life and learning potential.

Preparing for admission

Preparation for admission is the key to success. The following are points to consider:

- communication between parents and Early Years workers
- discussion with parents to allay any potential worries
- time for staff to update their own knowledge
- time for a child's specific visual needs to be understood, following liaison with any other involved professionals
- minor adjustment to toys may be required – there should be emphasis on sound-makers and bright coloured toys with moving parts
- ensuring light sources are adequate – especially in corridors, toilets and stairways
- assessment of the environment for safety hazards
- preparation of individual children – the importance of naming themselves to her
- preparation for introducing a visually impaired or blind child to the group.

Initial admission

A good settling-in procedure, with the reassuring presence of her parents, should allow a child to become confident with her new surroundings. Involve and listen to the parents as they will be aware of any specific areas that might pose problems for her.

Initially a safe corner could be sectioned off for her, allowing her the opportunity for exploration within a controlled environment. Individual or small groups of children can join her gradually to allow her to begin to meet her peers. Such a system would allow her to familiarise herself with some of the new toys and equipment available.

Encourage her to stamp the floor or tap a wall to identify the different surfaces she is meeting. Carpets, tiles, wooden floors and tarmac will all sound different and help her identify where she is. Give her other clues, too, such as sounds and textured wall areas at hand height and add bright or white tape or paint to the edges of tables and steps.

KEY POINT

Changes in the way a room is set up, chairs left out or clutter accumulating on the floor will all be potentially hazardous for the child.

Meeting and learning with her peers

■ Sing songs that use names of the children to help the child identify her friends.

A music session should include everyone

■ Choose stories that mention sounds or encourage staff and children to add their own voices and sound effects.
■ Encourage activities that children can enjoy equally together such as water and sand play.
■ Develop co-operative play such as see-saws and trikes with trailers, but always supervise well.

- Develop listening games such as sound lotto and remembering games such as 'My mother went to market'.
- Sing action songs together.
- Encourage children and staff always to identify themselves by name to her.

It may be helpful to spend time just observing the child and assessing at the beginning, learning what she actually can do.

Codes of behaviour must be applied to all children, including a child with a visual impairment. She, too, needs the security and stability of learning right from wrong. It would be additionally disabling for her, if your expectations were low and you allowed her impairment to be used as an excuse for unacceptable behaviour.

Braille

Some children will have insufficient sight to read print and may need to learn Braille. This requires the child to discriminate by touch between patterns made by sets of raised dots representing letters or words. Preparation for this means helping her identify shapes and objects by touch. Smaller and smaller objects are presented with increasingly subtle differences. Promoting fine motor development and strong fingers and hands through play will also provide a firm foundation for learning Braille.

An Early Years worker can also gain Braille skills through a distance learning course.

PROGRESS CHECK

What area of development needs stimulating to prepare a child to use Braille?

Managing glasses

If a child wears glasses check the following points:
- Know how often and when the glasses should be worn.
- Encourage parents to get a spare pair.
- Check the condition daily to ensure they are unbroken with screws tight and lenses still present!
- Confirm that the glasses are safe to be worn during all activities (even when the lenses are plastic).
- Check the comfort. Remember the child will grow out of her frames.
- When the glasses are taken off never put the lenses face down.
- Clean glasses regularly and with a non-scratch cleaner.
- Remember the child's prescription will probably need changing and her eyes retesting.
- Are you showing positive images of children with glasses in your displays?

GENERAL IMPLICATIONS

Visual impairment can delay a child's development, so stimulation and opportunities for play are important. Repetition and reinforcement of learning experiences may be needed for longer than for sighted children. Occasionally some aspects of behaviour, such as placing objects in the mouth or tapping and shouting for an echo, may be mistaken for a learning disability. Developmental stages may be different and pretend play may show itself in sounds rather than in action.

Specialist support and advice is important in ensuring that all her needs are both understood and met by all involved in her care.

Research suggests that more children have visual difficulties than have been identified, possibly between 17 and 22 per cent of school-age children. Sight screening is *not* routinely carried out in all schools and parents should be encouraged to take their children for free eye tests within the community, as a vital health check.

ADDITIONAL DEVELOPMENTS

Complex sensory rooms are available for some children, incorporating areas with music, fans, vibrating mats, feely boards, lasers, strip and bubble tube lights.

The National Library for the Blind has 3440 children's titles in Braille, including 'Two-ways', a series in which print and Braille are combined so they can be enjoyed by blind and sighted children together.

Increasingly, modern technology, especially sophisticated computer equipment, will be valuable in supporting learning. Closed circuit television has already been developed for use as a powerful microscope.

With the introduction of the SEN Code of Practice, local education authorities must obtain education advice from a teacher qualified to teach children who are visually impaired when undertaking a Statutory Assessment of Special Educational Needs.

CASE STUDY

When Jo was having her six-week developmental examination the family doctor noticed that her eyes seemed different and did not appear to be of the same size. Jo's mother, who had no other children, also confirmed that Jo had not yet smiled responsively for her. After further investigation it was discovered that Jo had no sight in one eye and only minimal peripheral vision in the other. She was registered as blind. This was an enormous shock and distress to her young mother, who felt the cause might have been due to the rubella she had contracted during her pregnancy.

1 How could you explain the importance of stimulating Jo's residual vision and other four senses to her mother?
2 What support could you give Jo's mother about providing a safe but stimulating and extending environment for her baby?

RESOURCES

LOOK
National Federation of Families with Visually Impaired Children
c/o Queen Alexandra College
49 Court Oak Road
Harborne
Birmingham B17 9TG
www.look-uk.org

RNIB National Library Service
PO Box 173
Peterborough
PE2 6WS
www.rnib.org.uk

Royal National Institute for the Blind
Head Office
105 Judd Street
London WC1H 9NE
www.rnib.org.uk

Spina bifida

Spina bifida is caused by a fault in the spinal column or backbone, when part of the rear section of one or more of the vertebrae (the thirty-three bones that make up the spine) fail to form properly. It is partially hereditary, and once there has been an affected pregnancy there is an increased risk to future babies. The incidence of having a child with a similar condition is one in thirty-five.

Spina bifida occurs between the fourteenth and twenty-eighth day after conception, when the baby is developing in the womb. The malformation is the result of a gap or split in the spinal column, which leaves the cord inadequately protected. It can be damaged or ruptured, resulting in:

- **paralysis**
- loss of sensation
- bladder and bowel control problems.

Spina bifida is the most common developmental problem of the central nervous system, occurring in up to 10 per cent of all births.

The causes of the condition are unknown but are thought to include both genetic and environmental factors:

- It occurs more often in white races.
- It occurs in babies born prematurely.
- It is more likely to re-occur in families who already have a child with the condition.

- Increasingly, diet at the time of conception and in the first twenty-five days of pregnancy, when the neural tube is developing, is considered to be important. Extra dietary folic acid (vitamin B9) is now universally prescribed. Women who have had a previous baby with a neural tube defect, or have a defect themselves, are advised to take 5 mg of folic acid for one month prior to conception and throughout the first twelve weeks of a pregnancy. This can reduce by 72 per cent the chances of a second baby being affected.

Babies born with spina bifida can also have the associated condition hydro-cephalus. This is often known as 'water on the brain' and occurs because there is an imbalance between the production and drainage of the special fluid (the cerebro-spinal fluid), which bathes the brain and lubricates the spinal cord. Swelling inside the brain develops, causing damage if left untreated.

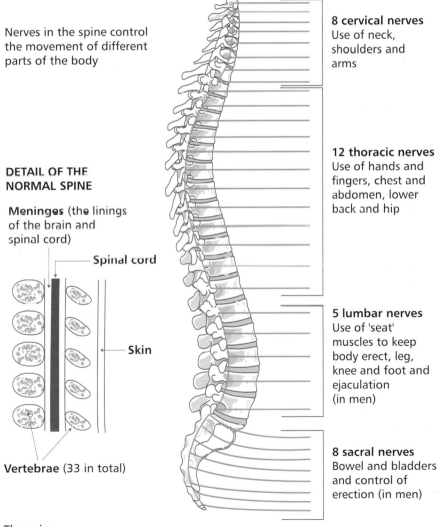

Nerves in the spine control the movement of different parts of the body

DETAIL OF THE NORMAL SPINE

Meninges (the linings of the brain and spinal cord)

Spinal cord

Skin

Vertebrae (33 in total)

8 cervical nerves
Use of neck, shoulders and arms

12 thoracic nerves
Use of hands and fingers, chest and abdomen, lower back and hip

5 lumbar nerves
Use of 'seat' muscles to keep body erect, leg, knee and foot and ejaculation (in men)

8 sacral nerves
Bowel and bladders and control of erection (in men)

The spine

WHAT HAPPENS

There are three main types of the condition.

Spina bifida occulta

Here only the vertebrae are affected, the condition is mild, common and rarely causes problems. It is thought to occur in one in ten of the population. Occasionally there is a slight dimple or small hair growth on the lower back. In some children the spinal cord may become caught against the vertebrae and, as growth increases, cause minor difficulties with bladder control and mobility.

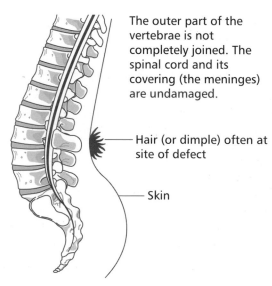

The outer part of the vertebrae is not completely joined. The spinal cord and its covering (the meninges) are undamaged.

Hair (or dimple) often at site of defect

Skin

Spina bifida occulta

Spina bifida cystica

Here a blister-like swelling occurs at the lower back, covered by a thin layer of skin. It can be either meningocele – the least common form – or myelomeningocele, the most common and most serious form.

Meningocele

Meningocele is the least common form of spina bifida cystica.

■ The sac will contain tissues that line the spinal cord (the meninges, see pages 365 and 367). These produce the cerebro-spinal fluid, which bathes and protects the brain and spinal cord.
■ Usually the nerves are undamaged.
■ Usually there is little disability.

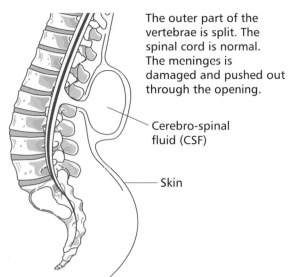

The outer part of the vertebrae is split. The spinal cord is normal. The meninges is damaged and pushed out through the opening.

Cerebro-spinal fluid (CSF)

Skin

Spina bifida cystica: meningocele

Myelomeningocele

Myelomeningocele is the most common and most serious form of spina bifida.

- Both the meninges and the cord protrude through the gap, which is covered with a thin membrane.
- The membrane may rupture and leak fluid, making the child vulnerable to infection, especially meningitis.
- The spinal cord will be damaged or not properly developed.
- There is always paralysis and loss of sensation below the damaged vertebra.
- A child may also have problems of bowel and bladder control.
- Two-thirds of children with this type of spina bifida will also have hydrocephalus.

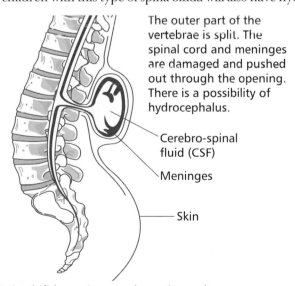

The outer part of the vertebrae is split. The spinal cord and meninges are damaged and pushed out through the opening. There is a possibility of hydrocephalus.

Cerebro-spinal fluid (CSF)

Meninges

Skin

Spina bifida cystica: myelomeningocele

How severely a child is affected will depend on the following two factors:

- the position of the lesion – any part of the spine may be affected and the higher in the spine the malformation, usually, the greater the effect. However occurrence in the lower spine is more common.
- how much damage there is to the spinal cord.

Cranium bifida

The bones of the skull fail to grow properly. The sac that forms sometimes contains tissues and fluid only and occasionally a very small and damaged brain that fails to develop.

The baby will either be stillborn or die shortly after birth.

PROGRESS CHECK

1 Why is a child with myelomeningocele more likely to be severely physically affected by spina bifida than a child with spina bifida occulta or a meningocele?
2 What is hydrocephalus?

DIAGNOSIS

Spina bifida can be detected while the baby is in the womb, but not treated.

After birth the more obvious malformations of the spine in spina bifida cystica are usually noted immediately. The neurological examination routinely given to all newborn babies will detect spina bifida occulata.

CARE

In a child who has a myelomeningocele, surgery is required to close the lesion. This is completed as soon after birth as possible for the following reasons:

- to prevent deterioration and further damage to the spinal cord
- to prevent the sac from bursting, leaving the child vulnerable to infection, especially meningitis
- to make handling and general personal care easier for all carers
- to improve appearance and help promote long-term self-esteem

On discharge home to the family, after surgery to close and repair a myelomening-ocele, a baby needs the following care:

- security, stimulation, love and her basic needs as a new baby met – feeding procedures will have to be adapted to avoid pressure on any wound
- to establish eye contact – she may spend time on her tummy initially
- appropriate toys provided, such as mobiles and musical toys
- care of any wound with strict implementation of hygiene procedures – any dressing required would be undertaken by a community nurse
- urine and faeces – kept away from any wound – baby is frequently cared for on her tummy, with her buttocks exposed. When healing is complete nappies

are used as usual. Sometimes the urine is removed by a catheter (a tube) into the bladder. If this is so, extra fluids will be needed to limit the increased chances of urinary infection.

Immediate and long-term care

In any condition where there is a loss of movement and sensation it is important to be aware of the dangers of pressure sores.

Pressure sores

A baby born with full sensation will automatically move to relieve weight, she will wriggle, squirm and eventually turn and sit. This is a natural way of preventing tissues being deprived of oxygen and sores developing. In a baby with paralysis the carer must undertake this for the baby, otherwise ulceration will occur. If this happens healing will take a considerable time and be difficult.

KEY POINTS

- A baby with paralysis and loss of sensation will feel no pressure or pain and so is especially vulnerable to sores.
- The baby will not indicate distress even if sores are present.
- The baby will be unable to discriminate between hot and cold and may be vulnerable to scalds and burns in the parts of her body that are paralysed.

GOOD PRACTICE

- Always check clothes are not rubbing or chaffing. Initially the baby may sleep on a sheepskin or have extra foam over the mattress for softness.
- Check the condition of the skin is healthy. Keep it dry, clean and moisturised, pay special attention to creases in ankles, knees, tips of nose, cheeks and chin. You may not be able to use a bath initially.
- Move her and change her position frequently.
- Watch for any signs of rubbing or pressure.

Movement

Muscles and limbs that do not move of their own accord must be exercised for the baby, by you. A physiotherapist will arrange passive exercises for you to undertake for her. These involve regularly gently moving the muscles and joints that she cannot move herself.

Position

The baby's body may be pulled into abnormal positions by gravity and the weight of her paralysed limbs. You will be taught how to position her to avoid this. Check that this is maintained. Especially vulnerable areas are the hip and ankle joints.

PROGRESS CHECK

1 What would lead you to think a child was showing signs of the start of pressure sores?
2 What equipment must you check to ensure friction is not caused?
3 Where are the vulnerable areas on her body?

Bladder management

A child who has lost sensation below the waist will have difficulty controlling her bowel and bladder needs. There are several reasons why managing this is important:

- Failure to empty the bladder regularly leaves her vulnerable to infection.
- The smell of urine is demoralising for her and may affect her developing social relationships.
- Effective management will keep her skin healthy and prevent sores.
- Failure to provide her with extra fluids may cause kidney infections.

For effective management one of the following may be necessary:

- A catheter (a tube) is used to empty the bladder regularly during the day, often every three to four hours.
- A catheter is left in the bladder continuously and left to drain into a bag.
- Boys may have a penile sheath, which covers the penis and drains into a bag.
- Medication may be prescribed by the family doctor.
- Occasionally various surgical techniques are undertaken.
- Pads and special pants may be used.

Your role is to:

- support the child in whatever system is chosen
- learn about the techniques and help required
- encourage the child in managing this herself as she grows.

Bowel management

A diminished sensation means the child is unaware when she needs to pass stools. Learning control over this aspect of her life prevents:

- embarrassment and loss of self-esteem
- leaking into her clothes
- constipation.

Help that can be offered includes:

- teaching the child to sit on the lavatory at a set time each day, usually following a certain meal
- teaching her pushing techniques.

Further help sometimes includes:

- enemas or suppositories to stimulate the bowel
- medication
- bowel washouts
- surgery.

Your role as an Early Years worker is important:

■ Offer her a high-fibre diet with plenty of fluids to prevent constipation.
■ Encourage exercise, both to help elimination and prevent her becoming overweight.
■ Learn about and support her in her programme and techniques.

Help the child to become independent

KEY POINT

Most children with spina bifida do develop routines of control over the personal needs aspect of their lives.

GOOD PRACTICE

■ Your support in helping a young child manage her personal needs will affect how she regards herself. Be sensitive and careful in your choice of language.
■ Always find privacy when helping her meet her needs.

Mobilisation

For a child who has a paraplegia (no movement or sensation below the waist) mobility is primarily achieved through the use of wheelchairs. Children who have more controlled movement may be helped by using crutches and frames.

Both occupational therapists and physiotherapists will be involved in deciding the most effective way of improving mobility.

Make sure that your environment is wheelchair friendly (see Chapter 7, pages 267–8).

Focus attention on the parts of her body that the child can control.

ONGOING MANAGEMENT

Planning and preparation before a child starts in a pre-school or school group will be needed. The more independent she is allowed to be the more confident she will become. Good communication and liaison will be essential.

Specific areas that will need consideration are:

- toilet needs
- mobility and access
- specific health needs
- continuation of programmes of care such as physiotherapy and occupational therapy
- any special dietary requirements.

For a child who is using a wheelchair or crutches for mobility all carers need to develop awareness of how much help to offer and when. Often only verbal guidance is needed.

Becoming wheelchair proficient and being able to manage small steps and uneven surfaces with confidence will need teaching. A child from the age of five can manage to push up slopes and control her chair on inclines. Young children in wheelchairs usually are accepted well into group situations, a 'watching' eye needed only to ensure safe play for all.

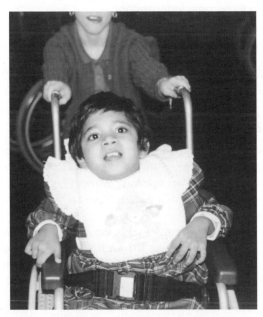

Young children in wheelchairs are well accepted by their peers

- Always keep the wheelchair in good condition.
- Keep any used cushions clean and change covers frequently. This is especially important if bowel and bladder control are not complete.

Activity
Create a raised garden that is easily accessible for a child in a wheelchair. Involve the children in planning, choosing and planting. Find plants that have different scents and offer a range of tactile experiences.

Hand skills
Some children with spina bifida are less skilful and dextrous manually than their peers of similar age. At the same time they are more dependent on their upper limbs as they need strength and power for controlling wheelchairs and crutches. Activities to develop fine motor movement should be developed and additional sensory input arranged:

- play with textured materials
- finger painting
- sand and water experience
- games and activities that encourage the development of two hands such as ball games and Stickle Bricks and Duplo play
- games to encourage fine finger movement such as finger puppets and pegboards
- encouragement in dressing, doing up buttons, zips and laces and using knives and forks.

A child with such a special need may be physically slow, so make sure you allow sufficient time for her to move around a building and prepare for activities, mealtimes, etc. Do not hurry her up or do everything for her, but try setting achievable goals for her to reach.

KEY POINT

Some children with spina bifida follow a conductive education approach to promote mobility (see pages 390–1).

Hydrocephalus

This is a condition where there is an imbalance between the production of cerebro-spinal fluid and its absorption over the surface of the brain and into the circulatory system.

WHAT HAPPENS

Cerebro-spinal fluid (CSF) is produced constantly inside each of the four spaces (the ventricles) in the brain. If a drainage path is obstructed then fluid accumulates in the ventricles causing them to swell and compress the surrounding brain tissue. In babies and young children the head size increases as the bones are still flexible and not fused.

The are several reasons why this may happen.

Congenital

Hydrocephalus may occur at birth but the reasons are often unknown.

Prematurity

A baby born early is very vulnerable. The brain is still actively developing, the blood vessels are fragile and easily damaged. If these break then clots can occur, blocking the flow of CSF and causing hydrocephalus.

Spina bifida

Babies born with spina bifida, especially with myelomeningocele and sometimes meningocele, often will have hydrocephalus. In addition to the lesion in the spinal cord there are also abnormalities in the physical structure of parts of the brain that develop before birth, which prevent adequate drainage of CSF. This can result in even further pressure on the brain.

Meningitis

When an infection of the meninges or linings of the brain and spinal cord occurs, the resulting debris and inflammation can block drainage pathways of CSF.

Brain and spinal tumours

Brain and spinal tumours can also cause compression and affect drainage of CSF.

Signs of hydrocephalus

These include:

- excessive head growth – all babies, from birth, should have their heads regularly measured and charted on a percentile chart for spurts of growth
- delayed closing of the anterior fontanelle in the skull – this is usually fully closed by 10–14 months
- a fontanelle that may be tense and bulging
- a fractious, restless baby, with a high pitched, shrill cry
- vomiting
- changes in the size of the pupils in the eye – they may be uneven

If untreated coma, seizures and death will occur.

Hydrocephalus produces delayed maturation of the brain and so all a child's senses may be affected to a degree.

- *Sight:* squint, double vision or nystagmus (rapid involuntary eye movements).
- *Sound:* initially a child might have a hypersensitivity to noise.
- *Touch and taste:* problems with shape, texture, temperature and taste.

- *Learning difficulties:*
  - short attention span
  - poor short-term memory
  - spatial awareness and visual perception problems
  - sequencing difficulties
  - delayed fine motor control.
- *Emotional problems:* the likelihood of behavioural difficulties is five times increased.

KEY POINT

Not every child will have all these difficulties and the levels of severity will vary widely.

DIAGNOSIS

Diagnosis is confirmed by a special brain scan. Early treatment is important to limit the possibility of brain damage.

CARE

The usual form of immediate treatment is the insertion of a shunting device by a surgical operation.

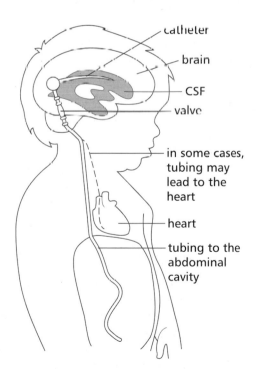

An example of a valve, or 'shunt', in place

This shunt diverts the accumulated CSF from the obstructed pathway and returns it to the bloodstream. It consists of a system of tubes with a valve to control the rate of drainage and prevent back-flow. It is inserted at the upper end into a brain ventricle and the lower end into either the heart or abdomen. The fluid collected is returned into the bloodstream. The shunt is not seen, as it is all completely enclosed in the child's body.

KEY POINT

A shunt does not cure hydrocephalus, and brain damage that has already occurred remains. A shunt's function is to prevent further damage happening.

Important signs that there may be something wrong with a shunt
Something wrong with a shunt is usually a blockage or infection. Remember each child is an individual and may present with different symptoms, however, the main signs to watch for are presented below.

Treatment
Treatment for a blockage is by surgery to replace or adjust the damaged shunt. Treatment for an infection is by surgery to remove the shunt, treating the infection with antibiotics and, when clear, inserting a new shunt.

Infants	Toddlers	Children
Enlargement of head	Head enlargement	Headache
Full tense fontanelle	Fever	Vomiting
Dividing skull sutures	Vomiting	Fever
Swelling or redness along tract of shunt	Headache	Irritability/sleepiness
	Irritability	Personality change
Fever	Swelling or redness	Loss of bladder and bowel control
Irritability	Seizures	Staggering
Seizures		Seizures
		Lethargy/loss of interest

Signs that there may be something wrong with a shunt

PROGRESS CHECK

1   You are a nanny caring for a new baby. What might indicate the baby was developing hydrocephalus?
2   You are an Early Years worker in an infant school – what might tell you a child of four with hydrocephalus has an infection in her shunt?

ONGOING MANAGEMENT

All the initial and ongoing management needed by a child with spina bifida will be required if both conditions are present.

A child with an obvious physical condition can have those physical needs met while her hidden ones are overlooked, for example any learning and emotional difficulties.

KEY POINT

The child will need full stimulation of all her senses – seeing, hearing, smelling, touching, tasting and moving – from her early years.

Check that the child is comfortable at any table for activities and that she can reach easily, manoeuvre her wheelchair and has access to all the equipment available.

The child needs release of tension by physical exercise and this will also help her develop spatial awareness.

Activity
Design a physical exercise programme for a child of five, with limited mobility, who is using either crutches or a wheelchair.

In your plan try to develop the child's gross motor skills, stamina, spatial awareness and concentration.

Could your plan include children without limited mobility? How could you adapt it to make the efforts required equal for all?

Remember to consider safety factors, an element of achievement and making it fun!

Other relevant issues on emotional management and behaviour are covered in Chapter 8. Information on the stimulation of vision and hearing, and the promotion of learning, can be found in this chapter in the sections on fragile X and Down syndrome.

GOOD PRACTICE

The visual aids, pictures, books, games and stories that you use should reflect the child's special condition, showing wheelchairs, crutches and frames. They should promote a positive image, with involved and fully participating children having individual likes, dislikes and wishes.

GENERAL IMPLICATIONS

The degrees of disability may vary enormously in a child with spina bifida and hydrocephalus. Many different professionals may be involved in her care and good communication and liaison between them, her parents and yourself will be especially important in helping the child's full development.

Sharing expertise and being able to ask questions will be necessary. No one will know all the answers and your input may be a vital part in preparation for her future.

Shona was a first baby born by normal delivery and her mother was discharged home immediately following the birth, as both she and her daughter appeared well.

Shona thrived during the first weeks of her life. At her routine six-week check at the local child health clinic, the doctor measured her head circumference as part of the normal screening procedure. On comparing the results of this measurement with those undertaken after her delivery it was noted there had been a considerable increase in the size of Shona's head, which had not been visually obvious.

Shona was referred immediately to a hospital where hydrocephalus was confirmed and a shunt inserted to drain the fluid and relieve pressure on her brain.

1 What ongoing observations will be needed to check the shunt is working effectively?
2 What other areas of Shona's development may possibly be affected by the discovery of her condition and how would you plan to meet these needs?

RESOURCES

The Association for Spina Bifida and Hydrocephalus (ASBAH)
42 Park Road
Peterborough PE1 2UQ
www.asbah.org

Cerebral palsy

Cerebral palsy (CP) is not a disease but a complex physical condition affecting a child's posture and movement. It is caused by damage or failure of the brain to develop in the specific area that controls movement.

Sometimes the area of the damage involves nearby parts of the brain, which can cause hearing impairment and perceptual difficulties. CP can cause a child to have difficulty in controlling her facial expression and in communicating. She may, as a result, be labelled as having learning difficulties where none exist.

CP is not usually inherited and can occur in any family regardless of sex, race or social background. It is thought that one in every 400 children is born with CP – a total of 1800 babies each year in Britain. It usually occurs at, or immediately after birth, but it can also happen following brain infections such as encephalitis or meningitis.

The range of the effects of the condition is enormous. Some children will appear to have no obvious disability apart from perhaps a mild clumsiness, while others will be severely disabled.

Associated difficulties that may also be present with CP

These can include:

- seizures: one in three children will also have epilepsy
- hearing impairment
- visual impairment – especially squints
- speech impairment – either delayed or indistinct speech
- perceptual difficulties/learning delay thought to involve up to 50 per cent of all children with CP. Some children, however, will have above average intellectual ability.

KEY POINTS

- There is no cure for the condition. It does not worsen as the child grows, but difficulties may become more apparent. Support and good management can ensure a child leads a full and active life.
- There is no relationship between physical appearance and intellectual ability.

WHAT HAPPENS

Anything that damages the growing brain may cause cerebral palsy. Often the reasons for this are unknown and it can occur before, during or after birth. The following are some of the known reasons for the condition.

Before birth

- Infections – especially rubella, toxoplasmosis and other viral infections
- Failure of the placenta to develop or function effectively
- Some drugs.

Around birth

- Prolonged or very difficult labour
- Prematurity
- Infections.

After birth

- Head injuries
- Infections such as meningitis
- Brain tumours.

KEY POINT

Whatever the reason for the damage to the brain, it does not get worse once it has happened; however, neither does it recover.

There are three main types of cerebral palsy thought to depend on which area or part of the brain has been affected (see page 380).

The three main types of CP are spastic cerebral palsy, athetoid cerebral palsy and ataxic cerebral palsy.

AREAS OF THE BRAIN AFFECTED BY CEREBRAL PALSY

Different areas of the brain are thought to be affected in the three major types of cerebral palsy.

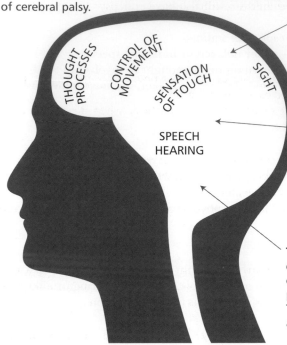

The cortex The outer layer of the brain – concerned with thought, movement and sensation.
Type of cerebral palsy: spasticity.

The basal ganglia In the middle of the brain below the cortex – concerned with the organisation of movement.
Type of cerebral palsy: athetosis.

The cerebellum At the base of the brain – concerned with organisation, coordination, posture and balance.
Type of cerebral palsy: ataxia.

THOUGHT PROCESSES

CONTROL OF MOVEMENT

SENSATION OF TOUCH

SIGHT

SPEECH HEARING

Spastic cerebral palsy

This is the most widely known and most common form of CP, affecting 50 to 60 per cent of all children with the condition.

Damage occurs to the cortex or outer brain layer, concerned with thought, movement and sensation. This results in abnormally strong tension in certain groups of muscles (this has been likened to muscle cramps) and sometimes pain. Attempts to move a joint cause muscles to contract and block the movement. Areas affected are arms and legs.

Arms

Arms are often held pressed against the body with the forearm bent at right angles to the upper arm and the hand bent against the forearm. The fist may be clenched tightly.

Legs

The legs are often less involved than the arms and the effect may be evident only when a child walks. The child may typically walk with legs wide apart and sometimes with arms outstretched.

With moderate involvement, movement may be slow and laboured with poor balance and a jerky motion.

Severe involvement, involving both legs, may result in 'scissoring', where the legs are crossed and the toes pointed.

Permanent contractures and resulting loss of mobility may develop without muscle training.

KEY POINTS

- The term 'spastic' should never be used as a noun – it is offensive to people with CP. It has been misused as a term of abuse.
- However, it is correct to use the term spasticity when describing the type of muscle tension in this sort of CP.

Athetoid cerebral palsy

This type of CP is thought to occur in 20–25 per cent of children with the condition. It results from damage to the basal ganglia in the brain, which results in involuntary, uncoordinated and uncontrolled movements of muscle groups. It is thought to be made worse by emotional stress.

All limbs

All limbs may be involved. Movement is uncontrolled, jerky and irregular, accompanied by twisting movements in the hands, involving the fingers and wrists.

Leg involvement

If the legs are involved then the child may walk in a writhing, lurching and stumbling manner, with noticeable difficulty in co-ordinating her arm movements.

KEY POINT

When calm and rested a child may walk well and when asleep or at rest may not show writhing hand movements.

Speech

This may be difficult to understand as the child's vocal cords and tongue may be affected. The likelihood of hearing impairment is increased.

KEY POINT

A child with athetosis will be delayed in her early physical development, slow to sit and 'floppy' in her muscle power. A child with spastic cerebral palsy will not show this.

Ataxic cerebral palsy

This type occurs between 1 and 10 per cent of children with CP. It results from damage to the cerebellum, which is concerned with balance.

Movement
The child typically finds difficulty in balancing and co-ordinating her movements. Often gross and fine control is affected. The child may walk with a high stepping motion.

Vision
Often nystagmus – rapid eye movement – is present.

Combination
In addition to the three identified types of CP around 15–40 per cent of all children will have a combination of effects.

Terms used to describe which area of the body is affected in cerebral palsy.

In **quadriplegia**, the most severe form of cerebral palsy, all four limbs are affected.
In **hemiplegia** one side of the body is affected.
In **paraplegia** the legs only are affected.

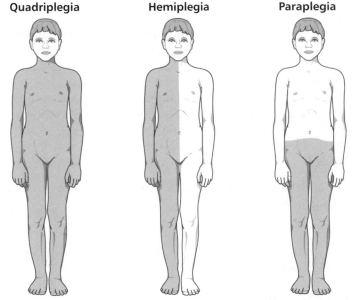

Quadriplegia   Hemiplegia   Paraplegia

Terms used to describe the areas of the body that are affected in cerebral palsy

DIAGNOSIS

Early signs
The following are early signs that might suggest a child may have CP:
- Asymmetry (unevenness) in movement or contour – creases in the groins or axillae may be different on each side of the body. One hand or limb moves more freely than the other.

- listlessness or irritability
- feeding difficulties – poor sucking or swallowing
- excessive or feeble cry
- long, thin baby who is slow to gain weight.

Later signs
These can include:
- failure to follow normal patterns of motor development
- persistence of primitive reflexes
- weakness
- early hand preference shown (often before 12–14 months of age)
- abnormal postures
- delayed or impaired speech.

GOOD PRACTICE

- Parents' anxieties about the progress of their child must always be acknowledged and investigated.
- Knowledge of the norms of development are essential for you in identifying a child who might have CP.

PROGRESS CHECK

1 What are the main early developmental differences you might notice between a child with spastic CP and a child with athetoid CP?
2 What differences might you notice when a child is at rest?

A child who is suspected of having CP will have a full developmental history taken and neurological examination by a paediatrician. An accurate assessment of a child's abilities will be made in conjunction with a variety of professionals, and in partnership with parents.

CARE

Early diagnosis allows for the following:
- the development of a programme of care, specific to a child's total individual needs and the identification of her particular strengths
- help to limit or prevent limb contractures (fixed abnormal limb positions)
- the development of maximum mobility, preventing restricted movement and faulty posture
- the identification and planning for any associated needs involving hearing, vision, speech and learning disability.

A parent may be supported by a variety of professionals depending on the specific needs of the individual child.

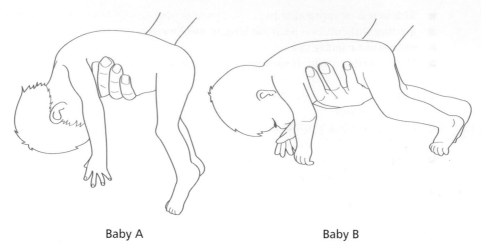

Baby A   Baby B

Both babies are the same age. Which type of cerebral palsy does baby A have?

KEY POINT

The degree to which a child is affected by CP varies enormously, depending on (a) the type of CP, (b) the location of the affected area of the brain and (c) the age at which the damage occurred.

Ensuring physical comfort and developing mobility

- Make sure you handle the limbs of a child affected with CP with care and attention and never hurry a movement. Always tell the child you are moving a limb.
- Try to maintain good body alignment to prevent contractures. Splints, casts, braces and wedges may all be used to help the child keep a comfortable position. Remember the stronger 'contracting' muscles are the most likely ones to pull a limb into an abnormal and potentially less useful position such as hips and knees becoming flexed and turned inwards – the classic 'scissoring' position.
- Certain situations, too, may produce tension and stress in the child, leading to increased muscle spasm. Know when this might happen and try to avoid it.
- If a spasm occurs never try and control it by force, but gently rock that part in spasm, as this often helps the muscles relax.
- When lying the child down, place her on her side to limit muscle spasm. As she grows older she may also be safe and comfortable on her stomach.
- Ensure you know how to lift correctly to prevent strain to your own back (see pages 268–9).
- When helping the child to stand, always position yourself in front of her. This encourages her to develop balance. Ensure her feet are firm to the floor with a wide base, check her body is leaning slightly forward and encourage her to take her own weight. Shoes must be well fitting and supportive. Specially adapted shoes may be advised.

- The usual baby pushchairs, car seats and body slings are suitable for initially getting around. These can be adapted to meet her growth. Always ensure you secure her correctly.
- Develop the child's confidence and independence in gaining mobility. Remember that fear and anxiety can increase spasms. Help her develop control over her own body by offering only essential support.

GOOD PRACTICE

- The physiotherapist will develop a programme using exercises and aids specific to the needs of the individual child.
- The physiotherapist will also teach you how to lift a child to ensure the child has the correct, safe support. This will help you to limit associated muscle tension and spasms which are different for each child.
- Your role is to understand this and know how to implement the care plan.

PROGRESS CHECK

1 What are the main points to remember when moving a child with CP?
2 How would you manage a child who was having a spasm?
3 What is the best position for a child to be placed in for rest?

BODY POSITIONS

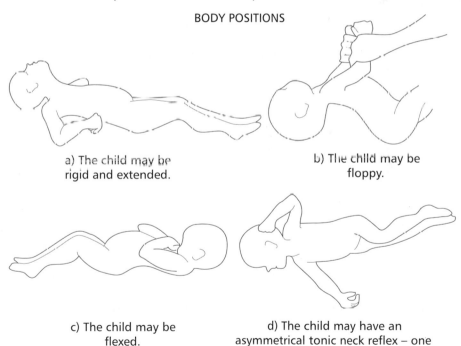

a) The child may be rigid and extended.

b) The child may be floppy.

c) The child may be flexed.

d) The child may have an asymmetrical tonic neck reflex – one arm is flexed, the other extended with the head turned towards it.

A child with CP may have fixed body positions or develop spasms. Consider this when giving support at mealtimes

Managing feeding

Initially some babies need to be fed by tube and this may lead to difficulty in the baby learning to suck. A mother will need understanding and support at this time. Tensions developing from such a situation are easily passed on to the baby.

A baby with CP may have fixed body positions or develop spasms. Consider this when supporting her at mealtimes (see below).

Early feeding

- A baby who is stiff will respond by further extension of her neck and arms when her mouth is open. So when feeding try to hold her so this cannot be achieved. Position her firmly in the crook of your arm, with her flexed arm tucked behind your back and the extended one flexed against her chest. When she is older she can be effectively supported in her own chair facing you.

- A baby who is floppy needs checking that she is well supported under the ribs to help her keep an upright position and extend her chest. Ensure there is good head support. Initially chewing may need to be encouraged by moving the jaw around. When she is using a chair, support her fully, possibly using an additional pillow and with her feet flat against the chair sides.

Weaning

Prompt weaning allows for the introduction of solids to help develop chewing and tongue control, which are important in promoting speech and for healthy teeth and gums. It is sometimes easier, but not advised, to continue with sloppy foods longer than for the ordinary child.

- Always make sure the child is comfortable, correctly positioned and can see well, before starting a meal so:
  - sit her in her own special chair
  - sit her well forward, with her elbows rested on the tray in front and feet flat on the foot rest
  - try to position the chair so that she can be a part of family meals
  - keep her head upright and in midline, to reduce the risk of choking.
- Use the time to talk, sing and encourage her development and make it fun.
- Always tell her what you are offering her.
- Check the temperature carefully.
- Allow plenty of time.
- Follow a usual weaning plan, with one food being introduced at a time, varying textures and tastes.
- Always use plastic or unbreakable spoons and beakers, as a strong bite reflex may be present, causing potential dangers.
- Place food far back on the tongue and to the side.
- Swallowing can be encouraged and the bite reflex overcome, if necessary, by rotating the lower jaw and firmly stroking upwards and backwards under the jaw.
- Crumbly foods can sometimes increase the chances of choking.

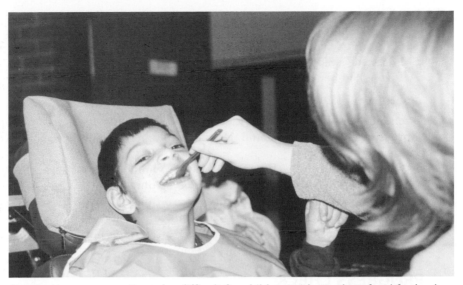

Swallowing can sometimes be difficult for children with CP. Place food far back and to the side if the child cannot manage alone

- As the child grows encourage her to hold the spoon. Help her grasp by checking the wrist is well back.
- Experiment with different types of spoons to find the most suitable for her – possibly ones with wide, shallow bowls and easy-grip rubberised handles.
- Use bowls with suction pads to prevent slipping.
- Encourage her to push food on to her spoon using another one or a fork. This also helps her use both sides of her body even if one is weaker.

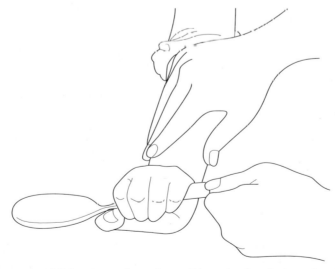

Encourage the child to keep the wrist well bent back to help maintain grasp

- Allow for mess and protect the child and the floor well.
- Make the time enjoyable to encourage her to try new foods and develop confidence with solids.
- Praise the child's efforts.
- If you feed her, sit at her side, always checking her position.

Drinking

Often the lower jaw is moved up and down as she drinks – this can be stopped by supporting the jaw from behind. Help her hold her mug and check her thumbs are turned *out*.

- Mugs should have two handles to promote symmetry and the use of both sides of the body. Weighted mugs may also be helpful.
- The tongue can continue to come forward (tongue thrust) in a child with CP and this can make both drinking and eating difficult. Sucking through a straw can help limit this and at the same time strengthen lips and palate muscles. Blowing bubbles can teach a sucking motion.

PROGRESS CHECK

What safety precautions must you be aware of when feeding a child with CP?

GOOD PRACTICE

- You should aim to promote independence at mealtimes, even if it is initially messier and takes longer than for a child who does not have CP.
- Mealtimes should be sociable, friendly times with opportunities to interact and learn.

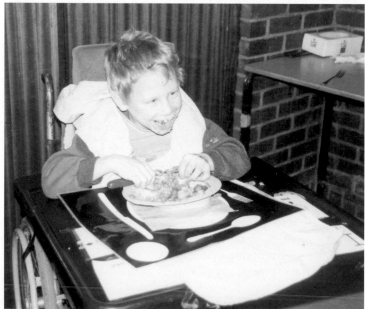

Mealtimes can provide taste, smell, language and tactile opportunities

Physical care

Dressing
- Aim to develop independence.
- Choose clothes that are easy to put on and take off.
- Put clothes on the affected limb first. Never pull her fingers as this will increase elbow flexion.
- Before putting on shoes and socks check her legs are bent. This will limit ankle and foot stiffness and toe curling.
- Encourage choice and involve her in selecting her own clothes.

Hygiene
- The usual routines will be required. Always use non-slip bath mats.
- In view of her reduced chewing capacity, pay special attention to dental care.
- As she grows and becomes heavier, adaptations to help at bathtimes may be advised by the occupational therapist.

Toileting
- Muscular tension may increase her difficulties in gaining bladder and bowel control. Exercises to help this may be advised by the physiotherapist.

Sleep routines
- Develop a settling routine involving a bath and relaxing story or song.
- Occasionally the child may find it difficult to settle. If she is less mobile than her peers she may just be less tired. Check her general comfort.
- If she has spastic CP she may need to be moved during the night to prevent spasms and make her comfortable.
- A special sleeping position may be recommended – usually on her side or tummy as she grows older.
- A Portage scheme is available in some areas for children with CP (see pages 176–9).

Play
As with any other child this is an important part of promoting her development.
- Check her position to ensure she is comfortable and well supported. Use wedges and standing frames to allow her access to toys. Remember, if she is placed on her back you may promote spasms.
- Encourage fine movements to develop hand control.
- Develop games to promote balance and control of movement.
- Stimulate and encourage her speech (see section on encouraging speech development, Chapter 8, pages 300–2). Liaise with the speech therapist (see sections on promoting oral speech, Chapter 8, pages 342–4, and managing hearing impairment, page 347).
- Swimming will both help movement and be fun.
- Short bursts of play are better than long sessions.
- Use music, stories and rhymes freely.

KEY POINTS

- The child may take longer to learn a game.
- She may tire more easily.
- Always praise and encourage effort.

Activity
Make a 'feely' box for a two-year-old child. Choose a variety of textures, shapes and sizes for your box.
  What areas of development could this box help?

GOOD PRACTICE

- A child with CP has the same needs as other children for love, security, stimulation and protection. Always apply routine rules and discipline as with any child.
- Treat the child as a unique and individual person with her own personality, likes and dislikes. This is especially important if she has communication difficulties.

ONGOING MANAGEMENT

Management issues of handling and promoting mobility, and developing independence and the self-esteem of a child with CP will continue throughout childhood.

Added difficulties will need to be addressed if identified (for hearing and visual impairments see pages 335–51 and 351–65; for learning difficulties see Down syndrome; and for managing behaviour problems see Chapter 8, pages 304–15).

Alternative approaches
A variety of therapies and treatments are used in the management of children with CP. They include the following.

Conductive education
Conductive education is becoming increasingly popular for children with CP or 'motor dysfunction'. It is an intensive teaching and learning system designed to enable children with disabilities to function more independently. A child is fully assessed before undertaking the programme, to ensure that she will benefit.

Conductive education was first developed in Hungary by Dr Andras Peto in 1952. Specially trained 'conductors' provide the child with a fully integrated day, without disruptions, from different professionals (speech, occupational and physiotherapists, etc.). The conductor's role is to be aware of, and develop all aspects of the child, through establishing a strong relationship with her, and many feel this is the key to the programme's success.

The following are the main aims of conductive education:

- to stimulate active exploration of the world through movement during the child's whole day

- to develop a routine to include a series of interlinked tasks undertaken with the child in different positions – lying, standing, etc.
- to encourage transferring skills learnt in these various positions to other activities, including educational ones, throughout the day. For example a child will sit at a table, lean forward to develop manipulative skills in matching or drawing and stand to paint at an easel. Thus sitting, leaning forward and standing are accompanied by manipulation, matching, memory skills and painting.
- to set achievable but increasingly demanding tasks and goals that cover both learning and motor development, so allowing the child to achieve success and raise self-esteem
- to assume movement and language are interconnected. The child is taught to use spoken language as a means of preparing herself mentally for movement – 'I stand up tall', etc.
- to look at the whole child, not just her special need
- to build on the child's interests and personality
- to provide the programme within a group of children with similar needs, so developing strong peer relationships and helping motivation
- to use a specially designed room to make progress from one activity to another streamlined. There are strategically placed bars and ladders for the child to hold on to.
- to encourage children to challenge their disability – to walk and not use a wheelchair, to speak and not use other forms of communication, etc.

Parents and carers play an important part in the programme; skills that are learnt by the child should be applied and reinforced in daily life.

The Bobath concept

Bobath therapy is designed to help a child with brain damage move more easily. It is integral to a child's daily routine, and uses play rather than 'exercises' in therapy. It aims to improve posture, reduce stiffness, increase muscle control and limit random muscle movements. Correct positioning and handling, at all times, is considered to be the key to enhanced movement. Specialist therapists have developed methods of handling using key points on the child's body. A child is taught to use her hands to aid herself in standing up and walking.

The involvement of families, and those who work with the child, is essential in this therapy. All are taught how to use the correct position for the child at all times, even when this feels 'unnatural'. The importance of persistence and effort is acknowledged to be vital in achieving improvement.

Botulinum Toxin A (BTA)

BTA is a drug, lasting up to sixteen weeks, which is injected deep into the muscles, either by local or general anaesthetic. It works by blocking the signal that the nerves are trying to pass to the muscles. Studies have shown that, in some children with CP, the result is reduced muscle tightness, and freer movements. It is thought the drug enables the muscles to stretch and so may reduce the risk of permanent contractures. It is used in conjunction with physiotherapy.

Patterning

The British Institute for Brain-Injured Children (BIBIC) is a charity whose work with brain injured children is based on the practices of a Philadelphian psychologist Doman-Delacato. It aims to help children's mobility through a series of exercises that 'teach' the undamaged part of the brain to take over the functions of the damaged part. Children who cannot voluntarily move their limbs are given intensive, frequent and repetitive rhythmic stimulation (patterning) to their limbs for up to eight hours a day. Cross-patterning involves the helpers moving the child's opposite arms and legs to prepare for balanced, co-ordinated walking. The therapy is controversial and can exhaust and distress the child. Many parents and carers find the commitment required time consuming and considerable, but can be rewarded by signs of achievement.

KEY POINTS

- Some treatments are available through the NHS, although provision is not universal.
- Not all therapies or treatments are suitable for all children and none are a cure for the condition. Their aims are to promote independence and enhance the quality of life for the child. SCOPE, the national organisation involved with CP (see Resources, page 393), advises families that before starting or paying for any treatment, advice should be sought from the child's GP, consultants or other health professional.

GENERAL IMPLICATIONS

A child with a severe disability can be a challenging and stimulating addition to a family, but exhausting – it is important to be sensitive to this. Respite care and holiday play schemes in which parents have confidence may be needed to allow time for families to refresh themselves.

Adaptations and changes to the home, together with information regarding benefits, may also be required as the child grows.

KEY POINT

The range of disability is enormous in CP. Many children will lead full and active lives with little effects from the condition, whereas other children will need some degree of lifelong support and protection.

ADDITIONAL DEVELOPMENTS

Sometimes drug therapy is needed to control epilepsy, and spasticity in limbs may be reduced with the use of muscle relaxants if a child is particularly distressed, but on the whole medicines are not routinely used for a child with CP.

Increasingly sophisticated technical developments are valuable for a child with CP. Microtechnology means computers can be worked with fingers, toes, tongues, voice and eye and breath movements, allowing access to the wider world. Communication aids now allow synthetic speech. Electric wheelchairs can even be worked with switches operated from the chin.

CASE STUDY

Mary was born prematurely with cerebral palsy and difficulties over feeding were immediately present. She was late in all aspects of her physical development, not sitting until she was eighteen months old and then only for a few seconds at a time. At four years old she was not yet walking unaided. She was alert and interested, but her speech was not distinct and although her parents understood exactly what she said, others did not. She could count, sing nursery rhymes and was always wanting more stories. She became frustrated and easily bored as she could not reach things in her surroundings easily.

Recently she has started attending a special playgroup where conductive educational methods are used. The individual attention and contact with other children have had a dramatic effect upon Mary. She sleeps much better, is keen to do things for herself and appears more tranquil. Her mother finds the respite from her loved, but demanding and increasingly heavy, daughter valuable, allowing her to give much needed attention to Mary's older brother of seven. The support from other parents attending the playgroup is helpful – 'knowing how she feels' is the way Mary's mother describes it.

1 What support could have been identified and organised earlier, both for Mary and her mother?
2 Which peripatetic therapists could have helped Mary in her home?

RESOURCES

The British Institute for Brain-Injured Children (BIBIC)
Knowle Hall
Knowle
Bridgwater
Somerset TA7 8PJ
www.bibic.org.uk

The Bobath Centre
250 East End Road
East Finchley
London N2 8AU
www.bobath.org.uk

The National Institute for Conductive Education
Cannon Hill House
Russell Road
Birmingham B13 8RD
www.conductive-education.org.uk

SCOPE
6 Market Road
London N7 9PW
www.scope.org.uk

Child abuse

Until comparatively recently society in general found it difficult to accept that children with special needs could be abused. However, children with differing disabilities are in fact at an increased risk of child abuse, the rate being 1.7 times higher than for children generally.

Many groups now consider that definitions of 'abuse' should be extended for children with a disability to include the following:

- lack of stimulation/supervision
- over-protection
- confinement to cot, bed or room/physical restraints such as strapping into chairs
- intrusive or insensitive medical photography or procedures
- incorrect drug use
- forced feeding, insensitive personal hygiene management, lack of privacy
- the withholding of aids such as wheelchairs, crutches, etc. in order to promote mobility.

Vulnerability of children with special needs

Children with special needs are particularly vulnerable because of the following:

- Intimate care in bathing, toileting and dressing, is often undertaken by someone else. This assisted care may continue for longer than would be expected for a child without special needs.
- Intimate contact in residential care may be undertaken by someone of the opposite sex.
- Children may be unable to speak out due to communication or speech difficulties, deafness or because they are withdrawn, allowing an abuser to continue unhindered.
- Low self-esteem in some children with disability may make it less likely they complain.
- Children in inclusive settings may be perceived as different and become the subject of bullying.

Vulnerability of parents/carers

The following are factors that place parents/carers under particular pressure:

- Children with behavioural difficulties may be particularly demanding for some carers.

- Children who need constant attention, especially at night, may increase pressure on families.
- Some physical and behavioural signs may be mistaken for complications of the condition itself.
- Parents and carers may be unaware of the impact of the condition itself.

GOOD PRACTICE

- Children with special needs must be cared for in an environment of dignity, respect and empowerment.
- Policies must be developed and adhered to in order to monitor children at particular risk of abuse.
- Early Years workers must consider their own feelings and attitudes to children with disability.
- Families and carers working with children with multiple and demanding needs must have support systems and networks available to them. Their needs, too, must be understood.
- The development of an ongoing programme of information regarding care of children with additional needs, should be undertaken.

RESOURCES

NSPCC
42 Curtain Road
London EC2A 3NH
www.nspcc.org.uk

Voice UK
The College Business Centre
Uttoxeter New Road
Derby DE22 3WZ
www.voiccuk.clara.net

This organisation supports and advises children and adults, with learning disabilities, who have been abused or have suffered violence.

KEY TERMS

You need to know what these words and phrases mean. Go back through the chapter and make sure that you understand:

astigmatism
asymmetry
auditory–oral approach
bilingualism
Bobath therapy
Braille
British Sign Language
cerebral palsy, ataxic CP, athetoid CP,
    spastic CP
child abuse (the wider definitions to
    be considered for children with
    special needs)
conductive education
conductive impairment
contractures
deaf culture

Down syndrome
fragile X
hearing impairment
heart lesions
myelomeningocele
otitis media with effusion
paralysis
patterning
pressure sores
ritualistic behaviour
sensory rooms
shunting device
spina bifida and hydrocephalus
squint
total communication
WHO definition of blindness

APPENDIX: Developmental norms

0–1 year

	Physical development (gross motor)	Physical development (fine motor)	Social and emotional development	Cognitive and language development
At birth	Reflexes: ■ Rooting, sucking and swallowing reflex ■ Grasp reflex ■ Walking reflex ■ Moro reflex If pulled to sit, head falls backwards If held in sitting position, head falls forward, and back is curved In supine (laying on back), limbs are bent In prone (laying on front), lies in fetal position with knees tucked up. Unable to raise head or stretch limbs	Reflexes: ■ Pupils reacting to light ■ Opens eyes when held upright ■ Blinks or opens eyes wide to sudden sound ■ Startled reaction to sudden sound ■ Eyes close to sudden bright light	Bonding/attachment	Cries vigorously, with some variation in pitch and duration
1 month	In prone, lifts chin In supine, head moves to one side Arm and leg extended on face side Begins to flex upper and lower limbs	Hands fisted Eyes move to dangling objects	Watches mother's face with increasingly alert facial expression Fleeting smile – may be wind Stops crying when picked up	Cries become more differentiated to indicate needs Stops and attends to voice, rattle and bell
3 months	Held sitting, head straight, back and neck firm. Lower back still weak When lying, pelvis is flat	Grasps an object when placed in hand Turns head right round to look at objects Eye contact firmly established	Reacts with pleasure to familiar situations/routines	Regards hands with interest Beginning to vocalise

0–1 year continued

	Physical development (gross motor)	Physical development (fine motor)	Social and emotional development	Cognitive and language development
6 months	In supine, can lift head and shoulders In prone, can raise up on hands Sits with support Kicks strongly May roll over When held, enjoys standing and jumping	Has learned to grasp objects and passes toys from hand to hand Visual sense well established	Takes everything to mouth Responds to different emotional tones of chief caregiver	Finds feet interesting Vocalises tunefully Laughs in play Screams with annoyance Understands purpose of rattle
9 months	Sits unsupported Begins to crawl Pulls to stand, falls back with bump	Visually attentive Grasps with thumb and index finger Releases toy by dropping Looks for fallen objects Beginning to finger-feed Holds bottle or cup	Plays peek-a-boo – can start earlier Imitates hand-clapping Clings to familiar adults, reluctant to go to strangers – from about 7 months	Watches activities of others with interest Vocalises to attract attention Beginning to babble Finds partially hidden toy Shows an interest in picture books Knows own name
1 year	Walks holding one hand, may walk alone Bends down and picks up objects Pulls to stand and sits deliberately	Picks up small objects Fine pincer grip Points at objects Holds spoon	Co-operates in dressing Demonstrates affection Participates in nursery rhymes Waves goodbye	Uses jargon Responds to simple instructions and understands several words Puts wooden cubes in and out of cup or box

1–4 years

	Physical development (gross motor)	Physical development (fine motor)	Social and emotional development	Cognitive and language development
15 months	Walking usually well established Can crawl up stairs frontwards and down stairs backwards Kneels unaided Balance poor, falls heavily	Holds crayon with palmar grasp Precise pincer grasp, both hands Builds tower of two cubes Can place objects precisely Uses spoon, which sometimes rotates Turns pages of picture book	Indicates wet or soiled pants Helps with dressing Emotionally dependent on familiar adult	Jabbers loudly and freely, with two–six recognisable words, and can communicate needs Intensely curious Reproduces lines drawn by adult
18 months	Climbs up and down stairs with hand held Runs carefully Pushes, pulls and carries large toys Backs into small chair Can squat to pick up toys	Builds tower of three cubes Scribbles to and fro spontaneously Begins to show preference for one hand Drinks without spilling	Tries to sing Imitates domestic activities Bowel control sometimes attained Alternates between clinging and resistance Plays contentedly alone near familiar adult	Enjoys simple picture books, recognising some characters Jabbering established 6–20 recognisable words May use echolalia (repeating adult's last word, or last word of rhyme) Is able to show several parts of the body, when asked Explores environment energetically
2 years	Runs with confidence, avoiding obstacles Walks up and down stairs both feet to each step, holding wall Squats with ease. Rises without using hands Can climb up on furniture and get down again Steers tricycle pushing along with feet Throws small ball overarm, and kicks large ball	Turns picture book pages one at a time Builds tower of six cubes Holds pencil with first two fingers and thumb near to point	Competently spoon feeds and drinks from cup Is aware of physical needs Can put on shoes and hat Keenly interested in outside environment – unaware of dangers Demands chief caregiver's attention and often clings Parallel play Throws tantrums if frustrated	Identifies photographs of familiar adults Identifies small-world toys Recognises tiny details in pictures Uses own name to refer to self Speaks in two- and three-word sentences, and can sustain short conversations Asks for names and labels Talks to self continuously

1–4 years continued

	Physical development (gross motor)	Physical development (fine motor)	Social and emotional development	Cognitive and language development
3 years	Competent locomotive skills Can jump off lower steps Still uses two feet to a step coming down stairs Pedals and steers tricycle	Cuts paper with scissors Builds a tower of nine cubes and a bridge with three cubes Good pencil control Can thread three large beads on a string	Uses spoon and fork Increased independence in self-care Dry day and night Affectionate and co-operative Plays co-operatively, particularly domestic play Tries to please	Can copy a circle and some letters Can draw a person with a head and two other parts of the body May name colours and match three primary colours Speech and comprehension well established Some immature pronunciations and unconventional grammatical forms Asks questions constantly Can give full name, gender and age Relates present activities and past experiences Increasing interest in words and numbers
4 years	All motor muscles well controlled Can turn sharp corners when running Hops on favoured foot Balances for three–five seconds Increasing skill at ball games Sits with knees crossed	Builds a tower of 10 cubes Uses six cubes to build three steps, when shown	Boasts and is bossy Sense of humour developing Cheeky, answers back Wants to be independent Plays games co-operatively Argues with other children but learning to share	Draws person with head, legs and trunk Draws recognisable house Uses correct grammar most of the time Most pronunciations mature Asks meanings of words Enjoys verses and jokes, and may use swear words Counts up to 20 Imaginative play well developed

4–7 years

	Physical development (gross motor)	Physical development (fine motor)	Social and emotional development	Cognitive and language development
5 years	Can touch toes keeping legs straight Hops on either foot Skips Runs on toes Ball skills developing well Can walk along a thin line	Threads needle and sews Builds steps with three–four cubes Colours pictures carefully Can copy adult writing	Copes well with daily personal needs Chooses own friends Well-balanced and sociable Sense of fair play and understanding of rules developing Shows caring attitudes towards others	Matches most colours Copies square, triangle and several letters, writing some unprompted Writes name Draws a detailed person Speaks correctly and fluently Knows home address Able and willing to complete projects Understands numbers using concrete objects Imaginary play now involves make-believe games
6 years	Jumps over rope 25 cm high Learning to skip with rope	Ties own shoe laces	Eager for fresh experiences More demanding and stubborn, less sociable Joining a 'gang' may be important May be quarrelsome with friends Needs to succeed as failing too often leads to poor self-esteem	Reading skills developing well Drawings more precise and detailed Figure may be drawn in profile Can describe how one object differs from another Mathematical skills developing, may use symbols instead of concrete objects May write independently
7 years	Rides a two-wheel bicycle Improved balance	Skills constantly improving More dexterity and precision in all areas	Special friend at school Peer approval becoming important Likes to spend some time alone Enjoys TV and books May be moody May attempt tasks too complex to complete	Moving towards abstract thought Able to read Can give opposite meanings Able to write a paragraph independently

GLOSSARY OF TERMS

Access
A way into; freedom to obtain or use something, for example, the environment, education, leisure facilities.

Advocacy
Speaking on behalf of, pleading for.

Advocate
Someone who pleads on behalf of another, for example a parent or professional carer for a child.

Biopsy
A procedure in which a small sample of tissue is removed and examined under a microscope.

Chromosome
A thread-like structure composed of deoxyribonucleic acid (DNA), carrying genetic material.

Congenital
Born with.

Contractures
Shortening of muscles causing limbs to remain in a fixed position.

Designated medical officer for SEN
A doctor, appointed by a health authority, to co-ordinate health care for children with special educational needs within that health authority.

Differentiation
Adapting and presenting the curriculum (Early Years or National) in a manner appropriate to a child's needs and abilities.

Discrimination
Unfair or unequal treatment of an individual or group of people on the grounds of disability, race, religion, gender or age.

Early Years
Generally, includes young children from birth up to eight years of age. The Department for Education and Skills identifies Early Years as from the age of three years up to the end of the reception years.

Eclectic
A combination of a variety of approaches to management.

Empower
To enable, to authorise.

Encopresis
Incontinence of faeces, faecal soiling.

Enuresis
Incontinence of urine, bedwetting.

Gene therapy
An experimental scientific technique currently under development for use in certain conditions. The aim is not to treat the symptoms of the condition but to correct the underlying cause. The therapy involves the addition of a healthy, working copy of a faulty gene, into the appropriate cell of the child.

Genes
Units of genetic material (DNA) carried at certain places on a chromosome and responsible for characteristics such as hair, eye and skin colour, blood group, body shape and size.

Genetics
The scientific study of inheritance. Human and medical genetics are concerned with the study of inherited disorders.

Genetic counselling
Advice on the possibility and probability of passing on inherited conditions and listening sympathetically to the concerns and anxieties of those seeking advice.

Inclusive environment
An environment that welcomes all children/adults, including those with disabilities and special needs, and is committed to caring for, valuing and respecting all children/adults equally.

Incontinence
Inability to control passage of urine or bowel movements.

Inherited
Passed down from one generation to another, for example genetic disorders.

Learning difficulties
Greater difficulty in learning than the majority of children of the same age or having a disability that prevents or hinders a child from using the educational facilities provided for children of the same age.

Ofsted (Office for Standards in Education)
A non-ministerial government department responsible for the inspection of all schools in England. Ofsted Early Years Directorate is responsible for the regulation of day care and childminding provision for children under the age of eight years in England.

Paralysis
Loss of sensation or movement.

Paraplegia
Paralysis of both legs, due to disorder or injury of the spinal cord.

Peripatetic teacher
A teacher who teaches children in a variety of settings such as school, day nursery or the home. Examples include peripatetic teachers for children with visual or hearing impairment.

Premature/pre-term
Refers to a baby born less than 37 weeks from the first day of the last menstrual period.

Respite care
A particular system of childcare and support for families with a child with special needs.

Special Educational Needs Co-ordinator
An identified member of staff in an Early Years education setting or a school, with responsibility for co-ordinating special educational provision within that setting or school.

Special Educational Needs Code of Practice
A document giving guidance to local education authorities (LEAs), schools and Early Years settings on their responsibilities towards children with special educational needs.

Statement of Special Educational Needs
A legal document that sets out a child's educational needs and the special help and provision the child should receive.

Statementing
The process of drawing up a statement of special educational needs.

Stereotyping
Having a fixed pre-conceived idea or image about a person or group of people; making assumptions.

Sure Start
A government programme that aims to address the issues of child poverty and social exclusion and to improve the health and well-being of young children and their families.

Syndrome
A combination of characteristics, signs and/or symptoms that indicate a particular disorder.

FURTHER READING

Cooke, C., Daone, L. and Morris, G. *'Stop Press'. A survey of how the press portray disabled people*, Scope, 2000

Department for Education and Skills (DfES), *The Special Educational Needs Code of Practice,* DfES/581/2001

Department for Education and Skills (DfES), *The Statutory Framework for the Early Years Foundation Stage*

Department of Health (DoH) *The Children Act*, HMSO, 1989

Drew, S. *Children and the Human Rights Act*, Save the Children, 2000

French, S. and Swan, J. *From a Different Viewpoint – the lives and experiences of visually impaired people*, Royal National Institute for the Blind (RNIB), 1997

Helman, C. *Culture, Health and Illness*, Hodder Arnold, 5 edn, 2007

Hobart, C., Frankel, J. and Walker, M. (Series Editor), *A Practical Guide to Activities for Young Children*, Nelson Thornes, 4th edn, 2009

Hobart, C., Frankel, J. and Walker, M. *Good Practice in Safeguarding Children*, 3rd edn, 2009

Kingsley, J., *Assessing Children in Need* ed. J. Horwath, National Society for the Prevention of Cruelty to Children (NSPCC), DoH and University of Sheffield, 2001

Lear, R. *Play Helps – toys and activities for children with special needs*, Butterworth Heinemann, 4th edn, 1996

Martin, D. *Teaching Children with Speech and Language Difficulties*, David Fulton, 2000

Mason, M. and Rieser, R. *Disability Equality in the Classroom: a human rights issue*, Disability Equality in Education, reprinted and updated 1992

Mencap, *On a Wing and a Prayer: inclusion and children with severe learning difficulties*, Mencap, 1999

Mukherji, P. *Understanding Children's Challenging Behaviour*, Nelson Thornes, 2001

National Deaf Children's Society (NDCS), *Hearing Aids*, NDCS, 2008

NDCS, *Playtime and Your Deaf Child*, NDCS factsheet, 2004

NDCS, *Sign Language*, NDCS factsheet, 2004

Pre-School Learning Alliance, *Inclusion in Early Years Settings*, Pre-School Learning Alliance, 2005

RNIB, *Improving Provision for Children with Visual Impairment and Multiple Disability*, RNIB, 1998 (pack containing a folder and three booklets)

RNIB and the British Toy and Hobby Association, *Playtime!*, RNIB, 2008

Saunders, K. *Happy Ever Afters – a storybook guide to teaching children about disability*, Trentham Books, 2000

St John Ambulance, St Andrew's Ambulance Association and British Red Cross Society, *First Aid Manual: The Step by Step Guide for Everyone*, Dorling Kindersley; 9th edn, 2009

Thacker, J., Strudwick, D. and Babbedge, E. *Educating Children with Emotional and Behaviour Difficulties – inclusive practice in mainstream schools*, Routledge & Falmer (School concern series), 2002

Wolfendale, S. *Special Needs in the Early Years – snapshots of practice*, Routledge & Falmer, 2000

OTHER RESOURCES

Usborne have a range of 'touchy-feely books'. See their catalogue at www.usborne.co.uk/catalogue

Ways of Reading is a guide to finding books for blind and partially sighted children, whether for pleasure, information or school work. It is a co-operative venture by Calibre Cassette Library, ClearVision, National Library for the Blind and the Royal National Insitute for the Blind. Copies are available in print, Braille or on tape. Contact the RNIB on 0845 702 3153.

USEFUL ADDRESSES

Listed below are the postal addresses of organisations and, where available, their website addresses. These organisations will provide general information regarding children and disabilities. Regional and local contact addresses, together with information in different languages, can often be accessed through the national website.

More specialist sources of information and advice are available at the end of each section in Part Two.

4Children
City Reach
5 Greenwich View Place
London E14 9NN
www.4children.org.uk

The Alliance for Inclusive Education
336 Brixton Road
London SW9 7AA
www.allfie.org.uk

CENMAC
Charlton School
Charlton Park Road
London SE7 8JB
www.cenmac.com
A central resource for service, advice and
assessment for pupils with physical
disabilities. This is primarily for inner
London, but can now offer assessment and
advice for pupils and parents from further afield

Centre for Studies on Inclusive Education
New Redland Building
Coldharbour Lane
Frenchay
Bristol BS16 1QU
www.csie.org.uk

Child Accident Prevention Trust
Canterbury Court
1–3 Brixton Road
London SW9 6DE
www.capt.org.uk

The Children's Legal Centre
University of Essex
Wivenhoe Park
Colchester
Essex CO4 3SQ
www.childrenslegalcentre.com

Contact a Family
209–211 City Road
London EC1V 1JN
www.cafamily.org.uk

The Council for Disabled Children
8 Wakely Street
London EC1V 7QE
www.ncb.org.uk/Page.asp?sve=785

Department for Children, Schools and Families
Sanctuary Buildings
Great Smith Street
London
SW1P 3BT
http://publications.dcsf.gov.uk

Disability Alliance
1st Floor East, Universal House
88–94 Wentworth Street
London E1 7SA
www.disabilityalliancc.org

Disability Equality in Education
Unit 1M Leroy House
436 Essex Rd
London N1 3QP
www.diseed.org.uk
Charity, based on the work of Richard Rieser
and Micheline Mason, providing training and
resources for schools, colleges and local education

Disability Equality Training Network
Leeds Centre for Integrated Living
Armley Grange Drive
Leeds LS12 3QH
www.leedscil.org.uk

Disability Resource Team
2nd Floor, 6 Park Road
Teddington
London TW11 0AA
www.disabilityresourceteam.com

Edu-Play
Morris Road
Leicester
LE2 6BR
www.edu-play.co.uk
Provides specialist early years
play equipment

Makaton
Manor House,
46 London Road
Blackwater
Camberley
Surrey GU17 0AA
www.makaton.org

MENCAP
123 Golden Lane
London EC1Y 0RT
www.mencap.org.uk

National Association of Toy and Leisure Libraries
68 Churchway
London NW1 1LT
www.natl.org.uk

National Children's Bureau
8 Wakely Street
London EC1V 7QE
www.ncb.org.uk

National Playbus Association
Brunswick Court
Brunswick Square
Bristol BS2 8PE
www.playbus.org.uk

Parents for Inclusion
Winchester House
Kennington Park Business Estate
Cranmer Road
London SW9 6EJ
www.parentsforinclusion.org

Persona Dolls Training 5
1 Granville Road
London N12 0JH
www.persona-doll-training.org

Play England
8 Wakley Street
London EC1V 7QE
www.playengland.org.uk

Play Leisure Advice Network (PLANET)
Save the Children
Cambridge House
Cambridge Grove
London W6 0LE
Tel: 020 8741 4054

Rights4Me
Office of the Children's Rights Director
Ofsted
33 Kingsway
London WC2B 6SE
www.rights4mc.org

Royal Society for the Prevention of Accidents
(RoSPA)
RoSPA House
Edgbaston Park
356 Bristol Road
Birmingham B5 7ST
www.rospa.com

Save the Children
1 St John's Lane
London EC1M 4AR
www.savethechildren.org.uk

SENSE
101 Pentonville Road
London N1 9LG
www.sense.org.uk

Useful websites

Department for Children, Schools and Families
www.dcsf.gov.uk/index.htm

Department of Health
www.dh.gov.uk

Department for Works and Pensions
www.dwp.gov.uk
Information on disability benefits

Charities Direct
www.charitiesdirect.com
Alphabetical list of all registered charities with their associated address and websites

Note: when using the internet, select your material carefully and remember that not all sites supply information that has been supported by wide research and academic scrutiny. However, government and established charities are excellent sources, and provide comprehensive, currect and accurate information.

INDEX

Page numbers in italics indicate tables or photographs.